Imprints 12

Imprints

Kathy Evans
Lori Farren
David Friend
Janet Hannaford
Stuart Poyntz
Jim Robson
Dom Saliani

CONSULTANT
Ann Manson

EDITORIAL TEAM
Joe Banel
Sandra McTavish
Diane Robitaille
Cathy Zerbst

gagelearning

Permissions Editor: Elizabeth Long
Photo Research: Patricia Buckley
Design, Art Direction, & Electronic Assembly: Wycliffe Smith Design Inc.
Cover Image: J.L. Stanfield/National Geographic/Firstlight.ca

IMPRINTS REVIEWERS

Gerry Bartlett, School District #2, NB
Janet Bent, Halifax Regional School Board, NS
Bryan Ellefson, Palliser Regional Schools, AB
Marg Frederickson, Burnaby School District #41, BC
Doreen Kennedy, Vancouver School District #39, BC
Yula Nouragas, York Region District School Board, ON
Jane Prosser, Saskatoon B of E, SK
Carol Ricker-Wilson, Toronto District School Board, ON
Mary Lou Souter, Upper Canada District School Board, ON
Carol Wadden, Avalon East School Board, NF

National Library of Canada cataloguing in publication data
Main entry under title:
Imprints 12: short stories, poetry, essays, media and drama

For use in grade 12.
Issued also in 2 vols.
ISBN 0-7715-0947-2
1. Readers (Secondary). I. Farren, Lori.
PE1121.I537 2002   428'.6   C2001-903082-7

We acknowledge the financial support of the Government of Canada through the Book Publishing Industry Development Program for our publishing activities.

ISBN 0-7715-0947-2
2 3 4 5 FP 05 04 03 02
Printed and bound in Canada

The selections collected in *Imprints* are drawn from a wide variety of sources. To respect the integrity of these sources, Gage has preserved the original spelling, grammar, and punctuation used by each author. Gage editorial style, however, is used throughout for activities and other text generated by Gage writers.

Table of Contents

Short Stories

Poetry

Essays and Other Non-Fiction

Media

Alternate Table of Contents

Short Stories

The universe is made of stories, not of atoms.

Muriel Rukeyser

Imagine what a marriage
proposal looks like in a society
where women rule.

Groom Service

by Michael Dorris

1

"She's a piece of pure quartz," Bernard's mother, Martha, said
to Marie's mother, Blanche. "A one-in-a-million that you find
after walking the beach for half your life with your eyes on the
ground. If I had a child like that I would keep her in a safe
place."

Blanche paused her blade midway down the side of the fish
she was scaling. Her face betrayed no expression except exer-
tion, and even in this intermission her teeth remained set, flex-
ing her jaw. The trader steel reflected what little light filtered
through the planks of the smokehouse, and the confined air still
smelled green. Blanche had hewn the boards with a mallet and
chisel in May, as soon as the ground firmed from the spring
runoff, and it took a while before the scent of fire crowded that
of drying wood. With her broad thumb she flicked a piece of fin
off the carved knife handle, then continued her motion.

Martha waited. She had all the time it took.

"You don't know," said Blanche. She shook her head as if
its secrets rolled like line-weights from side to side. She drew a
heavy breath. "You can't imagine. You with such a boy."

Martha sat straighter, all ears, while her hands continued to
explore, repairing the tears on the net that lay across her lap
and hid her pants and boots. Her fingers moved automatically,
finding holes, locating the ends of broken cord and twisting
them into square knots. She kept her nails sharp and jagged,
and when they weren't enough, she bowed her head and bit off
any useless pieces. This was mindless work, the labor of ten
thousand days, and could be done as easily in the dark as in the
light. It required no involvement. Her thoughts were elsewhere.

"You mean Bernard?" Her voice was wary. She had three sons and needed to be sure she knew the one Blanche had in mind.

"Ber-*nard*," Blanche nodded, giving the knife a last run, then inspecting the fish closely before tossing it into the large basket at her feet. The water slopped onto the floor and, from there, leaked to the shale ground inches below. Blanche arched her back and massaged her spine with her fist. With her other hand she reached for the cup of cooled tea that she had nursed for the past half-hour. Martha let the net rest and joined her.

"People talk about him, you know," Blanche said. "His looks, that goes without saying, but the other things too. The respect he pays the old folks. His singing. His calmness. His hunting skill. You must be proud."

Martha closed her eyes as if in great pain. "He is my punishment," she confessed, "but I don't know what I could have done so terrible as to deserve him. He stays out until morning. His hair is always tangled. I sometimes think that the game he brings home has died before he found it, the meat is so tough. You must have him confused with another boy. Or perhaps, with a girl like Marie, you find it hard to think ill of any child."

"Now you make fun of me," Blanche said. "It is well known that Marie has turned out badly. She is lazy and disrespectful, conceited and stubborn. I try my best to teach her, and so do my sisters and even my mother, but she folds her arms and stares at nothing. Hopeless. And she will never find a husband. A boy's mother would have to be desperate to send her son courting at my house."

"But not as desperate as a mother who could tolerate the thought of Bernard as a son-in-law," Martha said. "That would be true desperation. I will never be free of him. I will grow old with him at my side, and with no granddaughters or grandsons to comfort me."

"If only someone like your Bernard would find an interest in Marie," Blanche said as if she had not heard Martha. "If only some young man exactly like him would consent to live in my house, how I would welcome him. I would treat him as my own blood."

The two women met each other's gaze at last. Each held a cup to her lips, and after a few seconds, each drank. Each replaced her cup on the table between them. Each held her mouth firm. Blanche found her knife and reached for a new fish, cool and slippery as a stone over which much water has rushed. Martha shifted the net in her lap, moving a new section to the center. The smell of salt rose like steam as her hands went to work.

"I will speak to him," Martha said.

"And I to her," Blanche replied. "But I know her answer already. I have seen how she regards him."

"She will not be disappointed." Martha allowed one wave of pride to crest. "He's not so bad."

Blanche glanced up at Martha, then looked quickly back to her work. Bernard must be good indeed, she thought, if Martha could not better contain herself.

2

Bernard was drawing with charcoal on a piece of driftwood when his mother returned home. He was twenty-two, lean, and had large teeth. His eyes were dark beneath unusually thick brows, and his hands were long and broad. At the sound of Martha's step, he jumped to his feet and assumed the air of a person about to do something important. His fingers curved as if to hold a tool or a weapon and his eyes narrowed as if to see something far away. He was busy at nothing, his energy humming, ready for a focus. But for once she made no comment about his sloth. She did not despair at the time he wasted scratching on any smooth surface. She did not inspect his sketch and then toss it into the cooking fire. In fact, this afternoon she dealt with him rather mildly.

"Well, it's arranged," she announced. "I spent an endless morning with your future mother-in-law and before I left she had agreed to let you come to see Marie. Don't think it was easy."

Bernard's eyes followed his mother's movements as she crossed the floor and sat in exhaustion on the bed. She pushed off her boots, still caked with beach mud, and rubbed her feet together. She wore no socks.

"Marie?" he said at last. "She's too young. You should have asked me first."

Martha's glare clapped a hand over his mouth. In a moment, Bernard tried again.

"I know they're a good family. I know you want to do right for me. But you could … we could have discussed this. I mean, I think of her as a little girl, not a wife." The word, a stranger on Bernard's tongue, vibrated in the air.

"Stop whining." Martha lost patience. "Who do you 'think of' as a wife? *Doris?*"

Bernard blushed. He wasn't surprised that his mother knew about him and Doris, but it did not seem fair for her to mention it. Doris was a widow whose name brought nervous laughs to teenage boys and smiles of disapproval to everyone else. She was a woman almost twice

Bernard's age with a missing front tooth and eyes that sparked in his memory, a woman who had summoned him for an errand six months ago and whom he now loved better than he would have thought possible. But it was true: he had never thought of Doris as a wife.

"You should see yourself," Martha said. "Keep that face and you won't have to worry about marrying anyone. But don't expect me to support you forever." She noticed the driftwood, still on the floor, and nudged it with her toe to get a better view. Bernard had outlined the mountain across the bay from the village, and tucked a large sun behind its peak. When he drew it he thought it was his best work, but now its lines looked smudged and shaky. Martha leaned forward to pick it up and turn it over, as if expecting another illustration on the back. Finding none, she held it out for Bernard to take.

"Give this to your Doris," she said. "It looks like her under the blanket where she spends her time."

Bernard didn't move, but he watched the wood until his mother let it fall to the floor. He was angry at the shame he felt. He was angry that he knew it was just a matter of time until he would have to call on Marie. He was angry that his mother was right: his mountain *did* look like Doris, turned on her side.

3

When Blanche went into the house and told Marie that their problems were over, that Bernard, the catch of the village, would be courting, she expected some reaction, but her daughter simply folded her arms and stared at the fire.

"Don't you hear me?" Blanche demanded. "Bernard. Coming to see you. Can't you be happy? Can't you say something?"

Marie, however, only rolled her eyes and drummed her fingers against the pine bench upon which she sat. She wore a close-knit woven cap that, in combination with her unfortunately weak chin, made her head resemble an acorn. She was fifteen, just out of her confinement, trained for adulthood to the limits of Blanche and her sister's patience, but still a sulking child. At length she drew up her knees, circled them with her arms, and watched her mother from the corner of her eye.

> A good short story is a work of art which daunts us in proportion to its brevity … No inspiration is too noble for it; no amount of hard work is too severe for it.
> Elizabeth Stuart Phelps

Blanche stood across the long room, talking to her older sister Bonnie. She was not hard to overhear.

"Does she say 'thank you'? Does she appreciate what it means to her, to all of us, to get that damn Martha to agree? Does she care that Bernard could have any girl, from any family?"

Bonnie shook her head sadly. Her surviving children had all been boys and had long since moved to the houses of their wives' families, so she had no experience with reluctant girls, unless, she thought, she counted her memories of Blanche. But that would not do to say, especially not in earshot of Marie, who sat with her head cocked in their direction. Blanche's daughter was the hope of the next generation, the one who had to bring in a husband and produce more daughters than her mother or aunt, if the family was to regain its position. For a moment Bonnie thought of suggesting to Blanche that they present that information to Marie directly, to drop the shadows and point out both her responsibility and her power, but then she rejected the idea. The girl was impressed enough with herself as it was. Instead, Bonnie sympathized with her sister and cast occasional looks at her niece in hopes of catching on Marie's face a secret, a streak of pleasure.

4

"What am I supposed to do?" Bernard asked the next time his uncle visited. Bernard had waited for a private moment, and it came when, just before sleep, Theodore had stepped outside to relieve himself. The trees around the village seemed closer at night, taller, like the sides of a box.

From the darkness came rattling sounds of strangulation that Bernard eventually identified as the older man's yawn. When it, and the noise of splashing water, had abated, Theodore spoke. It was clear that he understood Bernard's problem.

"You do whatever they tell you and you hope they're not as bad as they could be," Theodore said. "You don't complain. You don't assume anything. You stay out of the way, because you never know what they're going to find to dislike. You be what they want."

"It's not fair." Bernard leaned against the side of the house and searched the sky. Thin clouds, silver as wet spiderwebs, passed in the night wind.

"That's true, but there are other things in the world besides owning real estate. Your true home will remain here at your mother's, just as it has been for me, but you can't *live* here forever. You need independence, distance, the chance to be a man in a place where you were never a boy.

Once you get yourself established, you'll understand what I mean. Your life is not all indoors. You'll hang around with your brothers-in-law, your uncles, your friends. Spend time at the men's house. Go to the sweat bath and gripe, or listen to the complaints of others and make jokes. In a year all your wife's family will care about is whether or not you bring in your share. By then you'll know what's what."

"But what if I don't get along with Marie?"

"*Do* get along with her. Get along with her mother. Get along with her auntie. But on your own time do what you want. It's not a big price to pay. It's a daughter-poor clan and the one they've picked out for you is going to control everything someday: rich fishing sites, a big house. Behave yourself now and you'll get your reward. It's not like you're marrying a youngest sister with no prospects."

Which was, Bernard knew, what had happened to Theodore. No wonder he was not more sympathetic.

"How do I tell Doris?" Bernard asked. This was something he had struggled with for days.

"Doris! She could have told *you*. It's good news to her. She gets a younger guy, fresh the way she likes them, and no hard feelings between you." Theodore laughed, and put an arm around Bernard's shoulders. "Listen to some advice, from your great-uncle through me to you," he said. "Groom service is the worst part, so make it as short as possible. Convince her family you won't be a pain in the ass to live with. Rule number one: appreciate everything they do. Compliment, compliment, compliment."

"Did you do that?" Bernard asked. "Did my mother's husband do that?"

"Do fish fry in hot grease? But don't take my word for it. Ask Pete. He's your father."

"I'd be embarrassed," Bernard said. "He and I never talk about serious matters. He's not of the clan."

"A man's a man," Theodore said.

5

"This is what you do," Martha instructed.

It was not yet light and she had awakened Bernard from a sound sleep. He blew into a cup of hot tea as he listened, let the darkness hide the resentment in his face.

"You go hunting and you catch something *good*, I don't care what. Something a little unusual. A beaver, maybe, or a goose. *Not* something small and easy. *Not* a squirrel. *Not* fish. You bring it home and I'll help you clean it. You leave a portion for me as if that's what you always do, to help provide for your family, but you take the best part and you set yourself in front of Blanche's door. You only speak if you're spoken to. You wait for *them* to ask *you*. And if they don't, which they won't right away, you act unconcerned. You do this every day until they invite you in, and then I'll tell you what to do next. This is your chance, so don't ruin it. Now move."

Bernard stepped out into the chill morning grayness, thought briefly of visiting Doris before he went hunting, but then abandoned the idea. He had heard through his mother's husband that Doris had made friends with a seventeen-year-old boy named James.

The dew from high grass had soaked through to Bernard's feet before he reached the edge of the woods. He realized his mother had forgotten to feed him breakfast, forgotten to make him a lunch. He heard a duck call from the lake and paused, but then continued on. He could hear his mother in his mind, and she said a duck wouldn't do.

6

"He's *there*!" Bonnie dropped the firewood she was carrying and rushed to Blanche's side.

Her sister was stirring a pot on the fire, as if what it contained were all that concerned her. "I have eyes," Blanche said. "Keep your voice down. He'll hear you."

"Did you see what he had?" Bonnie asked. "I got a glimpse of something flat and dark, but I didn't want him to catch me looking."

"I think it was a beaver tail. Would you believe, he had the nerve to hold it up to me and smile the first time I passed."

"No!"

"I thought he was better trained. It simply means he'll have to wait longer."

"Did Marie see him yet?"

"She won't go outside." Both sisters turned to the gloom in the rear of the room where Marie crouched, her head lowered over a stick game. Her long hair was loose and covered her shoulders like a shawl, her back to the doorway.

7

"Well, what happened?" Martha demanded when Bernard returned home late in the evening.

"Nothing happened," Bernard said, and threw himself down on his blankets. He raised an arm to cover his eyes, then turned to face the wall.

Martha spotted the sack her son had dropped on the floor and looked inside. The beaver tail and quarters were exactly as she had cleaned them that afternoon, and she took them out to add to the broth she had prepared.

"At least we'll eat well for a while," she said.

"I'm not hungry," Bernard replied, but his mother ignored him.

"Tell me everything."

"There's nothing to tell. I walked over there, dressed like I was going to a feast, carrying that beaver. I trapped it clean, surprised it so completely, there wasn't even adrenaline in its flesh. I thought they'd taste it, invite me to supper, but they walked by me like I wasn't there, their noses in the air."

"Whose noses?" Martha wanted to know.

"The mother and the aunt."

"Not the girl?"

"I saw no girl. I heard no girl."

"Ah," said Martha. "So she's shy. Good."

"Why good?"

"Because then she won't bully you at first, stupid boy. I've seen what happens to the husbands of the bold ones."

The smell of stewing meat filled the room, warm, rich, brown. Martha's husband Pete came into the house at the scent, tipped his head in his son's direction, and asked, "Hard day?"

8

For a week, then two weeks, the same pattern was repeated. Only the animals changed: they ranged from a porcupine to a hind quarter of caribou, from a fat grouse on a bad day to a string of matched silver salmon on a good one. Once Bernard thought he saw a black bear dive into the brush at the side of a stream, but he was momentarily afraid to investigate, and later berated himself. With a bear skin, he thought too late, he would have been irresistible and his long afternoons and evenings at Blanche's closed door would have been over.

As a month passed, Bernard gave up hope. He lost the alertness he had once felt when Blanche or Bonnie or Marie, the most unsympathetic of them all, approached, and he soon tired of the commiseration that Blanche's and Bonnie's husbands cast in his direction as they went about their business. They could remember, their expressions said, what it was like to wait outside this house, but there was nothing they could do. A word from them might slow the process rather than speed it up, might do more damage than good. If boredom was patience, Bernard achieved patience. If learning to exist without expectation of fulfillment was maturity, Bernard matured. At first he used his time to remember Doris, to wonder what she was doing and to regret not doing it with her. Later he thought about hunting, how he could have succeeded the times he had failed, how the animals behaved, how they smelled and sounded. Finally he found himself thinking about Pete, his father, in different ways than he ever had before. In Bernard's mind Pete became more than just his mother's husband; he became another man, an earlier version of Bernard, a fellow sufferer. It had not previously occurred to Bernard how hard it was to be forever a stranger in the house where you lived, to be always a half-visitor. He wondered how Pete stayed so cheerful, and wondered if his grandmother had kept his father waiting long at the doorway before inviting him inside. On an afternoon late in the second week, Bernard had a thought so profound, so unprecedented, that it straightened his back. What if, he wondered, his grandmother had not let Pete in at all? What if Pete had been judged inadequate? Where would that have left Bernard?

The next morning when he went hunting, Bernard returned to the place where he had seen the bear, hid himself behind a log, and waited.

9

"Did you hear?" Pete asked Theodore as they walked the trail from the sweat bath to their wives' houses.

"About Bernard's bear?"

"It must have weighed three hundred pounds. I didn't know Bernard had it in him."

"Have you forgotten what sitting in front of a house will drive you to? What did you catch to get inside Blanche's?"

"Nothing," Pete said. "It was me she couldn't resist."

"You forget," Theodore replied. "I was still a boy in that house. I recall their words of you. Let me see … I seem to remember some mention of the small size of certain of your parts."

"Poor brother-in-law," Pete said. "You still don't realize the lengths to which they went to avoid hurting your feelings! And how *is* your wife? How is the health of her many elder sisters? Is it true that they become stronger and more robust with every year?"

10

On the second day of the fifth week, just as she passed through the door, Blanche reached down her right hand and snagged one of the bear claws that rested in the basket by Bernard's leg. So quick was her movement, so apparently disconnected to the intent of her mind, so complete her distraction, that Bernard had to look twice to make sure it was gone. All the same, he felt a warm flush spread beneath the skin of his neck, and a feeling of inordinate pride suffused him so thoroughly that he had difficulty remaining still. He had been found worthy, and now it was only a matter of time.

Every day, with more pause and deliberation, Blanche browsed through his offerings and always selected some choice token. Her expression betrayed no gratitude, yet Bernard was sure that occasionally she was pleasantly surprised. Afraid to unbalance their precarious arrangement, he sat still as a listening hare in her presence. He kept his eyes lowered and held his breath until she had departed, but remained ever watchful for any cue that his probation had progressed. At last it came.

"Bernard!" Blanche said one day. She stood in the doorway, her hands on her hips, her head cocked to the side in amazement. "Is that you crouching there so quietly? Please, come in and share our supper, poor as it is. What a pleasure to see you."

Bernard rose slowly, stiff in his joints and half-skeptical that this was some joke, some new test, but when he entered the house, Blanche's hospitality continued and was joined by that of Bonnie, who sat by the fire trimming her husband's hair with a squeaking scissors. "Sit, sit," she motioned to a bench near the door. "What a shy boy you are. Luckily we have some nice moose to feed you."

Indeed they did. Bernard recognized the remains of the foreleg he had offered yesterday. Bonnie passed him a plate with a small portion of tough gristle, gray and cooled. He knew what to say.

"This is wonderful," he exclaimed. "The best I've ever tasted. What cooks you are. But you are too generous. Let me put some back in the pot."

When they refused, politely and with many denials of his compliments, Bernard made a great show of eating. The act of digestion absorbed his total concentration. He rubbed his stomach and cast his eyes to the ceiling in delight. With great subtlety he periodically raised his hand to his mouth, as if to wipe some grease, and used that motion to conceal the small bits of undigestible food he removed from his cheeks and tucked secretly into his pockets.

When he finished, Bernard sat nervously, breathless with anxiety. From the corner of the room he detected a space so devoid of movement that it attracted his attention. He looked, then quickly looked away. Yet his eyes still registered the image of Marie, her hair oiled and braided, wearing a new dress and a necklace made of bear claws, sitting as composed and shaded as a perfect charcoal sketch.

11

"You know, Pete," Martha said as she lay by her husband's side under a robe, "watching Bernard lately brings back memories."

"To me too. Your mother was a terror."

"I notice you still whisper such words, even though she's more than four years gone."

Pete shifted his position and propped on an elbow. In the moonlight Martha's face was seamless and young. A beam like the hottest part of a coal danced off her dark eye. He ran his fingers along her cheek and she turned her head in comfort. "You look the same as then," he said.

Martha caught his hand and brought it to her mouth, let it feel the smile.

"I pestered her, you know, to let you in," she said.

"You didn't care."

"I didn't care the day you found the eagle feathers? I didn't care the day you came an hour later than always?"

"It was raining," Pete said. "The ground was soft and I kept sinking to my knees. I couldn't arrive at your door covered in mud."

"I thought you weren't coming. I confronted my mother and told her that her slowness had cost me ..."

"Cost you what?" Pete asked, when Martha's silence persisted.

"Enough talk."

12

Marie watched the back of Bernard's head and admired the sleek sheen of his long hair, the play of muscles in his arms at his every movement. During the last month she had studied every part of him so completely that she could create him in her imagination whenever she chose, and lately she chose often. She had to fight not to laugh when they gave him the worst meat and he had to spit into his hand and act as though it were delicious. She watched the way his fingers held the plate, the way he sat so compact and attentive. She waited for the sound of his soft voice and wondered what he would say when he could speak in private. She made a game of observing his eyes until just the second before they turned to her, and believed she had been discovered only once.

13

Bernard ate almost all of his meals at Blanche's house now, and gradually became more relaxed. For one thing, his distribution increased in both quality and quantity, and he could now expect a reasonable piece of meat or salmon. For another, Blanche's and Bonnie's husbands had begun to join him on his hunts, to show him places to fish that only members of this household knew. He found he liked these men and began to call them "uncle."

Blanche herself still frightened him, but not all the time. There were moments when he found approval in her gaze, times when some word of hers sounded almost like a joke. Bonnie was warmer, more solicitous of his needs, more delighted at the food he brought, and Bernard regarded her as an ally.

As far as Marie was concerned, he still had no clue to her feelings. Even Pete and Theodore observed that this game was lasting longer than the usual and debated whether something might be wrong. They were full of advice for Bernard, full of ideas of how to please Marie, full of reminders that it was her agreement, more than anyone's, that was necessary. But no matter what Bernard did, Marie would not look at him or give him any sign of encouragement. He grew despondent, lost his appetite, found himself thinking once again of Doris and the ease of their association. Marie seemed totally beyond his reach, the focus of mystery and impossible desire. And so he was unprepared on the night, just before the first frost of winter, when, with shaking hands, Marie herself passed him a plate of food.

"This is for you," she said so softly he could barely hear, and she sat beside him while, slowly and with great emotion, he ate.

14

A year later, while waiting for the birth of Marie's first child, Blanche and Martha passed the time by nibbling strips of dried eel. Martha, who had no love for the oily skin, threw hers into the fire, where it sizzled briefly.

"The midwife predicts a girl," Blanche said. "When she spun the charm above Marie's stomach, it revolved to the left."

"A girl is most rewarding," Martha nodded. "But there is a special satisfaction in raising boys. So often I think of times when Bernard was young, so often I miss him around the house."

Blanche reached for another stick of *baleek* and did not answer. Her silence was immediately noticed, as she knew it would be.

"How is he doing?" Martha asked at last.

"He will learn," Blanche said. "He has potential. It is clear he cares greatly for Marie, and she is patient."

"That is one word for it." Martha tossed a handful of scraps into the flame and watched the light flare and dance. "Of course, Bernard was used to …" She shifted her weight, cleared her throat. "He had such a *happy* home that I'm sure it has taken some adjusting on his part in new surroundings."

"Yes, he *was* somewhat spoiled. But I think he has a good heart."

"As well he must, to remain loyal to such a chinless girl."

"One only hopes their child will inherit the mother's disposition and not be sulky and resentful of every request."

"One can but pray it will have the father's looks and personality."

A single rope of eel remained on the plate. Both women extended a hand toward it, hesitated, and withdrew. It rested between them as they cleaned their teeth with fine bone picks, carefully wiped their fingers, and when, at the sound of Marie's first muffled protest, they rose together and rushed to her side, it remained behind.

Michael Dorris was born in Kentucky, U.S., in 1945. He graduated from Yale University in 1970, taught at Franconia College, and founded the Native American Studies program at Dartmouth College, where he also taught. His works include the novels *The Crown of Columbus* (with Louise Erdrich), *A Yellow Raft in Blue Water*, and *Cloud Chamber*; a short story collection, *Working Men*; as well as non-fiction, essay collections, and a children's novel.

1. Response

a. As a reader, did you feel any connection to the character of Bernard? Did your reaction depend on your gender? Explain.

b. The author does not provide a specific setting for this story. What inferences can you make about where and when the events take place? Does the style of language reinforce the setting, or does it have a different purpose?

c. Describe the ritual of "groom service" outlined in this story. Is there a positive purpose to the ritual? Find specific evidence from the story to support your view. What relevance or message, if any, do you find in the story? Explain.
d. Describe the different relationships in this story and list their characteristics.

2. *Literature Studies* *Narrative Structure* "Groom Service" is told in sections resembling chapters. Analyse the narrative structure of the story, using a chart to present your findings. The chart should have four columns: Sections, Characters, Plot events, and Purpose of the sections. After you have completed the chart, ask yourself why Dorris may have used this particular structure to tell the story. Identify the narrative point of view and comment on whether it is appropriate for the purpose of the story.

3. *Critical Thinking* This story describes a *gynocentric society* (a society ruled by women) that is *matrilineal* (ancestry is traced through the maternal line). Working in a group, reread the story carefully and generate a list of the important rules and customs of this society. Which people seem to be the most influential? What seem to be the ideal characteristics for women? For men? Are there any aspects of this society that might be applied to our own society? Present your ideas in a brief, well-organized opinion piece. Be sure to support your arguments with solid evidence.

4. *Oral Language* *Interior Monologue* The character of Marie remains in the background and we learn very little about her. Choosing one of the scenes where Marie is present, write an interior monologue of her thoughts as the events unfold. Establish what you believe to be the tone of voice she would use within her own head. Do you think her true character is similar to or different from the way others perceive her? Read your interior monologue aloud to a small group. Afterward, explain why you characterized her as you did. Assess your delivery, considering how effectively you used voice, tone, volume, expressions, and gestures.

The Shining Houses

by Alice Munro

> "She could try all night and never find any words
> to stand up to their words, which came at her now
> invincibly from all sides: *shack, eyesore, filthy,
> property, value.*"

Mary sat on the back steps of Mrs. Fullerton's house, talking—or really listening—to Mrs. Fullerton, who sold her eggs. She had come in to pay the egg money, on her way to Edith's Debbie's birthday party. Mrs. Fullerton did not pay calls herself and she did not invite them, but, once a business pretext was established, she liked to talk. And Mary found herself exploring her neighbour's life as she had once explored the lives of grandmothers and aunts—by pretending to know less than she did, asking for some story she had heard before; this way, remembered episodes emerged each time with slight differences of content, meaning, colour, yet with a pure reality that usually attaches to things which are at least part legend. She had almost forgotten that there are people whose lives can be seen like this. She did not talk to many old people any more. Most of the people she knew had lives like her own, in which things were not sorted out yet, and it is not certain if this thing, or that, should be taken seriously. Mrs. Fullerton had no doubts or questions of this kind. How was it possible, for instance, not to take seriously the broad blithe back of Mr. Fullerton, disappearing down the road on a summer day, not to return?

"I didn't know that," said Mary. "I always thought Mr. Fullerton was dead."

"He's no more dead than I am," said Mrs. Fullerton, sitting up straight. A bold Plymouth Rock[1] walked across the bottom step and Mary's little boy, Danny, got up to give rather cautious chase. "He's just gone off on his travels, that's what he is. May of gone up north, may of gone to the States, I don't know. But he's not dead. I would of felt it. He's not old neither, you know, not old like I am. He was my second husband, he was younger. I never made any secret of it. I had this place and raised my children and buried my first husband, before ever Mr. Fullerton came upon the scene. Why, one time down in the post office we was standing together by the wicket and I went over to put a letter in the box and left my bag behind me, and Mr. Fullerton turns to go after me and the girl calls to him, she says, here, your mother's left her purse!"

Mary smiled, answering Mrs. Fullerton's high-pitched and not trustful laughter. Mrs. Fullerton was old, as she had said—older than you might think, seeing her hair still fuzzy and black, her clothes slatternly-gay,[2] dime-store brooches pinned to her ravelling sweater. Her eyes showed it, black as plums, with a soft inanimate sheen; things sank into them and they never changed. The life in her face was all in the nose and mouth, which were always twitching, fluttering, drawing tight grimace-lines down her cheeks. When she came around every Friday on her egg deliveries her hair was curled, her blouse held together by a bunch of cotton flowers, her mouth painted, a spidery and ferocious line of red; she would not show herself to her new neighbours in any sad old-womanish disarray.

"Thought I was his mother," she said. "I didn't care. I had a good laugh. But what I was telling you," she said, "a day in summer, he was off work. He had the ladder up and he was picking me the cherries off of my black-cherry tree. I came out to hang my clothes and there was this man I never seen before in my life, taking the pail of cherries my husband hands down to him. Helping himself, too, not backward, he sat down and ate cherries out of my pail. Who's that, I said to my husband, and he says, just a fellow passing. If he's a friend of yours, I said, he's welcome to stay for supper. What are you talking about, he says, I never seen him before. So I never said another thing. Mr. Fullerton went and talked to him, eating my cherries I intended for a pie, but that man would talk to anybody, tramp, Jehovah's Witness, anybody—that didn't need to mean anything."

[1]**Plymouth Rock:** a breed of chicken
[2]**slatternly-gay:** untidily colourful and showy

"And half an hour after that fellow went off," she said, "Mr. Fullerton comes out in his brown jacket and his hat on. I have to meet a man downtown. How long will you be, I said. Oh, not long. So off he goes down the road, walking down to where the old tram went—we was all in the bush then—and something made me look after him. He must be hot in that coat, I said. And that's when I knew he wasn't coming back. Yet I couldn't've expected it, he liked it here. He was talking about putting chinchillas[3] in the back yard. What's in a man's mind even when you're living with him you will never know."

"Was it long ago?" said Mary.

"Twelve years. My boys wanted me to sell then and go and live in rooms. But I said no. I had my hens and a nanny goat too at that time. More or less a pet. I had a pet coon too for a while, used to feed him chewing gum. Well, I said, husbands maybe come and go, but a place you've lived fifty years is something else. Making a joke of it with my family. Besides, I thought, if Mr. Fullerton was to come back, he'd come back here, not knowing where else to go. Of course he'd hardly know where to find me, the way it's changed now. But I always had the idea he might of suffered a loss of memory and it might come back. That has happened.

"I'm not complaining. Sometimes it seems to me about as reasonable a man should go as stay. I don't mind changes, either, that helps out my egg business. But this baby-sitting. All the time one or the other is asking me about baby-sitting. I tell them I got my own house to sit in and I raised my share of children."

Mary, remembering the birthday party, got up and called to her little boy. "I thought I might offer my black cherries for sale next summer," Mrs. Fullerton said. "Come and pick your own and they're fifty cents a box. I can't risk my old bones up a ladder no more."

"That's too much," Mary said, smiling. "They're cheaper than that at the supermarket." Mrs. Fullerton already hated the supermarket for lowering the price of eggs. Mary shook out her last cigarette and left it with her, saying she had another package in her purse. Mrs. Fullerton was fond of a cigarette but would not accept one unless you took her by surprise. Baby-sitting would pay for them, Mary thought. At the same time she was rather pleased with Mrs. Fullerton for being so unaccommodating. When Mary came out of this place, she always felt as if she were passing through barricades. The house and its surroundings were so self-sufficient, with their complicated and seemingly unalterable layout of vegetables and flower beds, apple and cherry trees, wired

---

[3]**chinchillas:** a squirrel-like rodent raised for its fur

chicken-run, berry patch and wooden walks, woodpile, a great many roughly built dark little sheds, for hens or rabbits or a goat. Here was no open or straightforward plan, no order that an outsider could understand; yet what was haphazard time had made final. The place had become fixed, impregnable, all its accumulations necessary, until it seemed that even the washtubs, mops, couch springs and stacks of old police magazines on the back porch were there to stay.

Mary and Danny walked down the road that had been called, in Mrs. Fullerton's time, Wicks Road, but was now marked on the maps of the subdivision as Heather Drive. The name of the subdivision was Garden Place, and its streets were named for flowers. On either side of the road the earth was raw; the ditches were running full. Planks were laid across the open ditches, planks approached the doors of the newest houses. The new, white and shining houses, set side by side in long rows in the wound of the earth. She always thought of them as white houses, though of course they were not entirely white. They were stucco and siding, and only the stucco was white; the siding was painted in shades of blue, pink, green and yellow, all fresh and vivid colours. Last year, just at this time, in March, the bulldozers had come in to clear away the brush and second-growth and great trees of the mountain forest; in a little while the houses were going up among the boulders, the huge torn stumps, the unimaginable upheavals of that earth. The houses were frail at first, skeletons of new wood standing up in the dusk of the cold spring days. But the roofs went on, black and green, blue and red, and the stucco, the siding; the windows were put in, and plastered with signs that said, Murry's Glass, French's Hardwood Floors; it could be seen that the houses were real. People who would live in them came out and tramped around in the mud on Sundays. They were for people like Mary and her husband and their child, with not much money but expectations of more; Garden Place was already put down, in the minds of people who understood addresses, as less luxurious than Pine Hills but more desirable than Wellington Park. The bathrooms were beautiful, with three-part mirrors, ceramic tile, and coloured plumbing. The cupboards in the kitchen were light birch or mahogany, and there were copper lighting fixtures there and in the dining ells. Brick planters, matching the fireplaces, separated the living rooms and halls. The rooms were all large and light and the basements dry, and all this soundness and excellence seemed to be clearly, proudly indicated on the face of each house—those ingenuously similar houses that looked calmly out at each other, all the way down the street.

Today, since it was Saturday, all the men were out working around their houses. They were digging drainage ditches and making rockeries and clearing off and burning torn branches and brush. They worked with competitive violence and energy, all this being new to them; they were not men who made their livings by physical work. All day Saturday and Sunday they worked like this, so that in a year or two there should be green terraces, rock walls, shapely flower beds and ornamental shrubs. The earth must be heavy to dig now; it had been raining last night and this morning. But the day was brightening; the clouds had broken, revealing a long thin triangle of sky, its blue still cold and delicate, a winter colour. Behind the houses on one side of the road were pine trees, their ponderous symmetry not much stirred by any wind. These were to be cut down any day now, to make room for a shopping centre, which had been promised when the houses were sold.

And under the structure of this new subdivision, there was still something else to be seen; that was the old city, the old wilderness city that had lain on the side of the mountain. It had to be called a city because there were tramlines running into the woods, the houses had numbers and there were all the public buildings of a city, down by the water. But houses like Mrs. Fullerton's had been separated from each other by uncut forest and a jungle of wild blackberry and salmonberry bushes; these surviving houses, with thick smoke coming out of their chimneys, walls unpainted and patched and showing different degrees of age and darkening, rough sheds and stacked wood and compost heaps and grey board fences around them—these appeared every so often among the large new houses of Mimosa and Marigold and Heather Drive—dark, enclosed, expressing something like savagery in their disorder and the steep, unmatched angles of roofs and lean-tos; not possible on these streets, but there.

"What are they saying?" said Edith, putting on more coffee. She was surrounded in her kitchen by the ruins of the birthday party—cake and molded jellies and cookies with animal faces. A balloon rolled underfoot. The children had been fed, had posed for flash cameras and endured the birthday games; now they were playing in the back bedrooms and the basement, while their parents had coffee. "What are they saying in there?" said Edith.

Words set things in motion. I've seen them doing it.
Words set up atmospheres, electrical fields, charges.
Toni Cade Bambara

"I wasn't listening," Mary said, holding the empty cream pitcher in her hand. She went to the sink window. The rent in the clouds had been torn wide open and the sun was shining. The house seemed too hot.

"Mrs. Fullerton's house," said Edith, hurrying back to the living-room. Mary knew what they were talking about. Her neighbours' conversation, otherwise not troubling, might at any moment snag itself on this subject and eddy menacingly in familiar circles of complaint, causing her to look despairingly out of windows, or down into her lap, trying to find some wonderful explanatory word to bring it to a stop; she did not succeed. She had to go back; they were waiting for cream.

A dozen neighbourhood women sat around the living room, absently holding the balloons they had been given by their children. Because the children on the street were so young, and also because any gathering-together of the people who lived there was considered a healthy thing in itself, most birthday parties were attended by mothers as well as children. Women who saw each other every day met now in earrings, nylons and skirts, with their hair fixed and faces applied. Some of the men were there too—Steve, who was Edith's husband, and others he had invited in for beer; they were all in their work clothes. The subject just introduced was one of the few on which male and female interest came together.

"I tell you what I'd do if I was next door to it," Steve said, beaming good-naturedly in expectation of laughter. "I'd send my kids over there to play with matches."

"Oh, funny," Edith said. "It's past joking. You joke, I try to do something. I even phoned the Municipal Hall."

"What did they say?" said Mary Lou Ross.

"Well, *I* said couldn't they get her to paint it, at least, or pull down some of the shacks, and they said no they couldn't. I said I thought there must be some kind of ordinance applied to people like that and they said they knew how I *felt* and they were very *sorry*—"

"But no?"

"But no."

"But what about the chickens, I thought—"

"Oh, they wouldn't let you or me keep chickens, but she has some special dispensation about that too, I forgot how it goes."

"I'm going to stop buying them," Janie Inger said. "The supermarket's cheaper and who cares that much about fresh? And my God, the smell. I said to Carl I knew we were coming to the sticks but I somehow didn't picture us next door to a barnyard."

"Across the street is worse than next door. It makes me wonder why we ever bothered with a picture window, whenever anybody comes to see us I want to draw the drapes so they won't see what's across from us."

"Okay, okay," Steve said, cutting heavily through these female voices. "What Carl and I started out to tell you was that, if we can work this lane deal, she has got to go. It's simple and it's legal. That's the beauty of it."

"What lane deal?"

"We are getting to that. Carl and I been cooking this for a couple of weeks, but we didn't like to say anything in case it didn't work out. Take it, Carl."

"Well, she's on the lane allowance, that's all," Carl said. He was a real estate salesman, stocky, earnest, successful. "I had an idea it might be that way, so I went down to the Municipal Hall and looked it up."

"What does that mean, dear?" said Janie, casual, wifely.

"This is it," Carl said. "There's an allowance for a lane, there always has been, the idea being if the area ever got built up they would put a lane through. But they never thought that would happen, people just built where they liked. She's got part of her house and half a dozen shacks sitting right where the lane has to go through. So what we do now, we get the municipality to put through a lane. We need a lane anyway. Then she has to get out. It's the law."

"It's the law," said Steve, radiating admiration. "What a smart boy. These real estate operators are smart boys."

"Does she get anything?" said Mary Lou. "I'm sick of looking at it and all but I don't want to see anybody in the poorhouse."

"Oh, she'll get paid. More than it's worth. Look, it's to her advantage. She'll get paid for it, and she couldn't sell it, she couldn't give it away."

Mary set her coffee cup down before she spoke and hoped her voice would sound all right, not emotional or scared. "But remember she's been here a long time," she said. "She was here before most of us were born." She was trying desperately to think of other words, words more sound and reasonable than these; she could not expose to this positive tide any notion that they might think flimsy and romantic, or she would destroy her argument. But she had no argument. She could try all night and never find any words to stand up to their words, which came at her now invincibly from all sides: *shack, eyesore, filthy, property, value.*

"Do you honestly think that people who let their property get so rundown have that much claim to our consideration?" Janie said, feeling her husband's plan was being attacked.

"She's been here forty years, now we're here," Carl said. "So it goes. And whether you realize it or not, just standing there that house is bringing down the resale value of every house on this street. I'm in the business, I know."

And these were joined by other voices; it did not matter much what they said as long as they were full of self-assertion and anger. That was their strength, proof of their adulthood, of themselves and their seriousness. The spirit of anger rose among them, bearing up their young voices, sweeping them together as on a flood of intoxication, and they admired each other in this new behaviour as property-owners as people admire each other for being drunk.

"We might as well get everybody now," Steve said. "Save going around to so many places."

It was supper time, getting dark out. Everybody was preparing to go home, mothers buttoning their children's coats, children clutching, without much delight, their balloons and whistles and paper baskets full of jelly beans. They had stopped fighting, almost stopped noticing each other; the party had disintegrated. The adults too had grown calmer and felt tired.

"Edith! Edith, have you got a pen?"

Edith brought a pen and they spread the petition for the lane, which Carl had drawn up, on the dining-room table, clearing away the paper plates with smears of dried ice cream. People began to sign mechanically as they said goodbye. Steve was still scowling slightly; Carl stood with one hand on the paper, businesslike, but proud. Mary knelt on the floor and struggled with Danny's zipper. She got up and put on her own coat, smoothed her hair, put on her gloves and took them off again. When she could not think of anything else to do she walked past the dining-room table on her way to the door. Carl held out the pen.

"I can't sign that," she said. Her face flushed up, at once, her voice was trembling. Steve touched her shoulder.

"What's the matter, honey?"

"I don't think we have the right. We haven't the right."

"Mary, don't you care how things look? You live here too."

"No, I—I don't care." Oh, wasn't it strange, how in your imagination, when you stood up for something, your voice rang, people started, abashed; but in real life they all smiled in rather a special way and you saw that what you had really done was serve yourself up as a conversational delight for the next coffee party.

"Don't worry, Mary, she's got money in the bank," Janie said. "She must have. I asked her to baby-sit for me once and she practically spit in my face. She isn't exactly a charming old lady, you know."

"I know she isn't a charming old lady," Mary said.

Steve's hand still rested on her shoulder. "Hey what do you think we are, a bunch of ogres?"

"Nobody wants to turn her out just for the fun of it," Carl said. "It's unfortunate. We all know that. But we have to think of the community."

"Yes," said Mary. But she put her hands in the pockets of her coat and turned to say thank you to Edith, thank you for the birthday party. It occurred to her that they were right, for themselves, for whatever it was they had to be. And Mrs. Fullerton was old, she had dead eyes, nothing could touch her. Mary went out and walked with Danny up the street. She saw the curtains being drawn across the living-room windows; cascades of flowers, of leaves, of geometrical designs, shut off these rooms from the night. Outside it was quite dark, the white houses were growing dim, the clouds breaking and breaking, and smoke blowing from Mrs. Fullerton's chimney. The pattern of Garden Place, so assertive in the daytime, seemed to shrink at night into the raw black mountainside.

Reservoir by Michael Berger. Digital watercolour

Berger's image is strongly geometrical; identify the basic shapes he uses to construct this landscape. Are there any details in the image that work against its linearity? In a group, discuss the effect the work creates and the ideas the artist might be suggesting.

The voices in the living room have blown away, Mary thought. If they would blow away and their plans be forgotten, if one thing could be left alone. But these are people who win, and they are good people; they want homes for their children, they help each other when there is trouble, they plan a community—saying that word as if they found a modern and well-proportioned magic in it, and no possibility anywhere of a mistake.

There is nothing you can do at present but put your hands in your pockets and keep a disaffected heart.

Alice Munro's first collection of short stories, *Dance of the Happy Shades* (from which this story was taken), was published in 1968 and won a Governor General's Award. In 1977, Munro became the first Canadian to win the Canada-Australia Literary Prize. She went on to win two more Governor General's Awards for her collections, *Who Do You Think You Are?* and *The Progress of Love*.

1. Response
  a. Why is Mary interested in Mrs. Fullerton? How would you describe their conversation at the beginning of the story?
  b. What is revealed about Mrs. Fullerton through her reaction to Mr. Fullerton's leaving?
  c. Reread the first section of the story and note any examples of foreshadowing you can detect. Compare your findings with those of a classmate.
  d. What do you think is the significance of the story's title?
  e. "The Shining Houses" portrays an important conflict in a changing community. Summarize that conflict in your own words. To what degree does the story present both sides of the argument? Do you think the author favours one side over the other? Give evidence for your answer.

2. *Media* *Human Interest Story* Imagine you are a print or TV journalist working in the community described in "The Shining Houses." A group led by Carl and Janie has taken their plan for the lane to local council. Mrs. Fullerton is fighting the zone change. Create a human interest story about the conflict. Include quotations from, or an interview with, Mary and other residents. You can present your story either as a written article, or orally, as a live broadcast.

3. *Critical Thinking* With the growth of urban development in many areas of the country, we, as a society, are frequently asked to balance the desire for expansion with the desire for preservation. Are there examples of this opposition within your community? If you were a member of a town council, what would you want to see done in your area? In a group, create a set of guidelines for managing growth in your own community. If the group cannot reach a consensus, include a dissenting opinion with your guidelines. List those oral and group skills that you think you used effectively in this activity. What skills would you like to develop?

4. *Focus on Context* "The Shining Houses" appeared in *Dance of the Happy Shades*, published in 1968. During this time of intense social activism, women's roles were increasingly being scrutinized and critiqued. Examine the characters of Mrs. Fullerton, Mary, and Janie, commenting on the different characteristics and roles each woman represents. How is Mary different from her neighbours? Speculate on Munro's purpose in writing this story and creating these characters. Does understanding the context of the story increase your understanding or appreciation of it? Explain.

Theme Connections

- *"On the Rainy River,"* a story about societal pressures, page 70
- *"I Am a Rock,"* an ironic song about not needing others, page 225
- *"The Love Song of J. Alfred Prufrock,"* a poem about conformity, page 240
- *"Rink Rage,"* a magazine article about "mob" actions, page 320

Transients in Arcadia

by
O. Henry

New York, circa 1908, where the elegant Hotel Lotus offered a dream of luxury to those who could afford it.

There is a hotel on Broadway that has escaped discovery by the summer-resort promoters. It is deep and wide and cool. Its rooms are finished in dark oak of a low temperature. Home-made breezes and deep-green shrubbery give it the delights without the inconveniences of the Adirondacks.[1] One can mount its broad staircases or glide dreamily upward in its aërial elevators, attended by guides in brass buttons, with a serene joy that Alpine climbers have never attained. There is a chef in its kitchen who will prepare for you brook trout better than the White Mountains ever served, seafood that would turn Old Point Comfort—"by Gad, sah!"—green with envy, and Maine venison that would melt the official heart of the game warden.

A few have found out this oasis in the July desert of Manhattan. During that month you will see the hotel's reduced array of guests scattered luxuriously about in the cool twilight of its lofty dining-room, gazing at one another across the snowy waste of unoccupied tables, silently congratulatory.

Superfluous, watchful, pneumatically-moving waiters hover near, supplying every want before it is expressed. The temperature is perpetual April. The ceiling is painted in watercolors to counterfeit a summer sky across which delicate clouds drift and do not vanish as those of nature do to our regret.

---

[1]**Adirondacks:** a mountain range of north-eastern New York state

The pleasing, distant roar of Broadway is transformed in the imagination of the happy guests to the noise of a waterfall filling the woods with its restful sound. At every strange footstep the guests turn an anxious ear, fearful lest their retreat be discovered and invaded by the restless pleasure-seekers who are forever hounding Nature to her deepest lairs.

Thus in the depopulated caravansary the little band of connoisseurs jealously hide themselves during the heated season, enjoying to the uttermost the delights of mountain and seashore that art and skill have gathered and served to them.

In this July came to the hotel one whose card that she sent to the clerk for her name to be registered read "Mme. Héloise D'Arcy Beaumont."

Madame Beaumont was a guest such as the Hotel Lotus loved. She possessed the fine air of the élite, tempered and sweetened by a cordial graciousness that made the hotel employees her slaves. Bellboys fought for the honor of answering her ring; the clerks, but for the question of ownership, would have deeded to her the hotel and its contents; the other guests regarded her as the final touch of feminine exclusiveness and beauty that rendered the entourage perfect.

This super-excellent guest rarely left the hotel. Her habits were consonant with the customs of the discriminating patrons of the Hotel Lotus. To enjoy that delectable hostelry one must forego the city as though it were leagues away. By night a brief excursion to the nearby roofs is in order; but during the torrid day one remains in the umbrageous fastnesses of the Lotus as a trout hangs poised in the pellucid sanctuaries of his favorite pool.

Though alone in the Hotel Lotus, Madame Beaumont preserved the state of a queen whose loneliness was of position only. She breakfasted at ten, a cool, sweet, leisurely, delicate being who glowed softly in the dimness like a jasmine flower in the dusk.

But at dinner was Madame's glory at its height. She wore a gown as beautiful and immaterial as the mist from an unseen cataract in a mountain gorge. The nomenclature[2] of this gown is beyond the guess of the scribe. Always pale-red roses reposed against its lace-garnished front. It was a gown that the head-waiter viewed with respect and met at the door. You thought of Paris when you saw it, and maybe of mysterious countesses, and certainly of Versailles[3] and rapiers and Mrs. Fiske[4] and

---

[2]**nomenclature:** literally a system of names or terms used in a particular field of science or art; here used playfully to mean designer
[3]**Versailles:** a French palace just outside of Paris
[4]**Mrs. Fiske:** a famous American actor, playwright, and activist

rouge-et-noir.[5] There was an untraceable rumor in the Hotel Lotus that Madame was a cosmopolite, and that she was pulling with her slender white hands certain strings between the nations in the favor of Russia. Being a citizeness of the world's smoothest roads it was small wonder that she was quick to recognize in the refined purlieus of the Hotel Lotus the most desirable spot in America for a restful sojourn during the heat of midsummer.

On the third day of Madame Beaumont's residence in the hotel a young man entered and registered himself as a guest. His clothing—to speak of his points in approved order—was quietly in the mode; his features good and regular; his expression that of a poised and sophisti-cated man of the world. He informed the clerk that he would remain three or four days, inquired concerning the sailing of European steam-ships, and sank into the blissful inanition of the nonpareil hotel with the contented air of a traveller in his favorite inn.

The young man—not to question the veracity of the register—was Harold Farrington. He drifted into the exclusive and calm current of life in the Lotus so tactfully and silently that not a ripple alarmed his fellow-seekers after rest. He ate in the Lotus and of its patronym,[6] and was lulled into blissful peace with the other fortunate mariners. In one day he acquired his table and his waiter and the fear lest the panting chasers after repose that kept Broadway warm should pounce upon and destroy this contiguous but covert haven.

After dinner on the next day after the arrival of Harold Farrington Madame Beaumont dropped her handkerchief in passing out. Mr. Far-rington recovered and returned it without the effusiveness of a seeker after acquaintance.

Perhaps there was a mystic freemasonry between the discriminat-ing guests of the Lotus. Perhaps they were drawn one to another by the fact of their common good fortune in discovering the acme of summer resorts in a Broadway hotel. Words delicate in courtesy and tentative in departure from formality passed between the two. And, as if in the expedient atmosphere of a real summer resort, an acquaintance grew, flowered and fructified on the spot as does the mystic plant of the con-juror. For a few moments they stood on a balcony upon which the cor-ridor ended, and tossed the feathery ball of conversation.

"One tires of the old resorts," said Madame Beaumont, with a faint but sweet smile. "What is the use to fly to the mountains or the seashore

---

[5]**rouge-et-noir:** game of chance
[6]**He ate in the Lotus and of its patronym:** "he ate of the Lotus"; in Homer's *The Odyssey*, the lotus-eaters lived in a state of drug-induced bliss

to escape noise and dust when the very people that make both follow us there?"

"Even on the ocean," remarked Farrington sadly, "the Philistines[7] be upon you. The most exclusive steamers are getting to be scarcely more than ferry boats. Heaven help us when the summer resorter discovers that the Lotus is further away from Broadway than Thousand Islands or Mackinac."[8]

"I hope our secret will be safe for a week, anyhow," said Madame, with a sigh and a smile. "I do not know where I would go if they should descend upon the dear Lotus. I know of but one place so delightful in summer, and that is the castle of Count Polinski, in the Ural Mountains."

"I hear that Baden-Baden and Cannes are almost deserted this season," said Farrington. "Year by year the old resorts fall in disrepute. Perhaps many others, like ourselves, are seeking out the quiet nooks that are overlooked by the majority."

"I promise myself three days more of this delicious rest," said Madame Beaumont. "On Monday the *Cedric* sails."

Harold Farrington's eyes proclaimed his regret. "I too must leave on Monday," he said, "but I do not go abroad."

Madame Beaumont shrugged one round shoulder in a foreign gesture.

"One cannot hide here forever, charming though it may be. The château has been in preparation for me longer than a month. Those house parties that one must give—what a nuisance! But I shall never forget my week in the Hotel Lotus."

"Nor shall I," said Farrington in a low voice, "and I shall never *forgive* the *Cedric*."

On Sunday evening, three days afterward, the two sat at a little table on the same balcony. A discreet waiter brought ices and small glasses of claret cup.

Madame Beaumont wore the same beautiful evening gown that she had worn each day at dinner. She seemed thoughtful. Near her hand on the table lay a small chatelaine purse. After she had eaten her ice she opened the purse and took out a one-dollar bill.

"Mr. Farrington," she said, with the smile that had won the Hotel Lotus, "I want to tell you something. I'm going to leave before breakfast

---

[7]**Philistines:** ignorant and uncultured people
[8]**Thousand Islands or Mackinac:** popular holiday spots: The Thousand Islands community is in southeastern Ontario and upstate New York on the St. Lawrence River; "Mackinac" refers to Mackinac Island in Michigan.

in the morning, because I've got to go back to my work. I'm behind the hosiery counter at Casey's Mammoth Store, and my vacation's up at eight o'clock tomorrow. That paper dollar is the last cent I'll see till I draw my eight dollars salary next Saturday night. You're a real gentleman, and you've been good to me, and I wanted to tell you before I went.

"I've been saving up out of my wages for a year just for this vacation. I wanted to spend one week like a lady if I never do another one. I wanted to get up when I please instead of having to crawl out at seven every morning; and I wanted to live on the best and be waited on and ring bells for things just like rich folks do. Now I've done it, and I've had the happiest time I ever expect to have in my life. I'm going back to my work and my little hall bedroom satisfied for another year. I wanted to tell you about it, Mr. Farrington, because I—I thought you kind of liked me, and I—I liked you. But, oh, I couldn't help deceiving you up till now, for it was all just like a fairy tale to me. So I talked about Europe and the things I've read about in other countries, and made you think I was a great lady.

"This dress I've got on—it's the only one I have that's fit to wear— I bought from O'Dowd & Levinsky on the instalment plan.

"Seventy-five dollars is the price, and it was made to measure. I paid $10 down, and they're to collect $1 a week till it's paid for. That'll be about all I have to say, Mr. Farrington, except that my name is Mamie Siviter instead of Madame Beaumont, and I thank you for your attentions. This dollar will pay the instalment due on the dress tomorrow. I guess I'll go up to my room now."

Harold Farrington listened to the recital of the Lotus's loveliest guest with an impassive countenance. When she had concluded he drew a small book like a checkbook from his coat pocket. He wrote upon a blank form in this with a stub of pencil, tore out the leaf, tossed it over to his companion and took up the paper dollar.

"I've got to go to work, too, in the morning," he said, "and I might as well begin now. There's a receipt for the dollar instalment. I've been a collector for O'Dowd & Levinsky for three years. Funny, ain't it, that you and me both had the same idea about spending our vacation? I've always wanted to put up at a swell hotel, and I saved up out of my twenty per, and did it. Say, Mame, how about a trip to Coney Saturday night on the boat—what?"

The face of the pseudo Madame Héloise D'Arcy Beaumont beamed.

"Oh, you bet I'll go, Mr. Farrington. The store closes at twelve on Saturdays. I guess Coney'll be all right even if we did spend a week with the swells."

Below the balcony the sweltering city growled and buzzed in the July night. Inside the Hotel Lotus the tempered, cool shadows reigned, and the solicitous waiter single-footed[9] near the low windows, ready at a nod to serve Madame and her escort.

At the door of the elevator Farrington took his leave, and Madame Beaumont made her last ascent. But before they reached the noiseless cage he said: "Just forget that 'Harold Farrington,' will you? McManus is the name—James McManus. Some call me Jimmy."

"Good-night, Jimmy," said Madame.

---

[9]**single-footed:** walked with a rapid, regular step

O. Henry is the pseudonym of William Sydney Porter, who was born in North Carolina, U.S., in 1862. He worked in Texas as a clerk and bank teller for over ten years, but was charged with embezzling funds from the bank in 1896. Although the amount was minimal, he fled to the Honduras and only returned to Texas when he discovered that his wife was dying. He turned himself in after her death. Porter was released from prison after serving three years of his five-year sentence, and moved to New York City where he began to write full time. During his lifetime, he published ten collections of short stories and, after his death, a further four collections were published.

I. Response

a. Use a reference book to discover the appropriateness of the story's title.

b. What was your reaction to the opening paragraphs of the story and the emphasis on description of the setting? What do you think O. Henry was trying to accomplish?

c. How does O. Henry establish Madame Beaumont as a member of high society and therefore an acceptable guest in the Hotel Lotus? To what degree does he use the same techniques with Harold Farrington? Leaving the question of wealth aside, are the two characters portrayed as suitable guests? Explain.

d. Were you surprised by the confessions from Madame Beaumont and Mr. Farrington? Why or why not?

2. ***Vocabulary*** Reread the story and make a list of ten words with which you are unfamiliar, or which you are unused to seeing in print. Provide a definition and at least one synonym for each word. Rewrite three sentences from the story by substituting the synonym for the original word. How does this affect the tone of the sentences?

3. ***Literature Studies*** *Coincidence and Irony* O. Henry's writing often includes coincidences and irony. How does he use these devices in this story? With a partner, prepare a short presentation for the class, illustrating your findings. How would you rate your ability to analyse the literary devices an author uses?

4. ***Language Conventions*** *Register* Why is the **register** of the language so important to the story's effectiveness? Identify the moment when a new language register appears in the narrative. How would you describe each type of register? What effect does each register have on the reader? Given O. Henry's stature as a writer of short stories, do you believe his choice of register was intentional? Why or why not? Analyse the register you have used in a piece of writing, and assess whether it was an effective choice for your audience and purpose. Experiment with using a change in register, as O. Henry has done, to create a particular effect.

Register refers to the level of formality of language. Language can be characterized according to the social context for which it is appropriate. For example, language with a colloquial register might contain slang expressions and unconventional grammar.

5. ***Media*** *Ad* Reread O. Henry's description of the setting in the opening paragraphs. Using these details as background, create an ad campaign for the owners of the Hotel Lotus. The campaign should include ads in at least two media—radio, TV, magazines, or newspapers. Although you should avoid using too many direct quotations from the story, be sure to maintain a sense of the atmosphere of quiet opulence. Prepare your campaign for presentation to the whole class.

> My writing is full of lives I might have lived.
> —*Joyce Carol Oates*

For five years Kamau had been held as a political prisoner.
What would he find upon his return home?

The Return

by Ngugi wa Thiong'o

The road was long. Whenever he took a step forward, little clouds of dust rose, whirled angrily behind him, and then slowly settled again. But a thin train of dust was left in the air, moving like smoke. He walked on, however, unmindful of the dust and ground under his feet. Yet with every step he seemed more and more conscious of the hardness and apparent animosity of the road. Not that he looked down; on the contrary, he looked straight ahead as if he would, any time now, see a familiar object that would hail him as a friend and tell him that he was near home. But the road stretched on.

He made quick, springing steps, his left hand dangling freely by the side of his once white coat, now torn and worn out. His right hand, bent at the elbow, held onto a string tied to a small bundle on his slightly drooping back. The bundle, well wrapped with a cotton cloth that had once been printed with red flowers now faded out, swung from side to side in harmony with the rhythm of his steps. The bundle held the bitterness and hardships of the years spent in detention camps. Now and then he looked at the sun on its homeward journey. Sometimes he darted quick side-glances at the small hedged strips of land which, with their sickly-looking crops, maize, beans, and peas, appeared much as everything else did—unfriendly. The whole country was dull and seemed weary. To Kamau, this was nothing new. He remembered that, even before the Mau Mau emergency,[1] the over-tilled Gikuyu holdings[2] wore haggard looks in contrast to the sprawling green fields in the settled area.

A path branched to the left. He hesitated for a moment and then made up his mind. For the first time, his eyes brightened a little as he went along the path that would take him down the valley and then to the village. At last home was near and, with that realization, the faraway look of a weary traveller seemed to desert him for a while. The valley

---

[1] **Mau Mau emergency:** a violent rebellion aimed at ejecting white settlers from colonial Kenya, 1952–56
[2] **Gikuyu holdings:** lands farmed by the Gikuyu people, but controlled at the time by the English colonial government

and the vegetation along it were in deep contrast to the surrounding country. For here green bush and trees thrived. This could only mean one thing: Honia river still flowed. He quickened his steps as if he could scarcely believe this to be true till he had actually set his eyes on the river. It was there; it still flowed. Honia, where so often he had taken a bathe, plunging stark naked into its cool living water, warmed his heart as he watched its serpentine movement round the rocks and heard its slight murmurs. A painful exhilaration passed all over him, and for a moment he longed for those days. He sighed. Perhaps the river would not recognize in his hardened features that same boy to whom the riverside world had meant everything. Yet as he approached Honia, he felt more akin to it than he had felt to anything else since his release.

A group of women were drawing water. He was excited, for he could recognize one or two from his ridge. There was the middle-aged Wanjiku, whose deaf son had been killed by the Security Forces just before he himself was arrested. She had always been a darling of the village, having a smile for everyone and food for all. Would they receive him? Would they give him a "hero's welcome"? He thought so. Had he not always been a favourite all along the Ridge? And had he not fought for the land? He wanted to run and shout: "Here I am. I have come back to you." But he desisted. He was a man.

"Is it well with you?" A few voices responded. The other women, with tired and worn features, looked at him mutely as if his greeting was of no consequence. Why! Had he been so long in the camp? His spirits were damped as he feebly asked: "Do you not remember me?" Again they looked at him. They stared at him with cold, hard looks; like everything else, they seemed to be deliberately refusing to know or own him. It was Wanjiku who at last recognized him. But there was neither warmth nor enthusiasm in her voice as she said, "Oh, is it you, Kamau? We thought you—" She did not continue. Only now he noticed something else—surprise? fear? He could not tell. He saw their quick glances dart at him and he knew for certain that a secret from which he was excluded bound them together.

"Perhaps I am no longer one of them!" he bitterly reflected. But they told him of the new village. The old village of scattered huts spread thinly over the Ridge was no more.

He left them, feeling embittered and cheated. The old village had not even waited for him. And suddenly he felt a strong nostalgia for his old home, friends and surroundings. He thought of his father, mother and—and—he dared not think about her. But for all that, Muthoni, just as she had been in the old days, came back to his mind. His heart beat faster. He felt desire and a warmth thrilled through him. He quickened his step. He forgot the village women as he remembered his wife. He had stayed with her for a mere two weeks; then he had been swept away by the Colonial Forces.[3] Like many others, he had been hurriedly screened and then taken to detention without trial. And all that time he had thought of nothing but the village and his beautiful woman.

The others had been like him. They had talked of nothing but their homes. One day he was working next to another detainee from Muranga.[4] Suddenly the detainee, Njoroge, stopped breaking stones. He sighed heavily. His worn-out eyes had a faraway look.

"What's wrong, man? What's the matter with you?" Kamau asked.

"It is my wife. I left her expecting a baby. I have no idea what has happened to her."

Another detainee put in: "For me, I left my woman with a baby. She had just been delivered. We were all happy. But on the same day, I was arrested …"

And so they went on. All of them longed for one day—the day of their return home. Then life would begin anew.

Kamau himself had left his wife without a child. He had not even finished paying the bride-price. But now he would go, seek work in Nairobi,[5] and pay off the remainder to Muthoni's parents. Life would indeed begin anew. They would have a son and bring him up in their own home. With these prospects before his eyes, he quickened his steps. He wanted to run—no, fly to hasten his return. He was now nearing the top of the hill. He wished he could suddenly meet his brothers and sisters. Would they ask him questions? He would, at any rate, not tell them all: the beating, the screening and the work on roads and in quarries with an askari[6] always nearby ready to kick him if he relaxed. Yes. He had suffered many humiliations, and he had not resisted. Was there any need? But his soul and all the vigour of his manhood had rebelled and bled with rage and bitterness.

One day these wazungu[7] would go!

One day his people would be free! Then, then—he did not know what he would do. However, he bitterly assured himself no one would ever flout his manhood again.

He mounted the hill and then stopped. The whole plain lay below. The new village was before him—rows and rows of compact mud huts,

---

[3]**Colonial Forces:** the army of Kenya's British colonial government
[4]**Muranga:** district of central Kenya
[5]**Nairobi:** capital city of Kenya
[6]**askari:** a guard or soldier
[7]**wazungu:** Europeans, white people

crouching on the plain under the fast-vanishing sun. Dark blue smoke curled upwards from various huts, to form a dark mist that hovered over the village. Beyond, the deep, blood-red sinking sun sent out finger-like streaks of light that thinned outwards and mingled with the grey mist shrouding the distant hills.

In the village, he moved from street to street, meeting new faces. He inquired. He found his home. He stopped at the entrance to the yard and breathed hard and full. This was the moment of his return home. His father sat huddled up on a three-legged stool. He was now very aged and Kamau pitied the old man. But he had been spared—yes, spared to see his son's return—

Donkeys, Lamu, Kenya by Andrew Macara. Oil on canvas

This painting captures a moment in the everyday life of the town of Lamu, Kenya. What adjectives would you choose to describe this scene? Explain how the artist's use of colour is essential to the impression that the painting creates.

"Father!"

The old man did not answer. He just looked at Kamau with strange vacant eyes. Kamau was impatient. He felt annoyed and irritated. Did he not see him? Would he behave like the women Kamau had met at the river?

In the street, naked and half-naked children were playing, throwing dust at one another. The sun had already set and it looked as if there would be moonlight.

"Father, don't you remember me?" Hope was sinking in him. He felt tired. Then he saw his father suddenly start and tremble like a leaf. He saw him stare with unbelieving eyes. Fear was discernible in those eyes. His mother came, and his brothers too. They crowded around him. His aged mother clung to him and sobbed hard.

"I knew my son would come. I knew he was not dead."

"Why, who told you I was dead?"

"That Karanja, son of Njogu."

And then Kamau understood. He understood his trembling father. He understood the women at the river. But one thing puzzled him: he had never been in the same detention camp with Karanja. Anyway he had come back. He wanted now to see Muthoni. Why had she not come out? He wanted to shout, "I have come, Muthoni; I am here." He looked around. His mother understood him. She quickly darted a glance at her man and then simply said:

"Muthoni went away."

Kamau felt something cold settle in his stomach. He looked at the village huts and the dullness of the land. He wanted to ask many questions but he dared not. He could not yet believe that Muthoni had gone. But he knew by the look of the women at the river, by the look of his parents, that she was gone.

"She was a good daughter to us," his mother was explaining. "She waited for you and patiently bore all the ills of the land. Then Karanja came and said that you were dead. Your father believed him. She believed him too and keened for a month. Karanja constantly paid us visits. He was of your Rika,[8] you know. Then she got a child. We could have kept her. But where is the land? Where is the food? Ever since land consolidation,[9] our last security was taken away. We let Karanja go with her. Other women have done worse—gone to town. Only the infirm and the old have been left here."

---

[8]**Rika:** a Gikuyu social grouping similar to a clan
[9]**land consolidation:** redistribution of land, directed by the Kenyan government

He was not listening; the coldness in his stomach slowly changed to bitterness. He felt bitter against all, all the people including his father and mother. They had betrayed him. They had leagued against him, and Karanja had always been his rival. Five years was admittedly not a short time. But why did she go? Why did they allow her to go? He wanted to speak. Yes, speak and denounce everything—the women at the river, the village and the people who dwelt there. But he could not. This bitter thing was choking him.

"You—you gave my own away?" he whispered.

"Listen, child, child—"

The big yellow moon dominated the horizon. He hurried away bitter and blind, and only stopped when he came to the Honia river.

And standing at the bank, he saw not the river, but his hopes dashed on the ground instead. The river moved swiftly, making ceaseless monotonous murmurs. In the forest the crickets and other insects kept up an incessant buzz. And above, the moon shone bright. He tried to remove his coat, and the small bundle he had held on to so firmly fell. It rolled down the bank and before Kamau knew what was happening, it was floating swiftly down the river. For a time he was shocked and wanted to retrieve it. What would he show his—Oh, had he forgotten so soon? His wife had gone. And the little things that had so strangely reminded him of her and that he had guarded all those years, had gone! He did not know why, but somehow he felt relieved. Thoughts of drowning himself dispersed. He began to put on his coat, murmuring to himself, "Why should she have waited for me? Why should all the changes have waited for my return?"

Ngugi wa Thiong'o was born in Kenya in 1938. He received degrees from the Makerere University in Uganda in 1963 and the University of Leeds in England, in 1964. His first novel, *Weep Not, Child*, was published while he was studying in England. After returning to Kenya, he wrote his second novel, *The River Between*. Ngugi's work involves issues such as Kenyan independence and the Mau Mau rebellion of 1952–56. His novel, *Petals of Blood*, led to his imprisonment in 1978. His book, *Detained: A Writer's Prison Diary*, describes his prison experiences, and his later works include the novel *Matigari* and the play *Ngaahika Ndeenda (I Will Marry When I Want)*.

1. Response

a. Make a list of the hopes and fears that are occupying Kamau's mind upon his return to his village. Compare your list with a classmate's and discuss the similarities and differences.

b. At what point in the story did you first suspect that Kamau would face disappointment? What specific details triggered your suspicion?

c. Explain why the women by the Honia river react so coldly toward Kamau.

d. Do you think it was reasonable or unrealistic for Kamau to expect his wife, Muthoni, to wait for him? Why?

e. Reread the ending carefully. What choices does Kamau consider as he stands before the river? Why do you think he is "relieved" to see the end of the "small bundle" of his personal effects? In your own words, summarize the choice Kamau makes at this crucial moment in his life.

2. Literature Studies *Setting* Using specific references from the story, show how Ngugi's careful descriptions of the setting help to create the story's atmosphere and contribute to its meaning. Present your conclusions either orally or in written form; you might also create a visual component to support your presentation.

3. Focus on Context Use your research skills to prepare one or two pages of background information that you think would help a reader better understand "The Return." For example, you might provide details about some or all of the following: the author; Kenyan geography and culture; the historical setting; and the geopolitical issues the story raises.

4. Media *Analysing News Articles* With a partner, examine six news articles—from various newspapers, magazines, or Internet sites—about Africa. What conclusions can you reach about how Africa is represented in the news? How accurate do you think this portrayal is?

Belisa's words could improve dreams or drive away melancholy—or they could pierce like the sharpest daggers.

Two Words

by Isabel Allende

Translated from the Spanish by Margaret Sayers Peden

She went by the name of Belisa Crepusculario,[1] not because she had been baptized with that name or given it by her mother, but because she herself had searched until she found the poetry of 'beauty' and 'twilight' and cloaked herself in it. She made her living selling words. She journeyed through the country from the high cold mountains to the burning coasts, stopping at fairs and in markets where she set up four poles covered by a canvas awning under which she took refuge from the sun and rain to minister to her customers. She did not have to peddle her merchandise because from having wandered far and near, everyone knew who she was. Some people waited for her from one year to the next, and when she appeared in the village with her bundle underneath her arm, they would form a line in front of her stall. Her prices were fair. For five *centavos* she delivered verses from memory; for seven she improved the quality of dreams; for nine she wrote love letters; for twelve she invented insults for irreconcilable enemies. She also sold stories, not fantasies but long, true stories she recited at one telling, never skipping a word. This is how she carried the news from one town to another. People paid her to add a line or two: our son was born; so and so died; our children got married; the crops burned in the field.

---

[1] **Belisa Crepusculario:** In Spanish, *belleza* means *beauty*, and *crepúsculo* means *twilight*.

Wherever she went a small crowd gathered around to listen as she began to speak, and that was how they learned about each other's doings, about distant relatives, about what was going on in the civil war. To anyone who paid her fifty *centavos* in trade, she gave the gift of a secret word to drive away melancholy. It was not the same word for everyone, naturally, because that would have been collective deceit. Each person received his or her own word, with the assurance that no one else would use it that way in this universe or the beyond.

Belisa Crepusculario had been born into a family so poor they did not even have names to give their children. She came into the world and grew up in an inhospitable land where some years the rains became avalanches of water that bore everything away before them and others when not a drop fell from the sky and the sun swelled to fill the horizon and the world became a desert. Until she was twelve, Belisa had no occupation or virtue other than having withstood hunger and the exhaustion of centuries. During one interminable drought, it fell to her to bury four younger brothers and sisters; when she realized that her turn was next, she decided to set out across the plains in the direction of the sea, in hopes that she might trick death along the way. The land was eroded, split with deep cracks, strewn with rocks, fossils of trees and thorny bushes, and skeletons of animals bleached by the sun. From time to time she ran into families who, like her, were heading south, following the mirage of water. Some had begun the march carrying their belongings on their back or in small carts, but they could barely move their own bones, and after a while they had to abandon their possessions. They dragged themselves along painfully, their skin turned to lizard hide and their eyes burned by the reverberating glare. Belisa greeted them with a wave as she passed, but she did not stop, because she had no strength to waste in acts of compassion. Many people fell by the wayside, but she was so stubborn that she survived to cross through that hell and at long last reach the first trickles of water, fine, almost invisible threads that fed spindly vegetation and farther down widened into small streams and marshes.

Belisa Crepusculario saved her life and in the process accidentally discovered writing. In a village near the coast, the wind blew a page of newspaper at her feet. She picked up the brittle yellow paper and stood a long while looking at it, unable to determine its purpose, until curiosity overcame her shyness. She walked over to a man who was washing his horse in the muddy pool where she had quenched her thirst.

"What is this?" she asked.

"The sports page of the newspaper," the man replied, concealing his surprise at her ignorance.

The answer astounded the girl, but she did not want to seem rude so she merely inquired about the significance of the fly tracks scattered across the page.

"Those are words, child. Here it says that Fulgencio Barba knocked out El Negro Tiznao in the third round."

That was the day Belisa Crepusculario found out that words make their way in the world without a master, and that anyone with a little cleverness can appropriate them and do business with them. She made a quick assessment of her situation and concluded that aside from becoming a prostitute or working as a servant in the kitchens of the rich there were few occupations she was qualified for. It seemed to her that selling words would be an honourable alternative. From that moment on, she worked at that profession, and was never tempted by any other. At the beginning, she offered her merchandise unaware that words could be written outside of newspapers. When she learned otherwise, she calculated the infinite possibilities of her trade and with her savings paid a priest twenty *pesos* to teach her to read and write; with her three remaining coins she bought a dictionary. She pored over it from A to Z and then threw it into the sea, because it was not her intention to defraud her customers with packaged words.

One August morning several years later, Belisa Crepusculario was sitting in her tent in the middle of a plaza, surrounded by the uproar of market day, selling legal arguments to an old man who had been trying for sixteen years to get his pension. Suddenly she heard yelling and thudding hoofbeats. She looked up from her writing and saw, first, a cloud of dust, and then a band of horsemen come galloping into the plaza. They were the Colonel's men, sent under orders of El Mulato, a giant known throughout the land for the speed of his knife and his loyalty to his chief. Both the Colonel and El Mulato had spent their lives fighting in the civil war, and their names were ineradicably linked to devastation and calamity. The rebels swept into town like a stampeding herd, wrapped in noise, bathed in sweat, and leaving a hurricane of fear in their trail. Chickens took wing, dogs ran for their lives, women and children scurried out of sight, until the only living soul left in the market was Belisa Crepusculario. She had never seen El Mulato and was surprised to see him walking towards her.

"I'm looking for you," he shouted, pointing his coiled whip at her; even before the words were out, two men rushed her—knocking over her canopy and shattering her inkwell—bound her hand and foot, and threw her like a duffel bag across the rump of El Mulato's mount. Then they thundered off towards the hills.

Hours later, just as Belisa Crepusculario was near death, her heart ground to sand by the pounding of the horse, they stopped, and four strong hands set her down. She tried to stand on her feet and hold her head high, but her strength failed her and she slumped to the ground, sinking into a confused dream. She awakened several hours later to the murmur of night in the camp, but before she had time to sort out the sounds, she opened her eyes and found herself staring into the impatient glare of El Mulato, kneeling beside her.

"Well, woman, at last you have come to," he said. To speed her to her senses, he tipped his canteen and offered her a sip of liquor laced with gunpowder.

She demanded to know the reason for such rough treatment, and El Mulato explained that the Colonel needed her services. He allowed her to splash water on her face, and then led her to the far end of the camp where the most feared man in all the land was lazing in a hammock strung between two trees. She could not see his face, because he lay in the deceptive shadow of the leaves and the indelible shadow of all his years as a bandit, but she imagined from the way his gigantic aide addressed him with such humility that he must have a very menacing expression. She was surprised by the Colonel's voice, as soft and well modulated as a professor's.

"Are you the woman who sells words?" he asked.

"At your service," she stammered, peering into the dark and trying to see him better.

The Colonel stood up, and turned straight towards her. She saw dark skin and the eyes of a ferocious puma, and she knew immediately that she was standing before the loneliest man in the world.

"I want to be President," he announced.

The Colonel was weary of riding across that Godforsaken land, waging useless wars and suffering defeats that no subterfuge could transform into victories. For years he had been sleeping in the open air, bitten by mosquitoes, eating iguanas and snake soup, but those minor inconveniences were not why he wanted to change his destiny. What truly troubled him was the terror he saw in people's eyes. He longed to ride into a town beneath a triumphal arch with bright flags and flowers everywhere; he wanted to be cheered, and be given newly laid eggs and freshly baked bread. Men fled at the sight of him, children trembled, and women miscarried from fright; he had had enough, and so he had decided to become President. El Mulato had suggested that they ride to the capital, gallop up to the Palace and take over the government, the way they had taken so many other things without anyone's permission. The Colonel, however, did not want to be just another tyrant;

there had been enough of those before him and, besides, if he did that, he would never win people's hearts. It was his aspiration to win the popular vote in the December elections.

"To do that, I have to talk like a candidate. Can you sell me the words for a speech?" the Colonel asked Belisa Crepusculario.

She had accepted many assignments, but none like this. She did not dare refuse, fearing that El Mulato would shoot her between the eyes, or worse still, that the Colonel would burst into tears. There was more to it than that, however; she felt the urge to help him because she felt a throbbing warmth beneath her skin, a powerful desire to touch that man, to fondle him, to clasp him in her arms.

All night and a good part of the following day, Belisa Crepusculario searched her repertory for words adequate for a presidential speech, closely watched by El Mulato, who could not take his eyes from her firm wanderer's legs and virginal breasts. She discarded harsh, cold words, words that were too flowery, words worn from abuse, words that offered improbable promises, untruthful and confusing words, until all she had left were words sure to touch the minds of men and women's intuition. Calling upon the knowledge she had purchased from the priest for twenty *pesos*, she wrote the speech on a sheet of paper and then signalled El Mulato to untie the rope that bound her ankles to a tree. He led her once more to the Colonel, and again she felt the throbbing anxiety that had seized her when she first saw him. She handed him the paper and waited while he looked at it, holding it gingerly between thumbs and fingertips.

"What does this say?" he asked finally.

"Don't you know how to read?"

"War's what I know," he replied.

She read the speech aloud. She read it three times, so her client could engrave it on his memory. When she finished, she saw the emotion in the faces of the soldiers who had gathered round to listen, and saw that the Colonel's eyes glittered with enthusiasm, convinced that with those words the presidential chair would be his.

"If after they've heard it three times, the boys are still standing there with their mouths hanging open, it must mean the thing's damn good, Colonel," was El Mulato's approval.

> Literature is the human activity that takes the fullest and most precise account of variousness, possibility, complexity, and difficulty.
>
> Lionel Trilling

"All right, woman. How much do I owe you?" the leader asked.

"One *peso*, Colonel."

"That's not much," he said, opening the purse he wore at his belt, heavy with proceeds from the last foray.

"The *peso* entitles you to a bonus. I'm going to give you two secret words," said Belisa Crepusculario.

"What for?"

She explained that for every fifty *centavos* a client paid, she gave him the gift of a word for his exclusive use. The Colonel shrugged. He had no interest at all in her offer, but he did not want to be impolite to someone who had served him so well. She walked slowly to the leather stool where he was sitting, and bent down to give him her gift. The man smelled the scent of a mountain cat issuing from the woman, a fiery heat radiating from her hips, he heard the terrible whisper of her hair, and a breath of sweet mint murmured into his ear the two secret words that were his alone.

"They are yours, Colonel," she said as she stepped back. "You may use them as much as you please."

El Mulato accompanied Belisa to the roadside, his eyes as entreating as a stray dog's, but when he reached out to touch her, he was stopped by an avalanche of words he had never heard before; believing them to be an irrevocable curse, the flame of his desire was extinguished.

During the months of September, October and November, the Colonel delivered his speech so many times that had it not been crafted from glowing and durable words, it would have turned to ash as he spoke. He travelled up and down and across the country, riding into cities with a triumphal air, stopping in even the most forgotten villages where only the dump heap betrayed a human presence, to convince his fellow citizens to vote for him. While he spoke from a platform erected in the middle of the plaza, El Mulato and his men handed out sweets and painted his name on all the walls in gold frost. No one paid the least attention to those advertising ploys; they were dazzled by the clarity of the Colonel's proposals and the poetic lucidity of his arguments, infected by his powerful wish to right the wrongs of history, happy for the first time in their lives. When the Candidate had finished his speech, his soldiers would fire their pistols into the air and set off fire-crackers, and when finally they rode off, they left behind a wake of hope that lingered for days on the air, like the splendid memory of a comet's tail. Soon the Colonel was the favourite. No one had ever witnessed such a phenomenon: a man who surfaced from the civil war, covered with scars and speaking like a professor, a man whose fame spread to every corner of the land and captured the nation's heart. The press focused their attention on him. Newspapermen came from far away to interview him and repeat his phrases, and the number of his followers and enemies continued to grow.

"We're doing great, Colonel," said El Mulato, after twelve successful weeks of campaigning.

But the Candidate did not hear. He was repeating his secret words, as he did more and more obsessively. He said them when he was mellow with nostalgia; he murmured them in his sleep; he carried them with him on horseback; he thought them before delivering his famous speech; and he caught himself savouring them in his leisure time. And every time he thought of those two words, he thought of Belisa Crepusculario, and his senses were inflamed with the memory of her feral scent, her fiery heat, the whisper of her hair and her sweet mint breath in his ear, until he began to go around like a sleepwalker, and his men realized that he might die before he ever sat in the presidential chair.

"What's got hold of you, Colonel?" El Mulato asked so often that finally one day his chief broke down and told him the source of his befuddlement: those two words that were buried like two daggers in his gut.

"Tell me what they are and maybe they'll lose their magic," his faithful aide suggested.

"I can't tell them, they're for me alone," the Colonel replied.

Saddened by watching his chief decline like a man with a death sentence on his head, El Mulato slung his rifle over his shoulder and set out to find Belisa Crepusculario. He followed her trail through all that vast country, until he found her in a village in the far south, sitting under her tent reciting her rosary of news. He planted himself, straddle-legged, before her, weapon in hand.

"You! You're coming with me," he ordered.

She had been waiting. She picked up her inkwell, folded the canvas of her small stall, arranged her shawl around her shoulders, and without a word took her place behind El Mulato's saddle. They did not exchange so much as a word in all the trip; El Mulato's desire for her had turned into rage, and only his fear of her tongue prevented his cutting her to shreds with his whip. Nor was he inclined to tell her that the Colonel was in a fog, and that a spell whispered into his ear had done what years of battle had not been able to do. Three days later they arrived at the encampment, and immediately, in view of all the troops, El Mulato led his prisoner before the Candidate.

"I brought this witch here so you can give her back her words, Colonel," El Mulato said, pointing the barrel of his rifle at the woman's head. "And then she can give you back your manhood."

The Colonel and Belisa Crepusculario stared at each other, measuring one another from a distance. The men knew then that their leader would never undo the witchcraft of those two accursed words, because the whole world could see the voracious puma's eyes soften as the woman walked to him and took his hand in hers.

Isabel Allende was born in Lima, Peru, in 1942. After the fall of her uncle Salvador Allende's government, she moved with her family to Venezuela, where she worked as a journalist. She then lived in the U.S. until her exile ended in 1988. Her first novel, *La casa de los espíritus (The House of the Spirits)*, was made into a motion picture in 1993. Her other works include the novels *De amor y de sombra (Of Love and Shadows)*, *Eva Luna*, *El Plan Infinito (The Infinite Plan)*, and *Hija de la Fortuna (Daughter of Fortune)*; a short story collection; and the non-fiction memoir, *Paula*, about Allende's daughter who died from the genetic disorder porphyria. "Belisa" is an anagram of Isabel.

I. *Response*

a. "She made her living selling words." In your own words, describe Belisa's occupation. Why did she create this job for herself?

b. What evidence is there that Belisa has a remarkable ability with words? Provide at least three examples. Why is Belisa so popular with the people she travels among?

c. Why do you think Belisa decides to help the Colonel, despite his murderous reputation?

d. Suggest a possible symbolic meaning for the story based on what the two main characters seem to represent. What fundamental conflict(s) does the story convey?

2. *Literature Studies* Blended Genres "Two Words" combines the concrete detail of a realistic narrative with the exaggeration and improbability of a folk tale or tall tale. For each of these two aspects of the story, identify several quotations that serve as examples. What is your personal response to this blend of genres? What advantages do you think it offers a writer?

3. *Oral Language* Group Presentation In a group, select four or five individual words from the story that you think best describe Belisa. Some words should reflect other characters' views of her, while others should suggest her own perspective. Together, create an imaginative oral presentation that shows these different aspects of Belisa.

4. *Film Study* Assume that "Two Words" has been adapted into a feature-length film and create a storyboard for a movie trailer to represent it. Incorporate details and ideas from the story in your trailer.

5. *Writing* Journal Entry From the Colonel's point of view, write a journal entry that explains how Belisa has transformed him. Include the two words she has revealed to him, and the impact they have. Consider how your purpose and the role you have assumed will affect your writing.

> Her profession was words and she believed
> in them deeply. The articulation, interpretation,
> appreciation, and preservation of good words ...
> words could incite, soothe, destroy,
> exorcise, redeem.
>
> —Gail Goodwin

Theme Connections

- *"How Should One Read a Book?" an essay about the power of literature, page 261*
- *"Making Poetry Pay," an anecdote about the power of words, page 284*
- *"What Will Your Verse Be?" a movie monologue about the importance of language, page 514*

A Marker on the Side of the Boat

"By flashes of the long-range artilleries I could detect no personal shelters on either sidewalk. It was death's ideal coordinates."

by Bao Ninh

Translated from the Vietnamese by Linh Dinh

In my life, I've been here, there, but I've had few chances to visit Hanoi.[1] Once when I was little, once during the war, and a couple times years later. That's why, aside from Turtle Lake and Long Bien Bridge, I can only recall Hang Co Train Station and a street with trolley tracks on it. But in spite of this, when I shut my eyes to peer into the crevices of my memory, I can always conjure up, if only dimly, a general image of its streets. This remote, alien city, with which I have had no intimacy, had, over the years, silently insinuated itself into my consciousness as a beloved place. It is a love born out of nothing, less of an emotion than a light sensation, melancholic, plotless, a souvenir from my war-filled youth, a youth that although long-gone, still reverberates with its echoes. Like the sounds of rain, of wind blowing through a room or of leaves falling, never to be forgotten.

Twenty years have already passed. Hanoi back then and Hanoi today must be as different as sky and earth.

That day, I was driving my division commander from the battle of Quang Tri[2] to a meeting at military headquarters, outside the capital. We arrived to find the city in a state of siege. It was truly a life-and-death battle, a blood struggle which, after

[1] **Hanoi:** capital of Vietnam; also capital of North Vietnam from 1954–75
[2] **Quang Tri:** a Vietnamese province; site of a decisive North Vietnamese victory in 1972

twelve days and nights, would change the faces of both winner and loser. In such a dire situation, I did not dare request a leave to visit my village; I only asked for permission to go into the city to deliver a handful of letters given to me by my buddies who were from Hanoi. I wanted to visit each family so I could receive a letter in turn, to bring a little joy back to our soldiers. On Christmas day, I was given permission to go into town, and was told to be back by midnight.

Without knowing the neighborhoods, and with nine letters to deliver, I still wasn't worried. I thought I would find the first address, then ask for directions to go to the next one. I didn't anticipate having to slip each one of those letters under the door. That day, all of Hanoi seemed to have been abandoned.

By the time I had delivered my last letter, the sky was pitch-dark. The long, deserted street lay soaked in rain, punctuated by dim circles of streetlights. I asked for direction to Vong. A militiaman in a frond jacket kindly escorted me for a stretch. At a three-way intersection, before we parted, he pointed to the trolley tracks hugging the sidewalk and said to follow them to get to my destination.

Vietnamese Fleeing on Street, Saigon by unknown photographer.

With my helmet on and my collar up, I plunged into that fine gauze of drizzle. The night was chilly. The tracks were like a trail forging through the jungle of darkened houses. A city during wartime, on a precipice, abandoned. I walked on doggedly, my body numbed. There were endless dark stretches without a single pedestrian or a stall. The night exhaled its cold, wet air, soaking me right down to my empty stomach. My joints felt stiff, aching, as if ready to be jarred apart. A fever that had been simmering all evening crept up my spine. I couldn't stop shivering. My brain slowed down. My knees felt like buckling. I hadn't even walked that far, and already I was counting my steps. Without seeing where I was going, I almost ran into the front of a trolley, a black mass parked in the middle of the street.

I staggered onto the sidewalk and wobbled beneath the eaves of a house. With my back leaning against the door, teeth chattering, I slowly slid down until I was sitting on the wet step, cold as a block of ice. My heart was freezing. I groaned until I could groan no more. My shivering became more violent. My body temperature was at a dangerous level. I thought numbly:

"If I'm not careful this could be the end. Other people stricken with fever die on a hammock in the middle of a jungle. I'll die sitting up, certainly, to be metamorphosed into a rock in front of someone's door."

Above my head, the corrugated tin roof shivered. The wind blew the rain right onto the stoop. Already wet, I got wetter. Dizzy, breathing in gulps, I knew I had to marshal all my energy to get up and continue, but I had no willpower left. It was draining out of me like water from a broken vase. At that point, the door behind me inched open. I heard the noise but could make no sense of it. Unconsciousness, like a letting-go and a sigh of relief, seduced me from my own body …

Time stopped for I don't know how long. I opened my eyes slowly. My consciousness settled on a rim of light. Still wobbly, uncertain, I nevertheless knew I was indoors, and no longer delirious. The walls appeared to have been painted a pale green, although faded with time. The ceiling was dark. The warm air redolent of camphor.[3] I shifted lightly. The bed creaked beneath my body. I was under a blanket, with my head on a pillow: tranquil, dried, warm, it was unreal. I turned my body. On a night table by the corner of the room, a small oil lamp gave off a dirty yellow light. A clock kept time by monotonously ticking off the seconds. The sudden thought of time startled me; I groaned.

"Oh, Brother …" Someone's hand caressed my cheek, and a soft, soothing voice whispered, "You've recovered. I was really worried …"

---

[3]**camphor:** a strong-smelling medicinal compound

My heart froze, then beat wildly. I was embarrassed. What was happening; who was this woman?

"I …" I finally opened my mouth, tongue-tied, stuttering, "Where am I … Where is this?"

"This is my house, Brother." Her soft hand touched my forehead. "You are my guest."

I tried to regain my composure, my strength. Breathing deeply, I turned toward my hostess. She was sitting on the edge of the bed, with her face beyond the lamp's illumination. I could only make out her shoulders and her hair.

"You still have a touch of that fever, Brother, but you've gotten much better, luckily. You scared the hell out of me in the beginning. I was frightened to death."

"I'm in trouble …" I gasped, "It's past time for me to report back. I, I have to go …"

"Oh, Brother, you're in no shape to go anywhere. Outside, in the cold, you'll only get sick again. Besides, your clothes are being hung to dry in the kitchen. You can't wear them yet. They're still damp."

What? I realized what had happened. I quickly touched my thigh and chest, shuddering, wishing I could contract my body. Beneath the quilted blanket, I was practically naked. "I'll bring you some rice gruel from the kitchen, all right?" The woman spoke casually and got up from the bed. "There is a change of clothing by the pillow for you to wear. It's also an Army uniform."

Without taking the oil lamp, she turned and walked out the door into the darkness. I threw the blanket aside and sprang out of bed. The strong aroma of medicinal balm from beneath the blanket stung my eyes. I dressed quickly. The uniform, new, reeking of camphor, was a reasonable fit. Decked out like a soldier again, I seemed to have regained my strength, although my entire body ached, my head was numb, and a ringing lingered in my ears.

As tired as I was, I could detect, immediately, the smell of hot rice gruel as it was being brought into the room by my hostess. She walked softly, her clogs barely making a noise on the wooden floor. She placed the tray on the table and turned up the knob on the oil lamp.

"The rain has stopped," she said, then sighed, for no apparent reason.

In the dimness of that room, I stared silently. This wonderful stranger was like an illusion conjured up in front of my eyes. An unearthly illusion, kind and beautiful. Kind and beautiful, her face, her eyes and lips, although I never really had a chance to look at her. The moment had arrived for this city. Within a fraction of a second, there won't be time for heaven and earth to react, no time to even shudder.

Something monstrous, violent, suddenly stabbed the silence. Out of nowhere, a reconnaissance plane—just one—thunderously slashed its way across the sky, skimming the city's rooftops. Inside the room, even the oil lamp seemed to be holding its breath ...

"I think it's gone," she whispered, trembling, a pale smile on her face. "They're just trying to scare us."

"Yes," I said, "Only some spy trying to sneak up on us, don't ..."

I was trying to reassure her, to tell her there was nothing to be scared of, when the horrible air siren started wailing, interrupting my sentence. Although I had heard it many times in previous nights and had learned to anticipate the sound, the air siren still made my heart freeze. Never before had this messenger of death reverberated so terrifyingly. The way it howled and screamed—desperate, angry, hysterical—made people want to scream along with it. "B-52s,[4] B-52s, B-52s are coming!" the public speaker frantically blared. "B-52s! Ninety kilometers from Hanoi. Eighty kilometers."

"Those Americans!" I said. "They're coming. That last guy was a scout."

"Yes. It's the B-52s. One more night."

"We'll have to go to the shelter!" I couldn't hide my nervousness. "They're getting near. Quick!"

"But how are you feeling?" She sighed, filled with childish concern. "It's very cold outside."

My premonition of danger suddenly became more palpable. With my mouth dry, my throat contracted, the drum in my chest was banging away. Never before had my intuition deceived me.

"Eat some, Brother, while it's still hot ..."

"No!" I said, my voice hoarse, "Hot cold nothing! The bombs are falling soon. They're carpet-bombing[5] us!"

"How do you know?" she blurted in terror.

"I can smell it! Quick! To the shelter!" I practically shouted.

After blowing out the lamp, she grabbed me by the wrist and led me out of the room. My tenseness had been transferred to her. Gasping, her clogs beat a fierce rhythm on the floor. We went down the stairs, then had to pass through a long, narrow, wet corridor before making it to the street. The rain had stopped. The sky had cleared up somewhat. The air was crisp, transparent, eerie. In the middle of the street, right outside the door, the same trolley sullenly sat, like a stranded ship.

---

[4]**B-52s:** long-range bombers used by the U.S. Air Force
[5]**carpet-bombing:** systematic bombing used to devastate a large area

On the sidewalk, the personal shelter, cast out of cement, gaped open its black mouth.

"We should go to the public shelter, Brother," the woman said between quick breaths, "I never want to go inside one of these round ones. There's stagnant water at the bottom. It's gross."

"Now this!" I said, irritated.

"It's only down the street, Brother. Plus, there will be lots of people. It won't be so scary."

We lunged forward into the wind. The entire city was in hiding. In the deadly silence, there were only the two of us, a couple alone in the midst of terror. The seconds ticked by but our escape route seemed endless. A three-way intersection. Then a four-way intersection. The public shelter was nowhere in sight. Wearing those clogs, she couldn't run. But then, oh God, it was already too late to run. Artillery was opening up in the outlying areas. The loud roars of 100-millimeter guns going off in unison. Brilliant flashes. Flame arrows, in pairs, thunderously lunging upward, tearing into the cloud ceiling, leaving red trails behind them. Surrounded by the frantic sounds of our troops' firepower, I could sense what was about to happen in the sky above. I had seen much carnage on the battlefield as a foot soldier. I knew how much chance there is in life-and-death matters. For the two of us, I knew it was over. The bombs were about to fall right on that street.

Fate had wickedly placed us in the middle of a long street with no houses on either side, only high walls running into the distance. By the flashes of the long-range artilleries, I could detect no personal shelters on either sidewalk. It was death's ideal coordinates. A few more hurried steps would not have made a difference.

"They're dropping them!" I said and grabbed her arm.

"Brother, only a little more!"

"We don't have time," I calmly said, with unearthly composure. "The bombs are coming right now. Lie down, quickly, and don't panic."

She obediently lay down next to me, at the foot of a brick wall. She was very confused and only half-believed my deadly pronouncements. But I knew that, within ten seconds or less, the bombs would come. The B-52s, those monstrous dragons, sowers of terror, were no strangers to me. In the South, they would fly at a lower altitude during the day, in formations of three or six planes, arrogantly across the sky, sowing streaks of thick smoke behind them as their bombs rained down. These rains could collapse a side of a mountain, bury a stretch of a river or wipe out an entire forest. But this was no rain; the sky itself was falling. In the place of mountains and forests were houses and streets. The sky was one vast menace, and the city appeared as small as the palm of a hand. In the face of such destruction, I thought, how flimsy is human life. I tensed and waited.

It was as if I didn't hear the explosions. Although I was anticipating the noise, it still took me by surprise. My vision abruptly darkened. The earth shuddered, writhed. Space itself became distorted. Something burning, sharp, slapped me in the face. Heat from the bombs filled my lungs.

She rolled toward me, seeking shelter—her cold body pressing against mine; her breath on my stunned, sweaty face; her hair disheveled.

Another string of bombs came, this time appearing to be right on the other side of the wall. Earth, rocks, cement, roof tiles, houses, all blew up together. The heavens screamed, shattered. Waves of heat rolled across the earth's surface. Die now! Die now! Die..ie..ie. I clutched her, clenching my teeth, waiting for that split second when our bones and flesh would be torn asunder. The bombs came steadily, savagely, howling, exploding one after another. After every explosion, every wave of heat, our bodies coiled more tightly together. The crushing shift in atmospheric pressure left us reeling, stupefied.

Suddenly, death relaxed its claws. The big door in the sky was slammed shut. Silence. The explosion of the last bomb stopped all the others.

We continued to lie still, clutching each other. It was as if we had become paralyzed, incredulous at the fact that we were still alive. We kept in that position for a long time before she wriggled herself free from my grasp.

I slowly helped her to get up. With a shoulder of her shirt torn, her hair disheveled, fear in her eyes, she groped with her feet trying to find her clogs, those useless high-heeled clogs. Billows of thick smoke drifted by. There was a burnt smell of bomb powder in the air. The sky was a bruised red.

As the humming subsided in my ears, I could hear, from somewhere nearby, voices crying for help. The whole neighborhood quickly went into a clamor. A crowd emerged, frantically rushing forward with picks, shovels, crowbars and stretchers.

"Don't just stand there like that!" Someone angrily yelled, his voice hoarse, thick with pain. "The shelter has collapsed. People are dying right in front of you. Oh, God!"

"Oh, my God! I think it's the public shelter. There are so many people in there!" the woman blurted out.

"I'll have to go give them a hand. You go home first. I'll follow!" I said.

I released her hand and ran hastily after the crowd. As I ran, I turned back, motioned with my hand and shouted:

"Go home! Wait there for me!" Near the site of the explosion, before I was to plow into the smoking remnants of the freshly destroyed houses, I turned back one more time. After a hellish night, it was the last glimpse I had of my beloved and illusory figure.

But it shouldn't have been the last time. I should have been able to return to that same house, to the same room where I was the previous night, to see this woman again. It was morning, a long time after the all-clear signals. I followed the trolley tracks, retracing my path from the night before, to go back to her house.

I thought nothing at first when I had to step aside to dodge a trolley. It was cold and the street was empty. The old, rusty trolley lunged forward; the bell silent; its steel wheels shrieking, throwing off sparks; the engine making an ear-shattering racket. But as it passed me, I gave a little start, as if my heart had just been whipped.

The street was straight, endless, without intersections. On each side of the street, the same houses crowded into each other, all identical, monotonous: a gloomy, grouchy façade shaded by a rusty tin roof; three steps leading to a single door. In front of every house was a cement hole. Since the trolley, my only clue, was gone, all I knew for sure was which side of the street the house was on. Everything looked the same, the same uneven, broken sidewalk, with puddles of stagnant water; the same walls and leaky roofs; the same arjun trees and light poles.

Although I had no time to spare, I stalked back and forth on that street, brooding over my failure. I stared into the houses and at the faces of people coming out. By the time another trolley came clanking by, I had to give up. With a face still covered in soot and ash, limbs all scratched, and wearing tatters stained with blotches of blood from the night's victims, I trudged dejectedly along the trolley tracks toward my destination on the outskirts of the city.

After the war, on my rare visits to Hanoi, I would always return to that same street. I would simply walk down it, not to find anything or go anywhere. The last time I got off at Hang Co train station, I could no longer recognize my old street. Hanoi had abolished the trolleys. The streets were glamorous; the houses beautiful; life happy …

There may come a day when people will have a hard time imagining a period when this city went through what I saw twenty years ago, when I was a very young man. ◗

Bao Ninh was born in Hanoi in 1952. In 1969, he served in North Vietnam's Glorious 27th Youth Brigade during the Vietnam War and was one of the ten survivors of the five hundred youths who fought with the brigade. His first novel, *The Sorrow of War*, is a semi-autobiographical work about his war experiences, and has been translated into many languages. Ninh's works have been published in *Granta*; in the U.S. anthology *The Other Side of Heaven: Post-War Fiction by Vietnamese & American Writers*; and in the French anthology *Terres des Éphémères*. The title of this story refers to a folk tale about a fisherman who, to mark the spot where he dropped his sword into a lake, made a mark on the side of his boat.

1. Response

a. Reread the first paragraph of the story. What does it suggest about the narrator's feelings about the city of Hanoi?

b. What do you think is the predominant mood of this story? Select one passage that you think truly captures this mood and give reasons for your choice.

c. Explain the significance of the story's title.

d. Find at least one example of irony in the story. Clarify the nature of the irony to a partner.

e. Explain how the influence of chance or luck is such an important element in this story.

2. Focus on Context

Discuss the background information provided on Bao Ninh with a partner. Speculate on why Ninh wrote this story, and who his original audience was. How does the context in which you read the story—in a Canadian classroom, decades after the war—affect your appreciation of it?

3. **Language Focus** *Descriptive Language* Identify three passages in the story that, in your view, contain the most striking examples of effective descriptive language. For each of your examples, point out and explain the purpose behind the description and the specific techniques the author uses to achieve that purpose. Which different senses does the author appeal to? Prepare an oral reading of one of the passages; read expressively to capture the spirit of the description.

4. **Writing** *Survival Story* Like most survival stories, "A Marker on the Side of the Boat" contains a powerful external conflict. What is it? Are there other conflicts within the story as well? Write a survival story of your own in which one or more main characters must overcome an external conflict of some kind.

5. **Drama** *Setting the Stage* Use the details provided in the story to develop a sketch of a theatre or film stage for a production of "A Marker on the Side of the Boat." How will you represent the various locales? What details will you emphasize? How will you light the stage to create an effective mood? Present your sketch to a small group, explaining your choices.

6. **Visual Communication** *Examine Photo* What information does this documentary photo convey? What assumptions does it prompt you to make as a viewer? Explain how the composition of the photo increases its impact.

> My function as a writer is not story-telling
> but truth-telling: to make things plain.
> —Laura Riding Jackson

"All of us, I suppose, like to believe
that in a moral emergency
we will behave
like the heroes
of our youth ..."

On the Rainy River

by Tim O'Brien

This is one story I've never told before. Not to anyone. Not to
my parents, not to my brother or sister, not even to my wife. To
go into it, I've always thought, would only cause embarrassment for all of us, a sudden need to be elsewhere, which is the
natural response to a confession. Even now, I'll admit, the story
makes me squirm. For more than twenty years I've had to live
with it, feeling the shame, trying to push it away, and so by this
act of remembrance, by putting the facts down on paper, I'm
hoping to relieve at least some of the pressure on my dreams.
Still, it's a hard story to tell. All of us, I suppose, like to believe
that in a moral emergency we will behave like the heroes of our
youth, bravely and forthrightly, without thought of personal loss
or discredit. Certainly that was my conviction back in the summer of 1968. Tim O'Brien: a secret hero. The Lone Ranger. If
the stakes ever became high enough—if the evil were evil
enough, if the good were good enough—I would simply tap a
secret reservoir of courage that had been accumulating inside
me over the years. Courage, I seemed to think, comes to us in
finite quantities, like an inheritance, and by being frugal and
stashing it away and letting it earn interest, we steadily increase
our moral capital in preparation for that day when the account
must be drawn down. It was a comforting theory. It dispensed
with all those bothersome little acts of daily courage; it offered
hope and grace to the repetitive coward; it justified the past
while amortizing the future.

In June of 1968, a month after graduating from Macalester College, I was drafted to fight a war I hated.[1] I was twenty-one years old. Young, yes, and politically naive, but even so the American war in Vietnam seemed to me wrong. Certain blood was being shed for uncertain reasons. I saw no unity of purpose, no consensus on matters of philosophy or history or law. The very facts were shrouded in uncertainty: Was it a civil war? A war of national liberation or simple aggression? Who started it, and when, and why? What really happened to the USS *Maddox* on that dark night in the Gulf of Tonkin? Was Ho Chi Minh a Communist stooge, or a nationalist savior, or both, or neither? What about the Geneva Accords? What about SEATO and the Cold War? What about dominoes? America was divided on these and a thousand other issues, and the debate had spilled out across the floor of the United States Senate and into the streets, and smart men in pinstripes could not agree on even the most fundamental matters of public policy. The only certainty that summer was moral confusion. It was my view then, and still is, that you don't make war without knowing why. Knowledge, of course, is always imperfect, but it seemed to me that when a nation goes to war it must have reasonable confidence in the justice and imperative of its cause. You can't fix your mistakes. Once people are dead, you can't make them undead.

In any case those were my convictions, and back in college I had taken a modest stand against the war. Nothing radical, no hothead stuff, just ringing a few doorbells for Gene McCarthy, composing a few tedious, uninspired editorials for the campus newspaper. Oddly, though, it was almost entirely an intellectual activity. I brought some energy to it, of course, but it was the energy that accompanies almost any abstract endeavor; I felt no personal danger; I felt no sense of an impending crisis in my life. Stupidly, with a kind of smug removal that I can't begin to fathom, I assumed that the problems of killing and dying did not fall within my special province.

The draft notice arrived on June 17, 1968. It was a humid afternoon, I remember, cloudy and very quiet, and I'd just come in from a round of golf. My mother and father were having lunch out in the kitchen. I remember opening up the letter, scanning the first few lines, feeling the blood go thick behind my eyes. I remember a sound in my head. It wasn't thinking, it was just a silent howl. A million things all at

---

[1] **war I hated:** the Vietnam War, 1961–75; it began as a civil war between North and South Vietnam in the mid-1950s. By 1961, the Americans were actively involved in the war on the side of the South Vietnamese.

once—I was too *good* for this war. Too smart, too compassionate, too everything. It couldn't happen. I was above it. I had the world dicked—Phi Beta Kappa and summa cum laude and president of the student body and a full-ride scholarship for grad studies at Harvard. A mistake, maybe—a foul-up in the paperwork. I was no soldier. I hated Boy Scouts. I hated camping out. I hated dirt and tents and mosquitoes. The sight of blood made me queasy, and I couldn't tolerate authority, and I didn't know a rifle from a slingshot. I was a *liberal*, for Christ sake: If they needed fresh bodies, why not draft some back-to-the stone-age hawk? Or some dumb jingo in his hard hat and Bomb Hanoi button? Or one of LBJ's pretty daughters? Or Westmoreland's whole family—nephews and nieces and baby grandson? There should be a law, I thought. If you support a war, if you think it's worth the price, that's fine, but you have to put your own life on the line. You have to head for the front and hook up with an infantry unit and help spill the blood. And you have to bring along your wife, or your kids, or your lover. A *law*, I thought.

I remember the rage in my stomach. Later it burned down to a smoldering self-pity, then to numbness. At dinner that night my father asked what my plans were.

"Nothing," I said. "Wait."

I spent the summer of 1968 working in an Armour meatpacking plant in my hometown of Worthington, Minnesota. The plant specialized in pork products, and for eight hours a day I stood on a quarter-mile assembly line—more properly, a disassembly line—removing blood clots from the necks of dead pigs. My job title, I believe, was Declotter. After slaughter, the hogs were decapitated, split down the length of the belly, pried open, eviscerated, and strung up by the hind hocks on a high conveyer belt. Then gravity took over. By the time a carcass reached my spot on the line, the fluids had mostly drained out, everything except for thick clots of blood in the neck and upper chest cavity. To remove the stuff, I used a kind of water gun. The machine was heavy, maybe eighty pounds, and was suspended from the ceiling by a heavy rubber cord. There was some bounce to it, an elastic up-and-down give, and the trick was to maneuver the gun with your whole body, not lifting with the arms, just letting the rubber cord do the work for you. At one end was a trigger; at the muzzle end was a small nozzle and a steel roller brush. As a carcass passed by, you'd lean forward and swing the gun up against the clots and squeeze the trigger, all in one motion, and the brush would whirl and water would come shooting out and you'd hear a quick splattering sound as the clots dissolved into a fine red mist. It was not pleasant work. Goggles were a necessity, and a rubber apron, but even so it was like standing for eight hours a day under a lukewarm blood-shower. At night I'd go home smelling of pig. I couldn't wash it out. Even after a hot bath, scrubbing hard, the stink was always there—like old bacon, or sausage, a dense greasy pig-stink that soaked deep into my skin and hair. Among other things, I remember, it was tough getting dates that summer. I felt isolated; I spent a lot of time alone. And there was also that draft notice tucked away in my wallet.

In the evenings I'd sometimes borrow my father's car and drive aimlessly around town, feeling sorry for myself, thinking about the war and the pig factory and how my life seemed to be collapsing toward slaughter. I felt paralyzed. All around me the options seemed to be narrowing, as if I were hurtling down a huge black funnel, the whole world squeezing in tight. There was no happy way out. The government had ended most graduate school deferments; the waiting lists for the National Guard and Reserves were impossibly long; my health was solid; I didn't qualify for CO status[2]—no religious grounds, no history as a pacifist. Moreover, I could not claim to be opposed to war as a matter of general principle. There were occasions, I believed, when a nation was justified in using military force to achieve its ends, to stop a Hitler or some comparable evil, and I told myself that in such circumstances I would've willingly marched off to the battle. The problem, though, was that a draft board did not let you choose your war.

Beyond all this, or at the very center, was the raw fact of terror. I did not want to die. Not ever. But certainly not then, not there, not in a wrong war. Driving up Main Street, past the courthouse and the Ben Franklin store, I sometimes felt the fear spreading inside me like weeds. I imagined myself dead. I imagined myself doing things I could not do—charging an enemy position, taking aim at another human being.

At some point in mid-July I began thinking seriously about Canada. The border lay a few hundred miles north, an eight-hour drive. Both my conscience and my instincts were telling me to make a break for it, just take off and run like hell and never stop. In the beginning the idea seemed purely abstract, the word Canada printing itself out in my head; but after a time I could see particular shapes and images, the sorry details of my own future—a hotel room in Winnipeg, a battered old suitcase, my father's eyes as I tried to explain myself over the telephone.

[2]**CO status:** conscientious objector status. A conscientious objector resisted the war for reasons of religious or moral principle and could avoid military service.

I could almost hear his voice, and my mother's. Run, I'd think. Then I'd think, Impossible. Then a second later I'd think, *Run*.

It was a kind of schizophrenia. A moral split. I couldn't make up my mind. I feared the war, yes, but I also feared exile. I was afraid of walking away from my own life, my friends and my family, my whole history, everything that mattered to me. I feared losing the respect of my parents. I feared the law. I feared ridicule and censure. My home-town was a conservative little spot on the prairie, a place where tradition counted, and it was easy to imagine people sitting around a table down at the old Gobbler Café on Main Street, coffee cups poised, the conversation slowly zeroing in on the young O'Brien kid, how the damned sissy had taken off for Canada. At night, when I couldn't sleep, I'd sometimes carry on fierce arguments with those people. I'd be screaming at them, telling them how much I detested their blind, thoughtless, automatic acquiescence to it all, their simple-minded patriotism, their prideful ignorance, their love-it-or-leave-it platitudes, how they were sending me off to fight a war they didn't understand and didn't want to understand. I held them responsible. By God, yes, I *did*. All of them—I held them personally and individually responsible—the polyestered Kiwanis boys, the merchants and farmers, the pious churchgoers, the chatty housewives, the PTA and the Lions club and the Veterans of Foreign Wars and the fine upstanding gentry out at the country club. They didn't know Bao Dai[3] from the man in the moon. They didn't know history. They didn't know the first thing about Diem's tyranny, or the nature of Vietnamese nationalism, or the long colonialism of the French—this was all too damned complicated, it required some reading—but no matter, it was a war to stop the Communists, plain and simple, which was how they liked things, and you were a treasonous coward if you had second thoughts about killing or dying for plain and simple reasons.

I was bitter, sure. But it was so much more than that. The emotions went from outrage to terror to bewilderment to guilt to sorrow and then back again to outrage. I felt a sickness inside me. Real disease.

Most of this I've told before, or at least hinted at, but what I have never told is the full truth. How I cracked. How at work one morning, standing on the pig line, I felt something break open in my chest. I don't know what it was. I'll never know. But it was real, I know that much, it was a physical rupture—a cracking-leaking-popping feeling.

[3]**Bao Dai:** the last emperor of Vietnam. He abdicated his throne in 1945, but returned to power from 1949–55.

I remember dropping my water gun. Quickly, almost without thought, I took off my apron and walked out of the plant and drove home. It was midmorning, I remember, and the house was empty. Down in my chest there was still that leaking sensation, something very warm and precious spilling out, and I was covered with blood and hog-stink, and for a long while I just concentrated on holding myself together. I remember taking a hot shower. I remember packing a suitcase and carrying it out to the kitchen, standing very still for a few minutes, looking carefully at the familiar objects all around me. The old chrome toaster, the telephone, the pink and white Formica on the kitchen counters. The room was full of bright sunshine. Everything sparkled. My house, I thought. My life. I'm not sure how long I stood there, but later I scribbled out a short note to my parents.

What it said, exactly, I don't recall now. Something vague. Taking off, will call, love Tim.

I drove north.

It's a blur now, as it was then, and all I remember is a sense of high velocity and the feel of the steering wheel in my hands. I was riding on adrenaline. A giddy feeling, in a way, except there was the dreamy edge of impossibility to it—like running a dead-end maze—no way out—it couldn't come to a happy conclusion and yet I was doing it anyway because it was all I could think of to do. It was pure flight, fast and mindless. I had no plan. Just hit the border at high speed and crash through and keep on running. Near dusk I passed through Bemidji, then turned northeast toward International Falls. I spent the night in the car behind a closed-down gas station a half mile from the border. In the morning, after gassing up, I headed straight west along the Rainy River, which separates Minnesota from Canada, and which for me separated one life from another. The land was mostly wilderness. Here and there I passed a motel or bait shop, but otherwise the country unfolded in great sweeps of pine and birch and sumac. Though it was still August, the air already had the smell of October, football season, piles of yellow-red leaves, everything crisp and clean. I remember a huge blue sky. Off to my right was the Rainy River, wide as a lake in places, and beyond the Rainy River was Canada.

For a while I just drove, not aiming at anything, then in the late morning I began looking for a place to lie low for a day or two. I was exhausted, and scared sick, and around noon I pulled into an old fishing resort called the Tip Top Lodge. Actually it was not a lodge at all, just eight or nine tiny yellow cabins clustered on a peninsula that jutted northward into the Rainy River. The place was in sorry shape. There was a dangerous wooden dock, an old minnow tank, a flimsy tar paper boathouse along the shore. The main building, which stood in a cluster of pines on high ground, seemed to lean heavily to one side, like a cripple, the roof sagging toward Canada. Briefly, I thought about turning around, just giving up, but then I got out of the car and walked up to the front porch.

The man who opened the door that day is the hero of my life. How do I say this without sounding sappy? Blurt it out—the man saved me. He offered exactly what I needed, without questions, without any words at all. He took me in. He was there at the critical time—a silent, watchful presence. Six days later, when it ended, I was unable to find a proper way to thank him, and I never have, and so, if nothing else, this story represents a small gesture of gratitude twenty years overdue.

Even after two decades I can close my eyes and return to that porch at the Tip Top Lodge. I can see the old guy staring at me. Elroy Berdahl: eighty-one years old, skinny and shrunken and mostly bald. He wore a flannel shirt and brown work pants. In one hand, I remember, he carried a green apple, a small paring knife in the other. His eyes had the bluish gray color of a razor blade, the same polished shine, and as he peered up at me I felt a strange sharpness, almost painful, a cutting sensation, as if his gaze were somehow slicing me open. In part, no doubt, it was my own sense of guilt, but even so I'm absolutely certain that the old man took one look and went right to the heart of things—a kid in trouble. When I asked for a room, Elroy made a little clicking sound with his tongue. He nodded, led me out to one of the cabins, and dropped a key in my hand. I remember smiling at him. I also remember wishing I hadn't. The old man shook his head as if to tell me it wasn't worth the bother.

"Dinner at five-thirty," he said. "You eat fish?"

"Anything," I said.

Elroy grunted and said, "I'll bet."

We spent six days together at the Tip Top Lodge. Just the two of us. Tourist season was over, and there were no boats on the river, and the wilderness seemed to withdraw into a great permanent stillness. Over those six days Elroy Berdahl and I took most of our meals together. In the mornings we sometimes went out on long hikes into the woods, and at night we played Scrabble or listened to records or sat reading in front of his big stone fireplace. At times I felt the awkwardness of an intruder, but Elroy accepted me into his quiet routine without fuss or ceremony. He took my presence for granted, the same way he might've sheltered a stray cat—no wasted sighs or pity—and there was never any talk about it. Just the opposite. What I remember more than anything is the man's willful, almost ferocious silence. In all that time together, all those hours, he never asked the obvious questions: Why was I there? Why alone? Why so preoccupied? If Elroy was curious about any of this, he was careful never to put it into words.

My hunch, though, is that he already knew. At least the basics. After all, it was 1968, and guys were burning draft cards, and Canada was just a boat ride away. Elroy Berdahl was no hick. His bedroom, I remember, was cluttered with books and newspapers. He killed me at the Scrabble board, barely concentrating, and on those occasions when speech was necessary he had a way of compressing large thoughts into small, cryptic packets of language. One evening, just at sunset, he pointed up at an owl circling over the violet-lighted forest to the west.

"Hey, O'Brien," he said. "There's Jesus."

The man was sharp—he didn't miss much. Those razor eyes. Now and then he'd catch me staring out at the river, at the far shore, and I could almost hear the tumblers clicking in his head. Maybe I'm wrong, but I doubt it.

One thing for certain, he knew I was in desperate trouble. And he knew I couldn't talk about it. The wrong word—or even the right word—and I would've disappeared. I was wired and jittery. My skin felt too tight. After supper one evening I vomited and went back to my cabin and lay down for a few moments and then vomited again; another time, in the middle of the afternoon, I began sweating and couldn't shut it off. I went through whole days feeling dizzy with sorrow. I couldn't sleep; I couldn't lie still. At night I'd toss around in bed, half awake, half dreaming, imagining how I'd sneak down to the beach and quietly push one of the old man's boats out into the river and start paddling my way toward Canada. There were times when I thought I'd gone off the psychic edge. I couldn't tell up from down, I was just falling, and late in the night I'd lie there watching weird pictures spin through my head. Getting chased by the Border Patrol—helicopters and searchlights and barking dogs—I'd be crashing through the woods, I'd be down on my hands and knees—people shouting out my name—the law closing in on all sides—my hometown draft board and the FBI and the Royal Canadian Mounted Police. It all seemed crazy and impossible. Twenty-one years old, an ordinary kid with all the ordinary dreams and ambitions, and all I wanted was to live the life I was born to—a mainstream life—I loved baseball and hamburgers and cherry Cokes—and now I was off on the margins of exile, leaving my country forever, and it seemed so impossible and terrible and sad.

I'm not sure how I made it through those six days. Most of it I can't remember. On two or three afternoons, to pass some time, I helped

Elroy get the place ready for winter, sweeping down the cabins and hauling in the boats, little chores that kept my body moving. The days were cool and bright. The nights were very dark. One morning the old man showed me how to split and stack firewood, and for several hours we just worked in silence out behind his house. At one point, I remember, Elroy put down his maul and looked at me for a long time, his lips drawn as if framing a difficult question, but then he shook his head and went back to work. The man's self-control was amazing. He never pried. He never put me in a position that required lies or denials. To an extent, I suppose, his reticence was typical of that part of Minnesota, where privacy still held value, and even if I'd been walking around with some horrible deformity—four arms and three heads—I'm sure the old man would've talked about everything except those extra arms and heads. Simple politeness was part of it. But even more than that, I think, the man understood that words were insufficient. The problem had gone beyond discussion. During that long summer I'd been over and over the various arguments, all the pros and cons, and it was no longer a question that could be decided by an act of pure reason. Intellect had come up against emotion. My conscience told me to run, but some irrational and powerful force was resisting, like a weight pushing me toward the war. What it came down to, stupidly, was a sense of shame. Hot, stupid shame. I did not want people to think badly of me. Not my parents, not my brother and sister, not even the folks down at the Gobbler Café. I was ashamed to be there at the Tip Top Lodge. I was ashamed of my conscience, ashamed to be doing the right thing.

Some of this Elroy must've understood. Not the details, of course, but the plain fact of crisis.

Although the old man never confronted me about it, there was one occasion when he came close to forcing the whole thing out into the open. It was early evening, and we'd just finished supper, and over coffee and dessert I asked him about my bill, how much I owed so far. For a long while the old man squinted down at the tablecloth.

"Well, the basic rate," he said, "is fifty bucks a night. Not counting meals. This makes four nights, right?"

I nodded. I had three hundred and twelve dollars in my wallet.

Elroy kept his eyes on the tablecloth. "Now that's an on-season price. To be fair, I suppose we should knock it down a peg or two." He leaned back in his chair. "What's a reasonable number, you figure?"

"I don't know," I said. "Forty?"

"Forty's good. Forty a night. Then we tack on food—say another hundred? Two hundred sixty total?"

"I guess."

He raised his eyebrows. "Too much?"

"No, that's fair. It's fine. Tomorrow, though ... I think I'd better take off tomorrow."

Elroy shrugged and began clearing the table. For a time he fussed with the dishes, whistling to himself as if the subject had been settled. After a second he slapped his hands together.

"You know what we forgot?" he said. "We forgot wages. Those odd jobs you done. What we have to do, we have to figure out what your time's worth. Your last job—how much did you pull in an hour?"

"Not enough," I said.

"A bad one?"

"Yes. Pretty bad."

Slowly then, without intending any long sermon, I told him about my days at the pig plant. It began as a straight recitation of the facts, but before I could stop myself I was talking about the blood clots and the water gun and how the smell had soaked into my skin and how I couldn't wash it away. I went on for a long time. I told him about wild hogs squealing in my dreams, the sounds of butchery, slaughterhouse sounds, and how I'd sometimes wake up with that greasy pig-stink in my throat.

When I was finished, Elroy nodded at me.

"Well, to be honest," he said, "when you first showed up here, I wondered about all that. The aroma, I mean. Smelled like you was awful damned fond of pork chops." The old man almost smiled. He made a snuffling sound, then sat down with a pencil and a piece of paper. "So what'd this crud job pay? Ten bucks an hour? Fifteen?"

"Less."

Elroy shook his head. "Let's make it fifteen. You put in twenty-five hours here, easy. That's three hundred seventy-five bucks total wages. We subtract the two hundred sixty for food and lodging, I still owe you a hundred and fifteen."

He took four fifties out of his shirt pocket and laid them on the table.

"Call it even," he said.

"No."

"Pick it up. Get yourself a haircut."

The money lay on the table for the rest of the evening. It was still there when I went back to my cabin. In the morning, though, I found an envelope tacked to my door. Inside were the four fifties and a two-word note that said EMERGENCY FUND.

The man knew.

Looking back after twenty years, I sometimes wonder if the events of that summer didn't happen in some other dimension, a place where your life exists before you've lived it, and where it goes afterward. None of it ever seemed real. During my time at the Tip Top Lodge I had the feeling that I'd slipped out of my own skin, hovering a few feet away while some poor yo-yo with my name and face tried to make his way toward a future he didn't understand and didn't want. Even now I can see myself as I was then. It's like watching an old home movie: I'm young and tan and fit. I've got hair—lots of it. I don't smoke or drink. I'm wearing faded blue jeans and a white polo shirt. I can see myself sitting on Elroy Berdahl's dock near dusk one evening, the sky a bright shimmering pink, and I'm finishing up a letter to my parents that tells what I'm about to do and why I'm doing it and how sorry I am that I'd never found the courage to talk to them about it. I ask them not to be angry. I try to explain some of my feelings, but there aren't enough words, and so I just say that it's a thing that has to be done. At the end of the letter I talk about the vacations we used to take up in this north country, at a place called Whitefish Lake, and how the scenery here reminds me of those good times. I tell them I'm fine. I tell them I'll write again from Winnipeg or Montreal or wherever I end up.

On my last full day, the sixth day, the old man took me out fishing on the Rainy River. The afternoon was sunny and cold. A stiff breeze came in from the north, and I remember how the little fourteen-foot boat made sharp rocking motions as we pushed off from the dock. The current was fast. All around us, I remember, there was a vastness to the world, an unpeopled rawness, just the trees and the sky and the water reaching out toward nowhere. The air had the brittle scent of October.

For ten or fifteen minutes Elroy held a course upstream, the river choppy and silver-gray, then he turned straight north and put the engine on full throttle. I felt the bow lift beneath me. I remember the wind in my ears, the sound of the old outboard Evinrude. For a time I didn't pay attention to anything, just feeling the cold spray against my face, but then it occurred to me that at some point we must've passed into Canadian waters, across that dotted line between two different worlds, and I remember a sudden tightness in my chest as I looked up and watched the far shore come at me. This wasn't a daydream. It was tangible and real. As we came in toward land, Elroy cut the engine, letting the boat fishtail lightly about twenty yards off shore. The old man didn't look at me or speak. Bending down, he opened up his tackle box and busied himself with a bobber and a piece of wire leader, humming to himself, his eyes down.

It struck me then that he must've planned it. I'll never be certain, of course, but I think he meant to bring me up against the realities, to guide me across the river and to take me to the edge and to stand a kind of vigil as I chose a life for myself.

I remember staring at the old man, then at my hands, then at Canada. The shoreline was dense with brush and timber. I could see tiny red berries on the bushes. I could see a squirrel up in one of the birch trees, a big crow looking at me from a boulder along the river. That close—twenty yards—and I could see the delicate latticework of the leaves, the texture of the soil, the browned needles beneath the pines, the configurations of geology and human history. Twenty yards. I could've done it. I could've jumped and started swimming for my life. Inside me, in my chest, I felt a terrible squeezing pressure. Even now, as I write this, I can still feel that tightness. And I want you to feel it—the wind coming off the river, the waves, the silence, the wooded frontier. You're at the bow of a boat on the Rainy River. You're twenty-one years old, you're scared, and there's a hard squeezing pressure in your chest.

What would you do?

Would you jump? Would you feel pity for yourself? Would you think about your family and your childhood and your dreams and all you're leaving behind? Would it hurt? Would it feel like dying? Would you cry, as I did?

I tried to swallow it back. I tried to smile, except I was crying.

Now, perhaps, you can understand why I've never told this story before. It's not just the embarrassment of tears. That's part of it, no doubt, but what embarrasses me much more, and always will, is the paralysis that took my heart. A moral freeze: I couldn't decide, I couldn't act, I couldn't comport myself with even a pretense of modest human dignity.

All I could do was cry. Quietly, not bawling, just the chest-chokes.

At the rear of the boat Elroy Berdahl pretended not to notice. He held a fishing rod in his hands, his head bowed to hide his eyes. He kept humming a soft, monotonous little tune. Everywhere, it seemed, in the trees and water and sky, a great worldwide sadness came pressing down on me, a crushing sorrow, sorrow like I had never known it before. And what was so sad, I realized, was that Canada had become a pitiful fantasy. Silly and hopeless. It was no longer a possibility. Right

Fiction reveals truth that reality obscures.

Jessamyn West

then, with the shore so close, I understood that I would not do what I should do. I would not swim away from my hometown and my country and my life. I would not be brave. That old image of myself as a hero, as a man of conscience and courage, all that was just a threadbare pipe dream. Bobbing there on the Rainy River, looking back at the Minnesota shore, I felt a sudden swell of helplessness come over me, a drowning sensation, as if I had toppled overboard and was being swept away by the silver waves. Chunks of my own history flashed by. I saw a seven-year-old boy in a white cowboy hat and a Lone Ranger mask and a pair of holstered six-shooters; I saw a twelve-year-old Little League shortstop pivoting to turn a double play; I saw a sixteen-year-old kid decked out for his first prom, looking spiffy in a white tux and a black bow tie, his hair cut short and flat, his shoes freshly polished. My whole life seemed to spill out into the river, swirling away from me, everything I had ever been or ever wanted to be. I couldn't get my breath; I couldn't stay afloat; I couldn't tell which way to swim. A hallucination, I suppose, but it was as real as anything I would ever feel. I saw my parents calling to me from the far shoreline. I saw my brother and sister, all the townsfolk, the mayor and the entire Chamber of Commerce and all my old teachers and girlfriends and high school buddies. Like some weird sporting event: everybody screaming from the sidelines, rooting me on—a loud stadium roar. Hotdogs and popcorn—stadium smells, stadium heat. A squad of cheerleaders did cartwheels along the banks of the Rainy River; they had megaphones and pompoms and smooth brown thighs. The crowd swayed left and right. A marching band played fight songs. All my aunts and uncles were there, and Abraham Lincoln, and Saint George, and a nine-year-old girl named Linda who had died of a brain tumor back in fifth grade, and several members of the United States Senate, and a blind poet scribbling notes, and LBJ, and Huck Finn, and Abbie Hoffman, and all the dead soldiers back from the grave, and the many thousands who were later to die—villagers with terrible burns, little kids without arms or legs—yes, and the Joint Chiefs of Staff were there, and a couple of popes, and a first lieutenant named Jimmy Cross, and the last surviving veteran of the American Civil War, and Jane Fonda dressed up as Barbarella, and an old man sprawled beside a pigpen, and my grandfather, and Gary Cooper, and a kind-faced woman carrying an umbrella and a copy of Plato's *Republic*, and a million ferocious citizens waving flags of all shapes and colors—people in hard hats, people in headbands—they were all whooping and chanting and urging me toward one shore or the other. I saw faces from my distant past and distant future. My wife was there. My unborn daughter waved at me, and my two sons hopped up and down, and a drill sergeant named Blyton sneered and shot up a finger and shook his head. There was a choir in bright purple robes. There was a cabbie from the Bronx. There was a slim young man I would one day kill with a hand grenade along a red clay trail outside the village of My Khe.

The little aluminum boat rocked softly beneath me. There was the wind and the sky.

I tried to will myself overboard.

I gripped the edge of the boat and leaned forward and thought, *Now.*

I did try. It just wasn't possible.

All those eyes on me—the town, the whole universe—and I couldn't risk the embarrassment. It was as if there were an audience to my life, that swirl of faces along the river, and in my head I could hear people screaming at me. Traitor! they yelled. Turncoat! Coward! I felt myself blush. I couldn't tolerate it. I couldn't endure the mockery, or the disgrace, or the patriotic ridicule. Even in my imagination, the shore just twenty yards away, I couldn't make myself be brave. It had nothing to do with morality. Embarrassment, that's all it was.

And right then I submitted.

I would go to the war—I would kill and maybe die—because I was embarrassed not to.

That was the sad thing. And so I sat in the bow of the boat and cried.

It was loud now. Loud, hard crying.

Elroy Berdahl remained quiet. He kept fishing. He worked his line with the tips of his fingers, patiently, squinting out at his red and white bobber on the Rainy River. His eyes were flat and impassive. He didn't speak. He was simply there, like the river and the late-summer sun. And yet by his presence, his mute watchfulness, he made it real. He was the true audience. He was a witness, like God, or like the gods, who look on in absolute silence as we live our lives, as we make our choices or fail to make them.

"Ain't biting," he said.

Then after a time the old man pulled in his line and turned the boat back toward Minnesota.

I don't remember saying goodbye. That last night we had dinner together, and I went to bed early, and in the morning Elroy fixed breakfast for me. When I told him I'd be leaving, the old man nodded as if he already knew. He looked down at the table and smiled.

At some point later in the morning it's possible that we shook hands—I just don't remember—but I do know that by the time I'd finished packing the old man had disappeared. Around noon, when I took my suitcase out to the car, I noticed that his old black pickup truck was no longer parked in front of the house. I went inside and waited for a while, but I felt a bone certainty that he wouldn't be back. In a way, I thought, it was appropriate. I washed up the breakfast dishes, left his two hundred dollars on the kitchen counter, got into the car, and drove south toward home.

The day was cloudy. I passed through towns with familiar names, through the pine forests and down to the prairie, and then to Vietnam, where I was a soldier, and then home again. I survived, but it's not a happy ending. I was a coward. I went to the war.

Tim O'Brien was born in Minnesota, U.S., in 1946. He graduated in 1968, after which he was drafted and sent to Vietnam. His division became involved in the My Lai massacre in 1968, which he wrote about later. After Vietnam, O'Brien attended Harvard, eventually leaving to become a newspaper reporter with the *Washington Post*. He soon gave up reporting to write fiction full time after his first book, *If I Die in a Combat Zone, Box Me Up and Send Me Home*. His other novels include *Northern Lights*, *Going After Cacciato*, *The Nuclear Age*, *The Things They Carried*, and *In the Lake of the Woods*.

I. *Response*

a. In your own words, summarize the reasons the narrator gives for his opposition to the Vietnam War.

b. The narrator's job at the Armour Meat Factory in some ways anticipates the experience of fighting in Vietnam. How? Do you think the author was right to include the graphic descriptions of the slaughterhouse? Explain.

c. In your opinion, does the reader need to have a personal knowledge of the issues regarding the Vietnam War to appreciate this story? Why or why not?

d. Reread the opening paragraph of the story. Now that you have read the whole account, why do you think the narrator waited so long to tell his story?

e. In a group, identify and discuss the emotional changes the narrator experiences as he moves toward his final decision. In your opinion, should he have accepted his draft notice, or should he have sought sanctuary in Canada as a draft-dodger?

2. ***Research and Inquiry*** Using the Internet and other resources, prepare a presentation for the class on American draft-dodgers and the Vietnam War. Try to find out how many young men dodged the draft at that time and what their reasons were. What was the reaction in the United States to these men at the time? What was the reaction after the war? Did the phenomenon of draft-dodging affect life in Canada in any way? Explain.

3. ***Literature Studies*** *Fiction Versus Autobiography* When you read "On the Rainy River," did you think of it as a story or an autobiographical account? Why? Actually, the story is a hybrid—it is based on O'Brien's experiences, but is not necessarily true in every detail. What are the benefits of this approach, from a writer's perspective? What is your own evaluation of this approach?

4. ***Film Study*** The Vietnam War has been the subject of a number of excellent films, for example, *Full Metal Jacket, Platoon, Apocalypse Now!*, and *Born on the Fourth of July*. View one of these films or another film about this war. Examine the protagonist's life and decisions. Write a brief essay to assess the difficulties he or she faces both physically and psychologically.

5. ***Making Connections*** Use a word web to explore the connotations and ideas that are evoked by the word *river*. Next, in an essay format, compare and contrast the symbolic value of the Honia River in "The Return" with that of the Rainy River in "On the Rainy River." Did your word web help to raise your awareness of these symbolic values? Explain.

　　Alternatively, write an essay to compare and contrast the outlook on war presented by Bao Ninh in "A Marker on the Side of the Boat" with that presented by Tim O'Brien in "On the Rainy River." Include specific differences and similarities.

An unexpected sum of money propels
Mrs. Sommers into a most unusual day ...

A Pair of Silk Stockings

by Kate Chopin

*L*ittle Mrs. Sommers one day found herself the unexpected possessor of fifteen dollars. It seemed to her a very large amount of money, and the way in which it stuffed and bulged her worn old *porte-monnaie*[1] gave her a feeling of importance such as she had not enjoyed for years.

The question of investment was one that occupied her greatly. For a day or two she walked about apparently in a dreamy state, but really absorbed in speculation and calculation. She did not wish to act hastily, to do anything she might afterward regret. But it was during the still hours of the night when she lay awake revolving plans in her mind that she seemed to see her way clearly toward a proper and judicious use of the money.

A dollar or two should be added to the price usually paid for Janie's shoes, which would insure their lasting an appreciable time longer than they usually did. She would buy so and so many yards of percale[2] for new shirt waists[3] for the boys and Janie and Mag. She had intended to make the old ones do by skilful patching. Mag should have another gown. She had seen some beautiful patterns, veritable bargains in the shop windows. And still there would be left enough for new stockings—two pairs apiece—and what darning that would save for a while! She would get caps for the boys and sailor-hats for the girls. The vision of her little brood looking fresh and dainty and new for once in their lives excited her and made her restless and wakeful with anticipation.

---

[1]*porte-monnaie:* purse, wallet
[2]**percale:** a closely-woven cotton fabric
[3]**shirt waists:** a style of shirt popular in the late 1800s

The neighbors sometimes talked of certain "better days" that little Mrs. Sommers had known before she had ever thought of being Mrs. Sommers. She herself indulged in no such morbid retrospection. She had no time—no second of time to devote to the past. The needs of the present absorbed her every faculty. A vision of the future like some dim, gaunt monster sometimes appalled her, but luckily tomorrow never comes.

Mrs. Sommers was one who knew the value of bargains; who could stand for hours making her way inch by inch toward the desired object that was selling below cost. She could elbow her way if need be; she had learned to clutch a piece of goods and hold it and stick to it with persistence and determination till her turn came to be served, no matter when it came.

But that day she was a little faint and tired. She had swallowed a light luncheon—no! when she came to think of it, between getting the children fed and the place righted, and preparing herself for the shopping bout, she had actually forgotten to eat any luncheon at all!

She sat herself upon a revolving stool before a counter that was comparatively deserted, trying to gather strength and courage to charge through an eager multitude that was besieging breastworks[4] of shirting and figured lawn.[5] An all-gone limp feeling had come over her and she rested her hand aimlessly upon the counter. She wore no gloves. By degrees she grew aware that her hand had encountered something very soothing, very pleasant to touch. She looked down to see that her hand lay upon a pile of silk stockings. A placard near by announced that they had been reduced in price from two dollars and fifty cents to one dollar and ninety-eight cents; and a young girl who stood behind the counter asked her if she wished to examine their line of silk hosiery. She smiled, just as if she had been asked to inspect a tiara of diamonds with the ultimate view of purchasing it. But she went on feeling the soft, sheeny luxurious things—with both hands now, holding them up to see them glisten, and to feel them glide serpent-like through her fingers.

Two hectic blotches came suddenly into her pale cheeks. She looked up at the girl.

"Do you think there are any eights-and-a-half among these?"

There were any number of eights-and-a-half. In fact, there were more of that size than any other. Here was a light-blue pair;

---

[4]**breastworks:** chest-high counters (likened to the walls of a fort)
[5]**figured lawn:** cotton fabric woven with designs

there were some lavender, some all black and various shades of tan and gray. Mrs. Sommers selected a black pair and looked at them very long and closely. She pretended to be examining their texture, which the clerk assured her was excellent.

"A dollar and ninety-eight cents," she mused aloud. "Well, I'll take this pair." She handed the girl a five-dollar bill and waited for her change and for her parcel. What a very small parcel it was! It seemed lost in the depths of her shabby old shopping-bag.

Mrs. Sommers after that did not move in the direction of the bargain counter. She took the elevator, which carried her to an upper floor into the region of the ladies' waiting-rooms. Here, in a retired corner, she exchanged her cotton stockings for the new silk ones which she had just bought. She was not going through any acute mental process or reasoning with herself, nor was she striving to explain to her satisfaction the motive of her action. She was not thinking at all. She seemed for the time to be taking a rest from that laborious and fatiguing function and to have abandoned herself to some mechanical impulse that directed her actions and freed her of responsibility.

How good was the touch of the raw silk to her flesh! She felt like lying back in the cushioned chair and reveling for a while in the luxury of it. She did for a little while. Then she replaced her shoes, rolled the cotton stockings together and thrust them into her bag. After doing this she crossed straight over to the shoe department and took her seat to be fitted.

She was fastidious. The clerk could not make her out; he could not reconcile her shoes with her stockings, and she was not too easily pleased. She held back her skirts and turned her feet one way and her head another way as she glanced down at the polished, pointed-tipped boots. Her foot and ankle looked very pretty. She could not realize that they belonged to her and were a part of herself. She wanted an excellent and stylish fit, she told the young fellow who served her, and she did not mind the difference of a dollar or two more in the price so long as she got what she desired.

It was a long time since Mrs. Sommers had been fitted with gloves. On rare occasions when she had bought a pair they were always "bargains," so cheap that it would have been preposterous and unreasonable to have expected them to be fitted to the hand.

Now she rested her elbow on the cushion of the glove counter, and a pretty, pleasant young creature, delicate and deft of touch, drew a long-wristed "kid"[6] over Mrs. Sommers's hand. She smoothed it down over

---

[6]**kid:** kid gloves, made from the skin of a young goat

the wrist and buttoned it neatly, and both lost themselves for a second or two in admiring contemplation of the little symmetrical gloved hand. But there were other places where money might be spent.

There were books and magazines piled up in the window of a stall a few paces down the street. Mrs. Sommers bought two high-priced magazines such as she had been accustomed to read in the days when she had been accustomed to other pleasant things. She carried them without wrapping. As well as she could she lifted her skirts at the crossings. Her stockings and boots and well fitting gloves had worked marvels in her bearing—had given her a feeling of assurance, a sense of belonging to the well-dressed multitude.

She was very hungry. Another time she would have stilled the cravings for food until reaching her own home, where she would have brewed herself a cup of tea and taken a snack of anything that was available. But the impulse that was guiding her would not suffer her to entertain any such thought.

There was a restaurant at the corner. She had never entered its doors; from the outside she had sometimes caught glimpses of spotless damask[7] and shining crystal, and soft-stepping waiters serving people of fashion.

When she entered her appearance created no surprise, no consternation, as she had half feared it might. She seated herself at a small table alone, and an attentive waiter at once approached to take her order. She did not want a profusion; she craved a nice and tasty bite— a half dozen blue-points,[8] a plump chop with cress, a something sweet —a crème-frappée,[9] for instance; a glass of Rhine wine, and after all a small cup of black coffee.

While waiting to be served she removed her gloves very leisurely and laid them beside her. Then she picked up a magazine and glanced through it, cutting the pages[10] with a blunt edge of her knife. It was all very agreeable. The damask was even more spotless than it had seemed through the window, and the crystal more sparkling. There were quiet ladies and gentlemen, who did not notice her, lunching at the small tables like her own. A soft, pleasing strain of music could be heard, and a gentle breeze was blowing through the window. She tasted a bite, and she read a word or two, and she sipped the amber wine and wiggled her toes in the silk stockings. The price of it made no

---

[7]**damask:** fine table linen
[8]**blue-points:** a kind of oyster
[9]**crème-frappée:** a frozen dessert
[10]**cutting the pages:** At one time, the pages of some books and magazines were attached and had to be sliced apart along one or more sides.

difference. She counted the money out to the waiter and left an extra coin on his tray, whereupon he bowed before her as before a princess of royal blood.

There was still money in her purse, and her next temptation presented itself in the shape of a matinée poster.

It was a little later when she entered the theatre, the play had begun and the house seemed to her to be packed. But there were vacant seats here and there, and into one of them she was ushered, between brilliantly dressed women who had gone there to kill time and eat candy and display their gaudy attire. There were many others who were there solely for the play and acting. It is safe to say there was no one present who bore quite the attitude which Mrs. Sommers did to her surroundings. She gathered in the whole—stage and players and people in one wide impression, and absorbed it and enjoyed it. She laughed at the comedy and wept—she and the gaudy woman next to her wept over the tragedy. And they talked a little together over it. And the gaudy woman wiped her eyes and sniffled on a tiny square of filmy, perfumed lace and passed little Mrs. Sommers her box of candy.

The play was over, the music ceased, the crowd filed out. It was like a dream ended. People scattered in all directions. Mrs. Sommers went to the corner and waited for the cable car.

A man with keen eyes, who sat opposite to her, seemed to like the study of her small, pale face. It puzzled him to decipher what he saw there. In truth, he saw nothing—unless he were wizard enough to detect a poignant wish, a powerful longing that the cable car would never stop anywhere, but go on and on with her forever.

Kate Chopin was born in St. Louis, U.S., in 1850. Several of her stories were published in magazines such as *America,* the *St. Louis Post-Dispatch,* and *Vogue.* Her first novel, *At Fault,* was published privately, after which she submitted her novel *Young Dr. Gosse* to several publishers, but was unsuccessful. She went on to publish several other works, including her well-known novel, *The Awakening,* which received scathing reviews. She died in 1904. Although her work remained more or less forgotten for some time, *The Awakening* is now widely read, and regarded as an important feminist work.

1. *Response*
a. What details is the reader given about Mrs. Sommers' life before her shopping trip? Explain how these details are important to the story's meaning.
b. Mrs. Sommers "did not wish to act hastily, to do anything she might afterward regret." Find the point in the story where she abandons her careful planning. Based on what you know about Mrs. Sommers' character, and about people in general, do you find this shift convincing? Why or why not?
c. Reread the final paragraph of the story. What is the impact of closing the story in this manner?
d. This story was published in 1894. In your view, does it have any relevance for today's readers? Explain.

2. *Language Conventions* *Formal Tone* Select five specific examples that illustrate the formal diction and prose style Chopin uses in this story. Do you think the style is appropriate to Mrs. Sommers' situation and to the story's theme? Explain.

3. *Literature Studies* *Character Analysis* Write a character analysis of Mrs. Sommers in which you describe and explain how she changes in this story. Include specific references to details that illustrate the **dynamic** nature of her character. Do you think these changes are temporary or permanent?

A **dynamic character** is one who undergoes a significant and permanent change in personality or beliefs.

4. *Drama* *Improvisation* What will unfold when, wearing her new clothes, Mrs. Sommers returns home to her family but with all her money spent? In a group, improvise the scene. Before you make your presentation, have a group discussion in which you agree on the state of mind of each character.

5. *Making Connections* In "Transients in Arcadia" and "A Pair of Silk Stockings," the characters have a powerful desire for a moment of luxury and the appearance of upper-class distinction. What are the similarities and differences between Mrs. Sommers and Mamie Siviter? Imagine what the two women might say to each other if they met at the hosiery counter at Casey's store. With a partner, role-play the conversation.

Dressing Up for the Carnival

by Carol Shields

All over town people are putting on their costumes. Tamara has flung open her closet door; just to see her standing there is to feel a squeeze of the heart. She loves her clothes. She *knows* her clothes. Her favourite moment of the day is *this* moment, standing at the closet door, still a little dizzy from her long night of tumbled sleep, biting her lip, thinking hard, moving the busy hangers along the rod, about to make up her mind.

Yes! The yellow cotton skirt with the big patch pockets and the hand detail around the hem. How fortunate to own such a skirt. And the white blouse. What a blouse! Those sleeves, that neckline with its buttoned flap, the fullness in the yoke that reminds her of the Morris dances she and her boyfriend Bruce saw at the Exhibition last year.

Next she adds her new straw belt; perfect. A string of yellow beads. Earrings of course. Her bone sandals. And bare legs, why not?

She never checks the weather before she dresses; her clothes *are* the weather, as powerful in their sunniness as the strong, muzzy early morning light pouring into the narrow street by the bus stop, warming the combed crown of her hair and fuelling her with imagination. She taps a sandalled foot lightly on the pavement, waiting for the number 4 bus, no longer just Tamara, clerk-receptionist for the Youth Employment Bureau, but a woman in a yellow skirt. A passionate woman dressed in yellow. A Passionate, Vibrant Woman About To Begin Her Day. Her Life.

Roger, aged thirty, employed by the Gas Board, is coming out of a corner grocer's carrying a mango in his left hand. He went in to buy an apple and came out with *this*. At the cash register he refused

Business Man Wearing Mask by Curtis Parker.

a bag, preferring to carry this thing, this object, in his bare hand. The price was $1.29. He's a little surprised at how heavy it is, a tight seamless leather skin enclosing soft pulp, or so he imagines. He has never bought a mango before, never eaten one, doesn't know what a mango tastes like or how it's prepared. Cooked like a squash? Sliced and sugared like a peach? He has no intention of eating it, not now anyway, maybe never. Its weight reminds him of a first-class league ball, but larger, longer, smooth skinned, and ripely green. Mango, mango. An elliptical purse, juice-filled, curved for the palm of the human hand, his hand.

He is a man of medium height, burly, divorced, wearing an open-necked shirt, hurrying back to work after his coffee break. But at this moment he freezes and sees himself freshly: a man carrying a mango in his left hand. Already he's accustomed to it; in fact, it's starting to feel lighter and drier, like a set of castanets which has somehow attached itself to his left arm. Any minute now he'll break out into a cha-cha-cha right here in front of the Gas Board. The shrivelled fate he sometimes sees for himself can be postponed if only he puts his mind to it. Who would have thought it of him? Not his ex-wife Lucile, not his co-workers, not his boss, not even himself.

And the Borden sisters are back from their ski week in Happy Valley. They've been back for a month now, in fact, so why are they still wearing those little plastic ski passes on the zipper tabs of their jackets? A good question. I SKIED HAPPY MOUNTAIN these passes say. The Bordens wear them all over town, at the shopping centre, in the parking lot. It's spring, the leaves are unfolding on the hedges in front of the post office, but the Borden girls, Karen and Sue, still carry on their bodies, and in their faces too, the fresh wintry cold of the slopes, the thrill of powder snow and stinging sky. (The air up there chimes with echoes, a bromide of blue.) It would be an exaggeration to say the Borden sisters swagger; it would be going too far. They move like young ponies, quivery and thoughtful, with the memory of expended effort and banked curves. They speak to each other in voices that are loud and musical, and their skin, so clear, pink, bright, and healthy, traps the sunshine beneath its surface. With one hand, walking along, they stroke the feathering-out tops of hedges in front of the post office, and with the other they pull and tug on those little plasticized tags—I SKIED HAPPY MOUNTAIN. You might say it's a kind of compulsion, as though they can't help themselves.

And then there's Wanda from the bank who has been sent on the strangest of errands. It happened in this way: Mr. Wishcourt, the bank manager where Wanda works, has just bought a new baby carriage for his wife, or rather, for their new baby son, Samuel James. The baby carriage was an impulsive lunch-hour purchase, he explains to Wanda, looking shamefaced but exuberant: an English pram, high-wheeled, majestically hooded, tires like a Rolls Royce, a beauty, but the fool thing, even when folded up, refuses to fit in the back of his Volvo. Would she object? It would take perhaps three-quarters of an hour. It's a fine day. He'll draw her a plan on a sheet of paper, put an X where his house is. He knows how she loves walking, that she gets restless in the afternoon sometimes, sitting in her little airless cage. He would appreciate it so much. And so would his wife and little Sam. Would she mind? He's never before asked her to make coffee or do personal errands. It's against his policy, treating his employees like that. But just this once?

Wanda sets off awkwardly. She is, after all, an awkward woman, who was formerly an awkward girl with big girlish teeth and clumsy shoulders. The pram's swaying body seems to steer her at first, instead of *her* steering *it*. Such a chunky rolling oblong, black and British with its wambling,[1] bossy, outsized keel. "Excuse me," she says, and "Sorry." Without meaning to, she forces people over to the edge of the sidewalks, crowds them at the street corners, even rubs up against them with the big soft tires.

All she gets back are smiles. Or kindly little nods that say: "It's not your fault" or "How marvellous" or "What a picture!" After a bit she gets the hang of steering. This is a technical marvel she's pushing along, the way it takes the curbs, soundlessly, with scarcely any effort at all. Engineering at its most refined and comical. Her hands rest lightly on the wide white handlebar. It might be made of ivory or alabaster or something equally precious, it's so smooth and cool to the touch.

By the time Wanda reaches Pine Street she feels herself fully in charge. Beneath the leafy poplars, she and the carriage have become a single entity. Gliding, melding, a silvery hum of wheels and a faint, pleasing adhesive resistance as the tires roll along suburban asphalt. The weight of her fingertips is enough to keep it in motion, in control, and she takes the final corners with grace. Little Sam is going to love his new rolling home, so roomy and rhythmic, like a dark boat sailing forward in tune with his infant breathing and the bump-dee-bump of his baby heart.

She stops, leans over, and reaches inside. There's no one about; no one sees her, only the eyes inside her head that have rehearsed this small gesture in dreams. She straightens the blanket, pulling it smooth,

---

[1]**wambling:** wobbling, rolling

pats it into place. "Shhh," she murmurs, smiling. "There, there, now."

Mr. Gilman is smiling too. His daughter-in-law, who considers him a prehistoric bore, has invited him to dinner. This happens perhaps once a month; the telephone rings early in the morning. "We'd love to have you over tonight," she says. "Just family fare, I'm afraid, leftovers."

"I'd be delighted," he always says, even though the word *leftovers* gives him, every time she says it, a little ping of injury.

At age eighty he can be observed in his obverse infancy, metaphorically sucking and tonguing the missing tooth of his life. He knows what he looks like: the mirror tells all—eyes like water sacs, crimson arcs around the ears, a chin that betrays him, the way it mooches and wobbles while he thrashes around in his head for one of those rumpled anecdotes that seem only to madden his daughter-in-law. Better to keep still and chew. "Scrumptious," he always says, hoping to win her inhospitable heart, but knowing he can't.

Today he decides to buy her flowers. Why-oh-why has he never thought of this before! Daffodils are selling for $1.99 a half dozen. A bargain. It must be spring, he thinks, looking around. Why not buy two bunches, or three? Why not indeed? Or four?

They form a blaze of yellow in his arms, a sweet propitiating little fire. He knows he should take them home immediately and put them in water for tonight, but he's reluctant to remove the green paper wrapping which lends a certain legitimacy; these aren't flowers randomly snatched from the garden; these are florist's flowers, purchased as an offering, an oblation.[2]

There seems nothing to do but carry them about with him all day. He takes them along to the bank, the drugstore, to his appointment with the foot specialist, his afternoon card club at the Sunset Lodge. Never has he received more courteous attention, such quick service. The eyes of strangers appear friendlier than usual. "I am no worse off than the average person," he announces to himself. He loses, gracefully, at canasta, then gets a seat on the bus, a seat by the window. The pale flowers in his arms spell evanescence, gaiety. "Hello there," a number of people call out to him. He is clearly a man who is expected somewhere, anticipated. A charming gent, elegant and dapper, propounding serious questions, bearing gifts, flowers. A man in disguise.

Ralph Eliot, seventeen years old, six feet tall, killingly handsome, and the best halfback the school team has seen in years, has carelessly left his football helmet hanging on a hook on the back of his bedroom

---

[2]**oblation:** an offering or gift

door. An emergency of the first order; his ten-year-old sister Mandy is summoned to bring it to the playing field.

She runs all the way up Second Avenue; at the traffic light she strikes a pose, panting, then pounds furiously the whole length of Sargent Street, making it in four minutes flat. She carries the helmet by its tough plastic chin strap and as she runs along, it bangs against her bare leg. She feels her breath blazing into a spray of heroic pain, and as her foot rounds on the pavement a filament of recognition is touched. The exactitude of the gesture doubles and divides inside her head, and for the first time she comprehends *who* her brother is, that deep-voiced stranger whose bedroom is next to her own. Today, for a minute, she *is* her brother. *She* is Ralph Eliot, age seventeen, six feet tall, who later this afternoon will make a dazzling, lazy touchdown, bringing reward and honour to his name, and hers.

Susan Gourley, first-year arts student, has been assigned Beckett's *Waiting for Godot*.[3] She carries it under her arm so that the title is plainly visible. She is a girl with a look of lustreless inattention and a reputation for drowsiness, but she's always known this to be a false assessment. She's biding her time, waiting; today she strides along, *strides*, her book flashing under her arm. She is a young woman who is reading a great classic. Vistas of possibility unfold like money.

Molly Beale's briny old body has been propelled downtown by her cheerful new pacemaker, and there she bumps into Bert Lessing, the city councillor, whose navy blue beret, complete with military insignia, rides pertly over his left ear. They converse like lovers. They bristle with wit. They chitter like birds.

Jeanette Foster is sporting a smart chignon. Who does she think she *is*! Who *does* she think she is?

A young woman, recently arrived in town and rather lonely, carries her sandwiches to work in an old violin case. This is only temporary. Tomorrow she may use an ordinary paper bag or eat in the cafeteria.

We cannot live without our illusions, thinks X, an anonymous middle-aged citizen who, sometimes, in the privacy of his own bedroom, in the embrace of happiness, waltzes about in his wife's lace-trimmed nightgown. His wife is at bingo, not expected home for an hour. He lifts the blind an inch and sees the sun setting boldly behind his pear tree, its mingled coarseness and refinement giving an air of confusion. Everywhere he looks he observes cycles of consolation and enhancement, and now it seems as though the evening itself is about to alter its dimensions, becoming more (and also less) than what it really is. ❯

---

[3]**Beckett's *Waiting for Godot*:** famous absurdist drama, written in 1949

Carol Shields was born in Illinois, U.S., in 1935. She studied at Hanover College, the University of Exeter in England, and at the University of Ottawa, and moved to Canada in the 1950s. She has worked as a professor, lecturing at several Canadian universities, and is the author of a number of novels and short story collections. Her writing has won a Canada Council Major Award, the Canadian Author's Award, two National Magazine Awards, a CBC Award, and the Governor General's Award. Her books include *Small Ceremonies, Swann, The Box Garden,* and *Larry's Party.*

1. *Response*
a. Make a list of the characters in the story, jotting down what each is wearing or carrying, and what that tells you about the character. Do you see a pattern or progression from the first characters to those in the closing paragraphs? Again, jot down your ideas in your notebook.
b. Comment on the title of the story. What is "the carnival"?
c. What are some of the ideas this story seems to be expressing? What do you think Carol Shields' purpose was in writing it?
d. Did you like this story? Explain your answer. Have you read any other stories with a similar style?

2. *Literature Studies* *Short Story Elements* Which short story elements does "Dressing Up for the Carnival" contain? In your view, what is the predominant element? Explore these questions in a small group. One group member should be prepared to present your conclusions to the class. Include specific references to the story in your presentation.

3. *Writing* *Storytelling* Create another episode for "Dressing Up for the Carnival," exploring the perspective of another character placed in this town. You might imitate Shields' writing style and/or expand on her ideas or themes. After your writing is complete, go back to the story and see where your episode would best fit. Did you find it easy or difficult to match your writing with that of Shields? Explain.

4. ***Film Study*** With a partner, develop a proposal for a film adaptation of this story. How would a filmmaker capture the atmosphere of the story and convey the ideas Shields presents? Your proposal should consider some or all of the following aspects of the film: atmosphere, setting, character (who you would cast), dialogue (whether you would add conversation), music/sound effects, and film technique (camera angles, shots, editing techniques). It should also include a storyboard for one scene of the film. Present your proposal and storyboard to the class, giving your reasons for the choices you made.

5. ***Visual Communication*** *Illustrating the Story* In a sentence or two, state your ideas about what the painting that accompanies this story might be saying. Next, compare and contrast *Business Man Wearing Mask* by Curtis Parker with "Dressing Up for the Carnival." Consider content, style, and tone in your analysis.

Theme Connections

- *"Transients in Arcadia," a story in which characters present a false front to others, page 37*
- *"A Pair of Silk Stockings," a story in which a character tries to create a new self, page 86*
- *"On the Value of Fantasies," a poem about the importance of dreaming of better lives, page 184*
- *"The Love Song of J. Alfred Prufrock," a poem about keeping up appearances, page 240*
- *"Introducing Cyrano," a play excerpt in which physical appearance plays an important role, page 462*

The Spaces Between Stars

by Geeta Kothari

WATCHING THE FISH SQUIRM IN EVAN'S GLOVED HANDS, Maya was transfixed by the fish's suffering. It had stopped moving for a second, but now it was struggling, its tail flapping back and forth, as it twisted for freedom, unaware that the hook lodged deep in its gut wouldn't let go.

"It's dying," she said. "We should have pushed down the barbs like that woman in the store told us to."

Evan grunted and peered inside the fish's mouth.

"I know what I'm doing."

Maya knew he was determined to give her a genuine, all-American fishing trip, the kind he used to go on when he was a boy outdoors, and she was a girl indoors, watching TV. Long before Evan, there had been a boy on TV, a boy with long lanky hair that hung across one eye. He had flicked it back impatiently as he baited the hook, explaining to the camera that the "crick" was his favourite place. She remembered that word "crick" because some of the kids at school said it, kids who were unaware of her but whom she observed from a distance.

The small sunfish, a swath of green and gold, glistened in Evan's hand. The sun beat down on the top of Maya's head, searing her scalp. She felt dizzy and a wave of sadness passed over her as she stared at the helpless fish.

"It's dying."

Evan gently placed the sunfish in the water and cut the line. It swam off, seemingly recovered from its near-death experience.

To cook the fish he had caught, the boy on TV dug up some fresh clay, patted it into two flat rounds, stuck the fish between them and baked it in the flames of his campfire. In her dreams, Maya would camp by that "crick," fish and swim in it and sleep in a tent under the stars. How she would see the stars above her head while sleeping in a tent, she wasn't sure, but even in her fantasy life, she could not see herself sleeping without shelter.

Maya climbed back into the boat. Her line had been cut, and her mission had been achieved. She proved herself able to catch a fish, and now she wanted to go home. She handed Evan a turkey sandwich and looked over the side of the boat. Her fish, red at the gills, eyes bulging, floated towards them.

"Look," she said. "It died anyway."

Evan shrugged. "It was just a sunfish. They're everywhere."

Her guilt pressed against her temples, tightening like a vice around her head. Still she said nothing. She'd been the one who not only agreed but had been excited about going fishing. It had been one of the many activities forbidden to her during childhood. The expedition should have made her feel closer to Evan. Instead, Maya felt as if the parched brown hills surrounding the lake had sprung up between them. The inside of her skin itched, and she wanted to jump out of it, leave behind her body and the pervasive smell of dead fish.

She watched Evan eat his sandwich, oblivious to her inner turmoil as he basked in the sun. He was like that boy on TV. He was resourceful, knew how to do things that were beyond her realm of experience. He could pitch a tent, start a campfire, handle raw meat without feeling sick, open the hood of a car and see things. He could talk to strangers and get his way. Evan assumed he had the right number until told otherwise; he assumed cooperation and satisfaction, even when talking to the phone company about a bill. Making calls from one of her temporary jobs, Maya would begin her sentences with "I'm not sure …" and end them breathless, gasping for air, as she struggled to find the right words. Eventually, passed from one person to the next, trying to make herself understood, she would give up and leave the task for the next day. What looked like procrastination was something she couldn't begin to explain.

She had wanted to be that boy on TV, but what such boys were seemed hereditary, increasingly out of reach and unattainable. Instead, she forced herself through college and one dismal semester of graduate school. And then she married Evan.

They got home late in the afternoon, just as the thunder started rolling in. Evan shut himself in his study while Maya napped. The heat, the death of the fish, had exhausted her leaving her empty and dry inside.

Later, she made dinner, though she had no appetite or enthusiasm for the aloo gobi[1] and dal.[2] Nothing smelled or tasted right; the potatoes and cauliflower were mushy and the dal was limp and tasteless. Her shoulders felt sore from the sun, and the smell of blood lingered on her fingers. She felt dirty, stained by the death of the sunfish. She rubbed her fingers with lemon juice until her cuticles burned, and still they smelled.

Evan padded into the kitchen, his blond hair sticking up as if he'd been sleeping and pulled a beer out of the refrigerator.

"Indian food. What's the occasion?" He leaned against the counter and stretched his legs across the narrow passage. Everything about him was long, lean and graceful. Next to him, she felt like a clumsy baby elephant—small, dark, and always in his shadow.

"None. Should there be?"

"You never make it, that's all."

"That's because I can't." Her voice got tighter and she felt a rush of anger, making her face hotter above the steaming pots.

But Evan would not be drawn into a fight. "Don't forget, my folks are coming next week. And they want an answer about the trip."

Maya's stomach dropped. She'd forgotten both the ski trip at Christmas and the Everetts' impending visit.

Fortunately, the Everetts would stay with friends, as they always did. Though they'd never said anything, Maya sensed that she didn't keep house up to their standards. The brass incense holder, the small footstool inlaid with ivory, the embroidered mirror-work cushions, and the orange and red batik wall hangings had been passed on to her by her aunt, Shyamma. They seemed to go well with the reupholstered couch and chair from Evan's parents, but she was sure they didn't find the same comfort in this mixed decor.

Maya checked the cumin-flavoured rice. When she looked up, she noticed that Evan was still in the room, watching her as she moved from stove to sink, counter to kitchen table. "Are you all right?" he asked.

"Fine." He was the psychologist, she thought. Let him figure it out.

"Really?" He came over and kissed the back of her neck while she fluffed the rice. The individual grains had lost their definition and clung together, exactly what the recipe warned against.

"Allergies," she said, shrugging him off. Her long dark hair was coming out of its elastic band, sticking to the back of her sweaty neck.

---

[1] **aloo gobi:** a vegetable curry, mainly of cauliflower and potatoes
[2] **dal:** a dish containing lentils

His lips against her skin reminded her of the fish, gasping for breath.

She couldn't tell him. She couldn't admit her failure of will, of heart, in the great American outdoors. It was simply beyond her, to find the words for this thing she couldn't understand.

After dinner, Shyamma called.

First, she complained about the weather.

"Yesterday, I forgot to drink even one glass of water. Can you imagine? I nearly fainted in the kitchen."

"You have to pay attention, auntie." Maya could not call her Shyamma, the way Evan did, not out loud, even though Shyamma had told her to. "The heat isn't your friend, just because you don't like the cold."

Three, four times a week, Shyamma would call with a muted crisis or a question that needed an immediate response. A response, not an answer, Maya finally understood, and she listened, for Shyamma was the only family she had.

"And how is that husband of yours?"

"Fine. He's nearly finished." Evan was working on his dissertation, and it gave Shyamma great pleasure to finally have a PhD in the family. Evan's success made up nicely for the brilliant failure of Maya's academic career.

Maya wondered what Shyamma would say about her aborted conversion into a fisherwoman and her complicity in the death of the sunfish. What was okay for an Everett might be unacceptable for a Sohni. Shyamma was still a vegetarian. She prayed to her blue-faced gods and goddesses,[3] and every day at sunset, burnt sweetgrass and sage on a small piece of charcoal, carrying it reverently from room to room in the small house Maya had grown up in.

Shyamma asked about the Everetts, their two daughters, and everyone else under the Everett sun.

"Such a nice family." She sighed.

"Because they invite you to their stupid Christmas party?" Maya chewed a hangnail, enjoying the sharp pain that ran through her finger.

"Yes. And they always send me cards—Halloween, Easter, Christmas."

Holidays Shyamma used to dismiss as "Christian" or "American," having nothing to do with them. Not even a Christmas tree, Maya thought, and now she eats cookies shaped like Santa Claus and sings

---

[3]**blue-faced gods and goddesses:** Hindu deities such as Vishnu and Shiva are sometimes depicted with blue faces and skin.

"Away in the Manger" without hesitation. After five years, she knew the words by heart, just like everyone else at the party.

"And so," Shyamma finally said, "How are you?"

"Fine. We went fishing today."

"That's nice, bacchi."[4] Maya listened to the pots and pan clattering in the background. She doubted her aunt had heard her. Their conversation was over.

Shyamma had raised Maya alone, after her parents were killed in a plane crash. Rather than send Maya back to live with her paternal grandparents, Shyamma insisted on keeping her in the States. She herself didn't want to go back to India and marry the demented distant cousin her father had found for her.

"Understand," Shyamma once said, "I had a fellowship, and I was finally free. And I was afraid if I sent you to your father's people, we'd never see you."

They had been lonely in Erie. They knew no other Indian families with children. Most of Shyamma's friends were single women who worked full-time. She seemed not to miss her family whom they saw on rare visits to Delhi. Now, though, her loneliness had caught up with her. Maya heard it in the phone calls, the unasked "When are you next coming up?" During those cold, dreary winters, when the wind blew hard off the lake and kept them inside, Shyamma would tell Maya what a great life they had, how easy it was to be American, how good this country had been to her. But for Maya, growing up in a strict vegetarian household in Erie during the sixties was not fun. Her aunt, Shyamma, banned Oreos because they were made with lard. At barbecues and school picnics, Maya hid her plate, heavy with potato salad, corn on the cob, coleslaw and an empty hot dog bun. Shyamma saw to it that Maya ate nutritionally sound meals, overlooking the conflict between this and Maya's sole desire: to be like everyone else and not like her aunt, who still lived in the culture she'd left over thirty years ago.

On their last trip to Erie, Maya and Evan had found Shyamma chilled and sick with the flu. She had hid it from them, she said, because she was afraid they wouldn't come up. The walk at Presque Isle, promised to Evan, was put off; it was too cold, even if they were healthy, Shyamma insisted. They spent the whole weekend indoors. Evan paced the small living room and stared out the window the way Maya used to when she was a child. Shyamma lay on the couch,

---

[4]**bacchi:** girl, daughter

reading magazines and marking all the things she would someday buy, when she had enough money. Her salary from the hospital was never quite enough; she was a woman with foreign syntax and got paid less than any man in the same position.

Such was Shyamma's freedom.

Later, in bed, Evan asked Maya again about the ski trip. His parents wanted to take them to Banff at Christmas, where a friend of theirs would let them stay for free.

"I don't think so."

Evan sat up and looked at her. Maya kept her eyes focussed on her book and remained slouched against the headboard.

"You always said you wanted—"

"I'm too old. Why don't you go without me?"

Evan ran his hand through his hair. He looked at her for a minute and then got out of bed.

"Fine. You figure out a way to tell my parents why you're not coming."

Evan, Maya had learned a long time ago, was uninterested in confrontation, in talking things through. He left the room and she heard him go into his study. He would work for the next few hours, slip into bed after she'd fallen asleep, and dream through the conflict. The next morning, he'd act as if nothing had been said, and by evening he'd be asking her the same question again. And if she did not give him the answer he wanted, the whole scene would repeat itself, day after day, until one of them—usually Maya—gave in.

She woke up early the next morning. Next to her, Evan slept soundly. Maya pushed his thin hair off his face and traced the outline of his ear, half willing him to wake up. He turned over to his other side, pulling the sheet with him. When she slid out of bed, he didn't move.

Down in the kitchen, watching the sky get lighter over the river, she smelled it, the dead fish smell. She sniffed the carton of cream, her fingers, the tail of her long braid. She opened the refrigerator, scanning the shelves for any forgotten beans, unwrapped meat or cheese. She pulled open the vegetable bin, checking for wilted broccoli, mushy tomatoes and soggy lettuce. She threw out some mouldy cottage cheese and a dried-up piece of fudge cake.

Maya's feet stuck to the kitchen floor as she scrubbed the cabinet doors.

"You are so ungrateful," Shyamma used to say, when Maya was sixteen and came home at two in the morning, smelling of alcohol and back seat sex.

Maya shrugged. It didn't matter what she did, Shyamma would be there. They were family, blood in a world of strangers. Like fish, they swam in the same school, a school of two, but a school nonetheless, dodging predators, careful of false bait.

Maya had finally bitten. Life with Evan was too tempting, an easy guarantee that she would not end up like Shyamma. But the ski trip weighed on her, pulling her in a direction she wasn't sure she wanted to go. Evan's parents had welcomed her as easily as they welcomed Shyamma; now she wished for a little resistance—a disapproving arched eyebrow or a look of confusion when they saw her living room, would have been good. Instead, Pat had smiled into the tiny mirrors, and Evy nodded as he eased himself in his old chair. She and Shyamma had done everything to make themselves acceptable, so why should the mixed decor worry the Everetts?

Maya brushed her teeth until her gums bled and the brush hurt her cheek. Once on a bus she saw a man scratching his arms with a steel pick comb, running it up and down his forearm, until the skin was raised in thin red welts and looked ready to burst.

"Heroin addict," Shyamma said, after the man stumbled off the bus.

"How do you know?"

"When they need a fix, they itch so bad, they want to jump out of their skin. That was him."

Looking at her reflection in the bathroom mirror, Maya felt the same way. She wanted to be out of this skin, out of this life and into another, one that fit her, not one that she had to fit.

That night, when Evan asked again, Maya said, "I don't want to go."

She lay in bed, flat on her back. Light from the house next door cut through the open blinds, striping the rumpled cotton sheets. She stared at the ceiling, searching for the fluorescent stars Evan had pasted on it when they first moved in.

Evan rolled over on his side, facing her. "If it's the money—"

"It's not the money."

"Then what is it?"

Maya flopped over, turning her back to him. "When I was a kid, all I ever wanted was to go on our school ski trips. Every year they had one, and all the cool people went. Those who couldn't afford it did cross-country on their own. Shyamma wouldn't even let me do that. When I said she didn't trust me to take care of myself, she said it was the cold—too cold for me. She really meant it was too cold for her."

"So here's your chance," Evan said.

"I don't care anymore. I can't do it."

"You won't even try."

She turned to face him. In the dark, she couldn't read his expression, but she resisted the urge to turn the light on.

"Why is it so important that I ski?"

Evan sighed. "You're part of the family."

"Ralph doesn't ski. He's still part of the family isn't he?" Evan's older brother-in-law refused to put on skis for political and economic reasons that the entire family teased him about.

"He's just scared."

"So? I bet Anne isn't forcing him to go to Banff."

"Jesus." Evan punched his pillow. "You're the one who wanted to go fishing, you wanted to ski, and now you're blaming me." He left the room, slamming the door behind him, and then slamming his study door as well.

Maybe she was scared. What if she couldn't really be an Everett? She was still horrified by her participation in the death of another creature. It was all very well to kill a fish on television or buy it at the store, nicely cleaned and filleted, but this—this was the beginning of a cycle she'd never be able to escape.

But what was the alternative? Maya lay on her back. On the ceiling, the stars glowed. There was the Big Dipper, the Little Dipper, Orion, the archer. Evan had followed the instructions so precisely, the whole sky filled their ceiling. When she initially suggested it, she'd thought of scattering them where she pleased. While she was out one day, Evan put them up, arranging each and every one just so.

When she showed her surprise, he frowned and said, "But that's how they're supposed to be. Every star in its place."

And where was hers? She had thought with Evan she would find it. But only if she forgot where she'd been before, and now she found that forgetting incomplete.

The next morning, Maya woke up at dawn and was on the road before the sun had completely risen. She didn't want to give herself the chance to change her mind and seeing Evan would have done that. She drove north on 79, past Mars, Moon Township, and the shrine in the median at Zelienople. A marker for someone who had died on the road, the small fir tree was decorated for July 4—red, white, and blue tinsel draped over it and an American flag languidly moving in the slipstream of the big trucks that roared by. At Easter, pastel-coloured plastic eggs hung from its branches, and at Christmas someone garnished it with bright ornaments, including a gold angel for the top. She'd seen similar shrines on the Mass Pike and the New Jersey Turnpike, so unusual they'd caught her eye.

By the time she pulled into Shyamma's neat little driveway, with the marigolds lined up on either side, it was well past eight o'clock. She knew that Shyamma would be in the kitchen. Maybe she could talk her into making some masala chai,[5] something to wash her mouth of the terrible McDonald's coffee she'd had an hour ago.

Shyamma didn't look up from the counter where she was rolling out some dough.

"Evan called. He wants to know if you'll be home for dinner."

Her tone was accusing, on Evan's behalf.

"I left him a note."

Shyamma tucked a strand of hair behind her ear. Her hair was still black and shiny, a testament to the coconut oil she used regularly and rigorous brushing. Her small brown face was slack at the jaw and under the chin, but her cheeks were high and firm, turning into small apples when she smiled. She had a sweet smile, Evan said, like Maya. But neither of them was smiling now.

"Paratha?"[6]

"Stuffed kulcha."[7] Shyamma kept rolling the small rounds of springy dough.

"For breakfast?" Maya was used to seeing the stuffed bread on special occasions only.

"No one here to tell me I can't."

She put the water to boil, in a saucepan, Maya noticed with relief. If Shyamma was making masala chai, Maya was not in that much trouble.

"I killed a fish." The words sounded terrible out loud, damning, yet she understood in that moment why criminals often confessed. A fleeting lightness lifted in her as she waited for her aunt's absolution.

"Did you eat it?"

"No." What did her aunt think she was? "I tried to save its life."

Shyamma added two teaspoons of tea to the boiling water and some milk. She let it boil vigorously, like the chai-wallahs[8] back home did, in huge pots on single burners.

"Sounds like a contradiction."

"It was an accident."

They ate in silence, at the same formica-topped table Shyamma had bought twenty years ago at a yard sale. The kulcha was slightly burnt, crispy at the edges and soft in the middle. Maya couldn't remember

---

[5]**masala chai:** a hot, spiced, milky tea
[6]**Paratha:** a flaky, fried bread, sometimes mixed or stuffed with other ingredients
[7]**kulcha:** a flatbread, sometimes stuffed with other ingredients
[8]**chai-wallahs:** roadside tea merchants

when it had tasted so good. "You don't have to come here every time you want a stuffed kulcha."

Shyamma cleared the dishes as she spoke. Maya had the impression she was going somewhere, that she didn't want her to stay.

"I know." She had the recipe, carefully pasted into a notebook with a number of other recipes Shyamma had insisted on showing her. At the time, she'd resisted; it seemed unnecessary, going back to a time when girls were prepared for marriage. Now she understood Shyamma had not been preparing her for anyone but herself.

As it turned out, Shyamma did have plans. She was going to a friend's house to discuss their Christmas vacation, a cruise somewhere warm and tropical. Maya hid her surprise; the only holidays her aunt had ever taken were their trips to India. Not wanting to even slightly dissuade her, Maya said nothing. She took the leftover kulcha and headed home, with promises to bring Evan back in a few weeks.

When she got home, Evan was out. She went straight to the bedroom and dug around for the leftover stars stashed in her bedside table. She cleared off the table and stood on it; using the wall for balance, she added her own star to the cluster directly above her side of the bed.

All these years, she thought the answer lay in teaching Shyamma to love the cold. Maybe she was wrong.

Maya sat on the porch staring across the river. The sun had nearly set and the air felt like rain, heavy and full of promise. Her skin was clammy from the heat and humidity, but it didn't bother her. It reminded her of the way she felt in the monsoon, just before the rains came, turning the streets into muddy rivers that came up to her knees.

The door opened, and she saw Evan's shadow cast down the stairs. He stood for a moment in the doorway, drinking a beer.

"Nice night," he said.

His voice was low and cautious as he sat down next to her. Maya couldn't bring herself to look at his face, that sweet combination of dimples and blue eyes that showed his confusion no matter how hard he tried to hide it. Instead, she looked at his feet, grimy from a barefoot summer, the toenails ridged and hard, dirt rimming the cuticles. Later, maybe, his nails would scratch dully against her legs, her ankles, and the tops of her feet, leaving white lines and marks across her own dry brown skin, never hard enough to draw blood, but enough to mark Evan on her.

> Storytelling is the oldest form of education.
>
> Terry Tempest Williams

"Shyamma used to have a small shrine in the corner of our kitchen." Her voice was hoarse from thirst and silence. "Incense, flowers, an old calendar painting of Ganesh.[9] That's all. Whenever I had friends over, I'd try to keep them from going in there."

"Why?"

"So I wouldn't have to hear them laugh and say, 'Ew, what's that?' and then explain why my aunt was worshipping a god with an elephant head."

"The god of all beginnings and the remover of obstacles." Evan sat down next to her.

"Shyamma told you that."

"When we got married."

Maya smiled. At the time, she would have forbidden the mention of Ganesh or any other god at her wedding, yet Shyamma had managed to find a space for him.

"I'm going to the temple when she comes."

One day, Shyamma will be gone, she thought, and I want to be left with more than the calendar image of a pot-bellied, elephant god.

He took her hand and squeezed it. "Want me to come?" "No. But no more fishing trips, okay?"

Maya drew a sip of beer from the long-necked bottle, letting a few drops drip down her chin. She held the cool glass against her temple and watched the lights come on across the river, solitary stars dotting a dark, lonely land. Evan put his hand on the back of her neck and stroked the damp hairs hanging out of her bun. They sat for a long time in silence, listening to the cicadas buzzing in the still heat, waiting for the storm to break and the sky to clear.

---

[9]**Ganesh:** an elephant-headed Hindu deity, remover of obstacles

Geeta Kothari's fiction and non-fiction have appeared in several anthologies and journals, such as the *Toronto South Asian Review*, the *New England Review*, the *Kenyon Review*, and *Her Mother's Ashes*. She is the editor of the anthology *Did My Mama Like to Dance? and Other Stories about Mothers and Daughters*.

1. *Response*
a. Explain how the first paragraph symbolically captures one of the main themes of the story. Reread the story carefully, noting other passages or references that you think might have a symbolic meaning. Be prepared to present your ideas to a group or the class.
b. Why does Maya both envy and resent Evan?
c. Throughout her life, Maya has relied on others to give her a sense of direction. Give some specific examples. Do you think this is still true at the end of the story? Explain.
d. What are some of the decisions Maya has to make in this story, and what choices are available to her? Do you think she makes good or bad decisions? Why?
e. "The Spaces Between Stars" depicts a particular situation. Do you think the story has a broader relevance? Why?
f. Discuss whether you were able to connect with the story, and whether that, in turn, affected your enjoyment of it.

2. *Literature Studies* Story Endings
Some stories end with **closure**, while others are open-ended. What kind of ending does "The Spaces Between Stars" have? Give reasons for your answer, including specific references from the text. Is this a question that can be answered definitively? Why or why not?

Closure occurs when a story ends without ambiguity. The main crises and/or conflicts are neatly wrapped up and the reader has a sense that the story is truly finished. In an *open-ended story*, the reader is uncertain about what might happen next; several outcomes are possible.

3. *Writing* Letter
Adopt the persona of Maya and compose the letter she would write to Evan's parents to explain her decision not to participate in the family skiing trip in Banff. Your writing should reflect your audience and purpose.

4. *Critical Thinking*
In "The Spaces Between Stars," author Geeta Kothari explores some issues related to the mingling of different cultures. In a group, identify and discuss these issues. What are the main problems and challenges in Maya and Evan's marriage, and what solutions appear at the end of the story? Summarize your conclusions for the class.

The Chrysanthemums

by
John
Steinbeck

**Some people feel
a deep restlessness
for something
they can't quite name ...**

T HE HIGH GREY-FLANNEL FOG OF WINTER CLOSED OFF the Salinas Valley[1] from the sky and from all the rest of the world. On every side it sat like a lid on the mountains and made of the great valley a closed pot. On the broad, level land floor the gang ploughs[2] bit deep and left the black earth shining like metal where the shares had cut. On the foot-hill ranches across the Salinas River, the yellow stubble fields seemed to be bathed in pale cold sunshine, but there was no sunshine in the valley now in December. The thick willow scrub along the river flamed with sharp and positive yellow leaves.

It was a time of quiet and of waiting. The air was cold and tender. A light wind blew up from the southwest so that the farmers were mildly hopeful of a good rain before long; but fog and rain do not go together.

Across the river, on Henry Allen's foot-hill ranch there was little work to be done, for the hay was cut and stored and the orchards were ploughed up to receive the rain deeply when it should come. The cattle on the higher slopes were becoming shaggy and rough-coated.

---

[1]**Salinas Valley:** a fertile valley of central California, about 30 km inland from the coast
[2]**gang ploughs:** a plough with several blades, making parallel furrows

Elisa Allen, working in her flower garden, looked down across the yard and saw Henry, her husband, talking to two men in business suits. The three of them stood by the tractor-shed, each man with one foot on the side of the little Fordson.[3] They smoked cigarettes and studied the machine as they talked.

Elisa watched them for a moment and then went back to her work. She was thirty-five. Her face was lean and strong and her eyes were as clear as water. Her figure looked blocked and heavy in her gardening costume, a man's black hat pulled low down over her eyes, clod-hopper shoes, a figured print dress almost completely covered by a big corduroy apron with four big pockets to hold the snips, the trowel and scratcher, the seeds and the knife she worked with. She wore heavy leather gloves to protect her hands while she worked.

She was cutting down the old year's chrysanthemum stalks with a pair of short and powerful scissors. She looked down toward the men by the tractor-shed now and then. Her face was eager and mature and handsome; even her work with the scissors was over-eager, over-powerful. The chrysanthemum stems seemed too small and easy for her energy.

She brushed a cloud of hair out of her eyes with the back of her glove, and left a smudge of earth on her cheek in doing it. Behind her stood the neat white farmhouse with red geraniums close-banked around it as high as the windows. It was a hard-swept-looking little house, with hard-polished windows, and a clean mud-mat on the front steps.

Elisa cast another glance toward the tractor-shed. The strangers were getting into their Ford coupé. She took off a glove and put her strong fingers down into the forest of new green chrysanthemum sprouts that were growing around the old roots. She spread the leaves and looked down among the close-growing stems. No aphids were there, no sow bugs or snails or cutworms. Her terrier fingers destroyed such pests before they could get started.

Elisa started at the sound of her husband's voice. He had come near quietly, and he leaned over the wire fence that protected her flower garden from cattle and dogs and chickens.

"At it again," he said. "You've got a strong new crop coming."

Elisa straightened her back and pulled on the gardening glove again. "Yes. They'll be strong this coming year." In her tone and on her face there was a little smugness.

"You've got a gift with things," Henry observed. "Some of those

---

[3]**Fordson:** a brand of tractor made by the Ford Motor Company

yellow chrysanthemums you had this year were ten inches across. I wish you'd work out in the orchard and raise some apples that big."

Her eyes sharpened. "Maybe I could do it, too. I've a gift with things, all right. My mother had it. She could stick anything in the ground and make it grow. She said it was having planters' hands that knew how to do it."

"Well, it sure works with flowers," he said.

"Henry, who were those men you were talking to?"

"Why, sure, that's what I came to tell you. They were from the Western Meat Company. I sold those thirty head of three-year-old steers. Got nearly my own price, too."

"Good," she said. "Good for you."

"And I thought," he continued, "I thought how it's Saturday afternoon, and we might go into Salinas for dinner at a restaurant, and then to a picture show—to celebrate, you see."

"Good," she repeated. "Oh, yes. That will be good."

Henry put on his joking tone. "There's fights tonight. How'd you like to go to the fights?"

"Oh, no," she said breathlessly. "No, I wouldn't like fights."

"Just fooling, Elisa. We'll go to a movie. Let's see. It's two now. I'm going to take Scotty and bring down those steers from the hill. It'll take us maybe two hours. We'll go in town about five and have dinner at the Cominos Hotel. Like that?"

"Of course I'll like it. It's good to eat away from home."

"All right, then. I'll go get up a couple of horses."

She said: "I'll have plenty of time to transplant some of these sets, I guess."

She heard her husband calling Scotty down by the barn. And a little later she saw the two men ride up the pale yellow hillside in search of the steers.

There was a little square sandy bed kept for rooting the chrysanthemums. With her trowel she turned the soil over and over, and smoothed it and patted it firm. Then she dug ten parallel trenches to receive the sets. Back at the chrysanthemum bed she pulled out the little crisp shoots, trimmed off the leaves of each one with her scissors and laid it on a small orderly pile.

A squeak of wheels and plod of hoofs came from the road. Elisa looked up. The country road ran along the dense bank of willows and cottonwoods that bordered the river, and up this road came a curious vehicle, curiously drawn. It was an old spring-wagon, with a round canvas top on it like the cover of a prairie schooner. It was drawn by an old bay horse and a little grey-and-white burro. A big, stubble-bearded man sat between the cover flaps and drove the crawling team. Under-neath the wagon, between the hind wheels, a lean and rangy mongrel dog walked sedately. Words were painted on the canvas, in clumsy, crooked letters. "Pots, pans, knives, sisors, lawn mores, Fixed." Two rows of articles, and the triumphantly definitive "Fixed" below. The black paint had run down in little sharp points beneath each letter.

Elisa, squatting on the ground, watched to see the crazy, loose-jointed wagon pass by. But it didn't pass. It turned into the farm road in front of her house, crooked old wheels skirling[4] and squeaking. The rangy dog darted from between the wheels and ran ahead. Instantly the two ranch shepherds flew out at him. Then all three stopped, and with stiff and quivering tails, with taut straight legs, with ambassadorial dig-nity, they slowly circled, sniffing daintily. The caravan pulled up to Elisa's wire fence and stopped. Now the newcomer dog, feeling out-numbered, lowered his tail and retired under the wagon with raised hackles and bared teeth.

The man on the wagon seat called out: "That's a bad dog in a fight when he gets started."

Elisa laughed. "I see he is. How soon does he generally get started?"

The man caught up her laughter and echoed it heartily. "Some-times not for weeks and weeks," he said. He climbed stiffly down, over the wheel. The horse and the donkey drooped like unwatered flowers.

Elisa saw that he was a very big man. Although his hair and beard were greying, he did not look old. His worn black suit was wrinkled and spotted with grease. The laughter had disappeared from his face and eyes the moment his laughing voice ceased. His eyes were dark, and they were full of the brooding that gets in the eyes of teamsters and of sailors. The calloused hands he rested on the wire fence were cracked, and every crack was a black line. He took off his battered hat.

"I'm off my general road, ma'am," he said. "Does this dirt road cut over across the river to the Los Angeles highway?"

Elisa stood up and shoved the thick scissors in her apron pocket. "Well, yes, it does, but it winds around and then fords the river. I don't think your team could pull through the sand."

He replied with some asperity: "It might surprise you what them beasts can pull through."

"When they get started?" she asked.

He smiled for a second. "Yes. When they get started."

"Well," said Elisa, "I think you'll save time if you go back to the Salinas road and pick up the highway there."

---

[4]**skirling:** a wailing sound, like that made by bagpipes

He drew a big finger down the chicken wire and made it sing. "I ain't in any hurry, ma'am. I go from Seattle to San Diego and back every year. Takes all my time. About six months each way. I aim to follow nice weather."

Elisa took off her gloves and stuffed them in her apron pocket with the scissors. She touched the under edge of her man's hat, searching for fugitive hairs. "That sounds like a nice kind of way to live," she said.

He leaned confidentially over the fence. "Maybe you noticed the writing on my wagon. I mend pots and sharpen knives and scissors. You got any of them things to do?"

"Oh, no," she said quickly. "Nothing like that." Her eyes hardened with resistance.

"Scissors is the worst thing," he explained. "Most people just ruin scissors trying to sharpen 'em, but I know how. I got a special tool. It's a little bobbit kind of thing, and patented. But it sure does the trick."

"No. My scissors are all sharp."

"All right, then. Take a pot," he continued earnestly, "a bent pot, or a pot with a hole. I can make it like new so you don't have to buy no new ones. That's a saving for you."

"No," she said shortly. "I tell you I have nothing like that for you to do."

His face fell to an exaggerated sadness. His voice took on a whining undertone. "I ain't had a thing to do today. Maybe I won't have no supper tonight. You see I'm off my regular road. I know folks on the highway clear from Seattle to San Diego. They save their things for me to sharpen up because they know I do it so good and save them money."

"I'm sorry," Elisa said irritably. "I haven't anything for you to do."

His eyes left her face and fell to searching the ground. They roamed about until they came to the chrysanthemum bed where she had been working. "What's them plants, ma'am?"

The irritation and resistance melted from Elisa's face. "Oh, those are chrysanthemums, giant whites and yellows. I raise them every year, bigger than anybody around here."

"Kind of a long-stemmed flower? Looks like a quick puff of colored smoke?" he asked.

"That's it. What a nice way to describe them."

"They smell kind of nasty till you get used to them," he said.

"It's a good bitter smell," she retorted, "not nasty at all."

He changed his tone quickly. "I like the smell myself."

"I had ten-inch blooms this year," she said.

The man leaned farther over the fence. "Look. I know a lady down the road a piece, has got the nicest garden you ever seen. Got nearly every kind of flower but no chrysanthemums. Last time I was mending a copper-bottom washtub for her (that's a hard job but I do it good), she said to me: 'If you ever run acrost some nice chrysanthemums I wish you'd try to get me a few seeds.' That's what she told me."

Elisa's eyes grew alert and eager. "She couldn't have known much about chrysanthemums. You *can* raise them from seed, but it's much easier to root the little sprouts you see there."

"Oh," he said. "I s'pose I can't take none to her, then."

"Why yes you can," Elisa cried. "I can put some in damp sand, and you can carry them right along with you. They'll take root in the pot if you keep them damp. And then she can transplant them."

"She'd sure like to have some, ma'am. You say they're nice ones?"

"Beautiful," she said. "Oh, beautiful." Her eyes shone. She tore off the battered hat and shook out her dark pretty hair. "I'll put them in a flowerpot, and you can take them right with you. Come into the yard."

While the man came through the picket gate Elisa ran excitedly along the geranium-bordered path to the back of the house. And she returned carrying a big red flower-pot. The gloves were forgotten now. She kneeled on the ground by the starting bed and dug up the sandy soil with her fingers and scooped it into the bright new flower-pot. Then she picked up the little pile of shoots she had prepared. With her strong fingers she pressed them into the sand and tamped around them with her knuckles. The man stood over her. "I'll tell you what to do," she said. "You remember so you can tell the lady."

"Yes, I'll try to remember."

"Well, look. These will take root in about a month. Then she must set them out, about a foot apart in good rich earth like this, see?" She lifted a handful of dark soil for him to look at. "They'll grow fast and tall. Now remember this: In July tell her to cut them down, about eight inches from the ground."

"Before they bloom?" he asked.

"Yes, before they bloom." Her face was tight with eagerness. "They'll grow right up again. About the last of September the buds will start."

She stopped and seemed perplexed. "It's the budding that takes the most care," she said hesitantly. "I don't know how to tell you." She looked deep into his eyes, searchingly. Her mouth opened a little, and she seemed to be listening. "I'll try to tell you," she said. "Did you ever hear of planting hands?"

"Can't say I have, ma'am."

"Well, I can only tell you what it feels like. It's when you're picking off the buds you don't want. Everything goes right down into your fingertips. You watch your fingers work. They do it themselves. You can feel how it is. They pick and pick the buds. They never make a mistake. They're with the plant. Do you see? Your fingers and the plant. You can feel that, right up your arm. They know. They never make a mistake. You can feel it. When you're like that you can't do anything wrong. Do you see that? Can you understand that?"

She was kneeling on the ground looking up at him. Her breast swelled passionately.

The man's eyes narrowed. He looked away self-consciously. "Maybe I know," he said. "Sometimes in the night in the wagon there—"

Elisa's voice grew husky. She broke in on him: "I've never lived as you do, but I know what you mean. When the night is dark—why, the stars are sharp-pointed, and there's quiet. Why, you rise up and up! Every pointed star gets driven into your body. It's like that. Hot and sharp and—lovely."

Kneeling there, her hand went out toward his legs in the greasy black trousers. Her hesitant fingers almost touched the cloth. Then her hand dropped to the ground. She crouched low like a fawning dog.

He said: "It's nice, just like you say. Only when you don't have no dinner, it ain't."

She stood up then, very straight, and her face was ashamed. She held the flower-pot out to him and placed it gently in his arms. "Here. Put it in your wagon, on the seat, where you can watch it. Maybe I can find something for you to do."

At the back of the house she dug in the can pile and found two old and battered aluminum saucepans. She carried them back and gave them to him. "Here, maybe you can fix these."

His manner changed. He became professional. "Good as new I can fix them." At the back of his wagon he set a little anvil, and out of an oily tool-box dug a small machine hammer. Elisa came through the gate to watch him while he pounded out the dents in the kettles. His mouth grew sure and knowing. At a difficult part of the work he sucked his underlip.

"You sleep right in the wagon?" Elisa asked.

"Right in the wagon, ma'am. Rain or shine I'm dry as a cow in there."

"It must be nice," she said. "It must be very nice. I wish women could do such things."

"It ain't the right kind of a life for a woman."

Her upper lip raised a little, showing her teeth. "How do you know?

How can you tell?" she said.

"I don't know, ma'am," he protested. "Of course I don't know. Now here's your kettles, done. You don't have to buy no new ones."

"How much?"

"Oh, fifty cents'll do. I keep my prices down and my work good. That's why I have all them satisfied customers up and down the highway."

Elisa brought him a fifty-cent piece from the house and dropped it in his hand. "You might be surprised to have a rival some time. I can sharpen scissors, too. And I can beat the dents out of little pots. I could show you what a woman might do."

He put his hammer back in the oily box and shoved the little anvil out of sight. "It would be a lonely life for a woman, ma'am, and a scarey life, too, with animals creeping under the wagon all night." He climbed over the single-tree[5] steadying himself with a hand on the burro's white rump. He settled himself in the seat, picked up the lines. "Thank you kindly ma'am," he said. "I'll do like you told me; I'll go back and catch the Salinas road."

"Mind," she called, "if you're long in getting there, keep the sand damp."

"Sand, ma'am? ... Sand? Oh, sure. You mean around the chrysanthemums. Sure I will." He clucked his tongue. The beasts leaned luxuriously into their collars. The mongrel dog took his place between the back wheels. The wagon turned and crawled out the entrance road and back the way it had come, along the river.

Elisa stood in front of her wire fence watching the slow progress of the caravan. Her shoulders were straight, her head thrown back, her eyes half-closed, so that the scene came vaguely into them. Her lips moved silently, forming the words "Good-bye—good-bye." Then she whispered: "That's a bright direction. There's a glowing there." The sound of her whisper startled her. She shook herself free and looked about to see whether anyone had been listening. Only the dogs had heard. They lifted their heads toward her from their sleeping in the dust, and then stretched out their chins and settled asleep again. Elisa turned and ran hurriedly into the house.

In the kitchen she reached behind the stove and felt the water tank. It was full of hot water from the noonday cooking. In the bathroom she tore off her soiled clothes and flung them into the corner. And then she scrubbed herself with a little block of pumice, legs and thighs, loins and chest and arms, until her skin was scratched and red. When

---

[5]**single-tree:** the crossbar used to hitch a horse to a wagon or other vehicle

she dried herself she stood in front of a mirror in her bedroom and looked at her body. She tightened her stomach and threw out her chest. She turned and looked over her shoulder at her back.

After a while she began to dress, slowly. She put on her newest underclothing and her nicest stockings and the dress which was the symbol of her prettiness. She worked carefully on her hair, pencilled her eyebrows and rouged her lips.

Before she was finished she heard the little thunder of hoofs and the shouts of Henry and his helper as they drove the red steers into the corral. She heard the gate bang shut and set herself for Henry's arrival.

His step sounded on the porch. He entered the house calling: "Elisa, where are you?"

"In my room, dressing. I'm not ready. There's hot water for your bath. Hurry up. It's getting late."

When she heard him splashing in the tub, Elisa laid his dark suit on the bed, and shirt and socks and tie beside it. She stood his polished shoes on the floor beside the bed. Then she went to the porch and sat primly and stiffly down. She looked toward the river road where the willow-line was still yellow with frosted leaves so that under the high grey fog they seemed a thin band of sunshine. This was the only color in the grey afternoon. She sat unmoving for a long time. Her eyes blinked rarely.

Henry came banging out of the door, shoving his tie inside his vest as he came. Elisa stiffened and her face grew tight. Henry stopped short and looked at her. "Why—why, Elisa. You look so nice!"

"Nice? You think I look nice? What do you mean by 'nice'?"

Henry blundered on. "I don't know. I mean you look different, strong and happy."

"I am strong? Yes, strong. What do you mean 'strong'?"

He looked bewildered. "You're playing some kind of a game," he said helplessly. "It's a kind of play. You look strong enough to break a calf over your knee, happy enough to eat it like a watermelon."

For a second she lost her rigidity. "Henry! Don't talk like that. You didn't know what you said." She grew complete again. "I'm strong," she boasted. "I never knew before how strong."

Henry looked down toward the tractor-shed, and when he brought his eyes back to her, they were his own again. "I'll get out the car. You can put on your coat while I'm starting."

Elisa went into the house. She heard him drive to the gate and idle down his motor, and then she took a long time to put on her hat. She pulled it here and pressed it there. When Henry turned the motor off she slipped into her coat and went out.

The little roadster bounced along on the dirt road by the river, raising the birds and driving the rabbits into the brush. Two cranes flapped heavily over the willow-line and dropped into the riverbed.

Far ahead on the road Elisa saw a dark speck. She knew.

She tried not to look as they passed it, but her eyes would not obey. She whispered to herself sadly: "He might have thrown them off the road. That wouldn't have been much trouble, not very much. But he kept the pot," she explained. "He had to keep the pot. That's why he couldn't get them off the road."

The roadster turned a bend and she saw the caravan ahead. She swung full around toward her husband so she could not see the little covered wagon and the mis-matched team as the car passed them.

In a moment it was over. The thing was done. She did not look back.

She said loudly, to be heard above the motor: "It will be good, tonight, a good dinner."

"Now you've changed again," Henry complained. He took one hand from the wheel and patted her knee. "I ought to take you in to dinner oftener. It would be good for both of us. We get so heavy out on the ranch."

"Henry," she asked, "could we have wine at dinner?"

"Sure we could. Say! That will be fine."

She was silent for a while; then she said: "Henry, at those prize-fights, do the men hurt each other very much?"

"Sometimes a little, not often. Why?"

"Well, I've read how they break noses, and blood runs down their chests. I've read how the fighting gloves get heavy and soggy with blood."

He looked round at her. "What's the matter, Elisa? I didn't know you read things like that." He brought the car to a stop, then turned to the right over the Salinas River bridge.

"Do any women ever go to the fights?" she asked.

"Oh, sure, some. What's the matter, Elisa. Do you want to go? I don't think you'd like it, but I'll take you if you really want to go."

She relaxed limply in the seat. "Oh, no. No. I don't want to go. I'm sure I don't." Her face was turned away from him. "It will be enough if we can have wine. It will be plenty." She turned up her coat collar so he could not see that she was crying weakly—like an old woman. ▶

> Not that the story need be long, but it will take
> a long while to make it short.
>
> Henry David Thoreau

John Steinbeck was born in Salinas, California, in 1902. He was educated at Stanford University and worked as a fruit picker and ranch hand. His most well-known book, *The Grapes of Wrath*, won a Pulitzer Prize in 1940. Steinbeck won the Nobel Prize for literature in 1962. His works include *Tortilla Flat, Of Mice and Men, The Moon Is Down, Cannery Row, East of Eden,* and *The Winter of Our Discontent.* He also wrote an autobiographical account of a trip across the U.S. with his pet poodle, called *Travels With Charley.* A number of his books have been made into films.

1. *Response*
   a. When and where do you think "The Chrysanthemums" takes place? List specific phrases and words that help to establish the setting.
   b. What was your initial reaction to Elisa? Did your impression change as the story progressed?
   c. Explain the way in which the peddler manages to capture Elisa's attention and then nudge her into giving him a job. What can you infer about the peddler's character from this behaviour?
   d. At the end of the story, why do you think Elisa first shows interest in the fights, then adamantly changes her mind?
   e. What significance do the chrysanthemums have for Elisa? For Henry? For the peddler? Comment on whether Steinbeck chose an appropriate title for the story.

2. *Oral Language* Group Discussion "'I've never lived as you do, but I know what you mean. When the night is dark—why the stars are sharp-pointed, and there's quiet. Why, you rise up and up! Every pointed star gets driven into your body. It's like that. Hot and sharp and—lovely.'" In a group, discuss what Elisa means. Do you think the peddler knows, or cares, what she is saying? What do you think Elisa is revealing about herself? Have one group member present your group's conclusions to the class.

3. **Literature Studies** *Juxtaposition* Steinbeck uses **juxtaposition** to develop a contradictory impression of Elisa's character. Reread the story, noting the places where Elisa seems to be bold and confident, as well as the places where

Juxtaposition is the intentional placement of dissimilar words or ideas side by side for a particular purpose—to emphasize contrasting ideas, for example.

she seems tentative. Record your observations in a T-chart format, using specific references from the story. How is this juxtaposition related to the central ideas in the story? Would you describe Elisa as predominantly a strong or weak person? Give reasons for your answer.

4. **Writing** *Point of View* Steinbeck has used the third-person limited point of view to tell this story from Elisa's perspective. Using the same time frame and setting, write an alternative version of the story from Henry or the peddler's point of view. Be prepared to explain the reasons behind any changes you make to the story.

5. **Focus on Context** John Steinbeck wrote a number of novels and short stories set in the Salinas Valley of California—an area he knew from his own life. What conclusions can you draw from "The Chrysanthemums" about life in this region, especially for women? Read one other Steinbeck work set in this region, such as a short story from *The Pastures of Heaven* or an episode from *The Grapes of Wrath*, for example. Write a brief essay (one or two pages), in which you investigate the similarities and differences in the themes and situations portrayed in "The Chrysanthemums" and the other work you have read.

Theme Connections

Touching Bottom

by Kari Strutt

"How many fingers?" Dad asked at bath time.

I was afraid, but I ducked my head into the half-full white tub. I opened my eyes, then came up sputtering.

"Two."

"That's right." Then his hand, broad as a rainbow, covered my head all the way to my ears, and slicked back my sopping hair. He wrapped me in a clean yellow towel, and the fear, what was left of it, evaporated.

I could open my eyes under water.

The summer I turned seven I went to Camp Kinaird with fifty other girls. "Where young girls learn to swim," Dad quoted from the black text between the brochure photos of smiling kids.

"You should learn to swim," he said, "you never know when you'll end up in water that's over your head."

The camp instructors told me I was a good swimmer. My spindly arms cut the water like fins, and I could circle them at a furious pace. I learned to put my face in the water, turn my head for air. I was quick, like a water beetle, and I liked the feeling of the cool water pushing through my hair.

On the fifth day of swim lessons, the fat girl came to shore with a dark glistening streak on her back. Somebody shrieked, "You gotta leech on you," and the shoreline became a seething mass of squealing, blue-lipped girls. The terror rang in my ears long after the camp counsellor salted the girl's back and caught the writhing leech in an old tin can. She was still whimpering when we went to the cookhouse for lunch.

For the rest of the summer I refused to go in the water. The other girls backstroked and side stroked and perfected their Australian crawls. The fat girl and I sat on the dock watching a black bloodsucker make its way across a yellow plastic bowl lodged in the sandy bottom near shore.

That fall my Dad signed me up for Red Cross swimming lessons. In a pool.

"You can start again," Dad said. "I'm sure there are no leeches at the YMCA, but I'll come and watch, just to be sure."

When we got to the YMCA, Dad and I walked around the pool together, looking for leeches. I thought I saw one, but it was just a Band-Aid.

The pool water was clear blue-green and with my goggles on I could see the bottom. There were wide black lines painted along the length of it. I used the lines to make sure I was swimming straight. I finished all of the Red Cross lessons, then I joined a swim club and learned to race. I trained every day, back and forth in the pool, guided on either side by the lane markers—bright strings of plastic bubbles, led from below by the thick black lines. When I turned fourteen I trained twice a day, every morning at five-thirty and every evening at five. Dad drove me to practice after practice, day after day, year after year.

I was skinny and hungry all the time. I ate a lot, but it was never enough. Sometimes I swam the backstroke, staring at the pool ceiling and dreaming of macaroni and cheese. After practice I sliced wafers of cold butter, let them melt on my tongue.

I learned to swim a long ways, but I never did get comfortable in murky water: lakes, rivers, anywhere I couldn't see bottom. That kind of water made my throat open too wide to bring the air into my lungs, made me breathe fast, out of control.

That's why, when I think of California, I get queasy. I lived there for four years with my husband. He came to Canada on business, to the art gallery where I worked, and swept me away to Los Angeles on a blue wave of charm.

My Dad told me not to go, not to marry him. He said I would be sorry. He said, "His mid-life crisis will pass soon enough and you'll be stuck in California, like a fish out of water." He said he would not come to the wedding. He didn't. The day I got married I felt lonely and afraid.

I lived with my husband, my sister-in-law and Ian, in a house in the San Fernando Valley. The air is close in that valley, but the people are distant, separated from each other by car lengths and private desires.

My husband's sister was a loveless woman, no girlfriends and no boyfriends. She once called the police when she found a rat in the kitchen. She screamed into the phone, "He's in the house! He's in the house!"

"Where in the house?" they demanded.

"He's under the stove," she shrieked. When the 9-1-1 operators found out she was talking about a rat and not a violent perpetrator, they hung up on her. She stood on the front porch for four hours, sweat trickling into the small of her back, waiting for help that never arrived. After that, she refused to cook.

Ian was my husband's son from a previous marriage. The summer Ian was born, I got a new CCM bicycle and I built a tree fort with my friend Elaine.

Ian was a sensible boy, tall for his age. I weighed more than he did, but our eyes were level. We listened to music. I introduced him to albums he'd never heard before: the Roches, Penguin Café Orchestra and Philip Glass. We laughed at the same movies. *Better Off Dead, Buckaroo Banzai, Real Genius, The Big Snit*. Ian was a good kid, smart.

Ian's mom told me once, "Don't try to be his mother; he already has one." She was taking Ian away for the weekend and I was seeing him out the door, making sure he had pajamas and enough underwear. I didn't want to be his mother, I just wanted her to know that I was good to him.

One day, Ian, my husband and I went to the beach near the Santa Monica pier. It was a warm day and the Santa Ana winds whipped the water into frothy whitecaps.

Ian was frantic about swimming, desperate to be in the water. I didn't really want to go because of the kind of water it was. Murky. I said yes anyway because his father wouldn't go with him, and kids should have fun. I told him, "I'll swim with you, but not where it's over our heads."

Ian was not a good swimmer, but good enough to do a few lengths. We stayed close to shore and let the waves knock us over. I laughed because Ian was laughing and whooping. His happiness caught me by the arm and spun me around, breathless and grinning. Ian could do that to me.

He bounced up and down in the waist-deep water. "Look at that," he said, pointing a slender arm, scraped at the elbow, toward the open water. "That's so awesome." There were boys on belly boards, fifty yards out, catching the bigger waves.

"Let's go there," Ian said. "It's not that deep and the waves are better. Can we?"

"Nope." I shook my head and his smile faded. I grabbed his waist and tickled him, extracting more laughter and a desperate squirm. Kissed the top of his head, the smell of salt and sunshine.

"Please, please, can we go? I'll stay right beside you. Please?"

I didn't like the idea, but he was right about the waves.

I told him we had to go a little further up the beach, because I didn't want the belly boarders to run us over. We went south, down the shore, not more than thirty yards or so, wading into chest-high water until, clear of the boarders, we stopped to rest. We put our backs to the incoming waves, watched a gull rise and drift north.

I could see Ian's father on the beach. He was lying in the sand, pretending not to watch the bronzed, blonde girls playing beach volleyball. He was lying on his stomach, hiding his pot belly from the sun and from their view.

Ian and I started swimming out to the bigger waves, and everything seemed okay. It's hard to tell where you are in the ocean, no lane markers, no bottom lines.

I was swimming and wondering if, in California, it was okay for a married man to lie on the beach watching girls while his second wife entertained his son.

That's when I noticed Ian and I were being pulled out to sea. We'd taken only a few strokes, but we were nearly as far from shore as the boarders. A few seconds later, we passed them.

Ian didn't notice.

He kept swimming until I said, "Ian. Stop. Stand up."

I dropped my feet to bottom and felt my toes dragging through the sand, just briefly. Then the bottom dropped away and the water was over my head.

"Head back to shore, Ian," I called. A hollowness was opening in my throat. Ian turned around without argument.

"You're going to have to swim hard," I said. "We're in some kind of current."

Ian swam hard. I swam behind him, pushing him forward by the soles of his feet. I could see the boarders, forward, to our left. We swam for a long time. We didn't get any closer.

My husband was a dark mark on the beach. He seemed to be talking to one of the volleyball players. I could see her pale yellow hair. She was standing above him; hands on hips. He was sitting in the sand, legs bundled to chest. I buried my face in the water, swam hard for shore.

Ian's front crawl grew lame. He was breathing loud and fast, exhaling twice with every stroke. He couldn't drag his arms out of the water.

"Keep swimming, Ian," I growled.

"I can't."

"You have to."

Ian kept swimming. He knew we were in trouble.

I thought about jellyfish stings and, just once, leeches, breathed slowly, looked toward the beach. The volleyball girl was sitting by my husband; they sat face to face, laughing.

Ian started to cry.

"I have a cramp in my calf," he said.

I know how bad that can be, like a rod of hot iron right through the belly of the muscle.

"Float on your back for a while."

Ian tried, but the waves kept washing into his mouth, making him cough, weak and watery.

I lifted Ian's head out of the water and held it up, side stroking in the direction of shore. Not losing ground, not gaining ground, stroke after stroke. Something in my shoulder snapped, and the joint began to grind. My sides clenched in the first spasms of exhaustion. I tried to add it up. Nearly half an hour of swimming in place, fifteen minutes of pulling Ian. That was equivalent to three miles at least, so I still had two more miles left in me, maybe three.

I felt dizzy. The water felt so cold now.

I wanted to let Ian go. I could see his father, reaching to touch the bronze girl.

"Can you try again, Ian? Just swim for a minute."

"No, I'm too tired."

"Just try, for me."

I didn't wait for him to answer, I just let him go. I knew instantly that it was a mistake. He started to drift away from me, seaward. I watched the distance between us grow until he screamed.

"Mom, help."

"You can shave four seconds off your best one hundred-yard time if you pull harder. Slow your cadence, and pull like this."

"Okay, coach."

I pulled hard, body rigid, head down, breaking the waves. A sprint, anaerobic, no time to breathe, no need to breathe. But when I got there, Ian was already going under, his face distorted by panic. He grabbed onto me, snarled my limbs with his. He was trying to keep his head above water and he pushed me under. He held me there, and for a few seconds I waited, hoping he would settle. When I started to run out of air, I pulled myself downward, away from him, deeper into the water.

It surprised me when my toes hit the sand. The bottom had never been too far away, twelve or fifteen feet at most, the water not much deeper than the diving tank at the YMCA. I opened my eyes and looked up. The water felt quiet. I could see Ian, above me, silhouetted against the yellow ball of the sun. I was so tired, and it was so soft and warm under that deep blanket of water. I thought I would sleep, just for a minute or two, collect my strength for the swim back to shore. Already dreaming, my knees touched coarse sand.

Kitchen table. Cinnamon toast.

"How come I didn't win, Dad?"

"Did you do your best?" Melted butter and spiced sugar, turning liquid on my tongue.

"Yes."

Dad's eyes, wise, weariness in the corners. "To win, you have to give until it hurts, then give some more."

On the surface of the water, Ian was still. My chest roared hot. I pushed myself upward, off the bottom, toward the pale light and the dark shadow of a boy.

At surface, I dragged air into aching lungs.

Ian on his back. Floating.

"I thought you might be dead," he said almost matter-of-factly. "I did like you told me, I'm floating." His body convulsed with uncontrollable shivers.

"I'm sorry, Ian. I won't let you go again."

I lay on my back, and cradled Ian's head on my chest. I thought that if I could swim north, get closer to the boarders, I could yell for help. I kicked us northward, parallel to the beach.

I know about the currents now. Bands, sometimes as narrow as twenty or thirty feet across, that pull toward deeper water. Swim parallel to shore and you can be free of them in a minute. Swim toward shore and you battle the current until you die.

I kicked and looked at the sky. I breathed slowly. I kicked and kicked until both calves locked into tight balls. Lungs felt so hot, so full.

I thought of the distance swimmer I once saw on television. The TV crew filmed her as she swam from Cuba to Florida, a boat beside her, keeping pace. The boat supported a moving net, a box of iron mesh to keep away sharks and jellyfish. It must have been nice, that net. She would always know she was in the right place, in miles of open water, even without any bottom lines.

Ian was quiet, resting. His shivering had nearly stopped. It sounded like he was humming. I had the smell of macaroni and cheese in my nostrils, the taste of slick, warm butter on my tongue.

I lay on my back, kicking, pulling weakly at the water with one arm. I hadn't looked around for a while, maybe ten or fifteen minutes, but suddenly I could hear the boarders.

"Ian, can you swim for a second?"

"I don't think so."

I held Ian upright with one arm and turned onto my stomach. We nearly ran into a blond boy, perhaps fifteen.

"Please," I asked, "My son is exhausted. Can I use your board to tow him to shore?"

The boy said nothing, but piloted his board to me. He helped me heave Ian onto the board and together we towed it to shore.

As we made our way in, I could see my husband, his hand on the waist of the bronze girl, sliding it slowly over the slick skin of her belly toward her breast. She brushed his hand, in that "somebody might be watching" kind of way. Her bikini had a pattern of teddy bears on it.

When we got to shore, I thanked the blond boy. Then I threw up in the sand. Mostly salt water. I retched for a long time after my stomach was empty. There were wide bleeding welts on my arms and back, and one eye was swollen shut. My right shoulder felt splintered inside.

Ian sat with me and covered his ears with his hands as my stomach heaved again. He looked at my bleeding arms. "I did that, didn't I?" I nodded. He cried, and that hurt worse than the welts or my eye.

"Should I get my dad?" he asked.

I wheezed a shallow "Yes."

Ian stumbled away from me and came back a few minutes later with a towel. "Dad's busy right now. He said he'll be here in a minute. Are you okay? Are you going to throw up again?"

"I don't think so." The taste of bitter bile on my teeth and gums.

"Good." He plopped into the sand and took my hand. We huddled together and I wrapped the beach towel around us, held Ian close, our cool skin touching, warming. We sat, silent, watching the waves tumble onto the sand.

Three months later I divorced Ian's father. I wasn't allowed to see Ian any more. I came home.

Ian is a man now. Last year he came to visit me, all the way from California. He is tall, and handsome, and very smart. We went for long walks and sang all the old songs we could remember: *Cats*, The Roches, *Songs from Liquid Days*. We talked about when we lived together, about

Disneyland, and Magic Mountain and shopping at the Galleria. We talked about what he would do when he finished college, his career as a photographer, his desire to move to London. He told me about a girl he had fallen in love with, how she had broken his heart. He said nothing of his father. I didn't ask.

The day before he went back to California, Ian took my biggest yellow towel, rolled his bathing suit and a pair of goggles inside it, and drove me to the public swimming pool near my house. I watched him doing lengths from a seat in the gallery. He is a powerful swimmer now, with a broad back, strong limbs and a well-tuned front crawl. He raced in high school. "Like you did," he smiled, "but probably a lot faster."

I asked him that night, after dinner, if he ever swam in the water off the coast.

He swirled his fingertip in a drizzle of cheese sauce that edged his plate. "Only when I have to," he replied, licking his finger clean. "I don't like the ocean much. But if I ever have kids, I'll make sure they learn how to swim in surf. I'll make sure they know about the currents."

After breakfast the next morning Ian flew to California. I drove back to the pool.

The water is different now.

"Government legislation and chlorine restrictions," the lifeguard said, slapping a grey mop onto the white deck. "The public pools have all been retrofitted for salt water." He swabbed limply. "Just as sterile, and better for the environment."

The salt muddied the blue-green water, made it less clear. The lines on the bottom were blurry, even with goggles. But salt in the water makes a swimmer buoyant. I floated easily.

I swam a few slow miles. Moving like a kayak. Felt the simple pull of each arm, the smooth thrust forward, my head slicing the water like a prow, my spine, compressed by gravity, elongating. I watched the dark mass of my own shadow on the pool bottom follow me from end to end. I swam and swam until the nagging hunger returned; then I let it sit there, familiar.

A lukewarm shower in a cold locker room. I carefully dried myself with a clean towel, fresh from the dryer. I drenched my salt-parched skin with lotion, sweet-scented with orange and ylang[1] to protect it from the harsh, dry cold of autumn.

I can still swim quite a ways. ▶

---

[1] **ylang:** a scented oil derived from flowers

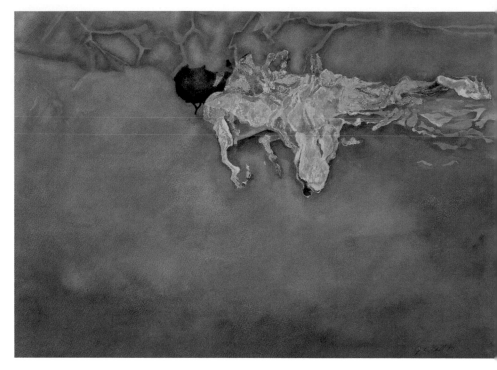

Swimmer in Yellow by Gareth Lloyd.

What techniques has the artist used to make *Swimmer in Yellow* visually interesting? Would you describe this work as a realistic painting? Explain your response, referring to specific elements of the painting.

Kari Strutt writes fiction and technical manuals. She lives in Calgary and is currently working on her first novel.

1. *Response*

a. The story begins with a retelling of some of the narrator's childhood memories. Is this an effective opening for a short story? Why or why not?

b. In your opinion, would this story be as effective if it were told in third-person narration? Explain.

c. Look for passages appearing in *italics*. What is different about these passages, and what functions do they serve?

d. What conflicts and complications are present in "Touching Bottom"? Describe the qualities that help the narrator to resolve these conflicts. Then, in a brief piece of personal writing, tell about a time when you needed the same qualities yourself.
e. What are some of the ways in which the narrator and Ian affected one another's lives? Support your opinion.

2. ***Literature Studies*** *Unifying Device* Describe the way in which Kari Strutt has used swimming as a **unifying device** within her story, from title to closing line. What are the most important narrative strands that are woven together? How does swimming function as a symbol, and what are the different meanings of the phrase "touching bottom"? Explain your ideas in a small group discussion.

A **unifying device** connects different parts of a narrative. It can be a metaphor, a symbol, an image, a character, or even an important word or phrase.

3. ***Drama*** *Reader's Theatre* In a group, prepare and perform a Reader's Theatre version of "Touching Bottom." In Reader's Theatre, the emphasis is on an expressive reading of narration and dialogue. Although physical movement is minimal, you may enhance the presentation with lighting, sound effects, or music. You may also edit the story somewhat to reduce the amount of narration.

4. ***Language Conventions*** *Pace and Flow* Using quotations from the story, show how Strutt uses sentence structure, punctuation, and paragraph breaks to shape the pace and flow of the story. For each example you choose, describe its important features (for example, comma use to break the sentence into short phrases) and then explain how those features influence the reader. Do you think the author does a good job of controlling the pace and flow of the story? Explain.

"Train rides seemed to open up
an unused store of associations,
provoking vivid flashes
of remembered sight."

The Forest of Arden

by Hannah Grant

PAUL WAS DREAMING OF A WOMAN STANDING IN A FIELD
with a gun. At first she was a small silhouette against a pinkish
dawn sky, smudged by dirt on the train window. She grew larger
and more distinct; he could see she wore rubber boots and a coat
over a loose dress or nightgown. She held the rifle loosely, all her
attention apparently focused on something beyond the train or
invisible to Paul. As the field and the woman rushed towards
him, he tried to determine whether she was actually moving; just
before the train brought them parallel, she vanished in a blur of
speed and he woke up.

The vibration of the train became the roar of a passing car.
He smelled exhaust in the cool air blowing in from the window;
somewhere down the street a child was crying. Faint music
from the next room meant that Gabriel was up and working.
Paul groped for the bedside clock and guessed seven thirty-two
or -three; untangling his legs from the sheets, he put his feet on
the floor. He no longer considered the extra few minutes of
sleepy half-consciousness he had enjoyed as a child, but for a
moment he sat on the edge of the bed, rubbing both hands
across his face, then stood up and walked out of his room. The
hall smelled of beer and laundry soap; he leaned against the
bathroom doorframe and reached sideways to turn both taps on
full. There was no need to hurry; he would have plenty of time
to catch the train.

The derailment which blinded Paul in the summer of his
eighth birthday happened during his first train ride. Chance
placed him in one of the two cars which were severely damaged.
After spending the afternoon of the first day in the observation

car, and the night with his family, he had finally decided to explore the front of the train. He was caught standing in the aisle, surrounded by strangers, when the wave of force tossed him sideways into a confusion of soft bodies and breaking glass. He remembered a prolonged shriek, and a shock which he could not remember either fading or ending. After that, of course, there was only darkness.

Paul stepped out of the bathroom just as Gabriel's radio erupted into the rest of the apartment, blasting out a Renaissance dance tune. Paul found Gabriel's relationship to music one of his most endearing qualities as a roommate. He produced it naturally or artificially wherever he went: he splashed and sang while washing; talked back to radio and television; cursed and laughed out loud; walked heavily, whistled, hummed. Sometimes he sang in his sleep. Paul could follow Gabriel's every movement through the apartment, calculate his mood, even recognize his voice from the other side of a concert hall.

Just now Gabriel was singing loudly, if incoherently, along with a soft drum rhythm, obscuring both the main recorder and harpsichord parts. The irregularities of his voice were echoed by the impact of his steps, and Paul kept a prudent distance as he followed the carolling, dancing Gabriel towards the kitchen. He reached the doorframe just as the exaggerated percussion of the finale was punctuated by the creak of the opening refrigerator.

"Hell, there's no milk!"

"Third shelf, behind two jars. Good morning."

Gabriel swore appreciatively. A second, slower tune began pouring in from the hall. Paul found the kettle, filled it and plugged it in; he found a cup, the instant coffee, a spoon and his chair. He let the music completely erase the echoes of the dream, the melody gradually replacing the almost subliminal memory of the sound of the train.

After the accident, the effects of concussion swept over him in waves, pulling him in and out of a coma for two days. He had so strongly associated the return of consciousness with the return of vision that later, trying to remember, he found it difficult to distinguish between this time and many of the days following. Once he had learned to identify his waking hours by the hiss of the air conditioner and the pain in his arm, he began to connect sight with his return home. He moved into his family's new house in the city with only the uncertain recollection of a photograph of the front of a building. For several years afterwards, it seemed to him at times that he had never really woken up and never gone home.

All at once the kettle began to whistle and the telephone rang; a split second later, whistle, recorder and harpsichord were overpowered by an eerie strain of East Indian sitar.[1] From the hall, Gabriel's voice claimed emphatically that he was not at home, while the real Gabriel knocked over his chair and barged across the kitchen, shouting at the telephone. Paul heard the sitar stop in mid-whine as Gabriel began an energetic monologue in French. After an equally incomprehensible shout of farewell, Paul heard the clatter of the hall closet opening and the front door slamming closed. Gabriel's footsteps on the metal stairwell clanged into silence like distant bells.

Gabriel, a graduate engineer, was now majoring in theatre arts; he had a vast, incompatible collection of acquaintances who appeared periodically and left obscure messages on his answering machine. When Gabriel was out of town, Paul was responsible for filing and selectively passing on these communications; he heard requests for help with surveying problems, demands for better speaking parts in *Hamlet*, instructions for the use of special effects such as lightning and small explosions. His position as a funnel for this stream of exotic visitors offset the combination of handicap and natural reticence which tended to let him slide into the careful circle of the blind.

Paul's studies in history required a lot of solitary reading, as did his work in the University Braille library. Outside of Gabriel's whirlwind of music and arguments, Paul's main solace was his collection of talking books. He would relax his cramped fingers, brew some herb tea and settle back in a cloud of fragrant steam to listen to *King Lear*, or a dramatic recital of *Beowulf* in Old English, or a commentary on Darwin's *The Origin of Species*, complete with recordings of bird calls. Shakespeare was Paul's favourite; he had versions of all the plays and sonnets. He had tried to explain his preference, and finally concluded that in Shakespeare, visual images were always more suggestive than descriptive: King Lear's storm of despair was only peripherally physical; Prospero's island and the forest of Arden were made up of selective associations, projections of worlds perceived in the mind. For Paul, visual images in literature were neither meaningless nor completely understandable: some triggered memory—sometimes sight, sometimes emotion; others did not. He found Shakespeare's symbolic landscapes especially comprehensive and real.

Paul's favourite sonnet was number 130, the one beginning:

> *My mistress' eyes are nothing like the sun;*
> *Coral is far more red than her lips' red: ...*

---

[1]sitar: a large stringed instrument originating in India

Paul's recording of this particular sonnet affected him to an extraordinary degree. Even more than the poetry, the voice of the reader, like music, seemed to enhance the significance of the words. It was a young woman's voice, slightly nasal but so clear and light as to be almost sexless; the self-conscious enunciation and mild distortion of the recording made it sound distant. Paul could imagine that he was hearing the woman for whom the sonnet had been written, reading it aloud for the first time, her voice blurred by centuries. The sonnet was part of a collection compiled by volunteer readers from the university; the reader of "Sonnet 130" was not named and did not appear on the rest of the recording. Paul had made several copies, as he was afraid of wearing out the original and being unable to replace it.

The sonnet had become so familiar that Paul found himself repeating it whenever he was slightly distracted, using it like a chant to measure distance when he was walking. Picking up his cane from the hall closet, he found his way down the stairs and out of the building. Turning left, he passed two lampposts:

> *If snow be white, why then her breasts are dun;*
> *If hairs be wires, black wires grow on her head.*

His relaxed mind offered him a brief view of snow-covered fields striped with a dark procession of pylons and connecting lines; the scene seemed to move past him before disappearing into his memory.

> *I have seen roses damasked, red and white,*
> *But no such roses see I in her cheeks;*

An imaginary smell of snow was replaced by the real, sweet scent coming from the flower stalls near the corner.

> *And in some perfumes is there more delight*
> *Than in the breath that from my mistress reeks.*

Paul felt the warm, malodorous rush of air coming up from the underground station and tapped his stick to find the first step down. He had memorized routes he could travel alone to get to the library and the university; today a friend was going to meet him at the link to the train station and travel with him to the conference.

Paul was no longer afraid of travelling by train, as repetition of the sightless experience had built up protective layers of routine. He now found it strangely exhilarating: the vibration, the press of people, the throbbing rattle of speed, all built and sustained an emotional tension and put Paul in a state of undefined expectation. He had discovered that train rides represented a way of reviving his memories. In addition to the dreams, train rides seemed to open up an unused store of associations, provoking vivid flashes of remembered sight. The effect sometimes lasted for several days. Paul had tried to explain the experience to Gabriel, who began referring to Paul's 'visions' as results of train 'trips.'

On the subway, Paul gripped the handle nearest the door, counting stops. He stepped out at the correct platform, inhaling the pervasive underground atmosphere of damp concrete and fighting the usual panic until he heard his friend's voice and felt a hand on his arm. As they headed for the ticket office, his apprehension suddenly produced the brilliant picture of a crowded station full of colour and movement. Some of the people Paul knew: he saw a ten-year-old friend who was now married, a neighbour with the dog he used to walk. Paul looked at other, strange faces and felt a mild unease. He climbed into his seat savouring the image; then he lost it as, with a starting jerk, the train began to move.

Paul returned from the conference feeling unhappy. Another student, a math major, had cornered Paul and forced him to discuss the different ways of presenting computerized geometry in Braille. Paul had lost interest in all but simple math when he had lost his sight. His pleasure in angles and lines had been purely visual; he could not understand the perspective of someone who had been blind from birth. As an added confusion, while the student was speaking, Paul involuntarily saw in perfect detail the figure of his father, twenty years earlier, as he had appeared trying to help Paul with his homework. As Paul watched helplessly, his father's image flickered and changed: his hair lengthened, then shortened as his skin darkened; his beard disappeared; a chequered shirt became striped, then was hidden under a sweater. Throughout these transformations, the young student's voice spoke as if from behind his father's face, which somehow managed to maintain an expression of earnest concern. Paul arrived back at the apartment with a sense of having lost something important, and by having it in the first place, had lost something else. For consolation he listened to ten of his favourite sonnets, ending with "Sonnet 130." Then he decided to go over the messages on the answering machine.

Gabriel had replaced the sitar with a sixteenth-century dulcimer;[2] a few delicate chords escaped before Paul pressed the correct button.

---

[2]**dulcimer:** a boxlike stringed instrument often played with mallets

A young woman's voice said clearly, "It's me." Paul was paralyzed; realizing he had missed the rest of the message, he rewound the tape. The slightly nasal intonation was unmistakable; Shakespeare's mistress was coming to collect her script at eight o'clock, as promised.

Her name was Emily Leonne; she was a forestry student who liked drama. She arrived still covered in pine needles from an afternoon field trip. When Paul let her in with a kind of horrified wonder, the scent of resin and damp earth streamed into the apartment. He thought he had opened the door to a forest. For a moment, he found himself looking into a stand of evergreens opposite that first platform, on that first day. A fox appeared at the edge of the tracks, loped neatly across and vanished into the trees.

Fantastically, the first word she spoke was his name. Gabriel must have told her. Her voice was gruffer, at once quicker and more hesitant than the recording.

> *I love to hear her speak, yet well I know*
> *That music hath a far more pleasing sound.*

When she agreed to go to a concert with him, Paul nearly drove Gabriel crazy with planning. He traced the route to the auditorium four times, counting blocks, turns, fire hydrants, streetlamps. Then he made himself sick worrying if she liked baroque music. Gabriel said if she didn't then what good was she anyway, and turned the radio up so that the bass thundered like a summer storm. Emily said she liked the concert and accepted a drink afterwards. After she left, Paul asked Gabriel what she looked like.

"Reddish hair; dark eyes—brown, I think."

Paul remembered the dark sleepers, the red flash of the fox.

> *I grant I never saw a goddess go:*
> *My mistress, when she walks, treads on the ground.*

He was silent, satisfied.

He asked her to another concert; in return, she brought him a pack of embossed cards and taught him to play poker with Gabriel. Paul gave her a necklace of agate, a cool, fluid weight of rounded stones; she arrived the next day with a balsam fir seedling from the nursery, carefully potted.

The first time Emily stayed the night, Paul remembered briefly as a revelation the red glow of closed eyelids. For the first time in years, he recognized the border between sleep and consciousness, then it faded into unimportance. He listened to Emily's heartbeat until it became a rhythm in a dream and he watched the shadows of trees passing, mile after mile, until the darkening sky made them indistinguishable.

Emily took Paul to the movies. They sat in the back and she whispered a blow-by-blow description of all the action she thought he was missing. These outings usually degenerated into normal back row foolishness when Emily began telling lies, giggling and commenting on their neighbours. As they walked out into the cold of the evening and on into the park (Emily still laughing), Paul felt as if the characters in the film with their choreographed ecstasy, and the other viewers with their cheerful passion, followed and surrounded them with the heady freshness of the new leaves.

She made him go to an evening of country dancing; she traced the patterns of each dance for him and taught him the steps. The other dancers whirled him around with congenial patronage. Paul could not decide whether he enjoyed himself or not; it was like being drunk. That night he dreamed of trying to keep his balance in a crowded corridor, jostled by faceless giants. He woke sweating, his heart beating quickly in time with the music.

Gabriel announced that as his current play was so successful he was going on tour. He left with a shout, his windbreaker rustling and snapping like the feathers of some huge bird. For a while it seemed to Paul that Gabriel still hovered in the apartment; half-eaten bags of cereal materialized from under cushions and the answering machine remained strongly vocal. Emily was much quieter than Gabriel, but no less detectable. Used to being untidy, she made an effort not to leave clothes on the floor where Paul might trip over them. As a result, all chairs and tables were carefully draped. Filmy scarves, work gloves, raincoats, all showed where Emily had just been, where she was going and where she was. Paul felt wonderfully secure, wrapped in this cocoon of reminders. Emily also filled the windowsills with small trees. For Paul, the apartment might have overlooked a vast wilderness; sun-warmed evergreen pervaded every room.

Emily read to him often. She agreed to tape other readings for him to keep, but only after some persuasion. Emily did not like her voice on recordings; she thought it sounded stilted, high-pitched, too childish. Paul had also noticed the difference between the live readings and the recordings. He loved Emily's voice and the possessive intimacy of listening to her, but he had come to realize that it was still the slightly distant, distorted voice that he found oddly compelling. Almost guiltily, he would take out his recordings and listen to them when she was away.

One day in the fall, Emily left early to catch the train for a foresters' clinic in the mountains. Paul got up late; he was still surprised by how much he noticed her absence. That evening, before she was due back —in a nostalgic, conspiratorial mood—he decided to listen to "Sonnet 130." He played the last lines through twice.

> *And yet, by heaven, I think my love as rare*
> *As any she belied by false compare.*

Paul reached over to open the window, spruce needles pricking his fingers. The wind that rushed in was cold; it was getting late. He sat back, breathing in the feral, resinous air, and felt vaguely anxious. The forest in his mind floated like a mirage on the other side of the tracks, silent and insubstantial.

When the telephone rang, Paul was so disoriented that it rang three times before he even reached the hall. He heard the answering machine click on and the throb of a drum mixed with the thick, green breath of the trees. Gabriel's voice announced his absence. The music paused, a note sounded and Paul heard Emily's voice, speaking against the noise of many other voices.

It seemed to Paul that he could still feel the resonance of the drum, but the tempo had become faster and steadier. His lungs filled with the cold of remembered snow. In his mind's eye he saw the fox, poised on the tracks. Fences began to writhe past him, stained pink by the dawn; trees shredded the sky around him; a flock of crows flew towards him at amazing speed. An ocean of white fields swelled up like a great tide and he saw the woman with the gun. For an instant, the skeleton of an abandoned barn framed the rising sun.

When Emily came in, a few minutes later, she was nearly knocked over as Paul grabbed at her and pressed his lips against her throat. He stumbled; his feet were tangled in long ribbons of tape and the remains of the stereo system. The answering machine lay sideways on the floor. There did not seem to be a way to tell her how, overwhelmed with visions, his heart pounding in time with the engine, he had suddenly seen his own face as he had last seen it, reflected in the train window. The telephone message sounded distant; the light voice spoke with nervous precision and sexless clarity. He heard the voice of this child, this eight-year-old self, distorted by the resonance of his own skull, saying:

"It won't be long. I'll be home soon." ❯

Hannah Grant has degrees from the University of St. Andrews, in Fife, Scotland, and the University of New Brunswick. Her short stories have been published in the journals *Voice*, *The Longmeadow Journal*, and *The Fiddlehead*. This story, "The Forest of Arden," was first published as the winner of the first Hemingway Prize offered in memory of Dan Hemingway, a student of the University of St. Andrews, and was later published in the collection *Coming Attractions '93.*

1. *Response*

a. Were there aspects of this story that you found difficult to understand? If so, explain what they were. What reading strategies helped you to deal with the story's complexities? Discuss your ideas in a group.

b. Explain the significance of the dream sequence with which the story opens.

c. In what way does the description in the second paragraph prepare the reader for the information about Paul's blindness? Why do you think the author withheld that information until the third paragraph?

d. How does the author integrate Shakespeare's "Sonnet CXXX" into the story? In a group, read the whole sonnet aloud, discuss its meaning, and comment on the functions it serves within the story.

e. What does Emily do to trigger Paul's final vision? What special significance does the vision hold for him?

2. *Literature Studies* Allusion

The title of this story is a literary **allusion** to a setting in one of Shakespeare's comedies. Using the Internet or other resources, identify which play the allusion refers to. If possible, find out whether Shakespeare's forest of Arden has a symbolic value that might contribute to the meaning of Grant's story. What other allusions does the story contain, and what do many of them have in common?

An **allusion** is a reference to another literary work, or a person, place, event, or object from history, literature, or mythology.

As you read this story,
consider how the images support
and complement the text.

Things That Fly

by Douglas Coupland

I'm sitting hunched over the living room coffee table on a Sunday night, in a daze, having just woken up from a deep deep sleep on a couch shared with pizza boxes and crushed plastic cherry yogurt containers. In front of me a TV game show is playing on MUTE and my head rests on top of my hands, as though I am praying, but I am not; I am rubbing my eyes and trying to wake up, and my hair is brushing the tabletop which is covered in crumbs and I am thinking to myself that, in spite of everything that has happened in my life, I have never lost the sensation of always being on the brink of some magic revelation—that *if only* I would look closely enough at the world, then that magic revelation would be mine—*if only* I could wake up just that little bit more, then … well—let me describe what happened today.

Today went like this: I was up at noon; instant coffee; watched a talk show; a game show; a bit of football; a religious something-or-other; then I turned the TV off. I drifted listlessly about the house, from silent room to silent room, spinning the wheels of the two mountain bikes on their racks in the hallway and

straightening a pile of CDs glued together with spilled Orange Crush in the living room. I suppose I was trying to pretend I had real things to do, but, well, I didn't.

My brains felt overheated. So much has happened in my life recently. And after hours of this pointlessness I finally had to admit I couldn't take being alone one more moment. And so I swallowed my pride and drove to my parents at their house further up the hill here on the North Shore: up on the mountain— up in the trees to my old house—my true home, I guess. Today was the first day when I could really tell that summer was over. The cold air sparkled and the maple leaves were rotting, putting forth their lovely reek, like dead pancakes.

Up on the mountain, my mother was in the kitchen making 1947-style cream cheese sandwiches with pimentos and no crusts to freeze in advance for her bridge friends. Dad was sitting at the kitchen table reading *The Vancouver Sun*. Of course they knew about what had happened recently and so they were walking on eggshells around me. This made me feel odd and under-the-microscope, so I went upstairs to sit in the guest room to look out the window at honking V's of Canada geese flying south toward the United States from northern British Columbia. It was peaceful to see so many birds flying—to see all these things in our world that can fly.

Mom had left the TV on in the bedroom, next room over. CNN was saying that Superman was scheduled to die later this week—in the sky above Minneapolis, and I was momentarily taken out of myself. I thought this was certainly a coincidence, because I had just visited the city of Minneapolis a month ago, on a business trip: a new crystal city, all shiny like quartz rising over the Midwest corn fields. According to the TV, Superman was supposed to die in an air battle over the city with a supremely evil force, and while I knew this was just a cheesy publicity ploy to sell more comics—and I haven't even *read* a Superman comic in two decades— the thought still made me feel bad.

And then the geese passed, and I sat watching the blue smoke linger down the mountain slopes from people burning leaves across the Capilano River. After a while I returned downstairs and Dad and I sat in the kitchen next to the sliding glass door and we fed the birds and animals on the back patio. We had grain and corn for the chickadees, juncos and starlings; and roasted peanuts for the jays and the black and grey squirrels. Such a sea of life! And I was glad for this activity because there is something about the animals that takes us out of ourselves and takes us out of time and allows us to forget our own lives.

Dad had placed a cob of corn on a stump for the jays, who bickered over it non-stop. And we threw peanuts to the jays and I noticed that when I threw two peanuts to a jay, it just sat there and couldn't decide which nut was juicier, so it became paralyzed with greed and couldn't take either of them. And we threw nuts to the squirrels, too, and they're so dumb that even if I hit them on the head with a nut, they couldn't find it. I just don't know how they've managed to survive these millions of years. Dad had also scattered sunflower seeds for a flying squirrel he has named Yo-yo who lives in the backyard. Yo-yo darted about the yard like a pinball.

Mom said that people are interested in birds only inasmuch as they exhibit human behavior—greed and stupidity and anger—and by doing so they free us from the unique sorrow of being human. She thinks humans are tired of having to take the blame all by themselves for the badness in the world.

I told Mom my own theory of why we like birds—of how birds are a miracle because they prove to us there is a finer, simpler state of being which we may strive to attain.

A good writer turns fact into truth.

Edward Albee

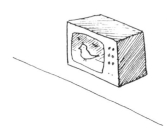

But anyway, I began feeling low again, and I felt I was making Mom and Dad feel uncomfortable because they were worrying I might go to pieces at any moment. I could see the relief on their faces when I laughed at the jays, like I'd been cured, and this depressed me, made me feel like a freak, and so I went back upstairs, into the TV room, turned on the TV and hid. I got to thinking about all of the bad stuff that had happened in life recently. It made me think of all of the bad things I had done to other people in my world—and there have been so many bad things I have done. I felt ashamed; I was feeling as though none of the good deeds I had ever done had ever mattered.

And on the TV there were still more birds! Such lovely creatures and I thought that we are so lucky to have the animals. What act of goodness did we as humans once commit to deserve such kindness from God?

There was a pretty grey parakeet who had learned to recognize human things—triangle shapes and car keys and the color blue—and to speak the words for them. This little parakeet worked so hard to remember these things, and it had an efficient faraway female voice like a telephone operator in Texas. The parakeet made me realize how hard it is to learn anything in life, and even then, there's no guarantee you might need it.

On another channel there were pictures of a zoo in Miami, Florida, which had been whacked by a hurricane and there were pictures of ducks and tall elegant birds swimming in the wreckage except they didn't know it was wreckage. It was just the world.

And then there was that same news story again about Superman's dying—except I realized I got the city wrong—he's supposed to die over *Metropolis*, not Minneapolis. But I was still sad. I have always liked the idea of Superman because I have always liked the idea that there is one person in the world who doesn't do bad things. And that there is one person in the world who is able to fly.

I myself often have dreams in which I am flying, but it's not flying the way Superman does. I simply put my arms behind my shoulders and float and move. Needless to say, it is my favorite dream.

Back on TV there were pictures of whooping cranes doing a mating dance and they were so sweet and graceful and I thought, "If only *I* could be a whooping crane and was able to float and fly like them, then it would be like always being in love."

And then I got just plain lonely and just so fed up with all the badness in my life and in the world and I said to myself, "Please, God, just make me a bird—that's all I ever really wanted—a white graceful bird free of shame and taint and fear of loneliness, and give me other white birds among which to fly, and give me a sky so big and wide that if I never wanted to land, I would never have to."

But instead God gave me these words, and I speak them here.

And I will add in closing that when I got back home tonight, I stepped through the door and over my messes; I fell onto the couch and into a sleep and then into a dream, and I dreamed that I was back in Minneapolis, back next to the corn fields. I dreamed I had

taken a glass elevator to the top of one of the city's green glass skyscrapers, to the very top floor, and I was running around that floor from one face of the skyscraper to another, frantic, looking through those big sheets of glass—trying to find a way to protect Superman. ❱

Douglas Coupland was born in 1961 on a Canadian military base in Germany. When he was four, he returned to Canada with his family. In 1984, he graduated from the Emily Carr College of Art and Design in Vancouver. After graduation, he studied abroad, eventually completing a two-year program in Japanese business science at a school in Japan. Although Coupland first became an artist, he is more famous for his writing. Of his nine novels to date, *Generation X, Life After God,* and *Lara's Book: Lara Croft and the Tomb Raider Phenomenon* are his most popular.

1. *Response*

   a. Make a list of the factual information the story provides about the narrator. Based on this list, what would you say about the amount and type of factual information the reader learns about the narrator?

   b. Reading between the lines, what do you think might have happened to the narrator in the recent past? What clues helped you reach those conclusions?

   c. The narrator tells this story as an extended flashback. Explain why you think this narrative technique is or is not appropriate to the story.

   d. Reread the story carefully. Do you see any signs that the narrator has found a possible remedy for his despair? Support your opinion with evidence from the text.

2. *Literature Studies* *Symbolism* The story contains several references to birds and to the comic-book character Superman. Reread the story carefully and suggest how these "things that fly" function as symbols. Do the symbols have more than one meaning? Explain how the symbols help to develop the meaning of the story.

3. **Language Conventions** *Conversational Tone* "Things That Fly" is written in a conversational tone. Find specific examples of techniques Coupland uses to create that feeling. Consider details such as sentence structure, punctuation, diction, and so on. Suggest some reasons why Coupland might have preferred a conversational tone. Do you think that the tone is effective? Why or why not?

4. **Visual Communication** *Line Drawings* Coupland's line drawings add an unusual visual element to this short story. In your view, do these illustrations add to or detract from the story? Explain.

   Write a brief story of your own (two or three pages) that contains a visual component—line drawings, colour illustrations, or special fonts, for example. Present your story to a group and explain what you were trying to accomplish with your visuals.

Once the disease of reading has laid hold upon the system it weakens it so that it falls easy prey to that other scourge which dwells in the inkpot and festers in the quill. The wretch takes to writing.

—Virginia Woolf

Theme Connections

- "Groom Service," a story about a young man who despairs of winning over the woman he loves, *page 12*
- "Transients in Arcadia," a story about a couple dissatisfied with their normal lives, *page 37*
- "The Return," a story in which one character faces despair and loneliness, *page 44*
- "Loneliness," a poem about loneliness, *page 244*
- "That's Extraordinary!" a radio play about a lonely woman, *page 423*

Could the fate
of the world
ultimately
depend on
the swing of
a golf club?

The Large Ant

by Howard Fast

There have been all kinds of notions and guesses as to how it would end. One held that sooner or later there would be too many people; another that we would do each other in, and the atom bomb made that a very good likelihood. All sorts of notions, except the simple fact that we were what we were. We could find a way to feed any number of people and perhaps even a way to avoid wiping each other out with the bomb; those things we are very good at, but we have never been any good at changing ourselves or the way we behave.

I know. I am not a bad man or a cruel man; quite to the contrary, I am an ordinary, humane person, and I love my wife and my children and I get along with my neighbors. I am like a great many other men, and do the things they would do and just as thoughtlessly. There it is in a nutshell.

I am also a writer, and I told Lieberman, the curator, and Fitzgerald, the government man, that I would like to write down the story. They shrugged their shoulders. "Go ahead," they said, "because it won't make one bit of difference."

"You don't think it would alarm people?"

"How can it alarm anyone when nobody will believe it?"

"If I could have a photograph or two."

"Oh, no," they said then. "No photographs."

"What kind of sense does that make?" I asked them. "You are willing to let me write the story—why not the photographs so that people could believe me?"

"They still won't believe you. They will just say you faked the photographs, but no one will believe you. It will make for more confusion, and if we have a chance of getting out of this, confusion won't help."

"What will help?"

They weren't ready to say that, because they didn't know. So here is what happened to me, in a very straightforward and ordinary manner.

Every summer, some time in August, four good friends of mine and I go for a week's fishing on the St. Regis chain of lakes in the Adirondacks. We rent the same shack each summer; we drift around in canoes and sometimes we catch a few bass. The fishing isn't very good, but we play cards well together, and we cook out and generally relax. This summer past, I had some things to do that couldn't be put off. I arrived three days late, and the weather was so warm and even and beguiling that I decided to stay on by myself for a day or two after the others left. There was a small flat lawn in front of the shack, and I made up my mind to spend at least three or four hours at short putts. That was how I happened to have the putting iron next to my bed.

The first day I was alone, I opened a can of beans and a can of beer for my supper. Then I lay down in my bed with *Life on the Mississippi*,[1] a pack of cigarettes and an eight-ounce chocolate bar. There was nothing I had to do, no telephone, no demands and no newspapers. At that moment, I was about as contented as any man can be in these nervous times.

It was still light outside, and enough light came in through the window above my head for me to read by. I was just reaching for a fresh cigarette, when I looked up and saw it on the foot of my bed. The edge of my hand was touching the golf club, and with a single motion I swept the club over and down, struck it a savage and accurate blow and killed it. That was what I referred to before. Whatever kind of a man I am, I react as a man does. I think that any man, black, white or yellow, in China, Africa or Russia, would have done the same thing.

First I found that I was sweating all over, and then I knew I was going to be sick. I went outside to vomit, recalling that this hadn't happened to me since 1943, on my way to Europe on a tub of a Liberty ship. Then I felt better and was able to go back into the shack and look at it. It was quite dead, but I had already made up my mind that I was not going to sleep alone in this shack.

---

[1] *Life on the Mississippi:* Samuel Clemens' (Mark Twain) memoir of his time as a steamboat pilot, published in 1875

I couldn't bear to touch it with my bare hands. With a piece of brown paper, I picked it up and dropped it into my fishing creel. That, I put into the trunk of my car, along with what luggage I carried. Then I closed the door of the shack, got into my car and drove back to New York. I stopped once along the road, just before I reached the Thruway, to nap in the car for a little over an hour. It was almost dawn when I reached the city, and I had shaved, had a hot bath and changed my clothes before my wife awoke.

During breakfast, I explained that I was never much of a hand at the solitary business, and since she knew that, and since driving alone all night was by no means an extraordinary procedure for me, she didn't press me with any questions. I had two eggs, coffee and a cigarette. Then I went into my study, lit another cigarette, and contemplated my fishing creel, which sat upon my desk.

My wife looked in, saw the creel, remarked that it had too ripe a smell, and asked me to remove it to the basement.

"I'm going to dress," she said. The kids were still at camp. "I have a date with Ann for lunch—I had no idea you were coming back. Shall I break it?"

"No, please don't. I can find things to do that have to be done."

Then I sat and smoked some more, and finally I called the Museum, and asked who the curator of insects was. They told me his name was Bertram Lieberman, and I asked to talk to him. He had a pleasant voice. I told him that my name was Morgan, and that I was a writer, and he politely indicated that he had seen my name and read something that I had written. That is formal procedure when a writer introduces himself to a thoughtful person.

I asked Lieberman if I could see him, and he said that he had a busy morning ahead of him. Could it be tomorrow?

"I am afraid it has to be now," I said firmly.

"Oh? Some information you require."

"No. I have a specimen for you."

"Oh?" The "oh" was a cultivated, neutral interval. It asked and answered and said nothing. You have to teach at least five semesters at a college to develop that particular "oh."

"Yes. I think you will be interested."

"An insect?" he asked mildly.

"I think so."

"Oh? Large?"

"Quite large," I told him.

"Eleven o'clock? Can you be here then? On the main floor, to the right, as you enter."

"I'll be there," I said.

"One thing—dead?"

"Yes, it's dead."

"Oh?" again. "I'll be happy to see you at eleven o'clock, Mr. Morgan."

My wife was dressed now. She opened the door to my study and said firmly, "Do get rid of that fishing creel. It smells."

"Yes, darling. I'll get rid of it."

"I should think you'd want to take a nap after driving all night."

"Funny, but I'm not sleepy," I said. "I think I'll drop around to the Museum."

My wife said that was what she liked about me, that I never tired of places like museums, police courts and third-rate night clubs.

Anyway, aside from a racetrack, a museum is the most interesting and unexpected place in the world. It was unexpected to have two other men waiting for me, along with Mr. Lieberman, in his office. Lieberman was a skinny, sharp-faced man of about sixty. The government man, Fitzgerald, was small, dark-eyed and wore gold-rimmed glasses. He was very alert, but he never told me what part of the government he represented. He just said "we," and it meant the government. Hopper, the third man, was comfortable-looking, pudgy, and genial. He was a United States senator with an interest in entomology, although before this morning I would have taken better than even money that such a thing not only wasn't, but could not be.

The room was large and square and plainly furnished, with shelves and cupboards on all walls.

We shook hands, and then Lieberman asked me, nodding at the creel, "Is that it?"

"That's it."

"May I?"

"Go ahead," I told him. "It's nothing that I want to stuff for the parlor. I'm making you a gift of it."

"Thank you, Mr. Morgan," he said, and then he opened the creel and looked inside. Then he straightened up, and the two other men looked at him inquiringly.

He nodded. "Yes."

The senator closed his eyes for a long moment. Fitzgerald took off his glasses and wiped them industriously. Lieberman spread a piece of plastic on his desk, and then lifted the thing out of my creel and laid it on the plastic. The two men didn't move. They just sat where they were and looked at it.

"What do you think it is, Mr. Morgan?" Lieberman asked me.

"I thought that was your department."

"Yes, of course. I only wanted your impression."

"An ant. That's my impression. It's the first time I saw an ant fourteen, fifteen inches long. I hope it's the last."

"An understandable wish," Lieberman nodded.

Fitzgerald said to me, "May I ask how you killed it, Mr. Morgan?"

"With an iron. A golf club, I mean. I was doing a little fishing with some friends up at St. Regis in the Adirondacks, and I brought the iron for my short shots. They're the worst part of my game, and when my friends left, I intended to stay on at our shack and do four or five hours of short putts. You see—"

"There's no need to explain," Hopper smiled, a trace of sadness on his face. "Some of our very best golfers have the same trouble."

"I was lying in bed, reading, and I saw it at the foot of my bed. I had the club—"

"I understand," Fitzgerald nodded.

"You avoid looking at it," Hopper said.

"It turns my stomach."

"Yes—yes, I suppose so."

Lieberman said, "Would you mind telling us why you killed it, Mr. Morgan?"

"Why?"

"Yes—why?"

"I don't understand you," I said. "I don't know what you're driving at."

"Sit down, please, Mr. Morgan," Hopper nodded. "Try to relax. I'm sure this has been very trying."

"I still haven't slept. I want a chance to dream before I say how trying."

"We are not trying to upset you, Mr. Morgan," Lieberman said. "We do feel, however, that certain aspects of this are very important. That is why I am asking you why you killed it. You must have had a reason. Did it seem about to attack you?"

"No."

"Or make any sudden motion toward you?"

"No. It was just there."

"Then why?"

"This is to no purpose," Fitzgerald put in. "We know why he killed it."

"Do you?" I nodded. "You're clearer on the subject than I am."

"The answer is very simple, Mr. Morgan. You killed it because you are a human being."

"Oh?" I borrowed that from Lieberman.

"Yes. Do you understand?"

"No, I don't."

"Then why did you kill it?" Hopper put in.

"I saw it," I answered slowly, "and somehow I knew that I must kill it. I didn't think or decide. I just grabbed the iron and hit it."

"Precisely," Fitzgerald said.

"You were afraid?" Hopper asked.

"I was scared to death. I still am, to tell the truth."

Lieberman said, "You are an intelligent man, Mr. Morgan. Let me show you something." He then opened the doors to one of the wall cupboards, and there stood eight jars of formaldehyde and in each jar a specimen like mine—and in each case mutilated by the violence of its death. I said nothing. I just stared.

Lieberman closed the cupboard doors. "All in five days," he shrugged.

"A new race of ants," I whispered stupidly.

"No. They're not ants. Come here!" He motioned me to the desk and the other two joined me. Lieberman took a set of dissection instruments out of his drawer, used one to turn the thing over, and then pointed to the underpart of what would be the thorax in an insect.

"That looks like part of him, doesn't it, Mr. Morgan?"

"Yes, it does."

Using two of the tools, he found a fissure and pried the bottom apart. It came open like the belly of a bomber; it was a pocket, a pouch, a receptacle that the thing wore, and in it were four beautiful little tools or instruments or weapons, each about an inch and a half long. They were beautiful the way any object of functional purpose and loving creation is beautiful—the way the creature itself would have been beautiful, had it not been an insect and myself a man. Using tweezers, Lieberman took each instrument out of the brackets that held it, offering each to me. And I took each one, felt it, examined it, and then put it down.

I had to look at the ant now, and I realized that I had not truly looked at it before. We don't look carefully at a thing that is horrible or repugnant to us. You can't look carefully at a thing through a screen of hatred. But now the hatred and the fear were diluted, and as I looked, I realized it was not an ant although like an ant. It was nothing that I had ever seen or dreamed of.

All three men were watching me, and suddenly I was on the defensive. "I didn't know! What do you expect when you see an insect that size?"

Lieberman nodded.

"What in the name of God is it?"

From his desk, Lieberman produced a bottle and four small glasses. He poured it and we drank it neat. I would not have expected him to keep good Scotch in his desk.

"We don't know," Hopper said. "We don't know what it is."

Lieberman pointed to the broken skull, from which a white substance oozed. "Brain material—a great deal of it."

"It could be a very intelligent creature," Hopper nodded.

Lieberman said, "It is an insect in developmental structure. We know very little about intelligence in our insects. It's not the same as what we call intelligence. It's a collective phenomenon—as if you were to think of the component parts of our bodies. Each part is alive, but the intelligence is a result of the whole. If that same pattern were to extend to creatures like this one—"

I broke the silence. They were content to stand there and stare at it.

"Suppose it were?"

"What?"

"The kind of collective intelligence you were talking about."

"Oh? Well, I couldn't say. It would be something beyond our wildest dreams. To us—well, what we are to an ordinary ant."

"I don't believe that," I said shortly, and Fitzgerald, the government man, told me quietly, "Neither do we. We guess. We comfort ourselves, too."

"If it's that intelligent, why didn't it use one of those weapons on me?"

"Would that be a mark of intelligence?" Hopper asked mildly.

"Perhaps none of these is a weapon," Lieberman said.

"Don't you know? Didn't the others carry instruments?"

"They did," Fitzgerald said shortly.

"Why? What were they?"

"We don't know," Lieberman said.

"But you can find out. We have scientists, engineers—good God, this is an age of fantastic instruments. Have them taken apart!"

"We have."

"Then what have you found out?"

"Nothing."

"Do you mean to tell me," I said, "that you can find out nothing about these instruments—what they are, how they work, what their purpose is?"

"Exactly," Hopper nodded. "Nothing, Mr. Morgan. They are meaningless to the finest engineers and technicians in the United States. You know the old story—suppose you gave a radio to Aristotle? What would he do with it? Where would he find power? And what would he receive with no one to send? It is not that these instruments are complex. They are actually very simple. We simply have no idea of what they can or should do."

"But there must be a weapon of some kind."

"Why?" Lieberman demanded. "Look at yourself, Mr. Morgan—a cultured and intelligent man, yet you cannot conceive of a mentality that does not include weapons as a prime necessity. Yet a weapon is an unusual thing, Mr. Morgan. An instrument of murder. We don't think that way, because the weapon has become the symbol of the world we inhabit. Is that civilized, Mr. Morgan? Or are the weapon and civilization in the ultimate sense incompatible? Can you imagine a mentality to which the concept of murder is impossible—or let me say absent. We see everything through our own subjectivity. Why shouldn't some other—this creature, for example—see the process of mentation[2] out of his subjectivity. So he approaches a creature of our world—and he is slain. Why? What explanation? Tell me, Mr. Morgan, what conceivable explanation could we offer a wholly rational creature for this," pointing to the thing on his desk. "I am asking you the question most seriously. What explanation?"

"An accident?" I muttered.

"And the eight jars in my cupboard? Eight accidents?"

"I think, Dr. Lieberman," Fitzgerald said, "that you can go a little too far in that direction."

"Yes, you would think so. It's a part of your own background. Mine is as a scientist. As a scientist, I try to be rational when I can. The creation of a structure of good and evil, or what we call morality and ethics, is a function of intelligence—and unquestionably the ultimate evil may be the destruction of conscious intelligence. That is why, so long ago, we at least recognized the injunction, 'Thou shalt not kill!' even if we never gave more than lip service to it. But to a collective intelligence, such as that of which this might be a part, the concept of murder would be monstrous beyond the power of thought."

I sat down and lit a cigarette. My hands were trembling. Hopper apologized. "We have been rather rough with you, Mr. Morgan. But over the past days, eight other people have done just what you did. We are caught in the trap of being what we are."

"But tell me—where do these things come from?"

_____

[2]**mentation:** thinking

"It almost doesn't matter where they come from," Hopper said hopelessly. "Perhaps from another planet—perhaps from inside this one—or the moon or Mars. That doesn't matter. Fitzgerald thinks they come from a smaller planet, because their movements are apparently slow on earth. But Dr. Lieberman thinks that they move slowly because they have not discovered the need to move quickly. Meanwhile, they have the problem of murder and what to do with it. Heaven knows how many of them have died in other places—Africa, Asia, Europe."

"Then why don't you publicize this? Put a stop to it before it's too late!"

"We've thought of that," Fitzgerald nodded. "What then—panic, hysteria, charges that this is the result of the atom bomb? We can't change. We are what we are."

"They may go away," I said.

"Yes, they may," Lieberman nodded. "But if they are without the curse of murder, they may also be without the curse of fear. They may be social in the highest sense. What does society do with a murderer?"

"There are societies that put him to death—and there are other societies that recognize his sickness and lock him away, where he can kill no more," Hopper said. "Of course, when a whole world is on trial, that's another matter. We have atom bombs now and other things, and we are reaching out to the stars—"

"I'm inclined to think that they'll run," Fitzgerald put in. "They may just have that curse of fear, Doctor."

"They may," Lieberman admitted. "I hope so."

But the more I think so, the more it seems to me that fear and hatred are the two sides of the same coin. I keep trying to think back, to recreate the moment when I saw it standing at the foot of my bed in the fishing shack. I keep trying to drag out of my memory a clear picture of what it looked like, whether behind that chitinous face and the two gently waving antennae there was any evidence of fear and anger. But the clearer the memory becomes, the more I seem to recall a certain wonderful dignity and repose. Not fear and not anger.

And more and more, as I go about my work, I get the feeling of what Hopper called "a world on trial." I have no sense of anger myself. Like a criminal who can no longer live with himself, I am content to be judged.

Howard Fast was born in 1914 in New York City. A high school drop-out, he published his first novel, *Two Valleys*, before his twentieth birthday and his most recent novel, *Greenwich*, in 2000. He is best known for his novels *Spartacus, Citizen Tom Paine,* and *The Last Frontier.* Along with his writing, Fast is known for his controversial membership in the Communist Party and for being awarded the Stalin Peace Prize.

I. *Response*
    a. What techniques does the author use to make an improbable situation seem believable? In your opinion, was he successful? Explain.
    b. In your opinion, is characterization an important element of this story? Why or why not?
    c. In your own words, summarize the philosophical perspective Howard Fast presents in "The Large Ant." What do you think his purpose was in writing the story, and why did he choose the science fiction genre to express his message?
    d. The characters in "The Large Ant" seem paralyzed by their dilemma. What course of action would *you* recommend to them?

2. *Critical Thinking* According to Fitzgerald, the government man, "'We can't change. We are what we are.'" Is humanity innately violent, and are we truly incapable of changing that? Discuss these issues in a small group.

3. *Focus on Context* Search for specific references, details, and behaviour in the story that imply that it took place many years ago. Make a list of the evidence you find and explain how it helps a reader identify the story's context. What reading and viewing skills do you rely on to help you identify the historical context for a particular literary or media work?

4. *Film Study* With a small group, brainstorm the titles for movies about encounters between humans and intelligent life from other planets. In these movies, what are some of the common human responses to alien life? Assess whether most of the movies support or refute Fast's message in "The Large Ant."

He was swimming for his life …

A Drowning

by Mark Ferguson

I watched him drown. The boat was far too close to the shore. There was engine trouble. I could see him working furiously trying to get it started. The seas were huge and the punt drifted in. All at once one swell broke, all round him, she went over, and I saw him leaping and thrown clear. Next I saw him there shocked in the water, but swimming evenly, fighting it, swimming away from the rocks, staying on top of the water, the white foam all over his darkly clad form like an otter in a brook. The next swell picked him up and swept in onto the low cliffs, onto the big black splintered rocks at their feet. Down he went a first time. I thought, I won't see him no more, but I was wrong. He came up a few yards shy of shore. I was shouting then. He was swimming mad out of there, swimming for his life, and another swell rolling in. It broke early, running down onto him like an avalanche for eighty or a hundred feet, a white wall tumbling and rushing forward to drown him. I saw him watching it come, paddling calmly out toward it and then I saw him duck under just as it struck where he had been. Smart, I was thinking, smart, but he was gone under a second time. I waited. The sea rose and boiled then sank away and back. The punt was already smashed, caught high up in the teeth of the land with tons and tons of water pouring back into the sea, off of the rocks and cliffs. The splintered wood of planks and torn brown strands of kelp in the blue-green.

He burst from below a second time, like a shot, his arm first, punching into air, swimming before he was even back on top of the water, swimming out to sea.

A third swell came then, larger than the others. I saw him see it. I saw him stop thrashing forward. I saw him turn sideways in the water, and look to the land, sizing up his chance. On it came. My arms jerked up—like a spasm and involuntary, waving for no reason really, a human impulse, a need to be recognized, to identify to him that I was there, even in the extraordinary circumstances. At all costs, waving only for him to notice me, to know that I was a witness. I did not speak, was not shouting, only my one big wave of both arms up over the head once. I left them up there, nothing but the helpless arms. I saw him then seeing me. He stared at me for one moment, held me in his eye, and there was no reproach, and no terror then, but something. Resignation maybe, like a tiredness, him knowing for an instant that I was something, a part of something back on land that he was really an incredibly long way off from. Never would he know it again. He was into something altogether different now. The connection between him and me, between his living breathing self and me, was pulled so thin and so taut in that moment, almost non-existent, not much longer now. No noise from him in the rueful moment, or maybe it was buried in the crashing seas and the jeering wind. And no noise from me, or maybe was I calling? And the speed was funny, the thing happening so slowly.

He went back to what he had been doing, what was really occupying him fully by then. He'd watch the third sea and then he'd watch the land, the sea, the land, and the sea seemed almost insane to me. Incredibly enough it seemed to keep on mounting, to keep growing, getting huge, getting heavy and dark—I know waves always do that when they come to the land—but this one time, this wave seemed ridiculous and wrong; it was breaking rules, the laws of waves or the rules had changed for that moment, and the fact that waves should rise up and break themselves onto the land seemed just then completely wrong, nothing only ugly and stupid. He looked so calm floating in the water, beautiful. As the beginning of the swell reached him, rising, I saw him treading calmly, now facing the land, his eyes fixed steadily on it. He must have chosen a spot he thought that he might just make, where he might just climb out of the wave and step magically back onto the land, soaked but safe. His whole thinking right then was determined by the concentration on that one wild hope. Then up he rose, and up he rose with the terrible sea. It rushed, it positively rushed on in then, gaining speed as it fell, and he had the whole crest to himself, that's how he rode in.

The world becomes utterly mute then, no sound, nothing, and I am the deafest one of them all, so utterly deaf it brings tears to my seeing eyes. That is how totally silent I remember it being. I see his face, his mouth open in a shout, half shock or surprise, half terror, his arms out meeting the crazy canted walls of rock, disappearing. I wonder can he still see his spot, can he still see that place he will land himself, step out of the sea? For how long does he think it will happen, for how long does he hold out, hold on to that one thought? Is it to the very last?

He was gone under for the third time, he disappeared completely then. He was out of sight and I never saw him then and he didn't come back up. How quiet was it? That total silence still when I turned away after a long time and he still hadn't resurfaced. I glanced back a few times, slowly climbing and clinging to the scrape and still no sign and a few times when I looked I thought, There. But when I looked a while it would just be a piece of wood or a this or a that. It stayed quiet like that for ages all the way back, and even when I got back, their voices at first were barely audible. They were talking but their voices were all really flat-sounding and seemed a long way off.

First person I met was John Mortimer waving from down a small pasture, feeding a horse out of a brin bag.[1] He shouts and I barely make him out. "Beautiful," he says, "Beautiful day." "Yes," I say. Because it was—it was still sunny and very breezy and dry and not too hot and it felt like it'd keep on like that another day or two for sure. All the women had their laundry and their fish out. I went home, told Dad and I stayed in the kitchen there with Mom and she got me some bread and jam and some tea and he went on to tell everyone else, to go and get a boat, try and find his body. The little cat had got in again, walking around the kitchen, meowing for supper. We ignored her for a long time till Mom said something offhand to her, and we had a little laugh, not paying attention then, and then Mrs. Abbott came in looking really very sad.

---

[1] **brin bag:** a sack made of burlap

Mark Ferguson lives in St. John's, Newfoundland and Labrador, and has been a member of The Burning Rock, a writer's collective, for a number of years. He is a short fiction writer whose work often has a St. John's or Placentia Bay setting.

1. *Response*
a. What is the impact of the opening line of the story?

b. What inferences about the narrator did you draw based on the information you were given? Compare your answers with those of a few other classmates. Why do you think the author gives so few details about the story's main characters?

c. What does the conclusion of the story suggest about the community in which the story takes place?

d. "A Drowning" explores one of the so-called "big questions": the question of mortality. In your journal or notebook, write a personal response to "A Drowning" and the message it conveys.

2. *Literature Studies* Plot
Would you agree with the suggestion that the climax of "A Drowning" seems to occur at the very beginning of the story? To answer the question, analyse the story's plot structure using a plot diagram. Compare your diagram with a partner's; did you reach the same conclusions? Once you have considered the plot as a whole, discuss whether Ferguson starts his story effectively. Be prepared to explain your ideas.

3. *Making Connections*
Use the Internet or other library resources to find the poem "Musée des Beaux Arts" by W. H. Auden and the painting "Fall of Icarus" by Pieter Breughel. What do these two works have in common with "A Drowning"? Present your ideas in the form of a brief written or oral report.

4. *Language Conventions* Verb Tense
At a decisive moment in the story, Ferguson switches the verb tense he is using. Identify where this occurs, explain how the verb tense changes, and create a convincing explanation for why the author might have used this technique. Does Ferguson continue with the new tense until the end of the story? Why or why not? Present your own opinion about the effectiveness of Ferguson's use of verb tense.

a form of a verb that relates it to time viewed as either as finite-past, present, or future

"I take my mother's hand in mine. Her hands are bony and crooked, her fingers rough and hard like wood."

Red Bean Ice

by Nancy Lee

I dress my daughter in a warm coat. November air has an angry bite. As I slip her knapsack onto her shoulders, we argue about a hat and scarf. I tell her to wear them; she says they are too itchy. We settle on the scarf. We are getting ready to visit my mother at the Chinese Centre. I call it the Centre because I cannot bear to call it the Home as everyone else does.

Two months ago, on a Saturday afternoon, my mother's stay in our home ended when a policeman presented her and my daughter at our front door. He had found them wandering around Chinatown; my mother, disoriented; my five-year-old, crying. The pockets of my daughter's coat were filled with candy. Her shoes were missing. I questioned my mother as to the whereabouts of the shoes. She shook her head and broke into an awkward smile. "What shoes?"

That night my husband and I fought. He had visited a care facility for my mother. I was furious that he had done so behind my back. He was pleased with himself: the green-eyed, blonde Canadian had found a good home for his Chinese mother-in-law. He had a colour brochure. They had medical staff; they spoke her language.

"I speak her language!" I shouted.

"She'll be with people her own age," he reasoned. "Maybe she already knows some of them."

"Just because we all look alike doesn't mean we know each other."

My daughter is straggling behind. I turn around and hold out my gloved hand.

"Come on."

She takes my hand but forces her weight onto it to slow us both down. "It's raining."

"I know it's raining. I told you to wear the hat." I pull my daughter along. Her feet stumble with reluctance.

"Why can't we go in the car?" Her knapsack has slipped down her arms, dangles in the crook of her elbow. She is hoping I will offer to carry it.

I resist the urge to baby her. "Because we're taking the bus."

"But why?" She swings her arm; the knapsack jerks and snaps between us.

"Because, it's fun."

It is a rainy Saturday morning. I am seven years old. My mother and I ride the number twenty-two bus to Chinatown.

My mother speaks to me quietly; her melodic Cantonese floats lightly between us. She does not look at me and I do not look at her. Instead, we watch the scenery drift by. Her counsel, an immigrant voice-over for the moving city at the window.

Kensington Community Centre. "Homework is very important. Smart girls study hard. Education is the most important thing."

The curve in the road as it changes from Knight Street to Clark Drive just before 12th Avenue. "You must be a good person in your heart. Even when bad things happen."

The turn onto Venables Street, where a bed warehouse is advertised by a dancing mattress with hands and feet. "Sometimes it is good to laugh, not be so serious about things."

The sharp right turn into Chinatown, the street signs in both English and Chinese. "It is very important to respect your elders. Be a good person." My mother whispers this last sentiment as if it is a secret not to be shared with the rest of the bus.

The first few houses at the entrance to Chinatown are frighteningly old and filthy. Most of them have porches on the verge of collapse and make-shift curtains torn from flags or bed sheets. Layers of paint peel, wooden boards hang, and on the porch sit battered pieces of indoor furniture; a rotting recliner, a festering love seat. My mother shakes her head and clicks her tongue in disgust. It shames her that the Chinese district is an area rimmed with drunks and vagrants.

After the houses, come the shops which stretch from one end of Chinatown to the other; grocery stores with dry goods piled onto their shelves and cardboard boxes of fresh produce spilling onto the sidewalk. I pull the string to ring the bell and my mother and I get off the bus.

We hold hands as we walk past the loud grocers. A Chinese man with a knife stands on the sidewalk and yells at my mother as we pass by. "Oranges on special today! Very sweet!" He offers my mother a single slice of orange on a large sharp blade. My mother nods; the fruit is sweet. My mother sifts through the oranges in the cardboard box.

"That one is sweet, but what about these?"

The man chuckles and cuts her a fresh orange from the box. My mother hands the slice to me.

"Sweet?"

I nod and chew the slice while my mother stuffs oranges into a plastic bag.

At the fish mongers, I watch lobsters and crabs in the giant tanks. Claws snapping, bodies climbing in slow motion. The old and damaged trapped in the bottom corners of the tank. My mother pokes the slimy silver bodies laid out on mounds of crushed ice. "Very fresh! Very fresh!" the man in the white coat shouts as he waves his knife at my mother.

"Too many bones," my mother says tersely. The man scans the fish, as if with x-ray vision, searches for one with fewer bones. Then he nods dramatically and pulls one from the pile, holds it up for my mother's inspection. My mother stares at the fish, and like the man, uses her magic Chinese sight to count the bones. She nods and tells him to leave the head on.

At the meat market, flattened ducks twirl in the window, Chinese sausages hang like thick beaded curtains. The smell is sweet, like soya sauce and honey.

"A pound of barbecued pork," my mother orders. The man with the cleaver reaches for a piece of meat, but my mother stops him. "Leaner," she says. The man nods and chooses another piece. I smile proudly at my mother's ability to choose what is best, feel sorry for those families whose mothers don't have the wisdom to say, "Leaner."

Our last stop before going home is the bakery. Arms stretched with bags of groceries, my mother and I sit down for a snack and a cup of tea. There are many bakeries in Chinatown and we try a different one each week. They are all similar, crowded, noisy with sugar-soaked air, and a wall-size selection of cakes and buns. We slide into a booth and my mother orders a curry puff and two cups of tea. I ask for the sponge cake that is shaped in a cone of wax paper. I like to peel back the paper and stroke the bubbly soft inside of the cake.

When our food arrives, I ask my mother, "Did you like curry puffs when you were a little girl?"

"No, when I lived in China, it was on a farm. We did not have cakes. But when I went to Hong Kong, then I liked red bean ice." My mother points to the tent card menu on our table. There is a photo of a parfait glass filled with red bean soup poured over crushed ice and topped with vanilla ice cream.

"In Hong Kong, your father and I were very poor. So, when we went out, your father would order a red bean ice for me and he would drink lemon-flavoured water. Your father is a good man."

After finishing her curry puff, my mother goes to the counter and orders a box of Chinese pastries to take home. She will pack them in my father's lunch.

My daughter cannot sit still on the bus. She crawls back and forth over my lap, interrogates the people around us.

"We have a car, you know. Do you have a car? What's your name?"

She rings the bell twice before our stop. The bus driver glares at me in the rear view mirror.

On the street, I hurry my daughter along. Shuffle her past the slouching addicts, the day-time prostitutes. She ignores my warnings and says hello to a freckled girl in a rabbit fur jacket. The girl waves.

We squeeze through the heavy glass door of the Chinese Centre. On my right hand, my daughter; my left hand balances my purse, her knapsack and her scarf. She runs ahead, then stops and waits for me at my mother's door.

I am struck by the smell as we enter my mother's room. An antiseptic odor tinged with sweetness, as if cleaning products have missed something ripe and sticky under the bed. When I first visited the Centre, I noticed the smell in the rooms of the other patients. I was sure my mother's room would smell different, light, flowery, like our home. I brought in plants and freshening sprays, but the plants disappeared every week and the sprays evaporated.

My daughter cups a hand over her nose and looks up at me with a crinkled grimace. She grips my fingers tight with her other hand as we approach my mother.

I sit in an orange plastic chair beside the bed and set our bags on the floor; my daughter climbs onto my lap. I take my mother's hand in mine. Her hands are bony and crooked, her fingers rough and hard like wood. They make me think of the wicked witches I read about in grade school, with their gnarled, restraining claws.

We speak in Cantonese. I ask my mother how she is. She says that she is fine, but her bones have been aching. My daughter leans back against my chest and clutches my free hand; she is afraid my mother will want to touch her. I tell my daughter to say hello to her grandma, I have taught her to say it in Cantonese, but she remains silent. My mother smiles at my daughter.

"Remember me?" my mother asks.

My daughter squints to understand the unfamiliar language. My mother's hand rises slowly off the bed and floats towards my daughter's face like a hypnotized wooden snake. My daughter presses herself against me as hard as she can, holds her body in complete stillness as my mother strokes her cheek.

"Beautiful girl," my mother whispers. "So beautiful."

My daughter tries to turn her face away from my mother's touch. My mother laughs.

"So shy," she says.

An attendant enters to tidy my mother's room. My mother calls her over.

"Have you met my family?" my mother asks.

"Every time they visit," the attendant jokes.

"She's not very bright," my mother whispers to me.

"Come," my mother says to the attendant, "let me introduce you."

The attendant comes to the bed. We smile apologies at each other.

"This is my daughter," my mother says, taking my daughter's small hand. I watch the soft white skin disappear into my mother's blotchy paw. My daughter is so still; I wonder if she has stopped breathing.

The attendant teases my mother.

"Isn't she a bit young to be your daughter?"

My mother stares at the attendant as if she had just said something very rude.

"Who," the attendant tries again as she points to me, "is this?"

"This is my sister. She came by boat from China to look after my daughter while I am in the hospital."

My mother thinks we are back in Hong Kong. The attendant leaves quietly. I take my mother's hand off my daughter's and hold it in my own.

"Mother, I am your daughter. This is my daughter, your grand-daughter."

My mother smiles and nods her head. I can not tell if she knows she has made a mistake, or if she thinks I have made one, or if she thinks I am playing a joke on her.

There is silence until I speak again. "Are you getting enough to eat?"

My mother gives me a puzzled look, then smiles. I wait for her answer, but she stares at me as if she is waiting for me to speak.

"Mother—"

"You know what they don't have here?"

"What?" I ask with some relief.

> Why do writers write? Because it isn't there.
>
> Thomas Berger

"Red bean ice." She smiles a broad smile. "Red bean ice," she says again as she reaches out a wooden finger to tickle my daughter. "Red bean ice."

My daughter tries to sit still, but my mother's finger makes her squirm and giggle.

"Red bean ice."

My daughter cackles and leans forward to try and tickle my mother.

"Red bean ice!" My daughter shouts, though the Chinese words are just sounds to her. "Red bean ice!"

My mother laughs. "Smart girl, smart girl." Her hand pats my daughter's knee.

There is a long silence as my mother smiles at my daughter and my daughter watches my mother's hand on her knee.

My daughter pulls my sleeve. "The book," she whispers. "Get the book."

I dig through her knapsack and find the book she has brought to read to her grandma.

My mother pats the edge of the bed and my daughter climbs up next to her. I note with envy that my daughter's body is still small and can easily fit into small places.

She holds the book halfway between herself and my mother, so my mother can look at the illustrations. She reads a line then points to the corresponding picture. My mother hasn't spoken English for over a year, but she nods on cue each time my daughter looks up at her. My mother strokes my daughter's hair and hums softly. My daughter leans into her and my mother rests her cheek on the top of my daughter's head. My daughter's lips move less and less with each turned page, her eyes close against her will as she trails her small finger under each line of words.

My mother lies back, eyes closed, soothing my daughter into sleep, patting her small thigh in a gentle rhythm. She holds my daughter against her and sings an old Cantonese lullaby. Her thin voice, a sweet, delicate melody.

I curl in my chair. What is this song? What is she remembering? The song that played the night she met my father and removed her new shoes under the table to be respectably shorter than him when she stood? The folk songs my father sang to his pregnant wife to keep her warm as they crossed the muddy choppiness of the Yangtze river on a cargo boat?

Often, my mother forgets she and my father had a child. I am used to being called a nurse or doctor, her best friend. I am not used to the darkness in her eyes when she thinks I am a stranger.

The afternoon light has grown dim with rain clouds. My mother and daughter are a silhouette against the window. They are caught in fairy tale sleep, deep and motionless; I almost believe nothing will wake them. But it is time for us to leave.

I lean forward in my chair, slip my hand under my mother's hand, lift it from my daughter's thigh. I hold my mother's hand in mine, this time feeling its true weight: bones, skin, old muscle. I raise her hand to my cheek and kiss the papery skin of her palm. I climb out of my chair and kneel down on the floor beside her bed. I lay my head on the mattress and press my mother's hand against my face.

I am remembering a rainy day, a crowded bus, my small body stretched across the seat. My head nestled in my mother's lap, her smooth hand stroking my face. The lulling hum of the bus engine. It is a long journey home.

Lunchtime by Gu Xiong. Woodcut

Where is the focal point of this work—to what part of the illustration are your eyes drawn? How does the artist create this focal point? Consider elements such as composition, line, shape, white space, and content.

Nancy Lee, author of poetry and fiction, has won awards for her writing. She works at the SFU Writing and Publishing program as an instructor and is currently writing a collection of short stories called *Dead Girls*.

I. *Response*

a. The plot of "Red Bean Ice" is divided into sections. Create a diagram that visually represents the way the plot is structured. In what way does the plot structure support one of the main ideas in the story?

b. Describe the narrator's behaviour in each section of the story. What inferences can you make about the narrator's character based on this analysis? Do you think the visit to the Chinese Centre was a good idea? Explain.

c. The narrator's husband appears briefly in the story. What is revealed through his presence?

d. Describe your personal reaction to the final section of the story. What mood or moods was the author trying to establish? Did you like the way the story ended and, in your view, was the conclusion effective? Give reasons for your answer.

2. *Literature Studies* *Proverbs* Nancy Lee includes a number of **proverbs** in the flashback segment of the story. Make a list of these proverbs and speculate on the functions they serve within the story. In a small group, brainstorm other proverbs with which you are familiar. Choose one or two of the proverbs that you think express valuable life lessons. Next, create a proverb of your own that captures one of the themes of "Red Bean Ice." Present the results of your discussion to the class.

A **proverb** is a short saying that expresses a basic truth or useful principle.

3. *Writing* *Memoir* Take this opportunity to portray, in writing, a special memory from your own life. Use vivid, descriptive language to capture the details of your experience, and include personal reflections that explain why that particular memory is significant to you. You can choose to share this piece of writing or keep it private.

Red Bean Ice • 171

4. ***Making Connections*** "Red Bean Ice" and "A Drowning" both focus on important questions that arise when life is ending. In a brief essay, explore how the two works are similar and different in terms of the situations and themes they present.

Fiction keeps its audience by retaining
the world as its subject matter. People like
the world. Many people actually prefer it to art
and spend their days by choice in the thick of it.

—Annie Dillard

Theme Connections

- *"Groom Service," a story about mother/child relationships, page 12*
- *"A Drowning," a story about the end of a life, page 160*
- *"The Circle Game," a song about the inevitability of the passing of time, page 180*
- *"Do Not Go Gentle Into That Good Night," a poem that dares one to defy death, page 209*
- *"The Five Stages of Grief," a poem detailing the grieving process, page 215*

Poetry

The essentials of poetry are rhythm,
dance, and the human voice.

Earle Birney

If a Poem Could Walk

It would have paws, not feet,
four of them
to sink into the moss
when humans blunder up the path.

Or hooves, small ones,
leaving half-moons in the sand.
Something to make you stop
                 and wonder
what kind of animal this is,
10   where it came from, where it's going.

It draws nearest when you are most alone.
You lay red plums on your blanket,
a glass of cool cider, two sugar cubes,

knowing it is tame and wild—
the perfect animal—
knowing it will stop for nothing
as it walks
             with its four new legs
right off the page

A poem can be many things/in miniature:
a short story/about people
a photograph/a surreal landscape
and perhaps an instant of ecstacy?
                —Dorothy Livesay

A poem should be equal to:
Not true.
           —Archibald MacLeish

Previous page:
Moon Dream, August by Tim Greyhavens. Iris print on canvas

The Carousel of Time

Life is like a carousel, forever turning and repeating its cycles. In the midst of growth and change, the poet finds opportunities for insight, foresight, and reflection.

I Grew Up

by Lenore Keeshig-Tobias

I

i grew up on the reserve
thinking it was the most
beautiful place in the world

i grew up thinking
i'm never going
to leave this place

i was a child
a child who would
lie under trees

watching wind's rhythms
sway leafy boughs
back and forth

back and forth
sweeping it seemed
the clouds into great piles

and rocking me as
i snuggled in the grass
like a bug basking in the sun

II

i grew up on the reserve
thinking it was the most
beautiful place in the world

i grew up thinking
i'm never going
to leave this place

i was a child
a child who ran
wild rhythms

through the fields
the streams
the bush

eating berries
cupping cool water
to my wild stained mouth

and hiding in the
treetops with
my friends

III

we used to laugh at teachers and
tourists who referred to
our bush as *forests* or *woods*

40 *forests* and *woods*
were places of
fairy-tale text

were places where people,
especially children, got lost
where wild beasts roamed

our bush was where we played
and where the rabbits squirrels
foxes deer and the bear lived

i grew up thinking
i'm never going   50
to leave this place

i grew up on the reserve
thinking it was the most
beautiful place in the world

Boys Playing Football by Allen Sapp. Acrylic on canvas

What specific techniques has the artist used to impart a sense of
movement and energy into his painting? What impression do you
think he is trying to convey about the game and the setting in
which it is taking place?

After the Wedding

by Marisa Anlin Alps

The first time I realized I was Chinese
I was seventeen, travelled east
to Toronto to celebrate my cousin's
marriage, the sole relation
from my branch of the family tree.
I'd never seen so many of my relatives
in one place, their unknown
faces swirling before me
and everyone there was Chinese.

10   Suddenly it hit me and I knew
I was too (or at least half)
a surprise since I've been everything else
for so long.

My mother says she feels more Canadian
than anything else, but perhaps we moved
to the island pockets of the west
coast to emulate her island childhood, a hint
of possibility in the Caribbean accents
slipping so easily around me, a little
20   like those split leaf plants
my grandmother smuggled into Trinidad,
the ones that grew, flourished
took over a whole corner of her lovely
garden and yet, I felt white
for the first time in my life, different
still from everyone around me, especially
during dim sum in Toronto's Chinatown
an intense experience with tripe and
chicken feet and the wonder
30   of what was not said.

dim sum: Chinese dumplings and other small delicacies

After the wedding, long and noisy tables
filled the banquet hall like sunflowers
pushing toward the centre of the dance
floor, couples whirling around the chairs.
My cousin asked me to dance but I was shy,
eyes downcast. *How did he see me?*

The flowers scented the air like wine,
voices like music, while others
flew I sat there on the edge, wonder pouring
40   from me, distant from the centre
I did not feel much, but I thought
I am Chinese
horizons shrinking
and changing before my eyes
a second wedding taking place
within me, two
inheritances exchanging vows.

Brian at Eighteen

by Rick Hillis

Brian, 18, spins
the basketball on the axis
of a finger

controls the angle of its revolution
(the crowd gasps)

This is his world
He dribbles it to the top of the key
It throbs the floor by his boot running shoe

      & he shields it with his body
10   which is thin in a way
time will make it forget

His bright red uniform sways like a sail
on his bones

in this vacuum of many held breaths

                  .   .   .

Brian, tired hero of morning
studies his hemisphere on a school library map
until he dreams
his footprints into Mexican sand

His thin body hunches over the world
20 His pencil arcs correctly calculating distance
not time

.   .   .

Brian wears gym shorts
spins the perfect leather world
on the axis of his finger

The bleachers are empty now
the gym hollow

It is June &

Brian feints
drives left, leaps, lets go

30 Ball arcing beneath dimmed lights
across lines & lines until it hits home

circles the rim around

In mid air Brian holds
this pose:

fingers of his right hand flung forward

of his left shielding his eyes
as if fending off a blow

or studying the lines
of his own palm

1. Response

a. Which of the three poems ("I Grew Up," "After the Wedding," or "Brian at Eighteen") were you best able to identify or connect with? Why?

b. Speculate on the purpose Lenore Keeshig-Tobias may have had in mind when she wrote "I Grew Up." Do you think the poem is autobiographical? Why or why not?

c. What interpretation would you offer for the last five lines of "After the Wedding"? Explain your interpretation and your reasoning to a partner.

d. Why do you think Rick Hillis chose to write "Brian at Eighteen"? Why do you think Hillis focusses on these particular moments in Brian's life? Who do you think Brian is?

2. Making Connections

In a group, compile a list of similarities and differences between "I Grew Up" and "After the Wedding." Consider poetic form and technique, and the possible purpose of the poets, as well as the ideas, feelings, and experiences described.

The Circle Game

by Joni Mitchell

Yesterday a child came out to wonder
Caught a dragonfly inside a jar
Fearful when the sky was full of thunder
And tearful at the falling of a star

Then the child moved ten times round the seasons
Skated over ten clear frozen streams
Words like when you're older must appease him
And promises of someday make his dreams

And the seasons they go round and round
10 And the painted ponies go up and down
We're captive on the carousel of time
We can't return we can only look
Behind from where we came
And go round and round and round
In the circle game

Sixteen springs and sixteen summers gone now
Cartwheels turn to car wheels thru the town
And they tell him take your time it won't be long now
Till you drag your feet to slow the circles down

20 And the seasons they go round and round
And the painted ponies go up and down
We're captive on the carousel of time
We can't return we can only look
Behind from where we came
And go round and round and round
In the circle game

So the years spin by and now the boy is twenty
Though his dreams have lost some grandeur coming true
There'll be new dreams maybe better dreams and plenty
30 Before the last revolving year is through

And the seasons they go round and round
And the painted ponies go up and down
We're captive on the carousel of time
We can't return we can only look
Behind from where we came
And go round and round and round
In the circle game

> Poetry is boned with ideas, nerved and blooded
> with emotions, all held together by the delicate,
> tough skin of words.
> —*Paul Engle*

Pride

by Marilyn Cay

he challenges his father
to arm wrestle
and the two ready themselves
at the kitchen table
this time
there is something about the son's calmness
that makes the father insist upon a fair start
his arm tense
the father breaks with speed
10   in order to put his son's arm down soundly

but he meets with iron this time
the two arms tremble, straight up and down
muscles bulging
hands gripping tightly

afterwards the mother says
the father was the big winner
even though it is her son
whose strength prevailed

1. **Response**
   a. Do you think the song "The Circle Game" expresses an optimistic or pessimistic outlook on life? Explain.
   b. In "Pride," the mother says, "the father was the big winner." What do you think she means by this comment?
   c. Reflect on your own life and identify one event that you feel represents an important moment in your growth toward independence. In a piece of personal writing, describe the event and explain what it means to you.

2. **Literature Studies** Understatement "Pride" is notable for its understatement. What details or events did the poet choose not to reveal, and how does this contribute to the understatement? In general, why is understatement an effective writing technique?

(More might be said
for fantasizing about space travel
or maybe about being a mermaid.)

I still hope (two months before my fifty-third birthday)
that I may yet meet that handsome stranger
all the fortunetellers have told me about;
that sometime my lottery ticket
30   will win a tax-free fortune,
and that my poems become household words
and make the next edition of Colombo's *Quotations.*

Colombo's Quotations: a reference work containing quotations by notable Canadians, edited by John Robert Colombo

I might as well believe in heaven, too,
for all the good it will do me to admit
statistics are against it.

1. **Response**
   a. "Silent, but …" and "There's Silence Between One Page and Another" express different perspectives on the meaning of silence. Which poem do you prefer? Explain.
   b. In your own words, summarize what "On the Value of Fantasies" says about dreams and fantasies. Do you agree with this message? Why or why not?
   c. In a group, create a brief oral presentation that shows how each of the four preceding poems has something to say about the theme of personal potential.

2. **Writing** *Letter* Write a letter to the teacher described in "On the Value of Fantasies," in which you comment on her point of view. To complete this task, you will need to assume a specific voice. For example, you may choose to pretend you are one of her students or an adult who heard the radio program.

3. **Visual Communication** *Illustration* Create an illustration that captures the visual imagery contained in "There's Silence Between One Page and Another." Present your work and explain how it is true to the poem.

The Swimmer's Moment

by Margaret Avison

For everyone
The swimmer's moment at the whirlpool comes,
But many at that moment will not say
"This is the whirlpool, then."
By their refusal they are saved
From the black pit, and also from contesting
The deadly rapids, and emerging in
The mysterious, and more ample, further waters.
And so their bland-blank faces turn and turn
10 Pale and forever on the rim of suction
They will not recognize.
Of those who dare the knowledge
Many are whirled into the ominous centre
That, gaping vertical, seals up
For them an eternal boon of privacy,
So that we turn away from their defeat
With a despair, not from their deaths, but for
Ourselves, who cannot penetrate their secret
Nor even guess at the anonymous breadth
20 Where one or two have won:
(The silver reaches of the estuary).

Symposium

by Paul Muldoon

You can lead a horse to water but you can't make it hold
its nose to the grindstone and hunt with the hounds.
Every dog has a stitch in time. Two heads? You've been sold
one good turn. One good turn deserves a bird in the hand.

A bird in the hand is better than no bread.
To have your cake is to pay Paul.
Make hay while you can still hit the nail on the head.
For want of a nail the sky might fall.

People in glass houses can't see the wood
10   for the new broom. Rome wasn't built between two stools.
Empty vessels wait for no man.

A hair of the dog is a friend indeed.
There's no fool like the fool
who's shot his bolt. There's no smoke after the horse is gone.

1. Response

a. "Symposium" is constructed of many different proverbs that have been patched together. Identify and complete as many of the proverbs as you can. In small groups, discuss the meaning of the proverbs and the poem.

b. Is "Symposium" a sonnet? Give reasons for your answer.

c. Compose two or three questions that, if answered, would help you better understand the meaning of "The Swimmer's Moment." In a group, try to answer one another's questions. Present your conclusions to the class.

2. Language Focus *Proverbs*

Using Internet or library resources, find proverbs from a variety of cultures; then write your own poem similar in style to "Symposium." As you select your proverbs, consider the message you wish your poem to convey. Be prepared to share the original completed proverbs. What do you think accounts for the continuing popularity of proverbs?

3. Oral Language *Choral Reading*

In a small group, prepare an expressive choral reading of either "Symposium" or "The Swimmer's Moment." Your reading should capture the mood of the poem, and be expressive and entertaining. Present your reading to the class.

A poet is someone who is astonished by everything.
—*Anonymous*

The Layers

by Stanley Kunitz

I have walked through many lives,
some of them my own,
and I am not who I was,
though some principle of being
abides, from which I struggle
not to stray.
When I look behind,
as I am compelled to look
before I can gather strength
10 to proceed on my journey,
I see the milestones dwindling
toward the horizon
and the slow fires trailing
from the abandoned camp-sites,
over which scavenger angels
wheel on heavy wings.
Oh, I have made myself a tribe
out of my true affections,
and my tribe is scattered!
20 How shall the heart be reconciled
to its feast of losses?
In a rising wind
the manic dust of my friends,
those who fell along the way,
bitterly stings my face.
Yet I turn, I turn,
exulting somewhat,
with my will intact to go
wherever I need to go,
30 and every stone on the road
precious to me.
In my darkest night,
when the moon was covered
and I roamed through wreckage,
a nimbus-clouded voice
directed me:

"Live in the layers,
not on the litter."
Though I lack the art
40   to decipher it,
no doubt the next chapter
in my book of transformations
is already written.
I am not done with my changes.

Young Soul

by Amiri Baraka (LeRoi Jones)

First, feel, then feel, then
read, or read, then feel, then
fall, or stand, where you
already are. Think
of your self, and the other
selves ... think
of your parents, your mothers
and sisters, your bentslick
father, then feel, or
10   fall, on your knees
if nothing else will move you,

then read
and look deeply
into all matters
come close to you
city boys—
country men

Make some muscle
in your head, but
20   use the muscle
in yr heart

1. Response

  a. "The Layers" contains a number of unusual images. Choose any three such images and discuss what ideas and feelings they convey to you.

  b. Examine "Young Soul," noting the way the words are placed on the page. Suggest possible reasons for the unconventional arrangement (remembering that there are no absolutely right or wrong answers).

  c. What does the word *bentslick* (from "Young Soul") suggest to you? Discuss a possible meaning for this invented word.

2. Literature Studies *Interpretation* In groups, discuss possible interpretations of these key lines: "Live in the layers,/not on the litter" ("The Layers") and "Make some muscle/in your head, but/use the muscle/in yr heart" ("Young Soul"). It is not your task to convince others of your point of view. Simply share your interpretation and listen carefully to the interpretations of others. Do you think listening to multiple interpretations is a helpful or distracting approach to understanding poems?

> Poetry is important. No less than science,
> it seeks a hold upon reality, and the closeness of its
> approach is the test of its success.
>
> —*Babette Deutsch*

Theme Connections

for all of the poems in the cluster "The Carousel of Time"
- *"On the Rainy River," a story about making decisions, page 70*
- *"The Spaces Between Stars," a story about determining one's personal identity, page 100*
- *"A New Perspective," an essay about growing up with an unwell parent, page 289*
- *"My Old Newcastle," a memoir about growing up in a particular place, page 296*
- *"Venus Sucked In," a radio play in which parental and other relationships play an important role, page 468*

Since Feeling Is First

More than any other literary form, poetry is used for the expression of powerful feelings. The poems that follow explore the complexities of love, passion, and devotion.

Since Feeling Is First

by E. E. Cummings

since feeling is first
who pays any attention
to the syntax of things
will never wholly kiss you;

wholly to be a fool
while Spring is in the world

my blood approves,
and kisses are a better fate
than wisdom
10   lady i swear by all flowers. Don't cry
—the best gesture of my brain is less than
your eyelids' flutter which says

we are for each other:then
laugh,leaning back in my arms
for life's not a paragraph

and death i think is no parenthesis

Love Is Not All

by Edna St. Vincent Millay

Love is not all: it is not meat nor drink
Nor slumber nor a roof against the rain;
Nor yet a floating spar to men that sink
And rise and sink and rise and sink again;
Love can not fill the thickened lung with breath,
Nor clean the blood, nor set the fractured bone;
Yet many a man is making friends with death
Even as I speak, for lack of love alone.
It well may be that in a difficult hour,
10   Pinned down by pain and moaning for release,
Or nagged by want past resolution's power,
I might be driven to sell your love for peace,
Or trade the memory of this night for food.
It well may be. I do not think I would.

Sonnet CXVI

by William Shakespeare

Let me not to the marriage of true minds
Admit impediments. Love is not love
Which alters when it alteration finds,
Or bends with the remover to remove:—
O no! It is an ever-fixèd mark   **mark:** beacon
That looks on tempests, and is never shaken;
It is the star to every wandering bark,   **wandering bark:**
Whose worth's unknown, although his height be taken.   lost ship

Love's not Time's fool, though rosy lips and cheeks
10   Within his bending sickle's compass come;   **compass:** range
Love alters not with his brief hours and weeks,
But bears it out ev'n to the edge of doom.
If this be error and upon me proved,
I never writ, nor no man ever loved.

Romeo and Juliet by Ford Madox Brown. Oil on canvas

In a group, discuss the archetypes, clichés, and/or stereotypes contained within this visual interpretation of the famous balcony scene from Shakespeare's *Romeo and Juliet*. How does this work compare with Lichtenstein's *Drowning Girl* (p. 201)?

1. Response

  a. What ideas or sentiments about love are suggested in Cummings' poem "Since Feeling Is First"? How do you feel about these ideas?

  b. Shakespeare's "Sonnet CXVI" is a popular choice as a reading at wedding ceremonies. Generate at least three reasons why you think this poem has attained this distinction.

  c. Do you think "Love Is Not All" is contradictory in its view of love? Explain.

2. Literature Studies *Comparison* Use a T-chart or other graphic organizer to show the similarities and differences between "Sonnet CXVI" and "Love Is Not All."

3. Writing *Imitation* Rewrite "Love Is Not All," using images and details from your own experience. You may choose to maintain the serious tone or create a humorous parody instead. Maintain the sonnet rhyme scheme and rhythm.

I Wish to Paint My Eyes

Anonymous Egyptian hieroglyphic text (circa 1500 B.C.E.)
Translated by Willis Barnstone

I wish to paint my eyes,
so if I see you, my eyes will glisten.
When I approach you and see your love,
you are richest in my heart.
How pleasant this hour is!
May it extend for me to eternity.

Meeting at Night

by Robert Browning

The grey sea and the long black land;
And the yellow half-moon large and low;
And the startled little waves that leap
In fiery ringlets from their sleep,
As I gain the cove with pushing prow,
And quench its speed i' the slushy sand.

Then a mile of warm sea-scented beach;
Three fields to cross till a farm appears;
A tap at the pane, the quick sharp scratch
10   And blue spurt of a lighted match,
And a voice less loud, thro' its joys and fears,
Than the two hearts beating each to each!

Sonnet XIV (If Thou Must Love Me)

by Elizabeth Barrett Browning

If thou must love me, let it be for nought
Except for love's sake only. Do not say,
"I love her for her smile—her look—her way
Of speaking gently—for a trick of thought
That falls in well with mine, and certes brought   **certes:** surely, certainly
A sense of pleasant ease on such a day."
For these things in themselves, Beloved, may
Be changed, or change for thee—and love, so wrought,
May be unwrought so. Neither love me for
10   Thine own dear pity's wiping my cheeks dry—
A creature might forget to weep, who bore
Thy comfort long, and lose thy love thereby!
But love me for love's sake, that evermore
Thou may'st love on, through love's eternity.

1. Response

   a. "I Wish to Paint My Eyes" was written almost 3500 years ago. In what ways are the sentiments expressed in this poem modern? What assumptions did you make about the speaker, and why?

   b. Every line of "Meeting at Night" contains imagery. Classify each of the images according to the sense(s) it appeals to.

   c. "Sonnet XIV" contains a logical argument. Summarize the argument in a few brief sentences.

2. Research and Inquiry Robert Browning and Elizabeth Barrett Browning were famous as poets and as a couple. Using online or print resources, compile a list of ten important and interesting facts for each of the Brownings. Do you think the details of their relationship affected the way their poetry was and continues to be regarded? Explain.

3. Critical Thinking Many of the poems in this section ("Since Feeling Is First") emphasize the idea that love is or should be eternal. Do you think this idea continues to be important in today's society? Express your answer in the form of a brief opinion piece or as a poem.

Poetry asks people to have values, form opinions, care about some other part of experience besides making money and being successful on the job.
—*Toi Derricotte*

The Passionate Shepherd to His Love

by Christopher Marlowe

Come live with me and be my Love,
And we will all the pleasures prove
That hills and valleys, dale and field,
And all the craggy mountains yield.

There will we sit upon the rocks
And see the shepherds feed their flocks,
By shallow rivers, to whose falls
Melodious birds sing madrigals.

madrigals: love songs

There will I make thee beds of roses
10   And a thousand fragrant posies,
A cap of flowers, and a kirtle
Embroidered all with leaves of myrtle.

kirtle: a dress or skirt

A gown made of the finest wool,
Which from our pretty lambs we pull,
Fair linèd slippers for the cold,
With buckles of the purest gold.

A belt of straw and ivy buds
With coral clasps and amber studs:
And if these pleasures may thee move,
20   Come live with me and be my Love.

Thy silver dishes for thy meat
As precious as the gods do eat,
Shall on an ivory table be
Prepared each day for thee and me.

The shepherd swains shall dance and sing
For thy delight each May-morning:
If these delights thy mind may move,
Then live with me and be my Love.

swains: lads

The Nymph's Reply to the Shepherd

by Sir Walter Raleigh

If all the world and love were young,
And truth in every shepherd's tongue,
These pretty pleasures might me move,
To live with thee and be thy love.

Time drives the flocks from field to fold,
When rivers rage, and rocks grow cold;
And Philomel becometh dumb;
The rest complains of cares to come.

The flowers do fade, and wanton fields
10   To wayward winter reckoning yields;
A honey tongue, a heart of gall,
Is fancy's spring, but sorrow's fall.

Thy gowns, thy shoes, thy beds of roses,
Thy cap, thy kirtle, and thy posies,
Soon break, soon wither, soon forgotten;
In folly ripe, in reason rotten.

Thy belt of straw and ivy buds,
Thy coral clasps and amber studs,
All these in me no means can move,
20   To come to thee and be thy love.

But could youth last, and love still breed,
Had joys no date, nor age no need,
Then these delights my mind might move
To live with thee and be thy love.

fold: a fenced enclosure

Philomel: the nightingale

1. *Response*
Discuss both Marlowe's "The Passionate Shepherd to His Love" and Raleigh's "The Nymph's Reply to the Shepherd," and their contrasting views of love.

2. *Literature Studies* Persona
What **persona** does Sir Walter Raleigh use in his reply to "The Passionate Shepherd to His Love"? In "The Nymph's Reply to the Shepherd," it is easy to distinguish between the poet and the speaker of the poem. Find a poem in this unit in which it is not clear whether the speaker is a persona or the poet him or herself. Why do you think it is an accepted critical practice to assume that the voice of the speaker of a poem is *not* necessarily the poet's own voice?

The **persona** is the voice or character that represents the narrator in a literary work. A persona is often described as a mask an author deliberately puts on in order to narrate a particular story or poem.

3. *Drama* Dialogue
In a group, prepare and present a dramatic reading of the two poems. In your reading, consider the poems as two sides of a single dialogue. You might use music, lighting, movement, and/or costume to enhance your work. Present your reading either as a live or videotaped performance.

4. *Focus on Context*
In *pastoral verse,* such as the two poems above, urban poets idealized life in the country, depicting happy shepherds playing music underneath the trees and pledging their undying love. Discuss this concept and these two examples.

Identify two or three areas of life that people tend to idealize today. How are these ideals expressed in our culture, and in what ways are they realistic or unrealistic?

Poetry is a matter of life,
not just a matter of language.
—*Lucille Clifton*

Variations on the Word Love

by Margaret Atwood

This is a word we use to plug
holes with. It's the right size for those warm
blanks in speech, for those red heart-
shaped vacancies on the page that look nothing
like real hearts. Add lace
and you can sell
it. We insert it also in the one empty
space on the printed form
that comes with no instructions. There are whole
10   magazines with not much in them
but the word *love*, you can
rub it all over your body and you
can cook with it too. How do we know
it isn't what goes on at the cool
debaucheries of slugs under damp
pieces of cardboard? As for the weed-
seedlings nosing their tough snouts up
among the lettuces, they shout it.
Love! Love! sing the soldiers, raising
20   their glittering knives in salute.
Then there's the two
of us. This word
is far too short for us, it has only
four letters, too sparse
to fill those deep bare
vacuums between the stars
that press on us with their deafness.
It's not love we don't wish
to fall into, but that fear.
30   This word is not enough, but it will
have to do. It's a single
vowel in this metallic
silence, a mouth that says
O again and again in wonder
and pain, a breath, a finger-
grip on a cliffside. You can
hold on or let go.

Drowning Girl by Roy Lichtenstein.

In your view, what is the tone of this work? Refer to the style of both the painting and the text in the speech balloon in your answer. Given that this work is considered Pop Art, what might some characteristics of the Pop Art style be? Do some research to confirm whether your suggestions are correct.

First Person Demonstrative

by Phyllis Gotlieb

I'd rather
heave half a brick than say
I love you, though I do
I'd rather
crawl in a hole than call you
darling, though you are
I'd rather
wrench off an arm than hug you
    though
10   it's what I long to do
I'd rather
gather a posy of poison ivy than
ask if you love me
so if my
hair doesn't stand on end it's
    because
I never tease it
and if my
heart isn't in my mouth it's
20   because
it knows its place
and if I
don't take a bite of your ear
    it's because
gristle gripes my guts
and if you
miss the message better get new
glasses and read it twice

I. *Response*

a. What observations and objections does Atwood raise about the use of the word *love* in "Variations on the Word *Love*"? Do you agree or disagree with her viewpoint? Explain.

b. What words would you use to describe the **tone** of "Variations on the Word *Love*"? Of "First Person Demonstrative"? How do these poems compare to most of the previous love poems in this section, in terms of tone? Which tone do you prefer, and why?

Tone is the implied attitude of the writer toward the subject or the audience.

2. *Writing* Poem   Study the structure of "First Person Demonstrative" carefully to note how the speaker expresses her or his love. Then write your own poem, following the original structure as closely as possible, using unconventional images of your own. You can retain the original first line and the last three lines.

3. *Media* Magazine Analysis   What point do you think Atwood is trying to make when she says, "There are whole/magazines with not much in them/but the word *love* ..."? Use an issue of a current popular magazine to support your interpretation of this line.

I write poetry in order to live more fully.
—*Judith Rodriguez*

Theme Connections

for all of the poems in the cluster "Since Feeling Is First"
- *"Transients in Arcadia," a story about a couple in love, page 37*
- *"The Spaces Between Stars," a story about relationship problems, page 100*
- *"Touching Bottom," a story in which a character falls in and out of love, page 124*
- *"The Raft," a burlesque act about a couple's first meeting, page 451*

Dover Beach

by Matthew Arnold

The sea is calm to-night.
The tide is full, the moon lies fair
Upon the Straits;—on the French coast, the light
Gleams, and is gone; the cliffs of England stand,
Glimmering and vast, out in the tranquil bay.
Come to the window, sweet is the night air!
Only, from the long line of spray
Where the sea meets the moon-blanched sand,
Listen! you hear the grating roar
10   Of pebbles which the waves suck back, and fling,
At their return, up the high strand,
Begin, and cease, and then again begin,
With tremulous cadence slow, and bring
The eternal note of sadness in.

Sophocles long ago
Heard it on the Ægæan, and it brought
Into his mind the turbid ebb and flow,
Of human misery; we
Find also in the sound a thought,
20   Hearing it by this distant northern sea.

The sea of faith
Was once, too, at the full, and round earth's shore
Lay like the folds of a bright girdle furled;
But now I only hear
Its melancholy, long, withdrawing roar,
Retreating to the breath
Of the night-wind down the vast edges drear
And naked shingles of the world.

Ah, love, let us be true
30   To one another! for the world, which seems
To lie before us like a land of dreams,
So various, so beautiful, so new,
Hath really neither joy, nor love, nor light,
Nor certitude, nor peace, nor help for pain;

moon-blanched: whitened or made pale by moonlight

Sophocles: ancient Greek dramatist (496–406 B.C.E.), author of *Oedipus Rex* and *Antigone*

girdle: a belt or sash

shingles: large, smooth stones; beaches consisting of such stones

And we are here as on a darkling plain
Swept with confused alarms of struggle and flight,
Where ignorant armies clash by night.

If There Be Sorrow

by Mari Evans

If there be sorrow
let it be
for things undone
undreamed
    unrealized
            unattained

to these add one:
love withheld
    restrained

1. *Response*
    a. According to the speaker of "Dover Beach," what is the importance of love? Would you call this poem a celebration of love? Why or why not?
    b. Choose one phrase or image from "Dover Beach" that you think captures the atmosphere of the poem best.
    c. Look carefully at the way in which both Arnold and Evans use rhyme in their poems. What similarities and differences do you see? Did you notice the presence of rhyme in these poems when you read them the first time? Do you think the poets have used rhyme effectively? Explain.

2. *Focus on Context* "Dover Beach" is widely considered to be one of the classics of English poetry. Using Internet or print resources, research this poem's place in our cultural history. Why do critics consider it to be so important? In a contemporary Canadian classroom, is this poem still important?

Grief of Mind

What pain can be greater than grief? These poems examine thoughts and emotions associated with mortality and loss. Some look beyond the limits of our knowledge, searching for purpose, peace, and hope.

Late Landing

by Julia M. Spicher

It's 1:30 and raining
as we wake above Pittsburgh,
but we feel back in Paris
asleep in hotel beds
dreaming of a rusty-lipped stewardess,
the long, black Atlantic
and naps in foam seats
that recline just so far.

We walk drugged, down the ramp
10 like game-show contestants
to an audience of parents,
wide waves and broad smiles.

Mom hugs me too hard
and wipes at her cheek—
was nine days that long?
I tell her I loved it,
did you get my postcards?
we drank coffee from bowls there,
and headlights were yellow,
20 Dad's in the car?

The wet trunk lid slams
and wipers start whining.
I shiver cold and numb.
Mom leans over the seat
and sighs for her secret,
"On the day that you left
Grandpa died."

Because I Could Not Stop for Death

by Emily Dickinson

Because I could not stop for Death—
He kindly stopped for me—
The Carriage held but just ourselves—
And Immortality.

We slowly drove—He knew no haste,
And I had put away
My labour and my leisure too,
For His Civility—

We passed the School, where Children strove
10   At Recess—in the Ring—
We passed the Fields of Gazing Grain—
We passed the Setting Sun—

Or rather—He passed Us—
The Dews grew quivering and chill—
For only Gossamer, my Gown—
My Tippet—only Tulle—

Tippet: a covering for the shoulders

Tulle: a fine netting used for veils and other clothing

We paused before a House that seemed
A Swelling of the Ground—
The Roof was scarcely visible—
20   The Cornice—in the Ground.

Cornice: moulding at the top of a wall

Since then—'tis Centuries—and yet
Feels shorter than the Day
I first surmised the Horses' Heads
Were toward Eternity—

Miss Dickinson Goes to the Office

by Gail White

Because I could not stop for lunch,
   it kindly stopped for me.
The lunch tray held a lemon sponge   **sponge:** sponge cake
   and watercress and tea.

I heard a fly buzz—in the Slaw—
   immortal for an hour.
The tea was hot—a small Brazil—
   although the cream was sour.

Since then 'tis centuries, yet each
10   seems shorter than the day
I first surmised the weekend was
   five working days away.

1. Response

a. Explain the significance of the title "Late Landing" and how effectively it reflects or reveals the poem.

b. Dickinson's "The Chariot" contains an unusual characterization of Death. In a group, complete a character sketch of Death as portrayed in the poem. What is the tone of this poem?

c. What aspects of "The Chariot" does Gail White imitate in her parody, "Miss Dickinson Goes to the Office"? Discuss the effectiveness and effect of this parody.

d. What does White's poem reveal about death or grieving?

2. Literature Studies

Atmosphere What details in "Late Landing" establish an atmosphere that is appropriate to the "secret" of the last two lines? Refer to specific words and phrases in your answer.

3. ***Focus on Context*** In a group, conduct some research on the poet Emily Dickinson. Create a mini-biography that summarizes what you feel are the ten most important details about her life and experience as a poet. As well, find a copy of the original published version of "The Chariot" and compare it to the version printed here. Which version do you prefer, and why?

Do Not Go Gentle Into That Good Night

by Dylan Thomas

Do not go gentle into that good night,
Old age should burn and rave at close of day;
Rage, rage against the dying of the light.

Though wise men at their end know dark is right,
Because their words had forked no lightning they
Do not go gentle into that good night.

Good men, the last wave by, crying how bright
Their frail deeds might have danced in a green bay,
Rage, rage against the dying of the light.

10   Wild men who caught and sang the sun in flight,
And learn, too late, they grieved it on its way,
Do not go gentle into that good night.

Grave men, near death, who see with blinding sight
Blind eyes could blaze like meteors and be gay,
Rage, rage against the dying of the light.

And you, my father, there on that sad height,
Curse, bless, me now with your fierce tears, I pray.
Do not go gentle into that good night.
Rage, rage against the dying of the light.

from *He Went Gentle*

by Geraldine Rubia

He went 'gentle into that good night'
and I would not wish it otherwise
for gentle he doubtless came
from that other night
his mother being oh so gentle
or, more precise, unruffleable,
and more or less gentle flowed his life.

Not all went well, far from it,
but the 'slings and arrows' evoked from him
10 no more than a shrug and a wry smile,
and though some would suggest
he forged the slings and arrows himself
who knows that it could have been
any other way.

Humor he had plenty of, though not
the rambunctious kind;
rather the kind that said to one
who smashed a glass on the kitchen floor
"Why wait till you had it washed and dried?"
20 That was it, really, in a nutshell;
it was always the irony he saw, never the tragedy.
Is there any tragedy after all
but the tragedy of no sense of humor?

1. *Response*
 a. Discuss the organization and structure of Dylan Thomas's
"Do Not Go Gentle Into That Good Night."
 b. Reread the last three lines of Rubia's "He Went Gentle"
and express the meaning in your own words.
 c. What significant similarities and differences are there in
the ideas and feelings expressed in "Do Not Go Gentle Into
That Good Night" and "He Went Gentle"? Which poem do
you prefer? Why?

2. **Oral Language** *Group Discussion* Verses 2–5 of "Do Not Go Gentle Into That Good Night" deal with the ways in which different types of people approach death. In a group discussion, clarify who these people are and describe the ways in which they approach death. Present your ideas to the class.

3. **Focus on Context** Using Internet or print resources, research the circumstances surrounding the writing of Thomas's "Do Not Go Gentle Into That Good Night." Does your response to the poem change as a result of the information you discovered? Explain.

The World

by Kathleen Raine

It burns in the void.
Nothing upholds it.
Still it travels.

Travelling the void
Upheld by burning
Nothing is still.

Burning it travels.
The void upholds it.
Still it is nothing.

10   Nothing it travels
A burning void
Upheld by stillness.

Reservoir Nocturne by Max Ferguson. Oil on panel

Do you think that this work is an appropriate companion piece
to the poem "Acquainted With the Night"? In your answer, refer
to specific elements of the painting and the poem.

Acquainted With the Night

by Robert Frost

I have been one acquainted with the night.
I have walked out in rain—and back in rain.
I have outwalked the furthest city light.

I have looked down the saddest city lane.
I have passed by the watchman on his beat
And dropped my eyes, unwilling to explain.

I have stood still and stopped the sound of feet
When far away an interrupted cry
Came over houses from another street,

10   But not to call me back or say good-by;
And further still at an unearthly height,
One luminary clock against the sky

Proclaimed the time was neither wrong nor right.
I have been one acquainted with the night.

Grief of Mind

by Edward de Vere, 17th Earl of Oxford

What plague is greater than the grief of mind?
    The grief of mind that eats in every vein;
In every vein that leaves such clots behind;
    Such clots behind as breed such bitter pain;
So bitter pain that none shall ever find,
What plague is greater than the grief of mind.

ABC

by Robert Pinsky

Any body can die, evidently. Few
Go happily, irradiating joy,

Knowledge, love. Most
Need oblivion, painkillers,
Quickest respite.

Sweet time unafflicted,
Various world:
X = your zenith.

1. Response

a. "Acquainted With the Night" describes the speaker's physical experiences very carefully, but leaves his/her state of mind unspoken. What thoughts or concerns might be responsible for taking the speaker repeatedly out into the night? Compare your ideas with those of a few classmates.

b. Select two of the four preceding poems and explain how the authors use repetition. Evaluate whether that repetition is appropriate and effective.

c. In groups, discuss the possible interpretations of the last line of Pinsky's poem "ABC."

2. Literature Studies *Enjambment* Identify examples of **enjambment** within "Acquainted With the Night." Prepare an oral reading of the poem that reflects the way enjambment affects the rhythm. Why do you think poets use enjambment in their work?

Enjambment occurs when there is no strong punctuation at the end of a line of poetry, allowing a phrase or sentence to carry through that line and into the next without a pause.

3. Vocabulary Using a word web, explore the meaning and connotations of the word *acquainted*. How does the meaning of this word help to shape the meaning of "Acquainted With the Night"? Use a thesaurus or other reference resource and list other words Frost could have used. For each of these alternatives, write a sentence explaining how the word might alter the poem's effect.

4. Writing *ABC Poem* Create a poem of your own that uses the same structure as Pinsky's "ABC." If necessary, use a dictionary or Internet resources to find interesting and unusual words for each letter of the alphabet. Remember that your poem, like Pinsky's, must develop one theme or topic. Ask a classmate to check the grammatical correctness of your work. What were the challenges you faced in writing this poem?

Poetry is a way of taking life by the throat.

—Robert Frost

The Five Stages of Grief

by Linda Pastan

The night I lost you
someone pointed me towards
the Five Stages of Grief.
Go that way, they said,
it's easy, like learning to climb
stairs after the amputation.
And so I climbed.
Denial was first.
I sat down at breakfast
10   carefully setting the table
for two. I passed you the toast—
you sat there. I passed
you the paper—you hid
behind it.
Anger seemed more familiar.
I burned the toast, snatched
the paper and read the headlines myself.
But they mentioned your departure,
and so I moved on to
20   *Bargaining*. What could I exchange
for you? The silence
after storms? My typing fingers?
Before I could decide, *Depression*
came puffing up, a poor relation
its suitcase tied together
with string. In the suitcase
were bandages for the eyes
and bottles of sleep. I slid
all the way down the stairs
30   feeling nothing.
And all the time Hope
flashed on and off
in defective neon.
Hope was a signpost pointing
straight in the air.
Hope was my uncle's middle name,
he died of it.

After a year I am still climbing,
though my feet slip
on your stone face.
The treeline
has long since disappeared;
green is a colour
I have forgotten.
But now I see what I am climbing
towards: *Acceptance*
written in capital letters,
a special headline:
Acceptance,
its name in lights.
I struggle on,
waving and shouting.
Below, my whole life spreads its surf,
all the landscapes I've ever known
or dreamed of. Below
a fish jumps: the pulse
in your neck.
Acceptance. I finally
reach it.
But something is wrong.
Grief is a circular staircase.
I have lost you.

Insouciance

by John W. Dickson

If the craven crow and the fierce-eyed hawk
    Swoop over the plain of my wasted years
And the bright plans dwindle to fancy talk
    And hope is restrained by a thousand fears,
Mrs. Brady would dash up the walk waving recipes
for fried crow and hawk stew and ask me to speak
at her Women's Club luncheon.

If Life throws up on my outstretched hand
    And Fate kicks the buttocks of my dreams
10   And my heart becomes a desert land
        Strewn with the bones of famished schemes,
Mrs. Brady would remark that there is so much of
that intestinal flu going around these days and
spend all afternoon showing me how bone chips can
make a delightful center-piece.

If the sun fades out in the black soot sky
    And the reaper comes, as he surely must,
Death-shroud draped over empty eye,
    Reducing endless time to dust,
20   Mrs. Brady would haggle with him a while and
finally agree to pay two dollars for the job
provided he doesn't forget that patch of grass
behind the garage and is sure to trim along the walk.

The Largest Life

by Archibald Lampman

There is a beauty at the goal of life,
A beauty growing since the world began,
Through every age and race, through lapse and strife
Till the great human soul complete her span.
Beneath the waves of storm that lash and burn,
The currents of blind passion that appal,
To listen and keep watch till we discern
The tide of sovereign truth that guides it all;
So to address our spirits to the height,
10   And so attune them to the valiant whole,
That the great light be clearer for our light,
And the great soul the stronger for our soul:
To have done this is to have lived, though fame
Remember us with no familiar name.

1. Response
   a. In "The Five Stages of Grief," Pastan uses imagery and figurative language to suggest what the speaker is feeling through the five stages of grief. For each stage, offer your own interpretation of what the speaker is experiencing. What conclusion does the speaker reach at the end of the journey? Do you think the poem ends on an optimistic or pessimistic note? Explain.
   b. What does the word *insouciance* mean? How does Dickson use juxtaposition within the poem to bring that meaning to life? Consider both the form of the poem and its content in your answer.
   c. Express the theme and message of Lampman's sonnet "The Largest Life" in your own words. Be concise; do not translate the poem line by line.

2. Drama *Dramatization* In a group, prepare and present a dramatization of "Insouciance." Through your reading, you should be able to create distinct personalities for the two outlooks on life that are present in each verse. You might also introduce the figures of the crow, the hawk, Life, Death, and Mrs. Brady into your dramatization.

3. Visual Communication Create a collage or PowerPoint presentation that captures the essence of some of your favourite poems in this section ("Grief of Mind"). Your work should contain appropriate visuals, brief quotations from the poems, and a personal commentary that reflects your own perspective.

Theme Connections

for all of the poems in the cluster "Grief of Mind"
- *"A Drowning," a story about a man drowning, page 160*
- *"Red Bean Ice," a story about an aging woman, page 164*
- *"Pierre Trudeau: He Has Gone to His Grace," a tribute to someone who has passed away, page 299, and other essays in the cluster "In Memory Of"*
- *"The Dashwoods' Fate Is Decided," a movie script which involves the death of a father, page 443*

The Good Life

What is the secret of the good life? What obstacles stand in the way of a good life?

The World Is Too Much With Us

by William Wordsworth

The world is too much with us; late and soon,
Getting and spending, we lay waste[1] our powers:
Little we see in Nature that is ours;
We have given our hearts away, a sordid boon![2]
This Sea that bares her bosom to the moon;
The winds that will be howling at all hours,
And are up-gathered now like sleeping flowers;
For this, for everything, we are out of tune;
It moves us not—Great God! I'd rather be
10   A Pagan suckled in a creed outworn;[3]
So might I, standing on this pleasant lea,[4]
Have glimpses that would make me less forlorn;
Have sight of Proteus[5] rising from the sea;
Or hear old Triton[6] blow his wreathèd horn.

[1]**lay waste:** destroy
[2]**boon:** benefit
[3]**suckled in a creed outworn:** raised to believe an obsolete religion
[4]**lea:** meadow
[5]**Proteus:** a Greek sea-god who could change his shape
[6]**Triton:** a Greek sea-god often portrayed with a trident and a seashell horn

Modern Edifices

by Maria Holod

In concrete, in iron,
up the stairs of stone,
between escalators
and elevators
in blinding neon
my world lost its way.
　　Smoky windows,
　　　　Smoky sky
　　for my world.
Artificially cool
air soaked
in metallic smell
spins around my world.
　　My papery world
　　my world in machines
　　my world in digits
　　my world, my world
At one time
my world was
in the sun
in the sky
in trees and birds
and in human beings.

1. *Response*
a. "The World Is Too Much With Us" and "Modern Edifices" make a similar criticism about modern life. Explain that criticism in your own words.
b. Which poem do you prefer? Explain.

2. *Film Studies* Imagine you are a screenwriter who wants to develop a movie that would communicate the theme of these poems. What story could you tell to bring that theme to life? How could you create a movie with mass appeal on this theme? Create a **synopsis** that would convince a producer to go ahead with the movie. Your synopsis should give the basic storyline, and as well, it might suggest a title and possible cast members.

A **synopsis** provides an overview or summary of a longer work.

3. *Focus on Context* William Wordsworth was an English Romantic poet. Using Internet or print resources, research the characteristics and major themes of the Romantic poets. Focus especially on how they felt about the city. Did researching the context of this poem help you to better appreciate or understand Wordsworth's sonnet? Explain.

When you write in prose you say what you mean.
When you write in rhyme you say what you must.
—*Oliver Wendell Holmes*

Kindly Unhitch That Star, Buddy

by Ogden Nash

I hardly suppose I know anybody who wouldn't rather be a
    success than a failure,
Just as I suppose every piece of crabgrass in the garden would
    much rather be an azalea,
And in celestial circles all the run-of-the-mill angels would
    rather be archangels or at least cherubim and seraphim,[1]
And in the legal world all the little process-servers hope to
    grow up into great big bailiffim and sheriffim.[2]
Indeed, everybody wants to be a wow,
But not everybody knows exactly how.
Some people think they will eventually wear diamonds instead
    of rhinestones
Only by everlastingly keeping their noses to their ghrinestones,
And other people think they will be able to put in more time
    at Palm Beach and the Ritz
By not paying too much attention to attendance at the office
    but rather in being brilliant by starts and fits.
Some people after a full day's work sit up all night getting a
    college education by correspondence,
While others seem to think they'll get just as far by devoting
    their evenings to the study of the difference in temperament
    between brunettance and blondance.
In short, the world is filled with people trying to achieve
    success,
And half of them think they'll get it by saying No and half of
    them by saying Yes,
And if all the ones who say No said Yes, and vice versa, such
    is the fate of humanity that ninety-nine percent of them
    still wouldn't be any better off than they were before,
Which perhaps is just as well because if everybody was a success
    nobody could be contemptuous of anybody else and
    everybody would start in all over again trying to be a
    bigger success than everybody else so they would have
    somebody to be contemptuous of and so on forevermore,
Because when people start hitching their wagons to a star,
That's the way they are.

---

[1] **cherubim and seraphim:** in the Bible, high-ranking angels
[2] **bailiffim and sheriffim:** wordplay on the legal terms *bailiff* and *sheriff*

To Be of Use

by Marge Piercy

The people I love the best
jump into work head first
without dallying in the shallows
and swim off with sure strokes almost out of sight.
They seem to become natives of that element,
the black sleek heads of seals
bouncing like half-submerged balls.

I love people who harness themselves, an ox to a heavy cart,
who pull like water buffalo, with massive patience,
10   who strain in the mud and the muck to move things forward,
who do what has to be done, again and again.

I want to be with people who submerge
in the task, who go into the fields to harvest
and work in a row and pass the bags along,
who are not parlor generals[1] and field deserters[2]
but move in a common rhythm
when the food must come in or the fire be put out.

The work of the world is common as mud.
Botched, it smears the hands, crumbles to dust.
20   But the thing worth doing well done
has a shape that satisfies, clean and evident.
Greek amphoras[3] for wine or oil,
Hopi[4] vases that held corn, are put in museums
but you know they were made to be used.
The pitcher cries for water to carry
and a person for work that is real.

[1]**parlor generals:** generals who avoid the battlefield
[2]**field deserters:** soldiers who flee during battle
[3]**amphoras:** two-handled jars
[4]**Hopi:** Aboriginal people of northeast Arizona

Thoughts

by Marty Robillard

There are so many things in life I want to do:
But some I don't have the courage to do,
Some I don't have the ability to do,
And others nobody will let me do.
　　So I fish.

1. **Response**
   a. What aspect of life does Nash poke fun at in "Kindly
   Unhitch That Star, Buddy"? Explain how the title of the poem
   makes an important contribution to its meaning.
   b. Select three images from "To Be of Use" that you
   think best capture the speaker's attitude toward work.
   Be prepared to explain your choices to the class.
   c. Do you agree with the basic message in Marty Robillard's
   poem "Thoughts"? Why or why not?

2. **Critical Thinking** In a brief essay, show how "To Be of Use"
   might be regarded as a response to "Kindly Unhitch That
   Star, Buddy." Use quotations from both poems as evidence
   to support your argument.

3. **Language Conventions** *Sentence Structure* Examine the
   punctuation in the final stanza of "Kindly Unhitch That Star,
   Buddy." How many sentences does the stanza contain? What
   is the technical term for this construction, and do you think
   it occurs accidentally or intentionally? Repunctuate the final
   stanza to correct it, and explain whether you think the
   poem is improved as a result.

> You will not find poetry anywhere
> unless you bring some of it with you.
> —*Joseph Joubert*

I Am a Rock

by Paul Simon

A winter's day
In a deep and dark December—
I am alone
Gazing from my window
To the streets below
On a freshly fallen silent shroud of snow.
I am a rock;
I am an island.

I build walls,
10   A fortress deep and mighty
That none may penetrate.
I have no need of friendship;
Friendship causes pain.
Its laughter and its loving I disdain.
I am a rock;
I am an island.

Don't talk of love.
Well, I've heard the word before;
It's sleeping in my memory.
20   I won't disturb the slumber
Of feelings that have died.
If I'd never loved, I never would have cried.
I am a rock;
I am an island.

I have my books
And my poetry to protect me.
I am shielded in my armour,
Hiding in my room,
Safe within my tomb.
30   I touch no one and no one touches me.
I am a rock;
I am an island.

And a rock feels no pain,
And an island never cries.

The World Is Not a Pleasant Place to Be

by Nikki Giovanni

the world is not a pleasant place
to be without
someone to hold and be held by

a river would stop
its flow if only
a stream were there
to receive it

an ocean would never laugh
if clouds weren't there
10   to kiss her tears

the world is not
a pleasant place to be without
someone

I. Response

a. What advice would you give to the speaker in "I Am a Rock"? Explain why you think that particular advice is appropriate.

b. Add two additional stanzas of your own to "The World Is Not a Pleasant Place to Be." Your stanzas can be inserted anywhere after the first verse and should be crafted to fit the structure and language of the poem. Comment on any insights you gained about the poem through this exercise.

2. *Making Connections* Simon's song lyric "I Am a Rock" was inspired by a quotation from the English poet, John Donne (1572–1631):

> No man is an island, entire of itself; every man is a piece of the continent, a part of the main; if a clod be washed away by the sea, Europe is the less, as well as if a promontory were, as well as if a manor of thy friend's or of thine own were; any man's death diminishes me, because I am involved in mankind; and therefore never send to know for whom the bell tolls; it tolls for thee.

What is Donne saying? How does the above quotation influence your interpretation of Simon's song?

3. *Language Conventions* *Punctuation and Capitalization* Examine "I Am a Rock" and discuss how it uses punctuation and capitalization. What are the general rules for capitalization within poems? Compare the punctuation and capitalization in "I Am a Rock" with that in "The World Is Not a Pleasant Place to Be." What is the effect of the punctuation and capitalization in each poem?

Poets aren't very useful
Because they aren't consumeful or produceful.

—*Ogden Nash*

Theme Connections

for all of the poems in the cluster "The Good Life"
- *"Groom Service," a story in which characters seek to improve their lives through the right marriage, page 12*
- *"The Shining Houses," a story in which the characters seek to improve their lives at the expense of others, page 26*
- *"Transients in Arcadia," a story in which the characters seek the good life, page 37*
- *"A Pair of Silk Stockings," a story in which a character seeks a luxurious escape from her everyday drudgery, page 86*
- *"Thoughts on Education," an essay that argues for improving one's life through public education, page 312*

I'm Sorry Says the Machine

by Eve Merriam

I'm sorry says the machine,
Thank you for waiting says the tape recording,
Trying to connect you says the voice in the
    vacuum at the end of the line.

I'm sorry that sister is not in working order.
Please verify your brother and try him again.
I'm sorry that mother is out of service.
Thank you for waiting, that father you have
    reached is a temporary disconnect.

10   I'm sorry that landlord is not in working order.
Please verify your neighborhood and try it again.
I'm sorry those repairs are out of service.
Thank you for waiting, that official you have
    reached is not reachable at this time.

I'm sorry that water is not in drinking order.
Please verify that sunlight and try it later.
I'm sorry that blue sky is out of service.
Thank you for waiting, those flowers and trees
    are permanently disconnected.

20   I'm sorry that country is not in working order.
I'm sorry that planet is out of service.
Please verify that godhead and try much later.
Thank you for waiting, that universe has been
    dis—.

All Watched Over by Machines of Loving Grace

by Richard Brautigan

I like to think (and
the sooner the better!)
of a cybernetic meadow
where mammals and computers
live together in mutually
programming harmony
like pure water
touching clear sky.

I like to think
10   (right now, please!)
of a cybernetic forest
filled with pines and electronics
where deer stroll peacefully
past computers
as if they were flowers
with spinning blossoms.

I like to think
(it has to be!)
of a cybernetic ecology
20   where we are free of our labors
and joined back to nature,
returned to our mammal
brothers and sisters,
and all watched over
by machines of loving grace.

1. Response
  a. How does Merriam craft "I'm Sorry Says the Machine" so that it builds to a climax? Did you like the way the poem ended? Why or why not?
  b. How do you read "All Watched Over by Machines of Loving Grace"? Do you take it at face value or read it ironically, or does it seem like an interesting but unrealistic vision of the future? Share your perspective on the poem in a group discussion.

2. Making Connections In what significant ways are the ideas and feelings expressed in "I'm Sorry Says the Machine" and "All Watched Over by Machines of Loving Grace" similar and/or different? Conclude your comparison with a statement about which poem you prefer and why.

3. Research and Inquiry Search current media works, either print or electronic, to find two reports on the effect of technology on the human or natural environment. One report should highlight a negative effect, the other a positive effect. Search especially for information "off the beaten path"—information that is not common knowledge (but be sure to verify the accuracy of this information). Present your findings to your classmates. As a class, you might create a technology bulletin board to display the information you gather.

> Poetry is the journal of a sea animal
> living on land, wanting to fly in the air.
> —*Carl Sandburg*

When I Heard the Learn'd Astronomer

by Walt Whitman

When I heard the learn'd astronomer,
When the proofs, the figures, were ranged in columns before me,
When I was shown the charts and diagrams, to add, divide,
    and measure them,
When I sitting heard the astronomer where he lectured
    with much applause in the lecture-room,
How soon unaccountable I became tired and sick,
Till rising and gliding out I wander'd off by myself,
In the mystical moist night-air, and from time to time,
Look'd up in perfect silence at the stars.

Advice to the Young

by Miriam Waddington

1
keep bees and
grow asparagus,
watch the tides
and listen to the
wind instead of
the politicians
make up your own
stories and believe
them if you want to
10   live the good life.

2
All rituals
are instincts
never fully
trust them
study to im-
prove biology
with reason.

3
Digging trenches
for asparagus
is good for the
muscles and
waiting for the
plants to settle
teaches patience
to those who are
usually in too
much of a hurry.

4
There is morality
in bee-keeping
it teaches how
not to be afraid
of the bee swarm
it teaches how
not to be afraid of
finding new places
and building them
all over again.

Warm Rain

by Midori Iwasaki

Warm
rain
runs
off fresh green boughs
and
wets
my
cheek

as I sail out
10   into
a
new
morning

1. *Response*

a. What kind of a person is the speaker in "When I Heard the Learn'd Astronomer"? List at least three character traits with details from the poem that support your conclusions.
b. Comment on the advice presented in "Advice to the Young." Does it seem useful or valuable to you? Explain.
c. Reread "Warm Rain" and select the one word that you think is the most important or interesting. Explain your choice.

2. *Writing* Poem

Each of the preceding three poems argues directly or indirectly in favour of direct experience with nature. Write a poem of your own, based on your personal experience, that makes the same point, or write a poem that refutes the other three poems. You can use one of these poems as a model, or choose another format.

{ Overwhelming Questions

Many poets explore, and may even answer, the overwhelming questions that trouble us all—who or what am I? Is there a purpose to life? What is the nature of happiness?

Original Thought

by The Four Dancers

Sometimes
it's hard
to raise a thought,
when you think
too hard,
thoughts create thinkers
or entangle non-thinkers
in chaos
with discordant rhymes,
thought takes the pen
and I wonder
sometimes
where thought even begins,
the norm think only in terms
of insanity
clustering pieces of thought
throughout their lives.

The luxury of unwrangling
stifled thought
may free the mind
allowing design
for creative communication,
silence,
one thought ebbs toward
    eternity,
threading the edge
of the thinker's mind
or
causing one to be fooled
by one's thought.
Thoughts captured in simplicity
hold glistening truths
to think
when the raising is hard.

10

20

30

Anything Worth Knowing?

by Kevin Major

In school that morning
he asked me, the teacher, what use it was for him
to know the parts of a worm
when his one use for worms was fishing.
I had no answer for him.
Except that some people want to know,
that the world is better for knowing.
If not him, then others were interested.

But that afternoon, after school
10   When he asked me, the learner, what use it was
for me to know the right way to bait a hook
("Your one use for worms is dissection")
I had an answer ready for him.
"Now I see that baiting hooks
destroys the crop, the gizzard, the dorsal ganglion!
Knowledge helps me understand the deadening of the
brain."

1. *Response*
   a. With a small group, discuss the poem "Original Thought"
   and what the poet might have been trying to achieve or
   capture.
   b. In a group, generate a list of effective strategies that would
   help readers to better understand a difficult poem such as
   "Original Thought." Present your conclusions to the class.
   c. In "Anything Worth Knowing?" how does the teacher
   respond to the student's two questions? What do you think
   of the teacher's answers?
   d. What essential question(s) does each poem ask? Is an
   answer provided?

2. *Critical Thinking* Reflect on your own attitudes about
   learning. What kind of knowledge is most important to you?
   Which learning experiences have been most satisfying? Summarize your ideas in a brief piece of personal writing, and
   describe at least two learning goals you have for the future.

Did I Miss Anything?

by Tom Wayman

Question frequently asked by students after
missing a class.

Nothing. When we realized you weren't here
we sat with our hands folded on our desks
in silence, for the full two hours

    Everything. I gave an exam worth
    40 per cent of the grade for this term
    and assigned some reading due today
    on which I'm about to hand out a quiz
    worth 50 per cent

Nothing. None of the content of this course
has value or meaning
Take as many days off as you like:
any activities we undertake as a class
I assure you will not matter either to you or me
and are without purpose

    Everything. A few minutes after we began last time
    a shaft of light descended and an angel
    or other heavenly being appeared
    and revealed to us what each woman or man must do
    to attain divine wisdom in this life and
    the hereafter
    This is the last time the class will meet
    before we disperse to bring this good news to all people
       on earth

Nothing. When you are not present
how could something significant occur?

    Everything. Contained in this classroom
    is a microcosm of human existence
    assembled for you to query and examine and ponder

    This is not the only place such an opportunity has been
       gathered

    but it was one place

    and you weren't here

What Is the Validity of Your Life?

by Dorothy Livesay

The validity of my life
is a few poems caught and netted
a few strong feelings
about love and dying
and loss—
a few tempestuous cloudbursts
because people couldn't be
as great as they might have been
if they'd never learned
10   to play games—
a few doubts
about my own importance—
a delight   delighting in
puffed redbreast on a tree
eyeing me   and his mate
and the crows in the jack pine squawking
because there's a small grey cat
on the garage roof
spitting at them.

20   The validity of my life
is whether you read this poem
or not
and whether it speeds
your arrow.

   a. What audience do you think would most enjoy reading
   the poem "Did I Miss Anything?" Give reasons for your
   answer. What other audiences might enjoy the poem?
   b. Describe the kinds of humour Wayman uses in "Did I Miss
   Anything?" In your own words, state the serious point he is
   arguing in his poem. Do you think his humorous approach is
   an effective way for him to express this point? Explain.
   c. Discuss the image contained in the final two lines of
   "What Is the Validity of Your Life?" In your opinion, what
   meaning is the poet trying to convey through this image?
   How effectively does the image convey this meaning?

Afternoons and Coffeespoons

by Brad Roberts

What is it that makes me just a little bit queasy?
There's a breeze that makes my breathing not so easy
I've had my lungs checked out with X rays
I've smelled the hospital hallways

Someday I'll have a disappearing hairline
Someday I'll wear pyjamas in the daytime

Times when the day is like a play by Sartre
When it seems a bookburning's in perfect order—
I gave the doctor my description
10   I tried to stick to my prescriptions

Sartre: Jean-Paul
Sartre (1905–1980),
French novelist and
philosopher

Someday I'll have a disappearing hairline
Someday I'll wear pyjamas in the daytime

Afternoons will be measured out
Measured out, measured with
Coffeespoons and T. S. Eliot

T. S. Eliot: Thomas
Stearns Eliot (1888–
1965), U.S.-born
English poet, dramatist,
and critic

Maybe if I could do a play-by-playback
I could change the test results that I will get back
I've watched the summer evenings pass by
I've heard the rattle in my bronchi ...
Someday I'll have a disappearing hairline
Someday I'll wear pyjamas in the daytime

Afternoons will be measured out
Measured out, measured with
20   Coffeespoons and T. S. Eliot

Old Man on Sea Shore, Saunton Sands, Devon by Bob Elsdale. Photo

What ideas about old age are communicated in this photo?
How specifically does the photo suggest those ideas? Gather
other images of older people from contemporary media works
and analyse them in the same way. Infer an audience and purpose
for each image. Draw at least two conclusions about social
attitudes toward aging, based on your analysis.

The Love Song of J. Alfred Prufrock

by T. S. Eliot

S'io credesse che mia risposta fosse
A persona che mai tornasse al mondo,
Questa fiamma staria senza più scosse.
Ma per cio che giammai di questo fondo
Non tornò viva alcun, s'i'odo il vero,
Senza tema d'infamia ti rispondo.[1]

Let us go then, you and I,
When the evening is spread out against the sky
Like a patient etherised[2] upon a table;
Let us go, through certain half-deserted streets,
The muttering retreats
Of restless nights in one-night cheap hotels
And sawdust restaurants[3] with oyster-shells:
Streets that follow like a tedious argument
Of insidious intent
10   To lead you to an overwhelming question …
Oh, do not ask, 'What is it?'
Let us go and make our visit.

In the room the women come and go
Talking of Michelangelo.

The yellow fog that rubs its back upon the window-panes,
The yellow smoke that rubs its muzzle on the window-panes
Licked its tongue into the corners of the evening,
Lingered upon the pools that stand in drains,
Let fall upon its back the soot that falls from chimneys,
20   Slipped by the terrace, made a sudden leap,
And seeing that it was a soft October night,
Curled once about the house, and fell asleep.

---

[1]**S'io credesse ... ti rispondo:** "If I believed that my response [to your question about why such a respected person as myself is in Hell] was being addressed to a person who would soon return to the world, my tongue would cease to speak. However, since no one can ever leave these depths, if what I hear is true, I will answer your question, without fear of ruining my reputation." A quotation from Dante's *Inferno*.
[2]**etherised:** made unconscious by an anaesthetic
[3]**sawdust restaurants:** cheap restaurants with sawdust over a rough floor

And indeed there will be time
For the yellow smoke that slides along the street
Rubbing its back upon the window-panes;
There will be time, there will be time
To prepare a face to meet the faces that you meet;
There will be time to murder and create,
And time for all the works and days of hands
30 That lift and drop a question on your plate;
Time for you and time for me,
And time yet for a hundred indecisions,
And for a hundred visions and revisions,
Before the taking of a toast and tea.

In the room the women come and go
Talking of Michelangelo.

And indeed there will be time
To wonder, 'Do I dare?' and, 'Do I dare?'
Time to turn back and descend the stair,
40 With a bald spot in the middle of my hair—
(They will say: 'How his hair is growing thin!')
My morning coat, my collar mounting firmly to the chin,
My necktie rich and modest, but asserted by a simple pin—
(They will say: 'But how his arms and legs are thin!')
Do I dare
Disturb the universe?
In a minute there is time
For decisions and revisions which a minute will reverse.

For I have known them all already, known them all—
50 Have known the evenings, mornings, afternoons,
I have measured out my life with coffee spoons;
I know the voices dying with a dying fall
Beneath the music from a farther room.
So how should I presume?

And I have known the eyes already, known them all—
The eyes that fix you in a formulated phrase,
And when I am formulated, sprawling on a pin,
When I am pinned and wriggling on the wall,
Then how should I begin
60 To spit out all the butt-ends of my days and ways?
And how should I presume?

And I have known the arms already, known them all—
Arms that are braceleted and white and bare
(But in the lamplight, downed with light brown hair!)
Is it perfume from a dress
That makes me so digress?
Arms that lie along a table, or wrap about a shawl.
    And should I then presume?
    And how should I begin?

          .   .   .   .

70   Shall I say, I have gone at dusk through narrow streets
And watched the smoke that rises from the pipes
Of lonely men in shirt-sleeves, leaning out of windows? ...

    I should have been a pair of ragged claws
Scuttling across the floors of silent seas.[4]

          .   .   .   .

And the afternoon, the evening, sleeps so peacefully!
Smoothed by long fingers,
Asleep ... tired ... or it malingers,
Stretched on the floor, here beside you and me.
Should I, after tea and cakes and ices,
80   Have the strength to force the moment to its crisis?
But though I have wept and fasted, wept and prayed,
Though I have seen my head (grown slightly bald) brought in
      upon a platter,
I am no prophet—and here's no great matter;
I have seen the moment of my greatness flicker,
And I have seen the eternal Footman hold my coat, and snicker,
And in short, I was afraid.

    And would it have been worth it, after all,
After the cups, the marmalade, the tea,
90   Among the porcelain, among some talk of you and me,
Would it have been worth while,
To have bitten off the matter with a smile,
To have squeezed the universe into a ball
To roll it toward some overwhelming question,

---

⁴ragged claws ... silent seas: an allusion to remarks made by Shakespeare's Hamlet

To say: 'I am Lazarus,[5] come from the dead,
Come back to tell you all, I shall tell you all'—
If one, settling a pillow by her head,
    Should say: 'That is not what I meant at all.
    That is not it, at all.'

    And would it have been worth it, after all,
100 Would it have been worth while,
After the sunsets and the dooryards and the sprinkled streets,[6]
After the novels, after the teacups, after the skirts that trail
        along the floor—
And this, and so much more?—
It is impossible to say just what I mean!
But as if a magic lantern[7] threw the nerves in patterns on
        a screen:
Would it have been worth while
110 If one, settling a pillow or throwing off a shawl,
And turning toward the window, should say:
    'That is not it at all,
    That is not what I meant, at all.'

                .   .   .   .   .

No! I am not Prince Hamlet, nor was meant to be;
Am an attendant lord, one that will do
To swell a progress, start a scene or two,
Advise the prince; no doubt, an easy tool,
Deferential, glad to be of use,
Politic, cautious, and meticulous;
120 Full of high sentence,[8] but a bit obtuse;
At times, indeed, almost ridiculous—
Almost, at times, the Fool.

    I grow old ... I grow old ...
I shall wear the bottoms of my trousers rolled.[9]

---

[5]**Lazarus:** In the Bible, Lazarus was brought back from the dead by Jesus.
[6]**sprinkled streets:** streets dampened with water to prevent dust
[7]**magic lantern:** a device used to project the image of a photograph onto a screen or wall
[8]**high sentence:** fine language used for serious ideas
[9]**the bottoms of my trousers rolled:** pants with cuffs (newly in fashion at the time)

Shall I part my hair behind? Do I dare to eat a peach?
I shall wear white flannel trousers, and walk upon the beach.
I have heard the mermaids singing, each to each.

I do not think that they will sing to me.

130 I have seen them riding seaward on the waves
Combing the white hair of the waves blown back
When the wind blows the water white and black.

We have lingered in the chambers of the sea
By sea-girls wreathed with seaweed red and brown
Till human voices wake us, and we drown.

Of our conflicts with others we make rhetoric;
of our conflicts with ourselves we make poetry.
—*William Butler Yeats*

Loneliness

by Emma LaRocque

Ah Loneliness,
How would I know
Who I am
Without you?

1. *Response*
a. Write a complete character sketch for Prufrock. For each detail or trait in your sketch, provide supportive details from the poem.
b. Do you think Prufrock ever reveals the nature of the "overwhelming question"? In a group, generate a list of overwhelming questions that a person like Prufrock might ask.
c. Prufrock and the speaker in "Afternoons and Coffeespoons" both speak of measuring out life "with coffee spoons." Write a brief explanation of what this metaphor suggests to you. In what way is the metaphor important to Eliot's poem and Roberts' song?
d. According to the speaker in "Loneliness," what role does loneliness play in our lives? Would Prufrock be comfortable speaking the words in LaRocque's poem? Explain.

2. *Research and Inquiry* Using Internet or print resources, research the many allusions that T. S. Eliot includes in "The Love Song of J. Alfred Prufrock." Write a paragraph in which you reflect on whether researching the allusions helped you to better understand and/or appreciate the poem.

3. *Making Connections* Poets and other writers often use a quotation or line from someone else's work to inspire them or provide a context for their own creations. Choose a phrase or line from one of your favourite poems in this poetry unit and use it as a starting point for a poem of your own. Use the quotation you have borrowed as an introduction, as T. S. Eliot does, or incorporate it directly into your poem, as Roberts does.

Theme Connections

for all of the poems in the cluster "Overwhelming Questions"
- *"On the Rainy River," a story about personal values and choices, page 70*
- *"The Spaces Between Stars," a story about values, page 100*
- *"The Large Ant," a story about the human condition, page 150*
- *"Living Like Weasels," an essay about the human condition, page 350*
- *"What Will Your Verse Be?" a movie monologue about discovering who you are, page 514*

Auto Wreck

by Karl Shapiro

Its quick soft silver bell beating, beating,
And down the dark one ruby flare
Pulsing out red light like an artery,
The ambulance at top speed floating down
Past beacons and illuminated clocks
Wings in a heavy curve, dips down,
And brakes speed, entering the crowd.
The doors leap open, emptying light;
Stretchers are laid out, the mangled lifted
10   And stowed into the little hospital.
Then the bell, breaking the hush, tolls once,
And the ambulance with its terrible cargo
Rocking, slightly rocking, moves away,
As the doors, an afterthought, are closed.

We are deranged, walking among the cops
Who sweep glass and are large and composed.
One is still making notes under the light.
One with a bucket douches ponds of blood
Into the street and gutter.
20   One hangs lanterns on the wrecks that cling,
Empty husks of locusts, to iron poles.

Our throats were tight as tourniquets,
Our feet were bound with splints, but now,
Like convalescents intimate and gauche,
We speak through sickly smiles and warn
With the stubborn saw of common sense,
The grim joke and the banal resolution.
The traffic moves around with care,
But we remain, touching a wound
30   That opens to our richest horror.

Already old, the question Who shall die?
Becomes unspoken Who is innocent?
For death in war is done by hands;

Suicide has cause and stillbirth, logic;
And cancer, simple as a flower, blooms.
But this invites the occult mind,
Cancels our physics with a sneer,
And spatters all we knew of denouement
Across the expedient and wicked stones.

Provisions

by Margaret Atwood

What should we have taken
with us? We never could decide
on that; or what to wear,
or at what time of
year we should make this journey

so here we are, in thin
raincoats and rubber boots

on the disastrous ice, the wind rising,

nothing in our pockets

10   but a pencil stub, two oranges
four toronto streetcar tickets

and an elastic band, holding a bundle
of small white filing-cards
printed with important facts.

1. *Response*
   a. Why do you think Karl Shapiro, in his poem "Auto Wreck," describes the accident scene in such detail? Which details made the strongest impact on you? Explain.
   b. What does the word *provisions* mean, and what connotations and associations does it carry for you? Use this information to comment on how the title shapes the meaning of Atwood's poem?

2. *Literature Studies* Analysis In a group, discuss and analyse "Auto Wreck" and "Provisions." For each poem, describe its literal and symbolic subject matter. What overwhelming question(s) is posed in each poem? Are any answers supplied, either directly or indirectly? As a final task, record the different personal reactions your group members had to these two works, and assess their effectiveness.

3. *Language Conventions* Descriptive Language Create a chart with the following headings: Nouns, Adjectives, Verbs, and **Verbals**. Use the chart to explore the descriptive language in "Auto Wreck," categorizing all the words in the poem that you think are unusual or especially well chosen. Explain what you learned about the poem by completing your chart.

Verbals look like verbs but function as other parts of speech. There are three kinds of verbals: infinitives, participles, and gerunds.

4. *Film Study* Many feature films contain protagonists who are faced with overwhelming questions relating to personal identity and one's place in the world. In a group, make a list of recent films that contain such a character. For each film, describe what questions of identity the character faced and explore how those questions were (or were not) resolved. Based on your discussion, are there any general observations you can make about the way our culture regards the quest for identity?

Poetry is the most direct and simple means of expressing oneself in words … If you listen to small children, and to the amount of chanting and singsong in their speech, you'll see what I mean.

—*Northrop Frye*

Circular Saws

by Fred Cogswell

When the circular saw
chewed up my fingernail
I said to myself
"This is a bad dream
and I shall wake up"
but I didn't
and in a few minutes
the pain began

10   after that, I had
a scar to remind me
not to go near
circular saws

But I soon found
they had ways
of disguising themselves
so that watch as I might
they were always
hurting me

20   now inside and out
I am covered with scars
but that is not
the worst I've learned
the worst thing is
that under the masks
I wear and without
intending to be
I am a circular saw

Night

by Yvonne Trainer

I was never afraid of the night
I'd sit on the farmhouse step and watch the stars
I'd count 5 up from the Big Dipper
to find the smaller one
the one with the bent handle
that leaked rain

I remember the white enamel dipper
that hung on a nail above the washstand
My Mother polishing it once a day
My Father chipping it when he threw it against the wall
in anger over something   I've forgotten
It doesn't matter

Still   light from the window
casts shadows over the yard
but the sky is calm
A whole universe
and nobody throws the stars
Everything has its place
          has order
Even the spaces belong.

Response

a. Which poem, "Circular Saws" or "Night," had the strongest impact on you after the first reading? Briefly explain why you think this was the case.

b. Reread "Night" carefully and then offer an interpretation of this particular phrase from the poem: "and nobody throws the stars."

c. Sometimes the questions a poem raises are implicit rather than explicit. What do you think the implicit questions are in "Circular Saws" and "Night"?

Poet Biographies

MARISA ANLIN ALPS graduated from Simon Fraser University and now works in the publishing industry. Her poetry is included in the collection *Breathing Fire: Canada's New Poets* and has also been broadcast on CBC radio.

MATTHEW ARNOLD (1822–88) was born in Laleham, England. He is best known as a poet but was also an influential critic, educator, and professor.

MARGARET AVISON was born in 1918 in Galt, Ontario. She lived as a child in Regina and Calgary, then returned to Ontario to go to school at the University of Toronto. Her poetry anthologies include *No time, Not Yet but Still, Winter Sun/The Dumbfounding: poems, 1940–66*, and *sunblue*.

AMIRI BARAKA (born LeRoi Jones in 1934) is a poet, activist, social critic, dramatist, and fiction writer. His work and life show his development through social discovery and rebellion, as well as a clear response to the injustice he faced every day.

RICHARD BRAUTIGAN was born in Tacoma, Washington in 1935. He was part of the Beat Movement during the fifties. His books include *The Hawkline Monster: a gothic western, Willard and His Bowling Trophies: A Perverse Mystery, Trout Fishing in America*, and *Revenge of the Lawn*.

ELIZABETH BREWSTER was born in New Brunswick in 1922. She has won numerous awards for her poetry, including the President's Silver Medal for Poetry and the Saskatchewan Arts Boards' Lifetime Award for Excellence in the Arts.

ELIZABETH BARRETT BROWNING was born in England in 1806. Her first poetry collection, *An Essay on Mind and Other Poems*, was published anonymously. In 1844, her collection, *Poems*, gained the attention of the poet Robert Browning. They eloped in 1846. Barrett's *Sonnets From the Portuguese*, dedicated to her husband, was published in 1850, and her verse novel, *Aurora Leigh*, in 1857.

ROBERT BROWNING, born in England in 1812, was a less recognized poet than his wife, Elizabeth Barrett Browning, during their lifetime. However, as a poet, he was considered famous enough to be buried in London's Westminster Abbey among the greatest figures in British history, following his death in 1889.

MARILYN CAY lives in Tisdale, Saskatchewan. She writes poetry and nonfiction and has published two books—*Farm* and *Pure and Startled Seconds*.

FRED COGSWELL, born in East Centreville, New Brunswick in 1917, was the editor of *The Fiddlehead* and two volumes of East Coast writing. He has won many awards, including the Bliss Carman Award for Poetry. His written works include *Watching an Eagle, As I See It*, and *In My Own Growing*.

LORNA CROZIER, along with other Saskatchewan writers, founded a monthly writing workshop jokingly named *The Moose Jaw Movement*. In 1992, her poetry collection, *Inventing the Hawk*, won the Governor General's Award.

EDWARD ESTLIN CUMMINGS is known as an experimental poet. Although his name often appears without capitalization, this was never at the legal request, or even wish, of Cummings himself. It was one publisher's style decision, which was adopted by subsequent publishers as the "correct" style.

EDWARD DE VERE, the 17th Earl of Oxford, was born in 1550 in Castle Heddingham in Essex, England. He acted and produced plays, as part of a court circle of writers. He died in 1604. The debate still rages over whether he was the author of Shakespeare's plays.

EMILY DICKINSON, born in 1830, remained in almost total physical isolation from the outside world most of her life. She was an extremely prolific poet, but was not publicly recognized during her lifetime. She died in 1886.

JOHN W. DICKSON was a Harvard professor, poet, and dramatist. He won the Pulitzer Prize for poetry.

THOMAS STEARNS ELIOT was born in Missouri in 1888, but settled in England in 1914. His first book of poems—*Prufrock and Other Observations*—immediately established him as a leading poet. He received the Nobel Prize for Literature in 1948, and died in London in 1965.

MARI EVANS wrote, produced, and directed the TV program *The Black Experience*, the play *River of My Song*, the musical *Eyes*, and the poetry collections *Nightstar* and *A Dark and Splendid Mass*.

THE FOUR DANCERS are H. Bear Bones, J.C. Rippling Water, Ola Hummingbird, and G. Walking in the Sky.

ROBERT FROST was born in San Francisco in 1874. His first two poetry collections—*A Boy's Will* and *North of Boston*—established his reputation as a poet. His later poetry collections won him more fame and honours, including four Pulitzer Prizes. He died in Boston in 1963.

NIKKI GIOVANNI is a writer of prose and of adult and children's poetry, and is also well known for her poetry recitals. She has received many awards for her written and performed poetry.

PHYLLIS GOTLIEB was born Phyllis Bloom in Toronto in 1926. Her books include the poetry collections *Within the Zodiac* and *Doctor UmLaut's Earthly Kingdom*; the science fiction novels *Sunburst, The Kingdom of the Cats, Flesh and Gold*, and *Violent Stars*; and the story anthologies *Son of the Morning and Other Stories* and *Blue Apes*. She has also written verse plays for the CBC.

RICK HILLIS wrote *The Blue Machines of Night* and *Limbo River*. He is a professor at Reed College in Portland, Oregon, currently teaching poetry, fiction, and screenwriting.

MARIA HOLOD was born in 1917 in Lviv, Western Ukraine. She graduated from the University of Lviv, then emigrated to Canada in 1948. Her writing has appeared in various anthologies and journals, and her book, *Chotyry pory roku (The four seasons)*, was published in 1978.

LENORE KEESHIG-TOBIAS has been a story-teller since she was a child; the oldest of ten children, she would amuse her younger brothers and sisters with stories. Keeshig-Tobias teaches oral studies at George Brown College in Toronto. She is interested in the oral traditions of a l l cultures, and has founded a society to preserve stories of the Trickster.

STANLEY KUNITZ was born in 1905 in Massachusetts. He went to school at Harvard where he received the Garrison Medal for Poetry. He wrote his first book of poems, *Intellectual Things*, before he was twenty-five. He won the Pulitzer Prize in 1959 for *Selected Poems: 1928–1958*. His work has been described as "combining a classical strength of language and vision which goes beyond the easier uses of irony and achieves the genuinely tragic." He is an active member of civil liberty and peace organizations.

ARCHIBALD LAMPMAN, born in 1861, in Morpeth, Canada West (a village near what is now Chatham, Ontario), attended Trinity College in Toronto, worked unsuccessfully as a teacher, but with greater success as a clerk in the post office in Ottawa—a post he held until his death in 1899. He was a writer of poetry, literary essays, and articles. He was one of the Confederation Writers, a group of poets that included Bliss Carman, Susanna Moodie, Charles G. D. Roberts, and Duncan Campbell Scott. His works include *Among the Millet, and Other Poems*, and *Lyrics of Earth*.

EMMA LaROCQUE is an expert on colonization and its impact on Aboriginal/White relations. She wrote *Defeathering the Indian* and many articles about Aboriginal literature, racism, and violence against women. Vicki Gaboreau and Peter Gzowski have both had her as a guest on their programs.

DOROTHY LIVESAY (1909–1996) was born in Winnipeg, Manitoba. She worked as a teacher from 1959 to 1963 in Northern Rhodesia (Zambia). She won the Governor General's Literary Award twice; in 1944 for *Day and Night*, and in 1947 for *Poems for People*.

VALERIO MAGRELLI was born in 1957 in Rome. Described as a post-modern or post-atomic poet, he wrote the poetry collection *The Contagion of Matter.*

KEVIN MAJOR, an important figure in Canadian young-adult literature, lives and writes in St. John's, Newfoundland and Labrador.

Born in 1564, CHRISTOPHER MARLOWE (the son of a shoemaker) had a brilliant but short career, with violence, heresy, and sedition playing a role. Marlowe was an innovative, intellectual thinker, writing the plays *Tamburlaine, Dr. Faustus, The Jew of Malta*, and *Edward II*. In 1593, Marlowe pointed out what he thought were inconsistencies in the Bible. On May 30 of that year, he was murdered at Bull's Tavern over an argument about the bill. Debate rages over whether Marlowe was deliberately provoked and murdered to prevent him revealing the names of fellow heretics, if arrested.

EDNA ST. VINCENT MILLAY, born in 1892, was a poet and playwright. In 1923, her fourth volume of poems, *The Harp Weaver*, was awarded the Pulitzer Prize.

As a young student, JONI MITCHELL thought she would be an artist; it was only as she became exposed to other musicians through the sixties that she began to turn to music, especially songwriting, as a career. She has produced more than twenty albums and is recognized as one of the most significant and consistent contributors of her generation. Her music often incorporates several styles and is hard to classify but is always captivating.

PAUL MULDOON was born in Ireland in 1951. He began writing poetry in Irish at the age of seventeen. His first volume of poetry, *New Weather*, was published in 1973 while he was still at university. After graduation he worked as a radio and TV producer for the BBC. He lives in the United States, and his poetry anthologies have won various awards.

OGDEN NASH was born in New York in 1902. He published his first book for children, *The Cricket of Caradon*, in 1925, and his first poem appeared in *The New Yorker* in 1932. Nash published nineteen books of poetry throughout his lifetime and is probably best known for his limericks.

MARGE PIERCY, born in 1936 in Detroit, Michigan, almost died from German measles and rheumatic fever as a child. She took refuge from illness in stories and books. She supported herself after college by working part-time at a number of jobs—secretary, clerk, faculty instructor, switchboard operator—while trying to write and publish poetry and fiction. She wrote the novels *Going Down Fast* and *Dance the Eagle to Sleep* while actively opposing American involvement in the Vietnam war.

ROBERT PINSKY'S (American Poet Laureate) poetry collections include *Jersey Rain, Sadness and Happiness, The Figured Wheel*, and *New and Collected Poems, 1966–1996*; he also wrote the non-fiction book *The Sounds of Poetry: A Brief Guide.*

KATHLEEN RAINE is a poet, scholar, and critic. She has won the Edna St. Vincent Millay Prize from the American Poetry Society, and the Harriet Monroe Prize. She lives in London, England. Her poetry is described as "a kind of mystical nature poetry ... immersed in the quiet air of solitude and imagination."

SIR WALTER RALEIGH is better known as an explorer, soldier, pirate, and adventurer than a poet. He was born in 1552 (some reports say 1554), in Devon. Raleigh fought with the French Huguenots in 1569. Then, with a half brother, Sir Humphrey Gilbert, he fought the Spanish at sea—an act of piracy that won him the favour of Queen Elizabeth I. He was sent to Ireland to suppress rebellion, which he did ruthlessly, and returned to London and the royal court still in favour. Expeditions he funded returned from Virginia (the "new world") with potatoes and tobacco. His star rose and fell during the years that followed. Unfortunately, on the queen's death, King James gained the throne and Raleigh was accused of treason and confined to the Tower of London (a prison) where he remained for thirteen years (writing his history of the world). In 1616, he was released to again mount an expedition to the "new world." On his return in 1618, Raleigh was executed.

Singer-songwriter BRAD ROBERTS is the lead vocalist of the Canadian rock group Crash Test Dummies. Roberts grew up in Winnipeg. In 1990, while still in university, he formed the Crash Test Dummies together with his brother, bassist Dan Roberts, and three friends. Roberts also performs as a soloist.

GERALDINE RUBIA, born in 1929 in Brooklyn, New York, now lives in Newfoundland and Labrador. She has written for radio, TV, and theatre.

WILLIAM SHAKESPEARE was born in 1564, in Stratford-on-Avon, England. He composed over a hundred sonnets between 1593 and 1601. These were written in the form of three quatrains and a rhyming couplet, now recognized as the Shakespearean sonnet. He died in 1616.

KARL SHAPIRO, born in 1913, began writing poetry while young. While serving in the army during WWII, the poems that he sent home to his fiancée were published. He returned from the war to find that he was a popular poet and he remained so, despite his stance against the poetic conventions and theories of the time.

TSUBOI SHIGEJI was born in 1889 in Japan. He wrote about the problems besetting the poor workers—and these views and writing led to his imprisonment.

PAUL SIMON grew up in the suburbs of New York City. His successful career as a singer and songwriter has spanned several decades. Simon is as acclaimed for his many enduring songs as he is for his musical innovations. Once part of folk-rock group Simon and Garfunkel, he has recorded many award-winning solo albums and has written music for films and stage.

DYLAN THOMAS was born in Wales in 1914. Although he excelled in English and reading, he dropped out of school when he was sixteen. His first book—*Eighteen Poems*—was published to great acclaim when he was twenty. He died in 1953 at the age of thirty-nine.

MIRIAM WADDINGTON was born in Winnipeg in 1917. She was the Canada Council Exchange Poet to Wales in 1980, and has been poetry editor of *Poetry Toronto*, and writer-in-residence at both the Windsor Public Library and the University of Ottawa.

TOM WAYMAN, born in Ontario in 1945, moved to Prince Rupert, British Columbia as a child, and then moved again, to Vancouver, when he was fourteen. He has written and published poetry collections, including *Paperwork, Did I Miss Anything?* and *The Astonishing Weight of the Dead*. He also writes essays and plays, and edits anthologies.

WALT WHITMAN is one of the most famous American poets of the nineteenth century. Born in 1819 in New York City, Whitman was a brilliant child and a voracious reader. He worked as a printer, teacher, journalist, and nurse, and cared deeply for the victims of war and slavery. His first and most popular book is *Leaves of Grass*. Whitman died in 1892.

WILLIAM WORDSWORTH was born in 1770 in England. Wordsworth's earliest poetry collections—*An Evening Walk* and *Descriptive Sketches*—were published in 1793. He died in 1850 and his most famous poem, *"The Prelude,"* was published posthumously by his wife.

Essays
and Other Non-Fiction

Essays are how we speak to one another in print...
a kind of public letter.

Edward Hoagland

> " ... we come to ask one another how we can pry open the door between our conscious and our subconscious, we come for reassurance that all our solitude and our word-wrestling is worthwhile."

What I've Learned From Writing

Speech by Shauna Singh Baldwin

When I was in school—in India in the '70s—my teachers were quite confident that "literature" was written outside the boundaries of the subcontinent, and that anything written in India was "only writing." I have learned from writing that the distinction is irrelevant. Writers don't write because some of us live outside India where writing is magically elevated to the status of "literature." Writers, whether we use narrative or not, write because it helps us make sense of the world, contribute to it, rail at it with a non-violent socially-acceptable weapon —language.

You would not attend writer's conferences if you did not believe in the power of the written word to transform your life, to raise your thoughts above the mundane tasks of working and cooking, sleeping, washing, cleaning, to offer some explanation, some semblance of meaning to the rhythm of each day. We writers begin as readers. At writer's conferences, we come to study the craft, we come to ask one another how we can pry open the door between our conscious and our subconscious, we come for reassurance that all our solitude and our word-wrestling is worthwhile.

I wanted to "be a writer" when I was eleven years old. But to be a writer, I thought I must have some experience to express, something I wanted to say that no one else had said. I wish I had known then, there is no original thought, because all we humans think and feel has been thought and felt so many times before, by so many generations. There is only original perspective, there are only permutations of scenarios. As

Note: "What I've Learned From Writing" was a keynote speech delivered at the Great Lakes Writer's Conference held June 1998 at Alverno College, Wisconsin.

I grew older, the cacophony of the world grew ever louder and soon it seemed all the things that needed to be said were being said by others, all the interesting stories had already been told, told so much better than I could tell them. I now know from other writers that even my experience in this is not unique. But at the time, I fell silent like a child who stops singing because the singers on the radio are so much better.

The challenge of the adult writer is to recover that child who was so confident, ask it what it still needs to say, and find out what shape to give its thoughts that will hold a reader's attention.

There is an old saying I've heard attributed to many famous writers, "Writing is when you sit before the typewriter and bleed." It is the cheapest form of therapy, but no one tells you this: you perform it on yourself, unattended, alone, and you suffer the consequences alone. I'd like to start a campaign to put warning labels on pens, pads, word processing software, and especially post-it notes!

When the urge to scribble turns coherent, it's really difficult to know where to begin. I kept a writer's journal sporadically through my teens converting personal angst, pain and fun times to text; I'm glad it was something no one read but I. But the habit was a good one and today I am never without my writer's journal. A writer's journal is different from a diary, because you fill it with description, not merely with events, but with thoughts, with the texture of the present. It becomes a treasury of moments when words sang.

I wrote poetry—who doesn't?—through school and college, and it wasn't till I was thirty that I attempted my first (non-fiction) book: *A Foreign Visitor's Survival Guide to America*. I wrote it with a co-author, who gave it balance in perspective and gave me confidence. When we began, it was from an artless confidence that we had something to say, that there was a gap in the universe where this book should be, and that we were the ones who had both the lived experience and the research capability to do it.

By the time we'd finished, we were amazed at how much the book had taught us: about ourselves; about our friendship; about our values; and view of the world; about the need for accuracy in word choice. When an editor challenged our ideas we had to agree upon and stand behind each word in that book. By the end of the process when we had internalized the *Chicago Manual of Style*, we knew we would never have written that book if we'd known how arduous the process would be.

So, what did I learn?

Begin with the desire to speak into silence, begin from passion.

My next book, *English Lessons and Other Stories*, is about Indian women in my three countries, India, Canada and the U.S.A. I began it in 1992 and it came to publication in 1996. In it, I began to move past my lived experience and personal problems to enter the earliest form of role-playing game, the virtual reality game that predates computers: the world of fiction. In doing so, a new question rose. No longer "what is writing," but "what makes writing memorable?"

To answer this I returned to dog-eared friends whose words were more likely to be highlighted than not, and I read and reread their wonderfully-scented yellowing pages to find the answer that worked for me: Writers we remember are those who set aside their egos, moved from the purely personal to address the human condition, writers who help us all with this daily business of living, to give us inspiration past entertainment, past culture, past their times.

I also had to find an acceptable answer to the question—for whom do you write? I'm a hybrid of three cultures, Indian, Canadian and American and I write from the perspective of all three. Today my answer is: I write for the people I love, a hybrid, global audience, for people interested in the process of becoming human, the ways in which we live, the influence of history, philosophy, culture, tradition and memory on our sense of self.

After my book of short stories, a novel came to me slowly. I call it *What the Body Remembers*. This novel moved into my life about two years ago and is still in residence in our home. It has to be fed in the morning and cleaned up in the evening. It began shyly, revealing itself in snatches: strange people were talking and I would write down what they said first and then ask myself, "which character is this?"

I now had to appreciate the distinction between a poem, a short story and a novel: Most poems without narrative are likely to be static, where the poet comments on a situation or presents a problem and solution but does not show change in setting, or events. In a short story, the writer's job is to open a window into a situation and let the reader be a voyeur of sorts. The reader's job is to find the significance, tie up loose ends—in short, the reader has the responsibility to imagine. A novel, on the other hand, allows a writer room to stretch, place to expound, philosophize, and here the worst sin the writer can commit is to lose sight of the story and the characters. The reader has far less responsibility to imagine in this form of writing. In the short story and in the novel, the writer is confined only by the first rule of drama: causality. In both short stories and novels there must be conflict, but for there to be drama, the reader must be able to see cause and effect—coincidence in narrative is not appreciated, it's too real. So in writing my novel, I found that it felt like coding a good piece of software, designing a system, building a house—in other words, it's like any other creative endeavor—every detail, every word, should be there for a reason.

Now I began to truly appreciate writers through the ages who wrote without word processors, all those writers who did their research without the Internet, the Milwaukee Public Library system and interlibrary loan, all the writers who travelled miles to interview their sources, instead of sending out an email or picking up the phone.

I hope you will not believe mine is the usual progression. Some writers are comfortable with novels immediately, some enjoy the short story form always, some stay with poems. There are pitfalls along the way: some people enjoy being writers more than they enjoy writing. Others prefer to have written than to write. Some of us get perfect manuscript syndrome. Some of us walk into bookstores and realise

Woman and Handwritten Letter by Brandtner and Staedeli. Photo

Explain the impact this photo has on you and suggest reasons for including it with this essay.

we're competing for limited shelf space with every writer who has ever written and we go home and get writer's block for a month. But it's all part of the game—we write because we need to. And if it were really that easy, wouldn't everyone be doing it? We take from the world and give back, hopefully with beauty and philosophy or entertainment value and our own unique perspective added along the way.

Though we may all hear the same words at this writer's conference, we each learn something unique. I think that's because each of us is at a different stage of readiness to receive from and give to the world.

I'm still developing as a writer, letting the process teach me empathy as I venture deeper into the minds and hearts of selves I might have been if I wasn't me. I'm no longer quite as concerned about who will read my work, or even if anyone will. When it's published, my novel will sit on an overloaded bookshelf and invite some seeking soul to read it, and I hope he or she will find my characters good company. For myself, I hope I will have moved on by then to another book.

Shauna Singh Baldwin was born in Montréal, Canada, but was raised in India. She worked as an independent public radio producer from 1991–1994. In 1974, she won the national Shastri Award (Silver Medal) for English Prose and in 1995, the Writer's Union of Canada Award for Short Prose.

1. *Response*
   a. This selection was the keynote speech given at a writer's conference. What advice from this selection do you think audience members would find most helpful? Explain why you think so.
   b. Were you surprised by anything Shauna Singh Baldwin had to say about writing? If so, explain your surprise to a partner.
   c. Reread two paragraphs from this speech aloud. What has the author done to make the speech effective? Consider techniques such as diction, rhythm, repetition, breaks or pauses in sentences, and parallel structure.

2. *Literature Studies* Structure With a partner, examine this speech and answer the following questions: How has this author structured her speech? What transition words does she use to connect each section of the speech? How is each section supported? Assess the effectiveness of the introduction and conclusion, the speech's overall structure, and its clarity, logical development, and supporting details.

What is the most important quality that a reader can possess? Read on to find out Virginia Woolf's opinion on the matter.

How Should One Read a Book?

Essay by Virginia Woolf

In the first place, I want to emphasise the note of interrogation at the end of my title. Even if I could answer the question for myself, the answer would apply only to me and not to you. The only advice, indeed, that one person can give another about reading is to take no advice, to follow your own instincts, to use your own reason, to come to your own conclusions. If this is agreed between us, then I feel at liberty to put forward a few ideas and suggestions because you will not allow them to fetter that independence which is the most important quality that a reader can possess. After all, what laws can be laid down about books? The battle of Waterloo was certainly fought on a certain day; but is *Hamlet* a better play than *Lear*? Nobody can say. Each must decide that question for himself. To admit authorities, however heavily furred and gowned, into our libraries and let them tell us how to read, what to read, what value to place upon what we read, is to destroy the spirit of free-dom which is the breath of those sanctuaries. Everywhere else we may be bound by laws and conventions—there we have none.

But to enjoy freedom, if the platitude is pardonable, we have of course to control ourselves. We must not squander our powers, help-lessly and ignorantly, squirting half the house in order to water a single rose-bush; we must train them, exactly and powerfully, here on the very spot. This, it may be, is one of the first difficulties that faces us in a library. What is "the very spot"? There may well seem to be nothing but a conglomeration and huddle of confusion. Poems and novels, histories and memoirs, dictionaries and blue-books; books written in all languages by men and women of all tempers, races, and ages jostle each other on the shelf. And outside the donkey brays, the women gossip at the pump, the colts gallop across the fields. Where are we to begin? How are we to bring order into this multitudinous chaos and so get the deepest and widest pleasure from what we read?

It is simple enough to say that since books have classes—fiction, biography, poetry—we should separate them and take from each what it is right that each should give us. Yet few people ask from books what books can give us. Most commonly we come to books with blurred and divided minds, asking of fiction that it shall be true, of poetry that it shall be false, of biography that it shall be flattering, of history that it shall enforce our own prejudices. If we could banish all such preconceptions when we read, that would be an admirable beginning. Do not dictate to your author; try to become him. Be his fellow-worker and accomplice. If you hang back, and reserve and criticise at first, you are preventing yourself from getting the fullest possible value from what you read. But if you open your mind as widely as possible, then signs and hints of almost imperceptible fineness, from the twist and turn of the first sentences, will bring you into the presence of a human being unlike any other. Steep yourself in this, acquaint yourself with this, and soon you will find that your author is giving you, or attempting to give you, something far more definite. The thirty-two chapters of a novel— if we consider how to read a novel first—are an attempt to make something as formed and controlled as a building: but the words are more impalpable than bricks; reading is a longer and more complicated process than seeing. Perhaps the quickest way to understand the elements of what a novelist is doing is not to read, but to write; to make your own experiment with the dangers and difficulties of words. Recall, then, some event that has left a distinct impression on you—how at the corner of the street, perhaps, you passed two people talking. A tree shook; an electric light danced; the tone of the talk was comic, but also tragic; a whole vision, an entire conception, seemed contained in that moment.

But when you attempt to reconstruct it in words, you will find that it breaks into a thousand conflicting impressions. Some must be subdued; others emphasised; in the process you will lose, probably, all grasp upon the emotion itself. Then turn from your blurred and littered pages to the opening pages of some great novelist—Defoe, Jane Austen, Hardy. Now you will be better able to appreciate their mastery. It is not merely that we are in the presence of a different person—Defoe, Jane Austen, or Thomas Hardy—but that we are living in a different world. Here, in *Robinson Crusoe*, we are trudging a plain high road; one thing happens after another; the fact and the order of the fact is enough. But if the open air and adventure mean everything to Defoe they mean nothing to Jane Austen. Hers is the drawing-room, and people talking, and by the many mirrors of their talk revealing their characters. And if, when we have accustomed ourselves to the drawing-room and its reflections, we turn to Hardy, we are once more spun round. The moors are round us and the stars are above our heads. The other side of the mind is now exposed—the dark side that comes uppermost in solitude, not the light side that shows in company. Our relations are not toward people, but toward Nature and destiny. Yet different as these worlds are, each is consistent with itself. The maker of each is careful to observe the laws of his own perspective, and however great a strain they may put upon us they will never confuse us, as lesser writers so frequently do, by introducing two different kinds of reality into the same book. Thus to go from one great novelist to another—from Jane Austen to Hardy, from Peacock to Trollope, from Scott to Meredith—is to be wrenched and uprooted; to be thrown this way and then that. To read a novel is a difficult and complex art. You must be capable not only of great fineness of perception, but of great boldness of imagination if you are going to make use of all that the novelist—the great artist—gives you.

But a glance at the heterogeneous company on the shelf will show you that writers are very seldom "great artists"; far more often a book makes no claim to be a work of art at all. These biographies and autobiographies, for example, lives of great men, of men long dead and forgotten, that stand cheek by jowl with the novels and poems, are we to refuse to read them because they are not "art"? Or shall we read them, but read them in a different way, with a different aim? Shall we read them in the first place to satisfy that curiosity which possesses us sometimes when in the evening we linger in front of a house where the lights are lit and the blinds are not yet drawn, and each floor of the house shows us a different section of human life in being? Then we are consumed with curiosity about the lives of these people—the servants gossiping, the gentlemen dining, the girl dressing for a party, the old woman at the window with her knitting. Who are they, what are they, what are their names, their occupations, their thoughts, and adventures?

> … writing is the enemy of forgetfulness, of thoughtlessness. For the writer there is no oblivion. Only endless memory.
>
> Anita Brookner

Biographies and memoirs answer such questions, light up innumerable such houses; they show us people going about their daily affairs, toiling, failing, succeeding, eating, hating, loving, until they die. And sometimes as we watch, the house fades and the iron railings vanish and we are out at sea; we are hunting, sailing, fighting; we are among savages and soldiers; we are taking part in great campaigns. Or if we like to stay here in England, in London, still the scene changes; the street narrows; the house becomes small, cramped, diamond-paned, and malodorous. We see a poet, Donne, driven from such a house because the walls were so thin that when the children cried their voices cut through them. We can follow him, through the paths that lie in the pages of books, to Twickenham;[1] to Lady Bedford's Park, a famous meeting-ground for nobles and poets; and then turn our steps to Wilton,[2] the great house under the downs, and hear Sidney[3] read the *Arcadia* to his sister; and ramble among the very marshes and see the very herons that figure in that famous romance; and then again travel north with that other Lady Pembroke,[4] Anne Clifford,[5] to her wild moors, or plunge into the city and control our merriment at the sight of Gabriel Harvey[6] in his black velvet suit arguing about poetry with Spenser. Nothing is more fascinating than to grope and stumble in the alternate darkness and splendour of Elizabethan London. But there is no staying there. The Temples[7] and the Swifts,[8] the Harleys[9] and the St. Johns[10] beckon us on; hour upon hour can be spent disentangling their quarrels and deciphering their character; and when we tire of them we can stroll on, past a lady in black wearing diamonds, to Samuel Johnson and Goldsmith[11] and Garrick,[12] or cross the channel, if we like, and meet Voltaire[13] and Diderot,[14] Madame du Deffand;[15] and so back to England and Twickenham—how certain places repeat themselves and certain names!—where Lady Bedford had her Park once and Pope lived later, to Walpole's home at Strawberry Hill. But Walpole[16] introduces us to such a swarm of new acquaintances, there are so many houses to visit and bells to ring that we may well hesitate for a moment, on the Miss Berrys'[17] doorstep, for example, when behold up comes Thackeray; he is the friend of the woman whom Walpole loved; so that merely by going from friend to friend, from garden to garden, from house to house, we have passed from one end of English literature to another and wake to find ourselves here again in the present, if we can so differentiate this moment from all that have gone before. This, then, is one of the ways in which we can read these lives and letters; we can make them light up the many windows of the past; we can watch the famous dead in their familiar habits and fancy sometimes that we are very close and can surprise their secrets, and sometimes we may pull out a play or a poem that they have written and see whether it reads differently in the presence of the author. But this again rouses other questions. How far, we must ask ourselves, is a book influenced by its writer's life—how far is it safe to let the man interpret the writer? How far shall we resist or give way to the sympathies and antipathies that the man himself rouses in us—so sensitive are words, so receptive of the character of the author? These are questions that press upon us when we read lives and letters, and we must answer them for ourselves, for nothing can be more fatal than to be guided by the preferences of others in a matter so personal.

But also we can read such books with another aim, not to throw light on literature, not to become familiar with famous people, but to refresh and exercise our own creative powers. Is there not an open window on the right hand of the bookcase? How delightful to stop reading and look out! How stimulating the scene is, in its unconsciousness, its irrelevance, its perpetual movement—the colts galloping round the field, the woman filling her pail at the well, the donkey throwing back his head and emitting his long, acrid moan. The greater part of any library is nothing but the record of such fleeting moments in the lives of men, women, and donkeys. Every literature, as it grows old, has its rubbish-heap, its record of vanished moments and forgotten lives told in faltering and feeble accents that have perished. But if you give yourself up to the delight of rubbish-reading you will be surprised, indeed you will be overcome, by the relics of human life that have been cast out to moulder. It may be one letter—but what a vision it gives! It may be a few sentences—but what vistas they suggest! Sometimes a whole story will come together with such beautiful humour and pathos and completeness that it seems as if a great novelist had been at work, yet it is only an old actor, Tate Wilkinson,[18] remembering the strange story of Captain Jones; it is only a young subaltern[19] serving under Arthur Wellesley[20] and falling in love with a pretty girl at Lisbon; it is only Maria Allen[21] letting fall her sewing in the empty drawing-room and sighing how she wishes she had taken Dr. Burney's good advice and had never eloped with her Rishy. None of this has any value; it is negligible in the extreme; yet how absorbing it is now and again to go through the rubbish-heaps and find rings and scissors and broken noses buried in the huge past and try to piece them together while the colt gallops round the field, the woman fills her pail at the well, and the donkey brays.

But we tire of rubbish-reading in the long run. We tire of searching for what is needed to complete the half-truth which is all that the Wilkinsons, the Bunburys, and the Maria Allens are able to offer us. They had not the artist's power of mastering and eliminating; they could not tell the whole truth even about their own lives; they have disfigured the story that might have been so shapely. Facts are all that they can offer us, and facts are a very inferior form of fiction. Thus the desire grows upon us to have done with half-statements and approximations; to cease from searching out the minute shades of human character; to enjoy the greater abstractness, the purer truth of fiction. Thus we create the mood, intense and generalised, unaware of detail, but stressed by some regular, recurrent beat, whose natural expression is poetry; and that is the time to read poetry when we are almost able to write it.

> Western wind, when wilt thou blow?
> The small rain down can rain.
> Christ, if my love were in my arms,
> And I in my bed again![22]

The impact of poetry is so hard and direct that for the moment there is no other sensation except that of the poem itself. What profound depths we visit then—how sudden and complete is our immersion! There is nothing here to catch hold of; nothing to stay us in our flight. The illusion of fiction is gradual; its effects are prepared; but who when they read these four lines stops to ask who wrote them, or conjures up the thought of Donne's house or Sidney's secretary; or enmeshes them in the intricacy of the past and the succession of generations? The poet is always our contemporary. Our being for the moment is centred and constricted, as in any violent shock of personal emotion. Afterwards, it is true, the sensation begins to spread in wider rings through our minds; remoter senses are reached; these begin to sound and to comment and we are aware of echoes and reflections. The intensity of poetry covers an immense range of emotion. We have only to compare the force and directness of

> I shall fall like a tree, and find my grave,
> Only remembering that I grieve,[23]

with the wavering modulation of

> Minutes are numbered by the fall of sands,
> As by an hour glass; the span of time
> Doth waste us to our graves, and we look on it;
> An age of pleasure, revelled out, comes home
> At last, and ends in sorrow; but the life,
> Weary of riot, numbers every sand,
> Wailing in sighs, until the last drop down,
> So to conclude calamity in rest,[24]

or place the meditative calm of

> whether we be young or old,
> Our destiny, our being's heart and home,
> Is with infinitude, and only there;
> With hope it is, hope that can never die,
> Effort, and expectation, and desire,
> And something evermore about to be,[25]

beside the complete and inexhaustible loveliness of

> The moving Moon went up the sky,
> And nowhere did abide:
> Softly she was going up,
> And a star or two beside—[26]

or the splendid fantasy of

> And the woodland haunter
> Shall not cease to saunter
>   When, far down some glade,
> Of the great world's burning
> One soft flame upturning
> Seems, to his discerning,
>   Crocus in the shade,[27]

to bethink us of the varied art of the poet; his power to make us at once actors and spectators; his power to run his hand into character as if it were a glove, and be Falstaff or Lear; his power to condense, to widen, to state, once and for ever.

"We have only to compare"—with those words the cat is out of the bag, and the true complexity of reading is admitted. The first process, to receive impressions with the utmost understanding, is only half the process of reading; it must be completed, if we are to get the whole pleasure from a book, by another. We must pass judgment upon these multitudinous impressions; we must make of these fleeting shapes one that is hard and lasting. But not directly. Wait for the dust of reading to settle; for the conflict and the questioning to die down; walk, talk, pull

> It is so unsatisfactory to read a noble passage
> and have no one you love at hand to share
> the happiness with you.
>
> Clara Clemens

the dead petals from a rose, or fall asleep. Then suddenly without our willing it, for it is thus that Nature undertakes these transitions, the book will return, but differently. It will float to the top of the mind as a whole. And the book as a whole is different from the book received currently in separate phrases. Details now fit themselves into their places. We see the shape from start to finish; it is a barn, a pig-sty, or a cathedral. Now then we can compare book with book as we compare building with building. But this act of comparison means that our attitude has changed; we are no longer the friends of the writer, but his judges; and just as we cannot be too sympathetic as friends, so as judges we cannot be too severe. Are they not criminals, books that have wasted our time and sympathy; are they not the most insidious enemies of society, corrupters, defilers, the writers of false books, faked books, books that fill the air with decay and disease? Let us then be severe in our judgments; let us compare each book with the greatest of its kind. There they hang in the mind, the shapes of the books we have read solidified by the judgments we have passed on them—*Robinson Crusoe, Emma, The Return of the Native.* Compare the novels with these—even the latest and least of novels has a right to be judged with the best. And so with poetry—when the intoxication of rhythm has died down and the splendour of words has faded, a visionary shape will return to us and this must be compared with *Lear*, with *Phedre*, with *The Prelude*; or if not with these, with whatever is the best or seems to us to be the best in its own kind. And we may be sure that the newness of new poetry and fiction is its most superficial quality and that we have only to alter slightly, not to recast, the standards by which we have judged the old.

It would be foolish, then, to pretend that the second part of reading, to judge, to compare, is as simple as the first—to open the mind wide to the fast flocking of innumerable impressions. To continue reading without the book before you, to hold one shadow-shape against another, to have read widely enough and with enough understanding to make such comparisons alive and illuminating—that is difficult; it is still more difficult to press further and to say, "Not only is the book of this sort, but it is of this value; here it fails; here it succeeds; this is bad; that is good." To carry out this part of a reader's duty needs such imagination, insight, and learning that it is hard to conceive any one mind sufficiently endowed; impossible for the most self-confident to find more than the seeds of such powers in himself. Would it not be wiser, then, to remit this part of reading and to allow the critics, the gowned and furred authorities of the library, to decide the question of the book's absolute value for us? Yet how impossible! We may stress the value of sympathy; we may try to sink our own identity as we read. But we know that we cannot sympathise wholly or immerse ourselves wholly; there is always a demon in us who whispers, "I hate, I love," and we cannot silence him. Indeed, it is precisely because we hate and we love that our relation with the poets and novelists is so intimate that we find the presence of another person intolerable. And even if the results are abhorrent and our judgments are wrong, still our taste, the nerve of sensation that sends shocks through us, is our chief illuminant; we learn through feeling; we cannot suppress our own idiosyncrasy without improvising it. But as time goes on perhaps we can train our taste; perhaps we can make it submit to some control. When it has fed greedily and lavishly upon books of all sort—poetry, fiction, history, biography—and has stopped reading and looked for long spaces upon the variety, the incongruity of the living word, we shall find that it is changing a little; it is not so greedy, it is more reflective. It will begin to bring us not merely judgments on particular books, but it will tell us that there is a quality common to certain books. Listen, it will say, what shall we call *this*? And it will read us perhaps *Lear* and then perhaps the *Agamemnon* in order to bring out that common quality. Thus, with our taste to guide us, we shall venture beyond the particular book in search of qualities that group books together; we shall give them names and thus frame a rule that brings order into our perceptions. We shall gain a further and a rarer pleasure from that discrimination. But as a rule only lives when it is perpetually broken by contact with the books themselves—nothing is easier and more stultifying than to make rules which exist out of touch with facts, in a vacuum—now at last, in order to steady ourselves in this difficult attempt, it may be well to turn to the very rare writers who are able to enlighten us upon literature as an art. Coleridge and Dryden and Johnson, in their considered criticism, the poets and novelists themselves in their unconsidered sayings, are often surprisingly relevant; they light up and solidify the vague ideas that have been tumbling in the misty depths of our minds. But they are only able to help us if we come to them laden with questions and suggestions won honestly in the course of our own reading. They can do nothing for us if we herd ourselves under their authority and lie down like sheep in the shade of a hedge. We can only understand their ruling when it comes in conflict with our own and vanquishes it.

If this is so, if to read a book as it should be read calls for the rarest qualities of imagination, insight, and judgment, you may perhaps conclude that literature is a very complex art and that it is unlikely that we shall be able, even after a lifetime of reading, to make any valuable contribution to its criticism. We must remain readers; we shall not put on the further glory that belongs to those rare beings who are also critics.

But still we have our responsibilities as readers and even our importance. The standards we raise and the judgment we pass steal into the air and become part of the atmosphere which writers breathe as they work. An influence is created which tells upon them even if it never finds its way into print. And that influence, if it were well instructed, vigorous and individual and sincere, might be of great value now when criticism is necessarily in abeyance; when books pass in review like the procession of animals in a shooting gallery, and the critic has only one second in which to load and aim and shoot and may well be pardoned if he mistakes rabbits for tigers, eagles for barndoor fowls, or misses altogether and wastes his shot upon some peaceful cow grazing in a further field. If behind the erratic gunfire of the press the author felt that there was another kind of criticism, the opinion of people reading for the love of reading, slowly and unprofessionally, and judging with great sympathy and yet with great severity, might this not improve the quality of his work? And if by our means books were to become stronger, richer, and more varied, that would be an end worth reaching.

Yet who reads to bring about an end, however desirable? Are there not some pursuits that we practise because they are good in themselves, and some pleasures that are final? And is not this among them? I have sometimes dreamt, at least, that when the Day of Judgment dawns and the great conquerors and lawyers and statesmen come to receive their rewards—their crowns, their laurels, their names carved indelibly upon imperishable marble—the Almighty will turn to Peter and will say, not without a certain envy when He sees us coming with our books under our arms, "Look, these need no reward. We have nothing to give them here. They have loved reading."

---

[1]**Twickenham:** city on the Thames, near London
[2]**Wilton:** town in England
[3]**Sidney:** Sir Philip Sidney (1554–1586), English poet, soldier, and statesman
[4]**Pembroke:** Sidney's sister was Mary, Countess of Pembroke, whose country house was at Wilton
[5]**Anne Clifford:** Anne Clifford Herbert, Countess of Pembroke (1590–1676); her diary was published in 1923
[6]**Gabriel Harvey:** English author (circa 1545–1630)
[7]**The Temples:** Sir William Temple (1628–1699), English author and statesman
[8]**the Swifts:** Jonathan Swift, *cf.* "A Modest Proposal" above
[9]**the Harleys:** Robert Harley, first Earl of Oxford (1661–1724), English statesman, left a valuable collection of manuscripts and pamphlets

[10]**the St. Johns:** Henry St. John, first Viscount Bolingbroke (1678–1751), English statesman and writer
[11]**Goldsmith:** Oliver Goldsmith (1728–1784), English poet, novelist, and dramatist
[12]**Garrick:** David Garrick (1717–1779), English actor
[13]**Voltaire:** born François Marie Arouet (1694–1778), French satirist, philosopher, and historian, known as Voltaire
[14]**Diderot:** Denis Diderot (1713–1784), French philosopher and encyclopedist
[15]**Madame du Deffand:** Marie de Vichy-Chamrond, Marquise du Deffand (1697–1780), witty and cynical Frenchwoman, leader in Parisian literary and philosophical circles
[16]**Walpole:** Horace Walpole, fourth Earl of Oxford (1717–1797), English author
[17]**the Miss Berrys:** Mary Berry (1763–1852), English authoress, and Agnes Berry (1764–1852), were both friends of Horace Walpole
[18]**Wilkinson:** English actor (1739–1803), fond of telling stories of real people, author of *Memoirs of His Own Life*; see V. Woolf's *Death of the Moth*
[19]**subaltern:** see *Memoirs and Literary Remains* of Lieutenant-General Sir Edward Henry Bunbury, bart. (1868)
[20]**Arthur Wellesley:** Duke of Wellington, English general and statesman (1769–1852)
[21]**Maria Allen:** see William S. Allen, *Memoirs of Mrs. Allen of Woodbread Hall, Staffordshire*, 1871; mentioned by V. Woolf in two essays in *Granite and Rainbow*. (With thanks to Professors James Hafley, Donald Weeks, and J. J. Wilson, for these and following identifications.)
[22]anonymous Renaissance lyric
[23]from John Ford's *Lovers' Melancholy*
[24]ibid.
[25]from Wordsworth's *Prelude*, Book VI
[26]from Coleridge's *Ancient Mariner*
[27]from Ebenezer Jones' *When the World Is Burning*

Virginia Woolf, British novelist, critic, and essayist, was born in 1882. She was a leader in the literary movement of modernism, and used a "stream of consciousness" technique in her writing, which revealed her characters' lives by representing the flow of their thoughts and perceptions. Her works include the novels *To the Lighthouse, Orlando,* and *Mrs. Dalloway,* and the essay, *"A Room of One's Own."*

1. Response

a. Using your own words, develop a short summary of Woolf's argument in this essay. Discuss your summary with a classmate.

b. Why does Woolf suggest that readers "try to become" the author they are reading? Do you agree with the point she is trying to make? Why or why not?

c. Find one analogy in the essay and explain to a partner why it is or is not effective.

d. What is Woolf's final answer to the question she raises in the title? Explain your own position on this question.

2. Making Connections Reread the fourth paragraph and consider what Woolf is saying about the different worlds a novelist creates. Do you agree or disagree with her point? Choose one novelist she mentions, or another classic novelist, and describe the world he/she creates for you. How do you respond to this world? Do you choose to read certain novels because of how much you enjoy the world they create? Explain.

3. Focus on Context In the fifth paragraph, Woolf refers to "These biographies and autobiographies, for example, lives of great men, of men long dead and forgotten ..." Why do you think she does not use the gender-neutral phrase "lives of great people"? Use Internet or print resources to research the life of this great woman—Virginia Woolf—and then write a report explaining her use of gender-biassed language.

4. Writing Essay Brainstorm some questions that you consider important or essential, like Woolf's question, "How should one read a book?" Develop an outline for an essay that explores possible answers to that question. Use your outline to help you write an essay. Your title could be the original question you posed.

Theme Connections

- *"Two Words,"* a story about the power of words, page 51
- *"Making Poetry Pay,"* an anecdote about the power of words, page 284
- *"What Will Your Verse Be?"* a movie monologue about the importance of language, page 514

Art History

Speech by Doreen Jensen

In my language, there is no word for "Art." This is not because we are devoid of Art, but because Art is so powerfully integrated with all aspects of life, we are replete with it. For the sake of brevity and clarity, I will use the word "Art" tonight.

This exhibition and forum, "Indigena," asks us to reflect on the impact of European colonization on indigenous cultures. In my talk, I'd like to offer a different perspective. I would like to remind you of the Art that the Europeans found when they arrived in our country.

The Europeans found Art everywhere. In hundreds of flourishing, vital cultures, Art was fully integrated with daily life. They saw dwellings painted with abstract Art that was to inspire generations of European painters. Ceremonial robes were intricately woven Art that heralded the wearers' identity and privilege in the community. Utilitarian objects, including food vessels, storage containers, and clothing, were powerfully formed and decorated with the finest, most significant Art.

Each nation had its theatre, music, and choreography. The first Europeans found hundreds of languages in use—not dialects but languages. And in every language, our Artists created philosophical argument and sacred ceremony, political discourse, fiction, and poetry.

The Europeans saw Earth Art and large-scale environmental Art projects. From the East to the West Coast, what were later called petroglyphs and pictographs recorded our histories. My own earliest memories of Art are of the tall sculptures that told the long histories of my people. These tall sculptures are called "totem poles," like the ones you see here in the Great Hall of the Museum of Civilization.

When the Europeans arrived, they found Aboriginal Artists creating beauty, culture, and historical memory. Art built bridges between human life and the natural world. Art mediated between material and spiritual concerns. Art stimulated our individuality, making us alert and alive. It affirmed our cultural identities.

I say all this to honour our cultural accomplishments. As Aboriginal Artists, we need to reclaim our own identities, through our work, our heritage and our future. We don't need any longer to live within others' definitions of who and what we are. We need to put aside titles that have been imposed on our creativity—titles that serve the needs of other people. For too long our Art has been situated in the realm of anthropology by a discourse that validates only white Artists.

Today there are many Art forms of the First Nations which are still not being recognized. Think of the exquisite sea grass baskets from the West Coast of Vancouver Island, the quill work and moose hair tufting Arts of the people east of the Rockies, and ceremonial robes, woven and appliquéd, throughout North America. Not surprisingly, these exquisite works of Art are mainly done by women.

Art can be a universal language which helps us bridge the gaps between our different cultures. But attitudes towards Art reveal racism. The first Europeans called our Art "primitive" and "vulgar." Today, people of European origin call our Art "craft" and "artifact."

Our elders have nurtured the important cultural traditions against tremendous odds. It is time for us to sit still, and let these powerful, precious teachings come to us. Our elders bequeathed us a great legacy of communication through the Arts.

Art is essential, for all of us. Artists are our spiritual advisers. In another five hundred years, who is going to remember Prime-Minister-What's-His-Name or Millionaire-What's-His-Name? Our cultural life— our Art—is all we will be remembered by.

I believe that culture is the soul of the nation. Canada *is* the First Nations. Canada *is* the English and the French who have struggled to make a new world here. Canada *is* also the other cultures who come to make a new life. The culture of the Indigenous people is the fertile soil where these new cultures are flourishing.

Think of the important Iroquois symbol of the eagle with five feathers in its talons. Because it is such a powerful image, the American government appropriated it to use as its insignia and cultural identity. This is just one tiny example of the unacknowledged appropriation of Indian Art which has nourished North American culture for five centuries.

As we enter this new age that is being called "The Age of Information," I like to think it is the age when healing will take place. This is a good time to acknowledge our accomplishments. This is a good time to share. We need to learn from the wisdom of our ancestors. We need to recognize the hard work of our predecessors which has brought us to where we are today. We need to look to the future, and to where we can incorporate our own wisdom and vision in a healing culture for all peoples.

During the Oka crisis, Canada's mask slipped to reveal the ugly and treacherous face of racism. At last, people could see the many injustices that need to be changed in order for Canada to become a strong country. Some cultural institutions have opened their doors a crack, and begun to take initiatives to mend the cultural fabric of Canada. All cultural institutions need to begin dialogues with Aboriginal people, and develop frameworks within which we can work together on a just representation of Aboriginal cultures.

First Nations Artists have something vitally important to offer—a new (or ancient) aesthetic, a way of understanding Art and the world that can heal this country, and help us all to find a place in it.

For North West Coast Indian Artists, the act of creativity comes from the cosmos. That is what I have been told by the old people. When I'm making Art, I am one with the universe. You can see it in the work, if you look with your heart, as well as your mind. If you really pay attention, you can "get the message"—and make it your own, without diminishing it or appropriating it.

If we pay attention, First Nations Art will remind us of this basic rule for being a human being: When I diminish others' "belongingness" in the universe, my own "belongingness" becomes uncertain.

Canada is an image which hasn't emerged yet. Because this country hasn't recognized its First Nations, its whole foundation is shaky. If Canada is to emerge as a nation with cultural identity and purpose, we have to accept First Nations Art, and what it has to tell us about the spirit and the land.

Our Art is our cultural identity; it's our politics. The late George Manuel said, "This land is our culture." I add to that, "Our culture is this land." Whether you acknowledge it or ignore it, the land and the culture are one. Land claims have to be settled, before Canadians can look at themselves in the mirror and see an image they would be proud to see.

George Erasmus said, "What has happened in the last five hundred years is not important. What is important is what we do in the next five hundred years."

Everywhere it is a time for choices. There is still white water ahead. The choices we make today can alter our course forever, not only nationally but throughout the world.

Today is a time to share, a time to enjoy the glory of your achievements. I congratulate all of you who have made this exhibition possible: the curators, the writers, and the museum. Most importantly, I thank you, the Artists—who have shared your personal visions.

Grizzly Bear Headdress, work in progress by Doreen Jensen.

Examine the above photos and write a description of the artwork they depict. Include your personal response to this work of art.

Doreen Jensen (originally Hahl Yee) is a graduate of the Kitanmax School of North West Coast Indian Art and has won many awards for her work. Her first language is Gitksan, and she describes herself as a "traditional Gitksan artist," working in the fields of sculpture, performance art, songs, dance, writing, and fabric art. Jensen actively promotes Aboriginal cultures and works toward getting contemporary Aboriginal art into Canada's major art museums.

I. *Response*
a. What is Doreen Jensen trying to get her audience to understand or accept? What are her main points?
b. Do you agree with Jensen's main points? Why or why not?
c. Consider the first sentence as an example of concise writing. What information is conveyed in just nine words?
d. Look up the words *indigenous* and *aboriginal* to find their roots, and to compare their meanings. Also look up *First Nations* and *Indian,* and find out more about their meanings and preferred usage.

2. *Oral Language* *Group Discussion* With three or four class-mates, respond to the following questions: What various forms does "art" encompass? How important is art to you? To your community or culture? Do you agree that art is all we will be remembered by? If so, what form or what particular piece of art would you choose to represent you and your community or culture?

3. *Literature Studies* *Persuasive Writing* In persuasive writing, writers state a thesis and provide support or evidence for their opinion. They often use logical reasoning and appeal to readers' emotions. Sometimes, they also predict any opposing viewpoints and refute them. Using the above criteria, assess the effectiveness of this selection.

4. *Focus on Context* Jensen delivered this as a talk at the Museum of Civilization in Hull, Québec, in 1992, for the opening of the display called "Indigena: Perspectives of Indigenous Peoples on Five Hundred Years." What clues are there in the selection that it was written for a specific purpose, and that it was an oral presentation? How has her context affected her content?

The artist, Gu Xiong, grew up in China during the
Cultural Revolution. During that time, the art he was
exposed to consisted mainly of postcards produced by
unknown artists during that period, and the works of the
Group of Seven. In fact, the Group of Seven paintings
formed his impressions of Canada. Gu Xiong produced
the following art exhibit with Canadian artist and curator
Andrew Hunter, to juxtapose the different images of
China and Canada that influenced them and their work.

Images From the
Cultural
Revolution

from an Art Exhibit
compiled by
Gu Xiong
and
Andrew Hunter

Mountains and Lake, 1929 by Lawren S. Harris.

只有解放全人類
才能最後解放無產
階級自己。

White Pine, circa 1957, by A. J. Casson.

Sunlight Tapestry, circa 1939, by A.Y. Jackson

Gu Xiong was born in the Sichuan province of the People's Republic of China in 1953. He was forced to flee China after the Tiananmen Square demonstrations in 1989. He now lives in Vancouver.

1. *Response*
   a. In your own words, explain why Gu Xiong and Andrew Hunter chose to display these Chinese postcards from the Cultural Revolution with works by the Group of Seven.
   b. Choose one image—either a postcard or painting—and record your response to it. How does the image make you feel? What does it make you think of? What does it remind you of? Share your response with a classmate.
   c. If the Group of Seven paintings were the only Canadian artwork Gu Xiong saw as a youngster, how do you think he would have felt about Canada?

2. *Research and Inquiry* Use the Internet or library resources to investigate one member of the Group of Seven or a Chinese artist of the Cultural Revolution. Find out what influenced the artist, and the effect his/her work has had on others. Develop a two-page report on the artist, including an assessment of one piece of his/her art.

3. *Visual Communication* Art Exhibit Create a visual essay that juxtaposes two major influences in your life. Write a fifty-word introduction to your essay explaining the images you have chosen.

4. *Film Study* Investigate the life of an artist as portrayed in movies by watching a movie like *My Left Foot, Frida, Pollock, Lust for Life, Artemesia,* or *Basquiat.* Investigate the artist's life further by examining some print texts as well, such as a biography or autobiography. In your opinion, what advantages and disadvantages does a movie have in offering a portrayal of the life of an artist?

Stone
Faces

from an Essay by Sharon Butala

"I am always trying to see this land as it must have
been before farmers plowed it, before domesticated
cattle came to graze it bare, before there were
highways, towns, power poles, and rows of gleaming
steel grain bins."

On a clear fall morning, I went to St. Victor Historic Petroglyphs Park
south of Moose Jaw. I climbed and climbed in my borrowed car to the
top of the Wood Mountain Uplands until I reached the park gate,
stopped, got out, found the stairs, and began the long climb on foot to
the top of the cliff where the glyphs are incised on the horizontal surface of the rock. I was the only person in the entire park, and, in the
stillness and the clarity of that morning, I felt my solitude gravely and
as a blessing.

At the top I stopped and looked around. The beautiful, treed village of St. Victor was lost in foliage below, and to the north and on an
angle beyond it Montague Lake shone softly. I could see for miles in
two directions where not a soul, a bird, a cow stirred. On the still air a
noise came faintly from the direction of the lake a mile or more away; I
listened hard, trying to identify it. At first I thought it was a farm dog
barking, then it seemed there was more than one voice and I thought,
oh, coyotes, but no, the sound came clearer and I realized it was geese,
pausing for water and to search out wheat kernels in the nearby farmer's
field that had been thrown over during combining, as sustenance to
strengthen them for their journey south. All alone and with no pressing
business, I took the time to gaze and gaze out across the landscape.
Soon two mule deer broke out of the brush below where I stood,
climbed a wooded ridge and disappeared over its crown.

Eventually I remembered to look at the glyphs, which were at my
feet immediately on the other side of the railing I was leaning on.

It took a moment, after that dazzling, endless view, to bring my mind and my eyes into focus so I could pick them out. Then I saw a human face staring up at me, carved when, no one is sure, and by whom, no one knows. Something unexpected gripped me quickly, hard, deep in my abdomen, a chill, a *frisson* of the numinous, and then let go.

In that silence and stillness I became aware of the sun hanging huge and yellow just above the back of my head, the guardian, the Other, the powerful and constant presence at that place. Its angled rays brought the many glyphs, invisible in higher light, into existence; each morning and each evening its rays created them anew: human hand-prints, faces and footprints, grizzly bear claws, bison hoofprints leading over the edge of the high cliff.

That year I had time to go to only one more prehistoric rock art site before winter snows covered them. This one is on another high, gently rounded, long hill, this time above a creek, and overlooks the small city of Swift Current. Here, two bison, their bodies chipped out of the rock till they form small basins, sat enigmatically just where they'd been for as long as two or three thousand years.

"Why would they do it?" an archaeologist asked me rhetorically. "They aren't work; that is, they don't produce food or clothing, or make houses. Think how hard this must have been to do, how long it must have taken. Their people must have seen it as important, and it follows, then, that these must have had to do with their spiritual life."

I am always trying to see this land as it must have been before farmers plowed it, before domesticated cattle came to graze it bare, before there were highways, towns, power poles, and rows of gleaming steel grain bins. I try to imagine it as the prehistoric people who lived here must have seen it and, from that, to feel what they might have felt. Now I rose from kneeling in the grass beside the stone bison and looked out toward the city where once there had been only uncounted hills and grass. At that moment it seemed less real than the petroglyph I'd come a hundred miles to see.

As I'd driven out of the yard that morning on my way to the edge of this distant city, the sun on my right was only a faint yellow gleam below the horizon, and on my left a white, three-quarter moon was riding the serpentine hills. For miles as I drove the deserted highway I watched the sun rise. First a red glow, then a radiant ruby arc like molten metal dissolving to gold at the edges, then the sun was above the horizon and too bright to look at. I began to watch its light pouring across the fields that flanked the highway, and beyond them the near hills, and behind them the land, as it lifted chunkily in blue folds toward the sky.

To ask what a carving in stone of a turtle, paintings or carvings of other animals and humans on or in stone, or human or animal footprints *mean* is to be distracted by something that seems to me irrelevant and unimportant. What matters is that they were *done* by humans like you and me. In such beauty there can be no response but awe. It was not an accident that all these sites had stunning views across miles of land with a clear view of the setting sun (sometimes the rising sun, I'm told) . . . It was the act of a people who, whether living ten thousand or two hundred years ago, knew desire and hope, remembered long and well, felt respect and reverence, had a sense of grace—had souls as puny and as magnificent, as various as ours.

Sharon Butala was born in Saskatchewan, Canada, in 1940 and attended the University of Saskatchewan. Her first novel, *Country of the Heart*, was nominated for the Books in Canada Best First Novel Award.

1. *Response*
   a. Have you ever seen a petroglyph? Describe or sketch it. How did your response to it compare with that of Butala?
   b. Butala's essay combines elements of descriptive and narrative essay techniques. Identify an exemplary passage for each type of essay.
   c. Find some photos or paintings of the Saskatchewan landscape. How do you relate to that landscape?

2. *Language Focus* Word Choices Professional writers make careful word choices to create exactly the image or message they want to get across to the reader. For example, consider Butala's use of the verbs "a cow *stirred*" and "light *pouring*." Substitute "moved" and "shining," respectively. Why are those verbs less effective?
   Choose a part of speech, such as a verb, adjective, adverb, or noun, and find examples in this essay of effective word choices for that part of speech. Try substituting other words to see how effective Butala's words are.

3. *Making Connections* With a partner, discuss "Art History" and "Stone Faces." Write a letter in role, from one author to the other, in which you comment on the other's selection and on how your ideas and opinions compare. Your partner can respond to your letter in role as the other author.

Langston Hughes was a central figure in the Harlem Renaissance—
a time of rising expression of African-American culture in the 1920s
and '30s. During the '30s and '40s, Hughes often went on tour to read
his poetry. In this selection, he recounts details
from his public readings.

Making Poetry Pay

Personal Essay
by Langston Hughes

By midwinter I had worked out a public routine of reading my poetry that almost never failed to provoke, after each poem, some sort of audible audience response—laughter, applause, a grunt, a groan, a sigh, or an "Amen!" I began my programs quite simply by telling where I was born in Missouri, that I grew up in Kansas in the geographical heart of the country, and was therefore very American, that I belonged to a family that was always moving; and I told something of my early travels about the Midwest and how, at fourteen, in Lincoln, Illinois, I was elected Class Poet for the eighth-grade graduating exercises, and from then on I kept writing poetry.

After this biographical introduction I would read to my audiences the first of my poems, written in high school, and show how my poetry had changed over the years. To start my reading, I usually selected some verses written when I was about fifteen:

I had my clothes cleaned
Just like new.
I put 'em on but
I still feels blue.

I bought a new hat,
Sho is fine,
But I wish I had back that
Old gal o' mine

I got new shoes,
They don't hurt my feet,
But I ain't got nobody
To call me sweet.

Then I would say, "That's a sad poem, isn't it?" Everybody would laugh. Then I would read some of my jazz poems so my listeners could laugh more. I wanted them to laugh a lot early in the program, so that later in the evening they would not laugh when I read poems like "Porter":

I must say,
Yes, sir,
To you all the time.
Yes, sir!
Yes, sir!

All my days
Climbing up a great big mountain
Of yes, sirs!

Rich old white man
Owns the world.
Gimme yo' shoes to shine.

Yes, sir, boss!
Yes, sir!

By the time I reached this point in the program my nonliterary listeners would be ready to think in terms of their own problems. Then I read poems about women domestics, workers on the Florida roads, poor black students wanting to shatter the darkness of ignorance and prejudice, and one about the sharecroppers of the Mississippi:

Just a herd of Negroes
Driven to the field,
Plowing, planting, hoeing,
To make the cotton yield.

When the cotton's picked
And the work is done,
Boss man takes the money
And you get none.

Just a herd of Negroes
Driven to the field.
Plowing, planting, hoeing,
To make the cotton yield.

Many of my verses were documentary, journalistic and topical. All across the South that winter I read my poems about the plight of the Scottsboro boys[1]:

Justice is a blind goddess.
To this we blacks are wise:
Her bandage hides two festering sores
That once perhaps were eyes.

Usually people were deeply attentive. But if at some point in the program my audience became restless—as audiences sometimes will, no matter what a speaker is saying—or if I looked down from the platform and noticed someone about to go to sleep, I would pull out my ace in the hole, a poem called "Cross." This poem, delivered dramatically, I had learned, would make anybody, white or black, sit up and take notice. It is a poem about miscegenation—a very provocative subject in the South. The first line—intended to awaken all sleepers—I would read in a loud voice:

My old man's a white old man....

And this would usually arouse any one who dozed. Then I would pause before continuing in a more subdued tone:

My old mother's black.

---

[1]**Scottsboro boys:** In 1931, in Alabama, nine black teenage boys were falsely accused of raping two white girls. The struggle for justice in the case went on for years.

Then in a low, sad, thoughtful tragic vein:

> *But if ever I cursed my white old man*
> *I take my curses back.*
>
> *If ever I cursed my black old mother*
> *And wished she were in hell,*
> *I'm sorry for that evil wish*
> *And now I wish her well.*
>
> *My old man died in a fine big house,*
> *My ma died in a shack.*
> *I wonder where I'm gonna die,*
> *Being neither white nor black.*

Here I would let my voice trail off into a lonely silence. Then I would stand quite still for a long time, because I knew I had the complete attention of my listeners again.

Usually after a résumé of the racial situation in our country, with an optimistic listing of past achievements on the part of Negroes, and future possibilities, I would end the evening with:

> *I, too, sing America.*
>
> *I am the darker brother.*
> *They send me*
> *To eat in the kitchen*
> *When company comes,*
> *But I laugh,*
> *And eat well,*
> *And grow strong.*
>
> *Tomorrow*
> *I'll sit at the table*
> *When company comes.*
> *Nobody'll dare*
> *Say to me,*
> *"Eat in the kitchen,"*
> *Then.*
>
> *Besides,*
> *They'll see*
> *How beautiful I am*
> *And be ashamed.*
>
> *I, too, am America.*

Langston Hughes was born in Missouri in 1902. He wrote novels, short stories, poetry, and plays, and his work was influenced greatly by jazz and blues. His works include the non-fiction titles, *I Wonder as I Wander*, and *The Langston Hughes Reader*. He died in 1967.

1. *Response*
   a. What would you say are some features of a personal essay? Why could this selection be considered a personal essay?
   b. What is the range of social issues that Hughes deals with in his poetry?
   c. What kind of reactions did Hughes seek in his public readings? What kind of reaction does he seek in this essay? How is the reader of the essay similar to the listener in the audience of his poetry reading? Do you think that he was successful in "making poetry pay"?

2. *Focus on Context* With a partner, read the biography of Hughes included above, and consider where and when he lived. If necessary, research his life further. Discuss what life would have been like for him as an African-American during that time period. How was his work affected by when and where he lived? How might readers at the time have been affected by his work? How are present-day readers affected by his work? Explain your personal response to one of the poems included in this selection.

3. *Language Conventions* Transitional Words In examining the pattern of the essay, you probably noted the use of words that marked a change in time, which helped you identify the chronology of events. Identify and list three of these words. Where do they appear in the paragraphs? How effective is their use? How effectively do you use transition words in your essay writing?

4. *Literature Studies* Essay Organization One of the ways of organizing an essay is through *chronological order*, meaning the writer examines a situation or event in the order in which it occurred. Trace the time pattern of this essay as it follows the pattern of Hughes's public readings. Then, consider how the poems work in the essay—how does each poem function in supporting Hughes's purpose?

As people grow up, they sometimes look back on their experiences and see them with new eyes.

A New Perspective

Essay by Janice E. Fein

Our lives are shaped by the seemingly insignificant events of our youth. My childhood has become a series of mental snips of celluloid edited from the long playing film entitled "Cheated in Life."

My mother is walking me to kindergarten. I'm sure it must be kindergarten. In future years it would become vitally important for me to remember just exactly when it was. If it were first or second grade we would have been walking in the opposite direction but I can clearly see each familiar house as we pass by: Leedom's, Neiman's, Salem's, yes, it was definitely kindergarten. The film clip does not take us to our final destination, nor does it begin at home. It's a simple walk down a simple block in time. I can still feel my left fingers cradled in the smooth grip of her hand, one not much bigger than that of my own. I actually feel the warmth of the rising sun on my face as I look up at her each time she speaks. Aha! It was kindergarten! The sun always rose from behind that row of houses. If we had been walking anywhere else, the sun would have been in her face, not mine. She never walked me to elementary school. She only walked me to kindergarten, and very possibly, only that one time. Was it the first day of school? Or Parent's Day? It was unimportant. What became important, in later years, was my ability to woefully lament, "I only remember my mother walking one time in my life. She walked me to kindergarten."

Thereafter, all recollections of her were in her hospital bed, a massive ugly thing that took up a good portion of my parents' room. The debilitating effects of rheumatoid arthritis confined her to that bed. There were, however, what she referred to as "good days," days in which she was able to drag herself from her bed and onto a small kitchen chair with curved metal legs. She would then muster enough energy to force her hips in an awkward motion. Each painful hip movement would inch the chair laboriously forward, commanding it to perform the tasks that her frozen arthritic joints could not accomplish. My friends never came to my room to play. To do so they would have to pass by my parents' room. I remember that bed and that chair as embarrassing eyesores and how, once again, I had felt cheated.

Connie had the best playroom in the neighborhood. She was my very best friend and every day after school I would race home to change clothes and, in a heartbeat, I was at her door. Half of her basement was converted into a wonderful playhouse with panelling, carpets, and lace curtains to match. I was sure that every toy ever created was in that room. Despite the lure of all those treasures, what I remember most were the marvelous sounds and smells that drifted down to us from the kitchen above. Pots and pans clanging, water rushing through the pipes, and best of all, Connie's mother humming softly as she worked. One particular evening, the aroma was so compelling that I had to ask. Connie wrinkled her nose in disgust and said, "Lasagna … again!" I pretended to have to use the bathroom so that I could pass through the kitchen and briefly glimpse what a lasagna looked like.

The oven timer was the saddest sound. When I heard it I knew what was coming next. "Connie, come wash up for supper," and I would have to leave. At a snail's pace, I would wander back to my own kitchen door. No wonderful aromas ever greeted me there. Sometimes there would be cold macaroni and cheese left over by one of my brothers or sisters. Most often I would prepare something on my own. Frozen hamburger patties, fish sticks, maybe I'll just have a can of soup. It never really mattered. It would never be lasagna. One evening, as I wander into my mother's room, bologna sandwich in hand, she shakes her head and says, "Is that the best you can find out there?" "I'm not very hungry," I lie. Only now can I see that the look in her eyes matched the despair in my heart, and yet, I felt cheated.

As childhood progressed, certain actions became innate. Handouts at school calling for volunteer room mothers and field trip chaperones were surreptitiously discarded along the nine-block journey home. I'll never forget those nine long blocks. In January and February they might just as well have been ninety! My classmates are piling into their mothers' warm waiting station wagons. I hunch my shoulders to my ears and silently watch as they disappear into the swirling gusts of snow. No steaming mug of hot cocoa is awaiting my arrival, just those sad eyes. Cheated.

I've rolled the film a thousand times. The scenes have never changed, only my perspective. It took the birth of my first child to truly see the whole picture. I've often tried to imagine what it would be like to see my son in pain and not be able to brush away a tear, mend a knee or simply hold him in my arms. I've seen the look in his eyes when he hit his first home run. I've "hugged him warm" on snowy days and "tickled him happy" when life was cruel. I've knelt with him to say his prayers and thanked God for my ability to do so. I may never understand why some of us are cheated in life. I only know, from this perspective, that I am not the one who was.

Janice E. Fein, born in 1948, graduated from the University of Akron in 1992. She works in the field of social services as a case worker for abused and neglected children.

1. *Response*
   a. What were the predominant emotions felt by the author in her early school days?
   b. What event determines the author's understanding of who was really "cheated" in life? Why do you think this particular event gives the author this insight?
   c. As you were reading the essay, what was your feeling toward the author? Did your opinion change? How does the author guide her readers toward feeling that way? Explain.

2. *Literature Studies Essay Structure* The author of this essay follows a traditional essay structure; one that can be used in any type of essay (personal, analytic, persuasive, argumentative, narrative).
   The *introduction*—(usually the first paragraph) clearly states the main idea or thesis.
   The *body*—(a series of paragraphs after the introduction) develops ideas or arguments to support the main idea or thesis.
   The *conclusion*—(usually the last paragraph) summarizes key points, provides a logical follow-up to the thesis and arguments, and is an insightful ending to the essay.
   Examine "A New Perspective" and identify each of the above parts or components; then consider the conclusion closely. How does it link to the introduction (a device called "closing by return")?

Only Daughter

Memoir by Sandra Cisneros

Once, several years ago, when I was just starting out my writing career, I was asked to write my own contributor's note for an anthology I was part of. I wrote: "I am the only daughter in a family of six sons. *That* explains everything."

Well, I've thought about that ever since, and yes, it explains a lot to me, but for the reader's sake I should have written: "I am the only daughter in a *Mexican* family of six sons." Or even: "I am the only daughter of a Mexican father and a Mexican-American mother." Or: "I am the only daughter of a working-class family of nine." All of these had everything to do with who I am today.

I was/am the only daughter and *only* a daughter. Being an only daughter in a family of six sons forced me by circumstance to spend a lot of time by myself because my brothers felt it beneath them to play with a *girl* in public. But that aloneness, that loneliness, was good for a would-be writer—it allowed me time to think and think, to imagine, to read and prepare myself.

Being only a daughter for my father meant my destiny would lead me to become someone's wife. That's what he believed. But when I was in fifth grade and shared my plans for college with him, I was sure he understood. I remember my father saying, "*Que bueno, mi'ja*, that's good." That meant a lot to me, especially since my brothers thought the idea hilarious. What I didn't realize was that my father thought college was good for girls—for finding a husband. After four years in college and two more in graduate school, and still no husband, my father shakes his head even now and says I wasted all that education.

In retrospect, I'm lucky my father believed daughters were meant for husbands. It meant it didn't matter if I majored in something silly like English. After all, I'd find a nice professional eventually, right? This allowed me the liberty to putter about embroidering my little poems and stories without my father interrupting with so much as a "What's that you're writing?"

But the truth is, I wanted him to interrupt. I wanted my father to understand what it was I was scribbling, to introduce me as "My only daughter, the writer." Not as "This is my only daughter. She teaches." *El maestra*—teacher. Not even *profesora*.

In a sense, everything I have ever written has been for him, to win his approval even though I know my father can't read English words, even though my father's only reading includes the brown-ink *Esto* sports magazines from Mexico City and the bloody *¡Alarma!* magazines that feature yet another sighting of *La Virgen de Guadalupe* on a tortilla or a wife's revenge on her philandering husband by bashing his skull in with a *molcajete* (a kitchen mortar made of volcanic rock). Or the *fotonovelas*, the little picture paperbacks with tragedy and trauma erupting from the characters' mouths in bubbles.

My father represents, then, the public majority. A public who is disinterested in reading, and yet one whom I am writing about and for, and privately trying to woo.

When we were growing up in Chicago, we moved a lot because of my father. He suffered periodic bouts of nostalgia. Then we'd have to let go our flat, store the furniture with mother's relatives, load the station wagon with baggage and bologna sandwiches, and head south. To Mexico City.

We came back, of course. To yet another Chicago flat, another Chicago neighborhood, another Catholic school. Each time, my father would seek out the parish priest in order to get a tuition break, and complain or boast: "I have seven sons."

He meant *siete hijos*, seven children, but he translated it as "sons." "I have seven sons." To anyone who would listen. The Sears Roebuck employee who sold us the washing machine. The short-order cook where my father ate his ham-and-eggs breakfasts. "I have seven sons." As if he deserved a medal from the state.

My papa. He didn't mean anything by that mistranslation, I'm sure. But somehow I could feel myself being erased. I'd tug my father's sleeve and whisper: "Not seven sons. Six! and *one daughter.*"

When my oldest brother graduated from medical school, he fulfilled my father's dream that we study hard and use this—our heads, instead of this—our hands. Even now my father's hands are thick and yellow, stubbed by a history of hammer and nails and twine and coils and springs. "Use this," my father said, tapping his head, "and not this," showing us those hands. He always looked tired when he said it.

Wasn't college an investment? And hadn't I spent all those years in college? And if I didn't marry, what was it all for? Why would anyone go to college and then choose to be poor? Especially someone who had always been poor.

Last year, after ten years of writing professionally, the financial rewards started to trickle in. My second National Endowment for the Arts Fellowship. A guest professorship at the University of California, Berkeley. My book, which sold to a major New York publishing house.

At Christmas, I flew home to Chicago. The house was throbbing, same as always; hot *tamales* and sweet *tamales* hissing in my mother's pressure cooker, and everybody—my mother, six brothers, wives, babies, aunts, cousins—talking too loud and at the same time, like in a Fellini film, because that's just how we are.

I went upstairs to my father's room. One of my stories had just been translated into Spanish and published in an anthology of Chicano writing, and I wanted to show it to him. Ever since he recovered from a stroke two years ago, my father likes to spend his leisure hours horizontally. And that's how I found him, watching a Pedro Infante movie on Galavision and eating rice pudding.

There was a glass filmed with milk on the bedside table. There were several vials of pills and balled Kleenex. And on the floor, one black sock and a plastic urinal that I didn't want to look at but looked at anyway. Pedro Infante was about to burst into song, and my father was laughing.

I'm not sure if it was because my story was translated into Spanish, or because it was published in Mexico, or perhaps because the story dealt with Tepeyac, the *colonia* my father was raised in, but at any rate, my father punched the mute button on his remote control and read my story.

I sat on the bed next to my father and waited. He read it very slowly. As if he were reading each line over and over. He laughed at all the right places and read lines he liked out loud. He pointed and asked questions: "Is this So-and-so?" "Yes," I said. He kept reading.

When he finally finished, after what seemed like hours, my father looked up and asked: "Where can we get more copies of this for the relatives?"

Of all the wonderful things that happened to me last year, that was the most wonderful.

Sandra Cisneros was born in Chicago, U.S. in 1954. She was instrumental in bringing the perspective of Chicana (Mexican-American) women into the field of literary feminism. Her first novel, *The House on Mango Street*, won the American Book Award from the Before Columbus Foundation in 1985.

1. *Response*
   a. What do you think the author was trying to achieve with this memoir? What was she exploring in her own life?
   b. In a few sentences, describe the picture you have in your mind of the father. Refer to the memoir for supporting details.
   c. Selecting details is important when framing your writing. What details does Cisneros use to describe her childhood, and what is her purpose? What details does she select for her adulthood, and what is her purpose?
   d. What are some variables that might contribute to people placing importance on one gender over the other?
   e. Why do you think it is so important for children, no matter their age, to seek the approval of their parents? If you think about yourself as a parent someday, what qualities will you look for in your children?

2. *Vocabulary* With a partner, examine how Cisneros embeds Spanish words and terms throughout the memoir. What effect does this have? What format of type lets readers know that a word is in a different language? How has the author provided the translations smoothly, so that she does not distract the reader? For those words for which she does not provide a translation, how are we able to guess at their meaning?

3. *Language Conventions* *Sentence Fragments* When we are learning to write, we are warned not to use sentence fragments. Experienced writers, however, sometimes use sentence fragments for specific effects. Identify three sentence fragments in this memoir and read them aloud, along with the sentences that precede and follow them. With a partner, analyse the effect sentence fragments have on the way the sentences sound, the tone of the memoir, and the author's meaning.

Canadian novelist David Adams Richards
describes Newcastle, New Brunswick—
the town of his childhood.

My Old Newcastle

Descriptive Essay by David Adams Richards

In Newcastle, N.B., which I call home, we all played on the ice floes in the spring, spearing tommy-cod with stolen forks tied to sticks. More than one of us almost met our end slipping off the ice.

All night the trains rumbled or shunted their loads off to Halifax or Montreal, and men moved and worked. To this day I find the sound of trains more comforting than lonesome. It was somehow thrilling to know of people up and about in those hours, and wondrous events taking place. Always somehow with the faint, worn smell of gas and steel.

The Miramichi is a great working river.

There was always the presence of working men and women, from the mines or mills or woods; the more than constant sound of machinery; and the ore covered in tarps at the side of the wharf.

But as children, sitting in our snowsuits and hats and heavy boots on Saturday afternoons, we all saw movies that had almost nothing to do with us. That never mentioned us as a country or a place. That never seemed to know what our fathers and mothers did—that we went to wars or had a flag or even a great passion for life.

As far as the movies were concerned, we were in a lost, dark country, it seemed. And perhaps this is one reason I write. Leaving the theatre on a January afternoon, the smell of worn seats and heat and chip bags gave way to a muted cold and scent of snow no movie ever showed us. And night came against the tin roofs of the sheds behind our white houses, as the long spires of our churches rose over the town.

Our river was frozen so blue then that trucks could travel from one town to the other across the ice, and bonfires were lit by kids skating; sparks rose upon the shore under the stars as mothers called children home at 9 o'clock.

All winter long the sky was tinted blue on the horizon, the schools we sat in too warm; privileged boys and girls sat beside those who lived in hunger and constant worry. One went on to be a Rhodes scholar, another was a derelict at 17 and dead at 20. To this day I could not tell you which held more promise.

Spring came with the smell of mud and grass burning in the fields above us. Road hockey gave way to cricket and then baseball. The sun warmed, the ice shifted and the river was free. Salmon and sea trout moved up a dozen of our tributaries to spawn.

In the summer the ships came in, from all ports to ours, to carry ore and paper away. Sailors smoked black tobacco cigarettes, staring down at us from their decks; blackflies spoiled in the fields beyond town, and the sky was large all evening. Cars filled with children too excited to sleep passed along our great avenues lined with overhanging trees. All down to the store to get ice cream in the dark.

Adolescent blueberry crops and sunken barns dotted the fields near the bay, where the air had the taste of salt and tar, and small spruce trees seemed constantly filled with wind; where, by August, the water shimmered and even the small white lobster boats smelled of autumn, as did the ripples that moved them.

In the autumn the leaves were red, of course, and the earth, by Thanksgiving, became hard as a dull turnip. Ice formed in the ditches and shallow streams. The fields became yellow and stiff. The sounds of rifle shots from men hunting deer echoed faintly away, while women walked in kerchiefs and coats to 7 o'clock mass, and the air felt heavy and leaden. Winter coming on again.

Now the town is three times as large, and fast-food franchises and malls dot the roadside where there were once fields and lumberyards. There is a new process at the mill, and much of the wood is clear-cut so that huge acres lie empty and desolate, a redundancy of broken and muted earth. The river is opened all winter by an ice-breaker, so no trucks travel across the ice, and the trains, of course, are gone. For the most part the station is empty, the tracks fiercely alone in the winter sun.

The theatre is gone now, too. And those thousands of movies showing us, as children filled with happy laughter someplace in Canada, what we were not, are gone as well. They have given way to videos and satellite dishes and a community that is growing slowly farther and farther away from its centre. Neither bad nor good, I suppose—but away from what it was.

David Adams Richards, writer of poetry, short stories, essays, and novels, was born in 1950. His work, *Nights Below Station Street*—the first in a trilogy—won the Governor General's Award in 1985. Several other literary awards followed, including the Canadian Authors Association Literary Award for Fiction in 1991, and the Alden Nowlan Award for Excellence in English Literary Arts in 1993. In 2000, Richards shared the Giller Prize (with Michael Ondaatje) for his novel, *Mercy Among the Children*.

1. *Response*
a. What do you think the author's purpose was in writing this essay? How does he feel about his home as an adult? Provide evidence from the essay to support your view.
b. This is a sample of a descriptive essay: The author has used vivid sensory details and images to describe the town of his memory. List images that appeal to each of the senses. Why do you think this kind of imagery is so evocative and effective?
c. The third paragraph is one short sentence. Comment on its function and its place in the essay.
d. Consider the title and the author's play on words. How does the structure of the essay reflect the idea of old and new?

2. *Literature Studies* *Essay Structure* The author uses a chrono-logical structure to develop this descriptive essay. Trace this order in the essay. What is the period of time in which the essay ends? What do you think of this structure? How does it suit the author's subject?

3. *Film Study* Reread the paragraphs in which movies are mentioned. The author suggests that the movies they saw as children in Canada were not at all reflective of their lives. Describe a movie that you think is a fairly realistic depiction of your life, or of the lives of people your age. Alternatively, think of some movies that are aimed at your age group and explain how they are *not* realistic. Do you have a preference? Do you think movies reflect who we are or who we want to be? Discuss your ideas in a group.

*Well-known journalist Rex Murphy pays tribute to
Canada's fifteenth prime minister on the day of his death:
September 28, 2000.*

Pierre Trudeau

He Has Gone to His Grace

Tribute by Rex Murphy

The sad vigil the country went on a few weeks ago this after-noon reached its inevitable conclusion. The largest, liveliest, smartest, fiercest and most graceful public figure that Canada has had in modern times, and probably ever, has made an end.

He walked outside the boundaries of expectation in almost everything he did. He was intense, private and reserved and gave himself to the one profession, the one vocation, that most depends on exhibition, attention and continuous display.

He was radiantly intelligent, a full intellectual, powered with jesuitical resources of argument and reason, yet—on so many occasions—was the most visceral and passionate of our public figures.

He hailed from the province that, with reason, nursed doubts about its place in Confederation, was burdened by fears of its future and destiny. Yet he of all Quebecers was the one most powered by the certitude, by the absolute confidence, that Quebecers were larger by being Canadians, and that a lack of confidence was more a failure of nerve than a matter of politics.

He bore a symbolic relationship with his time. This angular, complex, multifaceted personality seemed to say things to this country outside the words of his speeches or his policies. There was some element within him, or of him, that acted like a summons to the Canadian imagination; to live a little larger, think a little more carefully, or bring more courage or daring to our dreams.

Pre-eminently, his life and his public career revolved around the idea of Canada. In any turn of crisis or act of state, from the storm of the FLQ to patriation of the Constitution, Pierre Trudeau acted from a conception of the whole country, and a determination to give body to this country's often vague and drifting sense of itself.

He paid the country the deepest tribute a real politician can: he believed in it with his brain and his heart, and gave the wit of the one and the heat of the other to enlarging and enlivening its possibilities and our citizenship.

He was no neuter. It is one of the grandest things we will say of his memory that, at times, he antagonized as much as he inspired; our affection for Pierre Trudeau was turbulent and always interesting. If citizens of this day lament that leadership is a game of polls and cozy focus groups there will always be the example of this man to remind us that convictions can be set in bedrock, and that adherence to principles is the most enduring charisma.

Canadians first admired Pierre Trudeau, halted before his presence in a kind of happy awe. Over time as we learned him, and if it is not presumptuous, he learned us, the admiration melted into, I think, a dignified affection.

He left politics larger than he found it. He added to the dignity of public life and did not subtract from it. His life and career spoke to everyone of the sheer power of excellence as an ideal. In this wide, mixed and imposing country, for the time he was with us Canadians knew they had one touch of grandeur outside the landscape.

Passion, intellect, honour and courage were his hallmarks. He was, in public life, the best that we had. It was an honour and a joy that he was around and a real grief that today so much, so very much of what is best about us, has made farewell.

He has gone to his grace, and that leaves so much less of ours.

Rex Murphy, born in Carbonear, Newfoundland and Labrador, began his CBC career in the early 1970s as a commentator/ interviewer for *CBC Here and Now*. He wrote and hosted the documentary *The Last and the Best*, which covered Newfoundland and Labrador's twenty-fifth anniversary in Confederation, and which won a Wilderness Award.

1. *Response*
  a. Did this tribute help you to understand who Pierre Elliott Trudeau was? What additional information about him would you like to have? Where would you look for it?
  b. From reading this article, what aspect of Trudeau's accomplishments or his character impressed you most?
  c. What does the author mean by the second-last sentence: "He has gone to his grace ..."? How effective an ending do you think it is, and why?
  d. What do you think are the most important qualities a nation's leader should possess? Which leaders in the world today do you think demonstrate these qualities? List leaders, their qualities, and how these qualities are demonstrated.

2. *Focus on Context* What knowledge do you have of Pierre Elliott Trudeau? Consider his life (public and private) and his contributions. As a class, brainstorm your knowledge of Canadian Prime Ministers. Record and list the top three according to how much knowledge you have about them. How does your knowledge of Trudeau compare with your knowledge of the others? What might be some reasons for this?

3. *Language Conventions* *Parallelism* Rex Murphy makes use of **parallel structure** in this selection. Identify the paragraph openers that follow this structure and then note the change from that structure to a different one. Why might the author have chosen not to use the same structure for every paragraph?

Parallel structure is the repeated use of the same phrase or sentence, or the repeated use of a similar sentence structure. Parallel structure can be used to create balance or place emphasis on certain lines.

This tribute was written for broadcast on national TV. Read the essay again, aloud, listening to the delivery. How is this structure suitable for an oral tribute like this one?

4. *Writing* *Tribute* Think of a person "who has gone to his [her] grace" and commemorate that person in a tribute of your own. You could try using a similar parallel structure in an essay form, or you could use forms such as a letter or poem.

Eulogies and written tributes to those who have died create moving stories and memories of a person's life. Photos, too, can pay tribute. When well-chosen, even just a few photos can reveal a life to us. Consider these photos, published in a newspaper following the death of Canadian writer Mordecai Richler.

Mordecai in Memoriam

Photo Tribute from
The Toronto Star
Wednesday, July 4, 2001

Artist as a Young Man:
Mordecai Richler during
a pensive moment.

Widespread Appeal:
Richler reads to kids from one of his
best-loved stories, "Jacob Two-Two
and the Hooded Fang."

Back to His Roots: Looking out over
old Montréal neighbourhood, 1979.

Prix Parizeau: Mordecai Richler holds Aislin cartoon in Montréal spoofing Jacques Parizeau in 1996 with literary prize for Québec fiction in English. He called it the Prix Parizeau, given out by the Impure Wool Society, a thinly veiled reference to referendum-night remarks by the former Québec premier blaming the "ethnic vote" for the sovereigntists' defeat.

Family Toast: Richler with wife Florence and sons Noah (left) and Daniel.

Honoured: Richler receives honorary status from McGill University as university Chancellor Richard Pound looks on, in an undated photo.

Relaxed: Richler sits thoughtfully in a dressing room in Toronto, in undated photo.

Mordecai Richler was born in 1931 in Montréal, Canada. Before finishing his degree at Sir George Williams College in Montréal, Richler left for Europe, where he lived in London for twenty years. He achieved international acclaim with his novel, *The Apprenticeship of Duddy Kravitz*, set in Montréal and made into a film. His other works include novels *Cocksure* and *St. Urbain's Horseman*, which both won Governor General's Awards, and *Joshua Then and Now*, which was also made into a film. His essay collections include *Hunting Tigers Under Glass* and *Home Sweet Home: My Canadian Album*. Richler died in 2001. His fiction, essays, and columns revealed his outspoken and provocative nature.

1. *Response*
   a. Which of the photos would you say gives you the most information about Richler? Why? What information are you given?
   b. From these photos, what do you think Richler was like?
   c. Which photo do you like the most, and why?
   d. What, in particular, strikes you as interesting in these photos?
   e. There were probably thousands of photos from which editors could have chosen to pay tribute to Richler upon his death. Why do you think these were among those chosen?

2. *Making Connections* Mordecai Richler was a writer of varied genres: novels, screenplays, essays, and children's books. Read from some of Richler's works, as well as some of the biographical information on him. What do you learn about him that relates to what you perceived from the photos?

3. *Visual Communication* Photo Essay Create your own photo essay about a Canadian you admire—living or dead, famous or not. Use photos that you take, or photos collected from print or digital resources. Choose shots that help convey the character of the person. Consider also the placement of your photos: Do you want them in chronological order? Juxtaposed? Experiment with choice and placement until you have the effects you want.

   Alternatively, create a photo essay that pays tribute to your own life so far.

Frida Kahlo, a Mexican artist, died in 1954. In December 2001, the movie *Frida* was released to pay tribute to this popular artist. This article, published in April 2001, looks at some of the events surrounding the artist's popularity and the making of the movie.

Reviving Fridamania

Newspaper Article by Chris Kraul

Fridamania—the cult and the industry—may soon get a second wind.

Hollywood is finally making a movie on the tortured, colorful life of Mexican painter Frida Kahlo after a decade of abortive attempts. If the film is a hit, Mexico City could see a wave of Frida-inspired merchandising like the one that engulfed the capital a few years ago.

On an autumn day in 1997, you could on one day go to a Frida bar, see a Frida play, have a Frida dinner and load up on Frida T-shirts, calendars, cookbooks and key rings featuring her baleful, beetle-browed visage.

Overshadowed in her lifetime by her husband, the artist Diego Rivera, and ignored by the public for decades, Kahlo became an icon of popular culture. She was transformed into Mexico's Elvis, a "brand" that has sold several forests' worth of postcards, picture books and posters.

Fridamania began building in the late 1970s, spurred on by the interest of European feminists and Chicano muralists who saw her as a forerunner, said Raquel Tibol, author of *Frida Kahlo: An Open Life*. A 1983 biography by Hayden Herrera helped popularize the legend. Rivera willed all rights to his and Kahlo's images and intellectual property to the Mexican people after his death in 1957. And Mexico has made out handsomely, although not as well at it might have, because of weak copyright protection laws. To merchandise Kahlo legally, movie producers and souvenir manufacturers must pay royalties to the Mexican Central Bank.

Kahlo's house—la Casa Azul, or Blue House, where she lived, worked, was born and died—is Mexico City's Graceland, a museum now visited by an average of 300 pilgrims a day. They view the dozen Kahlo paintings on display, immerse themselves in the legend and pay homage to the artist's ashes—she died at age 47 in 1954—stored in an urn on the premises. But like all fads, Fridamania has subsided. Visits to the museum have declined 25 percent from the 1997 peak. Merchandisers report that demand for coasters, mirrors, calendars, key rings and desk

Frida Kahlo.

Use the imformation in the selection and in the above photo to write a 25-word description of Frida Kahlo.

calendars has slipped significantly. The onslaught of books and theatrical productions—the latter now numbering at least 60—has slowed.

Frida is still there, just not everywhere.

One place she is these days: the city of Puebla, where Miramax Films began shooting this month on its production, starring Mexican actress Salma Hayek. Release is expected early next year.

The vagaries of pop culture and merchandising fads aside, Kahlo, who overcame polio, an almost fatal bus accident and other setbacks to become an accomplished artist, remains a powerful cultural force here. Ask a dozen museum-goers, art experts and Frida merchants why that is, and you get a dozen different answers. "It was her attitude before life that appeals to people, that of an indefatigable fighter who struggled against physical problems, the shadow of her famous husband, the social restrictions of womanhood," said Luis-Martin Lozano, director of the Museum of Modern Art in Mexico City.

---

1. **Response**
   a. In your own words, write down five facts in your notebooks that you have learned about Frida Kahlo. Compare your facts with those of a classmate.
   b. What is *Fridamania*? How did it start?
   c. In your own words, define the term *powerful cultural force*.
   d. How and why are Mexicans paying tribute to Kahlo?

2. **Research and Inquiry** Investigate the life and work of Frida Kahlo further, using Internet and library resources. Begin by recording any questions you had about Kahlo after reading this article. Choose an innovative format in which to present your research to others—for example, a short biography, visual essay, or eulogy.

3. **Literature Studies** *Bias and Tone* Reread the article and identify both its **bias** and **tone**. Does the author admire Frida Kahlo? What do words like *Fridamania* imply about the author's attitude toward the artist? Does the article remain objective and impersonal? Discuss the article with a partner, analysing the effect of the author's bias and tone on the reader.

Bias is the author's inclination or preference toward one stance that makes it difficult or impossible to judge something fairly. For example, a fan of Sylvester Stallone may be unable to write an objective or balanced review of his work. **Tone** is the implied attitude of the writer toward the subject or audience. The tone of a piece can be described as *angry, satiric, joyful, serious,* and so on.

Rewrite one paragraph of the article, using an opposing tone or bias. Discuss the effectiveness of this rewrite with your partner.

Canadian poet Al Purdy, known as "a poet of the people," died in June 2001.

The Awkward Sublime

Tribute by Margaret Atwood

I began to read Al Purdy's poetry about the same time it changed from being odd and ungainly to being remarkable—in the early '60s. I was just into my 20s, writing a lot of poetry but not liking much of it; like most young poets then, I wanted to be published by Contact Press—a highly respected, poet-run cooperative—and I read everything they issued; and thus I read Al Purdy's *Poems for All the Annettes* in 1962, when it first came out.

Al Purdy, 1996, by Frank O'Connor. Photo

I was somewhat frightened by it, and did not fully understand what he was doing. This was a new sort of voice for me, an overpowering one, and a little too much like being backed into the corner of a seedy bar by a large, insistent, untidy drunk, who is waxing by turns both sentimental and obscene. For a young male poet of those days, this kind of energy and this approach—casual, slangy, subversive of recent poetic convention—could be liberating and inspirational, and some found in him an ersatz father figure. But for a young female poet—well, this was not the sort of father figure it would be altogether steadying to have.

Then, in 1965, *The Cariboo Horses*—Purdy's breakthrough book— came out, and I found that the drunk in the bar was also a major storyteller and mythmaker, though still wearing his offhand and rather shabby disguise. This was poetry for the spoken voice *par excellence*—not an obviously rhetorical voice, but an anecdotal one, the voice of the Canadian vernacular. Yet not only that either, for no sooner had Purdy set up his own limits than he'd either transcend or subvert them. He was always questioning, always probing, and among those things that he questioned and probed were himself and his own poetic methods. In a Purdy poem, high diction can meet the scrawl on the washroom wall, and, as in a collision between matter and anti-matter, both explode.

"[Purdy] wrote about going to good hockey games and fighting with the foreman at work ... the kind of things that occupy ordinary people."

—Howard White, president of Harbour Publishing

It would be folly to attempt to sum up Purdy's poetic universe: like Walt Whitman's[1] it's too vast for a précis. What interested him could be anything, but above all the wonder that anything at all can be interesting. He was always turning banality inside out. For me, he was, above all, an explorer—pushing into nameless areas of landscape, articulating the inarticulate, poking around in dusty corners of memory and discovering treasure there, digging up the bones and shards of a forgotten ancestral past. When he wasn't capering about and joking and scratching his head over the idiocy and pain and delight of being alive, he was composing lyric elegies for what was no longer alive, but had been—and, through his words, still is. For underneath that flapping overcoat and that tie with a mermaid on it and that pretence of shambling awkwardness—yes, it was a pretence, but only partly, for among other things Purdy was doing a true impersonation of himself—

there was a skillful master-conjurer. Listen to the voice, and watch the hands at work: just hands, a bit grubby too, not doing anything remarkable, and you can't see how it's done, but suddenly, where a second ago there was only a broken vase, there's a fistful of brilliant flowers.

---

[1] **Walt Whitman:** American poet who wrote the radical and influential *Leaves of Grass,* 1855

Margaret Atwood's poetic reputation was established in 1966 when *The Circle Game* won the Governor General's Award. She has published numerous books of poetry, including the well-known collection *The Journals of Susanna Moodie: Poems.* She is also an award-winning novelist, winning the Governor General's Award in 1985 for *The Handmaid's Tale* and the Booker Prize in 2000 for *The Blind Assassin.*

1. *Response*
a. What does Atwood focus on in her tribute to Al Purdy? Why do you think she does not mention other aspects of his life?
b. How did Atwood's attitude toward, and appreciation of, Al Purdy's poetry change over the years?
c. What do you think of the tribute's title, which can be considered an **oxymoron**? In your own words, explain what you think the title means and what it refers to.

An **oxymoron** is a figure of speech that is a combination of contradictory words. One of the most common examples of an oxymoron is "jumbo shrimp."

2. *Focus on Context* Consider Margaret Atwood and her contribution to Canadian literature. Do some research, including reading a bibliography of her writing. Does her stature as a writer affect your response to the tribute? Explain.

Theme Connections

- *"Two Words," a story about the clever use of language, page 51*
- *"The Chariot," a poem about death, page 207, and other poems in the cluster "Grief of Mind"*
- *"Making Poetry Pay," an anecdote that profiles a poet, page 284*

Use Internet or print resources to find out who Susanna Moodie was and when she lived. As you read the following essay, consider contemporary Canada and its attitudes toward education.

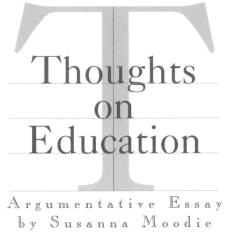

Thoughts on Education

Argumentative Essay
by Susanna Moodie

There is no calculating the immense benefit which the colony will derive from the present liberal provision made for the education of the rising generation.

A few years ago schools were so far apart, and the tuition of children so expensive, that none but the very better class could scrape money enough together to send their children to be instructed. Under the present system, every idle ragged child in the streets, by washing his face and hands, and presenting himself to the free school of his ward, can receive the same benefit as the rest.

What an inestimable blessing this is, and how greatly will this education of her population tend to increase the wealth and prosperity of the province! It is a certain means of calling out and making available all the talent in the colony; and as, thanks be to God, genius never was confined to any class, the poor will be more benefited by this wise and munificent arrangement than the rich.

These schools are supported by a district tax which falls upon the property of persons well able to pay it; but avarice and bigotry are already at work, to endeavour to deprive the young of this new-found blessing. Persons grumble at having to pay this additional tax. They say, "If poor people want their children taught, let them pay for it: their instruction has no right to be forced from our earnings."

What a narrow prejudice is this—what miserable, short-sighted policy! The education of these neglected children, by making them better citizens, will in the long run prove a great protection both to life and property.

Then the priests of different persuasions lift up their voices because no particular creed is allowed to be taught in the seminaries, and exclaim—"The children will be infidels. These schools are godless and immoral in the extreme." Yes; children will be taught to love each other without any such paltry distinctions as party and creed. The rich and the poor will meet together to learn the sweet courtesies of a common humanity, and prejudice and avarice and bigotry cannot bear that.

There is a spirit abroad in the world—and an evil spirit it is—which through all ages has instigated the rich to look down with contemptuous feelings of superiority on the humble occupations and inferior circumstances of the poor. Now, that this spirit is diametrically opposed to the benevolent precepts of Christianity, the fact of our blessed Lord performing his painful mission on earth in no higher capacity than that of a working mechanic ought sufficiently to show. What divine benevolence—what god-like humility was displayed in this heroic act! Of all the wonderful events in his wonderful history, is there one more astonishing than this—

> "That Heaven's high Majesty his court should keep
> In a clay cottage, by each blast controll'd—
> That Glory's self should serve our hopes and fears,
> And free Eternity submit to years?"

What a noble triumph was this, over the cruel and unjust prejudices of mankind! It might truly be termed the divine philosophy of virtue. This condescension on the part of the great Creator of the universe ought to have been sufficient to have rendered labour honourable in the minds of his followers; and we still indulge the hope that the moral and intellectual improvement of mankind will one day restore labour to her proper pedestal in the temple of virtue.

The chosen disciples of our Great Master—those to whom He entrusted the precious code of moral laws that was destined to overthrow the kingdom of Satan, and reform a degraded world—were poor uneducated men. The most brilliant gems are often enclosed in the rudest incrustations; and He who formed the bodies and souls of men well knew that the most powerful intellects are often concealed amidst the darkness and rubbish of uneducated minds. Such minds, enlightened and purified by his wonder-working Spirit, He sent forth to publish his message of glad tidings through the earth.

The want of education and moral training is the only *real* barrier that exists between the different classes of men. Nature, reason, and

Christianity recognise no other. Pride may say nay; but pride was always a liar, and a great hater of the truth. Wealth, in a hard, abstract point of view, can never make any. Take away the wealth from an ignorant man, and he remains just the same being he was before he possessed it, and is no way bettered from the mere circumstance of his having once been rich. But let that wealth procure for him the only true and imperishable riches—knowledge, and with it the power to do good to himself and others, which is the great end of moral and religious training—and a mighty structure is raised which death itself is unable to destroy. The man has indeed changed his nature, and is fast regaining the resemblance he once bore to his Creator.

The soul of man is of no rank, sex, or colour. It claims a distinction far above all these; and shall we behold its glorious energies imprisoned in the obscene den of ignorance and want, without making the least effort to enlighten its hideous darkness?

It is painful to reflect upon the vast barren wilderness of human intellect which on every side stretches around us—to know that thousands of powerful minds are condemned by the hopeless degradation of their circumstances to struggle on in obscurity, without one gleam of light. What a high and noble privilege has the Almighty conferred upon the wealthy and well-educated portion of mankind, in giving them the means of reclaiming and cultivating those barren minds, and of lifting them from the mire of ignorance in which they at present wallow, to share with them the moral dignity of thinking men!

A small portion of the wealth that is at present bestowed upon mere articles of luxury, or in scenes of riot and dissipation, would more than effect this great purpose. The education of the poorer classes must add greatly to the well-being and happiness of the world, and tend to diminish the awful amount of crimes and misery which up to the present moment has rendered it a vale of tears.

The ignorance of the masses must, while it remains, for ever separate them from their more fortunate brethren. Remove this stumbling block out of the way, and the hard line of demarcation which now divides them will soften, and gradually melt away. Their supposed inferiority lies in their situation alone. Turn to the history of those great men whom education has rescued from the very lowest walks of life, and you will find a mighty host who were in their age and day the companions, the advisers, the friends of princes—men who have written their names with the pen and the sword upon the pillars of time, and, if immortality can exist in a world of constant change, have been rendered immortal by their words or deeds.

Let poverty and bigotry do their utmost to keep such spirits, while living, in the shades of obscurity, death, the great equalizer, always restores to its possessors the rights of mind, and bids them triumph for ever over the low prejudices of their fellow-men, who, when reading the works of Burns or gazing on the paintings of Raphael, reproach them with the lowliness of their origin; yea, the proudest who have taste to appreciate their glorious creations rejoice that genius could thus triumph over temporary obstacles.

It has often been asserted by the rich and nobly-born, that if the poorer classes were as well educated as themselves, it would render them familiar and presumptuous, and they would no longer pay to their superiors in station that deference which must exist for the well-being of society. We view the subject with far other eyes, and conclude from analogy that that which has conferred such incalculable benefits on the rich, and helped mainly to place them in the position they now hold, could not be detrimental to the poor. The man who knows his duty is more likely to perform it well than the ignorant man, whose services are compulsory, and whose actions are uninfluenced by the moral responsibility which a right knowledge must give.

My earnest wish for universal education involves no dislike to royal rule, or for those distinctions of birth and wealth which I consider necessary for the well-being of society. It little matters by what name we call them; men of talent and education will exert a certain influence over the minds of their fellow-men which will always be felt and acknowledged in the world if mankind were equalized to-morrow. Perfect, unadulterated republicanism is a beautiful but fallacious chimera which never has existed upon the earth, and which, if the Bible be true (and we have no doubts on the subject), we are told never will exist in heaven. Still, we consider that it would be true wisdom and policy in those who possess a large share of the good things of this world, to make labour honourable, by exalting the poor operative into an intelligent moral agent. Surely it is no small privilege to be able to bind up his bruised and broken heart—to wipe the dust from his brow, and the tears from his eyes—and bid him once more stand erect in his Maker's image. This is, indeed, to become the benefactor both of his soul and body; for the mind, once convinced of its own real worth and native dignity, is less prone to fall into low and degrading vices, than when struggling with ignorance and the galling chain of despised poverty.

It is impossible for the most depraved votary of wealth and fashion *really* to despise a poor, honest, well-informed man. There is an aristocracy of virtue as well as of wealth; and the rich man who dares to cast undeserved contempt upon his poor but high-minded brother hears a voice within him which, in tones which cannot be misunderstood, reproves him for blaspheming his Maker's image. A glorious mission is conferred on you who are rich and nobly-born, which, if well and conscientiously performed, will make the glad arch of heaven ring with songs of joy. Nor deem that you will be worse served because your servant is a religious, well-educated man, or that you will be treated with less respect and attention by one who knows that your station entitles you to it, than by the rude, ignorant slave, who hates you in his heart, and performs his appointed services with an envious, discontented spirit.

When we consider that ignorance is the fruitful parent of crime, we should unite with heart and voice to banish it from the earth. We should devote what means we can spare, and the talents with which God has endowed us, in furthering every national and benevolent institution set on foot for this purpose; and though the progress of improvement may at first appear slow, this should not discourage any one from endeavouring to effect a great and noble purpose. Many months must intervene, after sowing the crop, before the husbandman can expect to reap the harvest. The winter snows must cover, the spring rains vivify and nourish, and the summer sun ripen, before the autumn arrives for the ingathering of his labour, and then the increase, after all his toil and watching, must be with God.

During the time of our blessed Lord's sojourn upon earth, He proclaimed the harvest to be plenteous and the labourers few; and He instructed his disciples to pray to the Lord of the harvest to send more labourers into the field. Does it not, therefore, behove those who live in a more enlightened age—when the truth of the Gospel, which He sealed with his blood, has been preached in almost every country—to pray the Father of Spirits to proportion the labourers to the wants of his people, so that Christian kindness, brotherly love, and moral improvement may go hand in hand, and keep pace with increasing literary and scientific knowledge?

A new country like Canada cannot value the education of her people too highly. The development of all the talent within the province will in the end prove her real worth, for from this source every blessing and improvement must flow. The greatness of a nation can more truly be estimated by the wisdom and intelligence of her people than by the mere amount of specie she may possess in her treasury. The money, under the bad management of ignorant rulers, would add but little to the well-being of the community, while the intelligence which could make a smaller sum available in contributing to the general good is in itself an inexhaustible mine of wealth.

If a few enlightened minds are able to add so much strength and importance to the country to which they belong, how much greater must that country become if all her people possessed this intelligence! How impossible it would be to conquer a country, if she could rely upon the united wisdom of an educated people to assist her in her hour of need! The force of arms could never subdue a nation thus held together by the strong hands of intellectual fellowship....

An ignorant man is incapable of judging correctly, however anxious he may be to do so. He gropes in the dark, like a blind man; and if he should happen to stumble on the right path, it is more by accident than from any correct idea which has been formed in his mind respecting it.

The mind which once begins to feel a relish for acquiring knowledge is not easily satisfied. The more it knows, the less it thinks of its own acquirements, and the more anxious it becomes to arrive at the truth; and finding that perfection is not a growth of earth, it carries its earnest longings beyond this world, and seeks it in communion with the Deity. If the young could once be fully persuaded that there was no disgrace in labour, in honest, honourable poverty, but a deep and lasting disgrace in ignorance and immorality, their education would be conducted on the most enlightened plan, and produce the most beneficial results.

The poor man who could have recourse to a book for amusement, instead of wasting a leisure hour in the bar-room of a tavern, would be more likely to promote the comfort and respectability of his family. Why should the labourer be debarred from sharing with the rich the great world of the past, and be unable to rank amongst his best friends the distinguished men of all creeds and countries, and to feel for these dead worthies (who, thanks to the immortal art of printing, still live in their works) the warmest gratitude and admiration? The very mention of some names awakens in the mind the most lively emotion. We recall their beautiful thoughts to memory, and repeat them with as much earnestness as though the dead spake again through our lips.

Of all the heaven-inspired inventions of man, there are none to which we are so greatly indebted as to the art of printing. To it we shall yet owe the emancipation of the larger portion of mankind from a state of mental and physical slavery. What floods of light have dawned upon the world since that silent orator, the press, set at liberty the imprisoned thoughts of men, and poured the wealth of mind among the famishing sons of earth! Formerly few could read, because manuscript books, the

A professional writer is an amateur who didn't quit.

Richard Bach

labours of the pen, were sold at such an enormous price that only men of rank or great wealth could afford to purchase them. The peasant, and the landholder who employed him, were alike ignorant; they could not obtain books, and therefore learning to read might well be considered in those dark ages a waste of time. This profound ignorance gave rise to all those superstitions which in the present enlightened age are regarded with such astonishment by thinking minds....

I have said more on this subject that I at first intended, but I feel deeply impressed with the importance of it; and, though I confess myself wholly inadequate to do it the justice it deserves, I hope the observations I have made will attract the attention of my Canadian readers, and lead them to study it more profoundly for themselves. Thanks be to God! Canada is a free country; a land of plenty; a land exempt from pauperism, burdensome taxation, and all the ills which crush and finally sink in ruin older communities. While the vigour of young life is yet hers, and she has before her the experience of all other nations, it becomes an act of duty and real *patriotism* to give to her children the best education that lies in her power.

Susanna Moodie, writer of poetry, short stories, articles, and novels, was born in Suffolk, England, in 1803. She became interested in humanitarian issues in the 1830s when her friend, the Scottish poet Thomas Pringle, introduced her to the injustices of slavery, and she wrote several anti-slavery tracts. In 1831, Pringle assisted Moodie in getting a collection of her poetry published. She moved to Canada with her husband in 1832, where they lived for six years on their bush farm. Her best-known book, *Roughing It in the Bush*, is a personal account of these difficult years spent in the Canadian wilderness. This was followed by *Flora Lyndsay; or Passages in an Eventful Life*, and *Life in the Clearings Versus the Bush*, which together create a trilogy about the immigration experience. Some of Moodie's novels include *Mark Hurdlestone; or The Gold Worshipper*, *Matrimonial Speculations*, and *Geoffrey Moncton; or The Faithless Guardian*. Moodie died in Toronto in 1885.

1. *Response*
    a. Is Susanna Moodie in favour of publicly-funded education? Why or why not?
    b. How convincing is Moodie's argument?
    c. Do you agree with Moodie's position? Explain your own viewpoint on the issue of publicly-funded education.
    d. Who was Moodie's original audience? What was her purpose in writing "Thoughts on Education"?

2. *Oral Language* *Group Discussion* Choose one passage within this essay and discuss Moodie's argument and viewpoint within a small group. Each group member should contribute one idea to this discussion. One member of your group can record the main points of your discussion. Another member can present these ideas to the class.

3. *Writing* *Letter* Write a letter to Susanna Moodie explaining the conditions of public education in your community in the present day. In your letter, incorporate a response to some of the points that Moodie raises.

4. *Language Focus* *Exclusive Language* Review the essay and consider the use of gender pronouns throughout. How does the language Moodie uses exclude particular people? What assumptions has the author made? Why or why not are these assumptions acceptable, given the context of this selection? In your own writing, what strategies do you use to maintain an inclusive tone or style?

Theme Connections

- *"Two Words," a story in which the main character is self-taught, page 51*
- *"Young Soul," a poem that extols the importance of reading but also feeling, page 189*
- *"Anything Worth Knowing" a poem about the value of education, page 235*
- *"Did I Miss Anything?" a poem about the value of education, page 236*
- *"Only Daughter," an essay that demonstrates the value of education, page 292*

Screaming, shouting, and hitting—
abusive parents are spoiling their kids' sports.

Rink Rage

Magazine Article by James Deacon,

with Brenda Branswell in Montréal,
Susan McClelland in Toronto,
and Darryl Smart in Port Dover

When the Delhi Legion peewees travelled down the highway to play the Port Dover Pirates in February 2001, there was a fair bit on the line for both teams. The series winners would advance to the semifinals of the Ontario Minor Hockey Association's AE Peewee playoffs.... So about 200 parents and fans crowded into the arena in Port Dover and arranged themselves in the stands according to their community affiliation.

It was typical of peewee games at that level—12- and 13-year-olds a notch above house league—enthusiastic if not always polished. Early on, the Pirates won most of the battles along the boards, and took the lead as well. The action got progressively rougher. Several Delhi supporters began hollering at the two referees to crack down on what they saw as the Pirates' overly aggressive body checking, and in fact, Port Dover incurred most of the penalties.

That didn't satisfy some Delhi supporters. With five minutes left, when a Delhi player was penalized for hitting from behind, both of Delhi's coaches strenuously argued the call and were ejected. That provoked a couple of hotheaded fans, who hurled coins and a plastic water bottle onto the ice. Finally, with one minute and 38 seconds to go and Port Dover up 2-0, one particularly loud Delhi fan tossed a broom onto the ice. That was it for the officials. They halted play and, unable to identify exactly who the main offenders were, simply ejected all 200 spectators. The local provincial police detachment sent officers to protect the referees as they left the arena.

On the ice, the players were stunned by what they heard and saw coming out of the stands. "You don't pay attention to that stuff usually, but a couple of people in the stands were getting real mad at the refs," says Pirate defenceman Colton Organ, 13. When the broom hit the ice, Organ says, "we all just kind of looked at each other and shook our heads." The majority of fans did the same. It was, as one of the more composed Delhi parents said afterwards, "embarrassing."

No kidding. It was just a peewee hockey game, for crying out loud. It was supposed to be fun, yet it deteriorated into yet another example of out-of-control adults ruining their own kids' games. The bad behaviour is so common in hockey that it even has its own name—rink rage. In other incidents, some B.C. referees boycotted youth games to protest abuse from fans. A coach in Quebec was hospitalized after being attacked between periods by the father of one of his players. In Ontario, a coach was charged with threatening to kill a teenage referee. In Winnipeg, a police constable—already suspended from the force for a previous assault conviction—was arrested and charged with threatening another parent during his nine-year-old son's hockey game. And the worst news is that rink rage isn't confined to the rink. Similarly ill-tempered adults can be found spoiling kids' enjoyment of youth soccer, basketball, baseball and football games, among others.

The offenders are few—the vast majority of parents are supportive of their kids without being disrespectful of coaches, referees or other fans. And extreme behaviour is rare. There are tens of thousands of kids' games played every year in a variety of sports, and referees and sports associations contacted by *Maclean's* estimate that they are forced to eject spectators perhaps one per cent of the time. "Most of us just come out to support our kids," Delhi fan David Edmonds said about the incident in Port Dover. "It's too bad, really, because it's just a couple of people making the rest of us look bad."

While their shrill heckling may not always be profane or abusive enough to cause ejection, it poisons the atmosphere and drives volunteer coaches and low-paid referees out of the game. The Canadian Hockey Association says harassment is a major cause of attrition among referees, about 30 per cent of whom quit every season. In soccer, it's just about as bad: Manitoba soccer officials say that two-thirds of new referees recruited and trained in the province leave by the end of their first year.

Not that there weren't leather-lunged louts in the good old days. But experts say hostile behaviour at youth games is far more pervasive —and sometimes violent—than it was a generation ago. Consider what happened in the summer of 2000 at a children's recreational hockey practice in Reading, Mass., north of Boston. One player's father was so abusive to the man supervising a pick-up game that the arena staff asked the father to leave the building. But the man, 42-year-old Thomas Junta, came back to confront the volunteer supervisor, 40-year-old Michael Costin. The hulking Junta, six-foot-one and 275 lb., beat Costin, a single father of four, into unconsciousness while a crowd of young kids—including two of the victim's sons—watched in horror. Doctors pronounced Costin dead at the hospital, and Junta was charged with manslaughter. "It is a terrible tragedy," says Fred Engh, president of the Florida-based National Alliance for Youth Sports. "But given what's been happening out there, it didn't surprise me."

On a flight home after the National Hockey League All-Star Weekend in Denver, a 10-year-old boy was going through his bag of loot. He had, among other things, trading cards, a bunch of autographs and a cool replica all-star jersey. "Have fun?" someone asked. "It was awesome," the boy replied. His dad, sitting next to him, frowned and explained wistfully that, because of the trip, the boy had to miss his team's Saturday game back home. "Dad, it was against the last-place team," said the son. "It's not like we were going to lose or anything." "I know, I know," the father said, "but you missed a great chance to pad your stats."

Huh? For the kid, a pass into all-star weekend was better than a blank cheque at Toys "R" Us. But the father saw a lost opportunity to bolster his son's CV and to impress higher-level coaches. Parents' inflated ambitions, experts say, contribute to the intensified atmosphere surrounding youth games. "We're out there to put on recreation programs for kids, so they can have their fun," says Orest Zaozirney of the Edmonton Minor Hockey Association. "But you get parents who think they've got the next Gretzky."

This isn't the first generation of sports parents with stars in their eyes. But now they have dollar signs, too. Even modestly successful

> Only amateurs say that they write for their own amusement. Writing is not an amusing occupation. It is a combination of ditch-digging, mountain-climbing, treadmill and childbirth. Writing may be interesting, absorbing, exhilirating, racking, relieving. But amusing? Never!
>
> Edna Ferber

professional athletes can make millions these days, and expansion in all leagues has provided more jobs than ever before. The kids begin to look like meal tickets, when in fact lottery tickets is a better comparison. The odds of making it to the pro ranks are infinitesimally small—the Canadian Hockey Association estimates that less than one per cent of hockey-playing kids make it to the NHL.

"I think parents' expectations are greater than they ever have been," says Steve Larmer, a 39-year-old retired NHL all-star who, among other things, is now a volunteer coach of a novice (age 7 to 8) team in Peterborough, Ont. "They expect more not just from their kids, but from coaches and referees, too." Guy Blondeau, executive director of Hockey-Quebec, which represents about 350 minor hockey associations in the province, just shakes his head. "If parents stopped for a few minutes to think about the chances of their children having a career," says Blondeau, "I think they would reduce those expectations by a lot."

For a variety of reasons, modern parents are playing a bigger role than ever in their kids' recreation. "They are way more involved now than they were when I was a kid," says Larmer. "That's good in some ways, but sometimes they take it too far." As if to protect their "investment" in their future star, some adults hound their kids' coaches, demanding more playing time, all while pushing the child to excel. And that, says Jean Cote, a psychology professor at Queen's University in Kingston, Ont., is likely the most counterproductive approach parents can take. There are exceptions, of course—tennis's phenomenal Williams sisters and their all-controlling father come to mind. But Cote has studied the families of elite athletes and says the most successful competitors typically come from homes where parents are supportive without pushing their child too hard, or hollering at referees, or interfering with coaches. Parents who get too involved, Cote says, risk turning the kid off sport altogether. "It is quite consistent throughout our studies with elite athletes," Cote says, "that at a critical point, their parents let them choose what they wanted to do."

Beyond high expectations, experts say, the main reason for the sideline conflicts plaguing recreational sports is society as a whole. If otherwise sensible people can be enraged by traffic or by airline delays, why not by what they see at sporting events? "We are seeing an erosion of civility in society as a whole," says Engh, "and sports just mirrors what is happening all around us."

At a bantam (age 13 to 14) AA game in Thetford Mines, Que., in October 2000, a father confronted his son's coach during the intermission after the boy sat out the first period. The man allegedly hit the coach, Pierre Morin, in the face and slammed him to the ground. The attacker was ejected from the building and the injured coach took his place behind the bench for the rest of the game. Afterwards, Morin was taken to hospital where he was diagnosed with a dislocated shoulder. Clement Lajoie was charged with assault and uttering threats of death or bodily harm. His bail conditions forbid him from entering an arena or attending his son's hockey games. The case has not yet gone to court.

Youth sport couldn't exist without its referees and coaches, yet for years the culture surrounding the games has, if anything, driven them away. Dick Derrett, technical administrator for player and referee development at Manitoba Soccer, says that, for officials, dealing with rowdy adults is an ongoing battle. "Some of these parents get it in their head to win, win, win, and they don't care about the kids," Derrett says. "A lot of foul language is used right in front of the kids. For a referee, it is very frightening to be subjected to someone like that, not knowing what they are going to do."

It's not like refs are getting rich. It's a big deal if they receive $20 each to call a game in minor hockey, and they have to supply their own gear, including the striped jerseys. Veteran refs say it can be a lot of fun when the kids play well, the game goes smoothly and the fans enjoy themselves. But too often there is harassment and verbal abuse. In Nanaimo, B.C., local referees boycotted a weekend series of minor hockey games to protest the vicious taunting from so-called fans. Some attacks are not directed at the officials. "I've seen parents fighting in the stands, and heard people yelling racial slurs," says Cam Johnston, a longtime minor-hockey official in Mississauga, Ont. "One time, I saw two mothers pushing and shoving each other after a game, and there were their kids, just tykes, watching and crying. It was just terrible."

Before the start of the 2000-2001 season, the Edmonton Minor Hockey Association introduced something new to its player-registration process. Parents wanting to enrol their kids had to first sign a pledge to behave themselves at games. If they refused to sign, their children were not allowed to play. Simple as that.

Many sports organizations are reluctant to crack down on the hotheads for fear of alienating their members. Youth sports would simply collapse without the help of parents who volunteer as ticket-takers, drivers, fund-raisers, administrators and coaches. While practically every association admits there's a serious problem, they invariably claim their own group of parents is just fine.

Still, zero tolerance is spreading. The fair-play program adopted in Edmonton was pioneered by the Dartmouth Whalers Minor Hockey

Association in Dartmouth, N.S., in 1994. It promotes sportsmanship and equal ice time for players, and respect and restraint among spectators. It has resulted in a dramatic decline in verbal harassment of players and officials, leading nearby associations, which were initially skeptical, to adopt the same rules. In Laval, Que., after police were called to break up a fight in the stands between two parents, Hockey Laval introduced a code of ethics for parents, players, coaches, administrators and officials, and promised that parents will be required to sign the good behaviour pledge. "We want to sensitize people," says Dominique Roy, director of operations at Hockey Laval.

Experts say that approach will work over time. "One of the things we have to do," says Dale England, vice-president of officiating for the Winnipeg Minor Hockey Association, "is to teach parents to respect the game, the coaches, the players and the referees—all the things that go into making this activity happen." Engh, author of *Why Johnny Hates Sports*, says proactive education of parents is the only way to restore order on the sidelines. "Why do parents behave the way they do?" Engh asks. "There are many reasons, but the main one is that no one has ever told them they can't."

That education process has been slow, so youth sport officials hope that the embarrassing string of incidents this winter might prompt more sports to introduce their own fair-play initiatives. Or perhaps they should just listen to kids like Port Dover winger Craig Pineo, 13, who was out there trying to play a game while adults were screaming epithets and throwing debris and ultimately causing the game to be stopped. "I couldn't believe it was happening," Pineo said. "We knew it had nothing really to do with us, but it got a little scary. We were winning the game, but we just wanted to get out of there." And that is just wrong.

1. *Response*
a. Summarize the thesis of this essay in your own words. Compare your wording with that of other students and discuss the differences.
b. Identify the authors' use of examples to support the thesis. Remember that examples can include any of the following: narration of events drawn from the writer's experience; or statistics, facts, analogies, quotations, and anecdotes of events or incidents in others' lives. How have the authors organized the examples throughout the essay?

c. What seem to be the causes of rink rage? Do you think rink rage can be prevented?

d. If the offenders are few, why is the behaviour tolerated by so many? How do parents and children behave in your local sport competitions?

e. Why do you think some parents put this pressure on their children?

2. *Visual Communication* Presentation Prepare a visual presentation to encourage the prevention of parental violence connected with sports. You can focus on one sport or on sports in general. Choose your intended audience and purpose, and a suitable format; for example, a cartoon lampooning parents' "support" at a sports competition; a brochure for handing out to parents; a how-to video for parents; a videotaped skit about the problem; a PowerPoint (or similar) presentation; or a poster of rules for behaviour. Include a commentary about why your presentation would be effective in stopping sports rage.

3. *Media* Studying Photos Study the photos and captions that appear in the sports pages of a variety of newspapers and sports magazines for a given number of days. Using a chart or other graphic organizer, make observations based on the following: What is the subject of the photos? How many of them are of body contact or roughness? What types of shots are they—close up, wide angle, or middle distance? What message is conveyed by the caption? Is there a difference between the kind of shots taken of women's sport as opposed to men's? Study your findings and, in an oral report, share your overall observations.

Then, assume that you are the photo editor of the sports page for your community's weekly newspaper. Using photos that you clip from newspapers and magazines, digital photos, and/or photos that you shoot, choose five photos that you would use on your sports page, and explain why you chose them.

Theme Connections

- *"The Shining Houses,"* a story in which people behave badly, page 26
- *"The Large Ant,"* a story about violence and human nature, page 150
- *"Peace a Hard Sell to Skeptical Youth,"* an article about encouraging youth to act for peace, page 407

A simple cup of coffee turns out to be
not so simple after all.

Coffee

Process Analysis by Alan Durning

Beans

I brewed a cup of coffee. It took 100 beans—about one fortieth of the beans that grew on the coffee tree that year. The tree was on a small mountain farm in the region of Colombia called Antioquia. The region was cleared of its native forests in the first coffee boom three generations ago. These "cloud forests" are among the world's most endangered ecosystems.

The beans ripened in the shade of taller trees. Growing them did not require plowing the soil, but it did take several doses of insecticides, which were synthesized in factories in the Rhine River Valley of Europe. Some of the chemicals entered the respiratory systems of farm workers. Others washed downstream and were absorbed by plants and animals.

The beans were picked by hand. In a diesel-powered crusher they were removed from the fruit that encased them. They were dried under the sun and shipped to New Orleans in a 132-pound bag. The freighter was fueled by Venezuelan oil and made in Japan. The shipyard built the freighter out of Korean steel. The Korean steel mill used iron mined on tribal lands in Papua New Guinea.

At New Orleans the beans were roasted for 13 minutes at temperatures above 400 degrees F. The roaster burned natural gas pumped from the ground in Oklahoma. The beans were packaged in four-layer bags constructed of polyethylene, nylon, aluminum foil and polyester. They were trucked to a Seattle warehouse and later to a retail store.

Bag

I carried the beans out of the grocery in a brown paper bag made at an unbleached kraft paper mill in Oregon. I transported them home in an automobile that burned one sixth of a gallon of gasoline during the five-mile round-trip to the market.

Grinder

In the kitchen, I measured the beans in a disposable plastic scoop molded in New Jersey and spooned them into the grinder. The grinder was assembled in China from imported steel, aluminum, copper, and plastic parts. It was powered by electricity generated at the Ross Dam on the Skagit River.

I dumped the coffee into a gold-plated mesh filter made in Switzerland of Russian ore. I put the filter into a plastic-and-steel drip coffee maker.

I poured eight ounces of tap water into the appliance. The water came by pipe from the Cedar River on the west slope of the Cascade Mountains. An element heated the water to more than 200 degrees F. The hot water seeped through the ground coffee and dissolved some of its oils and solids. The brew trickled into a glass carafe.

Paper Cups

The coffee mugs were all dirty so I poured the coffee into a paper cup. The cup was made from bleached wood pulp in Arkansas. A fraction of the chlorine in the bleach was discharged from the pulp mill into the Arkansas River. In the river, the chlorine ended up as TCDD, which is often simply called dioxin. It is the most carcinogenic substance known.

Cream

I stirred in one ounce of cream. The cream came from a grain-fed dairy cow in the lowlands north of Seattle. The cow liked to graze on a stream bank and walk in the stream. This muddied the water and made life difficult for native trout.

The cow's manure was rich in nitrogen and phosphorus. The soils of the pasture where the cow grazed were unable to absorb these quickly enough, so they washed into the stream when it rained. The infusion of nutrients fertilized algae, which absorbed a larger share of the oxygen dissolved in the water. The shortage of oxygen made life more difficult for native trout.

Sugar

I measured out two tablespoons of sugar. It came from the canefields south of Lake Okeechobee in Florida. These plantations have deprived the Everglades of water, endangering waterfowl and reptile populations.

Alan Durning went to Washington D.C. after college, where he worked at the Worldwatch Institute as a research assistant. At the age of 21, his article on the dangers to the environment of animal farming, published in the *Los Angeles Times*, attracted national interest. Durning continued his work at Worldwatch, researching and publishing articles, and his book, *How Much Is Enough?: The Consumer Society and the Future of the Earth*, was published in 1992.

I. *Response*

a. In this selection, the author details the processes that occur for him to have a cup of coffee. Briefly outline the steps in this process.

b. What do you think Durning's purpose was in writing this? Explain the impression you are left with after reading it.

c. Do you think that the ending provides a satisfactory conclusion? Explain.

d. What environmental or ecological dangers does the author cite in this selection?

2. *Making Connections* With four or five classmates, discuss the following questions: What foods are manufactured in your area? What foods are imported to your area from other regions of Canada? From North America? From other continents? How much attention do you usually give to the source of what you eat and how it got to your table? Why might it be important to know where the food you eat comes from?

3. *Literature Studies* *Process Analysis* The type of organization or pattern for this selection is called **process analysis**. Look through some essay collections, magazines, or newspapers to find other examples of process analysis. Choose one to focus on and identify the steps in the process, perhaps by using a flow chart.

A **process analysis** shows how something is done. It gives information about a process, usually in the same order as the process itself.

4. *Language Conventions* *Passive Voice* Alan Durning uses the passive voice in several paragraphs—something most writers usually try to avoid because it makes the writing less vivid and lively. Study the third, fourth, sixth, and ninth paragraphs, and identify the use of this voice. When the author uses "I" in the sentences, what voice does he use? What is the effect of this choice of voice and of sentence construction?

Blue Gold

"Canadians have something we need, and I don't mean hockey players."

Argumentative Essay
by Jim Hightower

Should we invade Canada with armed forces? Sure, they're nice people, and ever so peaceable. (It's going to be hard to work up much xenophobic hatred toward a country that thinks "jeepers" is an expletive, and that has "Be Polite" in its constitution.) But Canadians have something we need, and I don't mean hockey players. "Blue gold," it's been dubbed by a Canadian newspaper, but it's far more valuable than that implies, because the world can do without gold.

Water. That's what Canada has that parts of our country and much of the world might literally kill for.

Hell, you say, water's everywhere. Yes, but as Canada's Maude Barlow points out, less than half of 1 percent of all the water on the globe is drinkable. An author and agitator for common sense, Barlow heads the Council of Canadians and is founding chair of Action Canada Network, two grassroots groups working for progressive policies. "Worldwide, the consumption of water is doubling every 20 years," she writes in a stunning report called "Blue Gold: The Global Water Crisis." In a very short while, most of the world's people will face shortages or absolute scarcity. This is not a matter of seeing more stories of wretched African children dying in horrible droughts, but of imminent water crises in America (the Southwest, Florida, and California especially), Southern Europe, India, England, China, and other nations not usually thought of as facing massive water shortages.

Canada, on the other hand, has a blessing of *agua fresca*. Some 20 percent of the world's entire supply of fresh water is in its winding rivers and countless lakes. This reality has not dawned on Canadians alone; others are casting their eyes northward. But it's not countries making invasion plans—it's corporations.

To get their hands on the gold, the corporate grubbers first have to change how drinking water is managed. Instead of letting countries treat it as a commonly held resource allocated for the general good, they want it considered as a commodity traded by private investors for profit. Like oil or pork bellies ... only this is your drinking water they want to privatize. Will it surprise you to learn that those bratty globalization twins, NAFTA and the World Trade Organization, contain provisions that advance the commodity concept? Both baldly assert that "water, including ordinary natural water of all kinds," is merely one form of "goods," subject to the new rules of global trade.

We're talking about bulk sales here: not Evian, but whole lakes and aquifers bought and mined, rivers siphoned off, the Great Lakes themselves on the market. Barlow and others report that multinationals are ready to use supertankers, pipelines, canals, river rerouting, and other mammoth schemes to shift the product from the water-rich to those willing to pay top dollar:

- Nordic Water Company totes H_2O from Norway to thirsty Europe across the sea in giant, floating plastic bags.
- Global Water Corporation, a Canadian firm, has cut a deal with Sitka, Alaska, to haul 18 billion gallons of water per year from nearby Blue Lake to China—"Water has moved from being an endless commodity that may be taken for granted to a rationed necessity that may be taken by force," says GWC's chilling statement.
- The Great Recycling and Northern Development Canal involves building a dike across James Bay to capture water from 20 rivers that feed it, converting the bay into a giant reservoir, then building a network of canals, dams, and locks to move the water 400 miles south to Georgian Bay, where it would be "flushed through" the Great Lakes into pipelines that would take it to America's Sun Belt for lawn watering, golf course sprinkling, and other essentials.
- The McCurdy Group of Newfoundland hopes to "harvest" some 13 billion gallons of water a year from one of that province's lakes, pipe it to the coast, pump it into old oil tankers, and ship it to the Middle East for a hefty profit.
- One Monsanto executive, seeing a multibillion-dollar business opportunity, says bluntly: "Since water is as central to food production as seed is, and without water life is not possible, Monsanto is now trying to establish its control over water.... Monsanto [has launched] a new water business, starting with India and Mexico, since both these countries face water shortages."

> What is written without effort is in general read without pleasure.
>
> Samuel Johnson

"Canada," barked editor Terence Corcoran of the *Financial Post* in a 1999 editorial, "is a future OPEC of water"; he urged that the country begin trading this commodity. But thanks to citizen groups like Maude Barlow's, the Great Canadian Water Sale-a-Thon has yet to begin; their vigilance has produced a temporary moratorium on bulk sales. This might be a good place to add that Maude, and Canadians generally, are not saying, "It's our water and the rest of the world can go suck eggs." To the contrary, they are pushing for a public policy of sharing their bounty to meet the global water crisis, allocating water particularly to help those in need.

But the pressure is intense to simply let "the market" decide who needs it. And the big stick of "free trade" is being wielded to turn the water loose. Sun Belt Water Inc., based in Santa Barbara, California, has filed the first NAFTA water case. It had an agreement with a British Columbia company to ship water in tankers from B.C. to Southern California. But such an outcry ensued when the scheme became public that the provincial government enacted a moratorium on all water exports. The corporation sued Canada in 1998, claiming that its future profits were "expropriated" by British Columbia's export moratorium and that, under NAFTA's Chapter 11, the nice people of Canada owed it $468 million.

Money isn't enough, though. Sun Belt CEO Jack Lindsey is also outraged at what he perceives as Canadian stinginess: "California has 33 million people—more than the entire population of Canada. This is expected to double in the next 20 years, and they have been living in a permanent drought condition. In 20 years, the shortfall in California will be 4 million acre-feet of water [per year]—1 percent of what spills into the Pacific Ocean from British Columbia—and they're saying, 'Sorry, you can't have it?'" Such a humanitarian. Jack just wants a few drops for California's poor parched people.

What a crock. Bulk water deals have nothing to do with global need and everything to do with global greed. Privateers will deliver the water to whoever will pay the most—like Silicon Valley's water-gobbling high-tech companies and agribusiness corporations that suck up aquifers like insatiable sponges. Then there is Lindsey's snide comment about water that just "spills into the Pacific Ocean," a common refrain, as if water that isn't being used commercially is being "wasted." Never mind that water running to the sea is essential to the ecological cycle, delivering nutrients, sustaining fishing economies, replenishing wetlands, and doing much more useful chores than fattening the wallets of would-be water barons.

Jim Hightower is a radio commentator, bestselling author, and public speaker. This selection was taken from his book, *If the Gods Had Meant Us to Vote They Would Have Given Us Candidates.*

1. **Response**
   a. Discuss your response to this essay. How did you feel toward the author? Did this feeling change at any point? Explain.
   b. Is Canada being selfish with its policies concerning its "blue gold"?
   c. Why is the citizenry's vigilance important to the issue of water trade?

2. **Literature Studies** *Argumentative Essay* "Blue Gold" is an example of an argumentative essay. David G. Pitt writes, "Argumentative prose aims not so much to explain something as to convince or persuade others ..." These writing techniques can include making effective word choices; using irony; using the element of surprise or shock; using *hyperbole* (exaggeration); using the imperative voice; and using examples such as facts, statistics, events in real life, or quotations. With this list of techniques in mind, skim the essay to find out how Hightower has presented his argument and analyse its effectiveness.

3. **Oral Communication** *Discussion* Have a round-table discussion on the sale of water, with fellow students representing different countries. You should research the country's water resources and any policies on water consumption, and be prepared to present that country's needs and its possible stance on the issue.

4. **Media** *Ad* Create an ad based on your study of this essay and the water issue. You could, for example, promote Canada's sale of water; urge Canadians to resist the sale of their water; urge people to conserve water; promote the appreciation of our natural resources; or focus on the need for water in countries with few water resources.

5. **Making Connections** What do you think Alan Durning's ("Coffee") response might be to this essay? Support your response by thoroughly examining the opinions given in both "Blue Gold" and "Coffee." How does the way in which each writer presents his thesis differ?

*Mary Schäffer, photographer and pioneer at the turn
of the century, explored the Alberta rocky mountains
and captured an "unmapped country" on film.*

Hunter of
Peace

Photo Essay by Mary Schäffer

Here's to a life of unnumbered
summers in the mountains,
with stars above by night,
sunshine and soft winds by day,
with the music of the waters
at our banquet.
Civilisation!
How little it means
when one has tasted
the free life of the trail!

Mary Schäffer Warren was born in Pennsylvania, U.S., in 1861. She was an explorer, watercolour painter, and photographer, returning time and again to Canada where she hiked the trails through the Canadian Rockies. She wrote the books *Untrodden Paths in the Canadian Rockies, Old Indian Trails,* and *A Hunter of Peace*, as well as many articles about the wildflowers and countryside of Saskatchewan and the Rockies. She died in 1939.

1. Response
   a. Explain what you think the title "Hunter of Peace" means, given the introductory text and photos.
   b. What would you say is the thesis of this photo essay? Express it by giving the essay a new title. You could also use a subtitle, if necessary.
   c. What inferences or assumptions do you make from the photos? For example, what does the mood of the people seem to be? Who are they? What might their purpose be?
   d. Imagine you are in one of the photos. Quickly, record the first words that come to your mind.

2. *Focus on Context* What do you find out about Mary Schäffer from reading and viewing this essay? Use Internet and library sources to find out more about this photographer. Write a short biography for Schäffer, explaining how her photographic work was affected by her surroundings and the time in which she lived. What was her purpose in creating the photos? Who was her audience?

3. *Visual Communication* *Photo Essays* Research to find another photo essay—other than the ones in this anthology —that appeals to you, on any subject, for example, showing another period in history or another location. Present this photo essay to a partner, explaining why it appeals to you.
   Alternatively, create a photo essay to represent a period in history, a particular landscape, or a subject of your own. Take your own photos, if feasible, or select print and digital photos. Try a variety of sources. Make decisions about whether or not to include text, whether to use black and white or colour, or both, and about the placement of the photos. Do not forget to include a title. Ask a peer to assess your photo essay and its effectiveness.

4. *Film Study* Choose one of these photos and consider the story it suggests to you. Jot down notes on the story and use them to develop a movie proposal or treatment (an outline for a movie that is used to sell the movie to a producer). Your proposal should include a title, list of characters, setting, storyline, and probable target audience.

Worms
and the Soil

Expository Essay by Charles Darwin

Worms have played a more important part in the history of the world than most persons would at first suppose. In almost all humid countries they are extraordinarily numerous, and for their size possess great muscular power. In many parts of England a weight of more than ten tons of dry earth annually passes through their bodies and is brought to the surface on each acre of land; so that the whole superficial bed of vegetable mould passes through their bodies in the course of every few years. From the collapsing of the old burrows the mould is in constant though slow movement, and the particles composing it are thus rubbed together. By these means fresh surfaces are continually exposed to the action of the carbonic acid in the soil, and of the humus-acids[1] which appear to be still more efficient in the decomposition of rocks. The generation of the humus-acids is probably hastened during the digestion of the many half-decayed leaves which worms consume. Thus the particles of earth, forming the superficial mould, are subjected to conditions eminently favorable for their decomposition and disintegration. Moreover, the particles of the softer rocks suffer some amount of mechanical trituration[2] in the muscular gizzards of worms, in which small stones serve as mill-stones.

The finely levigated[3] castings,[4] when brought to the surface in a moist condition, flow during rainy weather down any moderate slope; and the smaller particles are washed far down even a gently inclined surface. Castings when dry often crumple into small pellets and these are apt to roll down any sloping surface. Where the land is quite level and is covered with herbage, and where the climate is humid so that much dust cannot be blown away, it appears at first sight impossible that there should be any appreciable amount of subaerial[5] denudation; but worm castings are blown, especially whilst moist and viscid, in one uniform direction by the prevalent winds which are accompanied by rain. By these several means the superficial mould is prevented from accumulating to a great thickness; and a thick bed of mould checks in many ways the disintegration of the underlying rocks and fragments of rock.

The removal of worm castings by the above means leads to results which are far from insignificant. It has been shown that a layer of earth, two tenths of an inch in thickness, is in many places annually brought to the surface per acre; and if a small part of this amount flows, or rolls, or is washed, even for a short distance down every inclined surface, or is repeatedly blown in one direction, a great effect will be produced in the course of ages. It was found by measurements and calculations that on a surface with a mean inclination of 9°26', two and four tenths cubic inches of earth which had been ejected by worms crossed, in the course of a year, a horizontal line one yard in length; so that 240 cubic inches would cross a line 100 yards in length. This latter amount in a damp state would weigh $11\frac{1}{2}$ pounds. Thus a considerable weight of earth is continually moving down each side of every valley, and will in time reach its bed. Finally this earth will be transported by the streams flowing in the valleys into the ocean, the great receptacle for all matter denuded from the land. It is known from the amount of sediment annually delivered into the sea by the Mississippi, that its enormous drainage-area must on an average be lowered .00263 of an inch each year; and this would suffice in four and a half million years to lower the whole drainage-area to the level of the seashore. So that, if a small fraction of the layer of fine earth, two tenths of an inch in thickness, which is annually brought to the surface by worms, is carried away, a great result cannot fail to be produced within a period which no geologist considers extremely long.

Archaeologists ought to be grateful to worms, as they protect and preserve for an indefinitely long period every object not liable to decay, which is dropped on the surface of the land, by burying it beneath their castings. Thus, also, many elegant and curious tessellated[6] pavements and other ancient remains have been preserved; though no doubt the worms have in these cases been largely aided by earth washed and blown from the adjoining land, especially when cultivated. The old tessellated pavements have, however, often suffered by having subsided unequally from being unequally undermined by the worms. Even old massive walls may be undermined and subside; and no building is in this respect safe, unless the foundations lie six or seven feet beneath the surface, at a depth at which worms cannot work. It is probable that many monoliths[7] and some old walls have fallen down from having been undermined by worms.

Worms prepare the ground in an excellent manner for the growth of fibrous-rooted plants and for seedlings of all kinds. They periodically expose the mould to the air, and sift it so that no stones larger than the particles which they can swallow are left in it. They mingle the whole intimately together, like a gardener who prepares fine soil for his choicest plants. In this state it is well fitted to retain moisture and to absorb all soluble substances, as well as for the process of nitrification.[8] The bones of dead animals, the harder parts of insects, the shells of land-molluscs, leaves, twigs, etc., are before long all buried beneath the accumulated castings of worms, and are thus brought in a more or less decayed state within reach of the roots of plants. Worms likewise drag an infinite number of dead leaves and other parts of plants into their burrows, partly for the sake of plugging them up and partly as food.

The leaves which are dragged into the burrows as food, after being torn into the finest shreds, partially digested, and saturated with the intestinal and urinary secretions, are commingled with much earth. This earth forms the dark colored, rich humus which almost every-where covers the surface of the land with a fairly well-defined layer or mantle. Von Hensen placed two worms in a vessel eighteen inches in diameter, which was filled with sand, on which fallen leaves were strewed; and these were soon dragged into their burrows to a depth of three inches. After about six weeks an almost uniform layer of sand four tenths of an inch in thickness was converted into humus by having passed through the alimentary canals of these two worms. It is believed by some people that worm burrows, which often penetrate the ground almost perpendicularly to a depth of five or six feet, materially aid in its drainage; notwithstanding that the viscid castings piled over the mouths of the burrows prevent or check the rainwater directly entering them. They allow the air to penetrate deeply into the ground. They also greatly facilitate the downward passage of roots of moderate size; and these will be nourished by the humus with which the burrows are lined. Many seeds owe their germination to having been covered by castings; and others buried to a considerable depth beneath accumulated castings lie dormant, until at some future time they are accidentally uncovered and germinate.

The challenge of nonfiction is to marry art and truth.

Phyllis Rose

Worms are poorly provided with sense-organs, for they cannot be said to see, although they can just distinguish between light and darkness; they are completely deaf, and have only a feeble power of smell; the sense of touch alone is well developed. They can therefore learn little about the outside world, and it is surprising that they should exhibit some skill in lining their burrows with their castings and with leaves, and in the case of some species in piling up their castings into tower-like constructions. But it is far more surprising that they should apparently exhibit some degree of intelligence instead of a mere blind instinctive impulse, in their manner of plugging up the mouths of their burrows. They act in nearly the same manner as would a man, who had to close a cylindrical tube with different kinds of leaves, petioles,[9] triangles of paper, etc., for they commonly seize such objects by their pointed ends. But with thin objects a certain number are drawn in by their broader ends. They do not act in the same unvarying manner in all cases, as do most of the lower animals; for instance, they do not drag in leaves by their foot-stalks, unless the basal part of the blade is as narrow as the apex, or narrower than it.

When we behold a wide, turf-covered expanse, we should remember that its smoothness, on which so much of its beauty depends, is mainly due to all the inequalities having been slowly leveled by worms. It is a marvelous reflection that the whole of the superficial mould over any such expanse has passed, and will again pass, every few years through the bodies of worms. The plough is one of the most ancient and most valuable of man's inventions; but long before he existed the land was in fact regularly ploughed, and still continues to be thus ploughed by earth-worms. It may be doubted whether there are many other animals which have played so important a part in the history of the world, as have these lowly organized creatures. Some other animals, however, still more lowly organized, namely corals, have done far more conspicuous work in having constructed innumerable reefs and islands in the great oceans; but these are almost confined to the tropical zones.

---

[1]**humus-acids:** acids in the humus, a brown or black substance resulting from the partial decay of leaves and other vegetable matter
[2]**trituration:** rubbing or grinding into very fine particles or powder
[3]**levigated:** ground to a fine, smooth powder
[4]**castings:** things thrown off or ejected
[5]**subaerial:** beneath the air, hence on the surface
[6]**tessellated:** laid out in a mosaic pattern of small, square blocks
[7]**monoliths:** in architecture, single large blocks of stone
[8]**nitrification:** impregnation of soil with nitrates, which serve as fertilizers
[9]**petioles:** the stalks to which leaves are attached

Charles Darwin was born in Shropshire, England, in 1809. After his education at Edinburgh and Oxford, he joined the English survey ship *HMS Beagle* on a voyage around the world. As a naturalist, he was expected to observe and report on the diverse geological formations, fossils, and living organisms found on the different islands and continents they visited. Darwin is best known for his controversial theories on evolution. In 1859 and 1871, he published his theories in *On the Origin of Species by Means of Natural Selection* and *The Descent of Man*. He died in 1882.

1. *Response*
   a. Why is Darwin so fascinated by worms?
   b. How do you feel about worms? Were your feelings toward worms changed by the information given in this essay? Explain.
   c. What is the thesis of this essay? Do you think Darwin proves this thesis? Explain.
   d. Summarize the main points of this essay.

2. *Focus on Context* Tell a partner everything you know about Charles Darwin. Listen as your partner does the same. Now, research to find out more about who Darwin was, and the time in which he lived. Discuss how this contextual knowledge influences your understanding or appreciation of "Worms and the Soil."

3. *Writing* Character Sketch Use the information in the essay and your imagination to develop a fictional character sketch for a worm protagonist or antagonist. Your story could be a horror, fantasy, drama, comedy, adventure, et cetera. Use your character sketch to develop a short story, movie treatment, novel outline, poem, or another format of your choice.

4. *Language Conventions* Indicative Mood Examine the use of indicative mood or mode (a verb form showing the manner of action—stating a fact or asking a question) within the essay. How is this mood appropriate to the purpose and content of the essay? What other mood is used in the essay (check a writer's handbook to find out the characteristics of imperative and subjunctive moods)? Where else would you expect to use indicative mood? How do you use indicative mood in your own writing?

A rocket launched into the aurora borealis
during a two-year peak in its activity
is helping scientists unravel the mysteries
of the northern lights.

Night
Spirits

Magazine Article by Candace Savage

One of the pleasures of a Canadian winter is the night. Stars spangle the heavens, and between their radiant points, the universe flows outward into endless black. We look up and feel ourselves falling into cosmic emptiness—blank space without matter or movement. But then, if luck is with us, the sky begins to ripple with soft, shimmering curtains of light that fill this seemingly empty cosmos with energy and life. Aurora borealis, or the northern lights. So faint they are seldom seen in summer, these luminous wraiths are a gift of winter's darkness.

The northern lights stand at the boundary between visible and invisible worlds, giving us a glimpse into a little-known universe. In times past, people thought that the lights must be spirits: fairies, magic beasts or bright souls. Even today, while scientists have a good idea of the physical forces involved, they still view the spectacle of the aurora with old-fashioned awe.

Physicist Dave Knudsen, an assistant professor in the department of physics and astronomy at the University of Calgary, is a case in point. Raised in Iowa (where the aurora rarely appears), he was in his twenties before he first saw the northern lights in action. Yet, despite the novelty of the experience, Knudsen was never in any doubt about what he was looking at. "I've always been driven by a desire to understand electricity and magnetism," he explains, "and this was so obviously a display of electromagnetism. I knew there must be basic laws governing it, but it was so inexplicably complex. My mind was just racing with excitement!"

To Knudsen, the northern lights are more than a source of delight. To him they are a manifestation of turbulent forces that bluster and roil throughout the dark universe. "If you go even 100 kilometres above Earth, to the base of the auroral curtains," he says, "you already find yourself in a different world. The behaviour of the physical system is dramatically different there than what we find here on the ground. It's not hard to imagine that things get even more interesting and complex as you move farther out."

With this thought in mind, Knudsen recently initiated a multi-million-dollar international research project known as GEODESIC or, to give its full moniker: Geo-electrodynamics and Electro-Optical Detection of Electron and Suprathermal Ion Currents. The effort literally got off the ground in February 2000, when Knudsen and his team launched a sounding rocket (built by Winnipeg's Bristol Aerospace) from the Poker Flat rocket range, near Fairbanks, Alaska. The main purpose of the six-year study is to investigate the otherworldly behaviour of charged particles in and around the auroral curtains.

Space is occupied not by the solids, liquids and gases that we earthlings know so well. Instead, it is filled with a fourth state of matter known as plasma—a kind of improbably thin, electrically active vapour. Although natural plasmas are rare on Earth (found only in exotic phenomena such as ball lightning), they are exceedingly common in space. In fact, about 99 percent of the matter in the universe is thought to exist in the plasma state. Unlike air, which is electrically inert, plasmas consist of charged molecules and atoms that not only respond to familiar physical forces (such as pressure and gravity) but are also highly sensitive to electromagnetic fields. Pushed and pulled by all these conflicting forces, plasma is even more chaotic and dynamic than air, many times more changeable than weather.

Yet all the cosmic *Sturm und Drang*[1] of the plasma might pass us by unnoticed—if it weren't for the aurora. Like whitecaps on a storm-tossed sea, the northern lights are the visible crests of invisible plasma waves that batter Earth. (Much of this bombardment originates in the sun, which spews out streams of plasma as the so-called solar wind.) Drawn toward the polar regions of Earth along magnetic lines of force, plasma cascades ever downward until—about 1,000 kilometres overhead—it begins to run into atmospheric gases. As high-speed electrons in the plasma collide with oxygen and nitrogen in the air, the gases receive an energetic jolt, which they emit as faint bursts of colour

---

[1] *Sturm und Drang:* German, meaning, literally, storm and stress. Refers to a literary movement in Germany in the late eighteenth century.

(greenish white for oxygen, pink for nitrogen). When millions of ener-gized molecules go off at the same time, the night sky begins to dance with all the tumultuous vigour of the plasma currents. Down on Earth, we look up and emit gasps of delight.

If we want to understand the cosmic forces that whirl through space, we cannot do better than to study auroral displays. "The north-ern lights provide us with a natural laboratory for studying plasma struc-tures," says Knudsen. We can be pretty sure that whatever is simmering in the northern lights is boiling over somewhere else in the universe." For example, there are fine structures within the aurora—tubes less than 50 metres across—that appear to serve as a kind of charged-particle gun, or accelerator. Through some unknown mechanism, these tubes transfer energy from plasma to atmospheric ions and send them zooming off into outer space. If Knudsen and his GEODESIC colleagues can figure out how these accelerators work, they will have made a small contribution to understanding the northern lights and a larger one to solving an outstanding problem in plasma physics.

Northern Lights, Alberta, Canada by Daryl Benson. Photo

Examine this photo and record your thoughts and feelings on its content and composition. Use these notes to create a piece of writing (short story, folk tale, poem, essay, et cetera) that explores the impact that the northern lights have on humanity.

As the GEODESIC rocket blasted off from Poker Flat and through a display of northern lights, its payload of sensitive instruments took a rapid-fire series of measurements, at the rate of about 10 million bits per second. Translated into graphical images, these data trace the moment-by-moment behaviour of charged particles in a series of accelerators. The entire mission, from takeoff to crash landing in the frozen Beaufort Sea, took 17 minutes flat. But decoding and figuring out what the data mean will keep Knudsen and his colleagues busy until about 2003.

Meanwhile, Knudsen is preparing an instrument for another rocket that will be launched from Norway's Svalbard Archipelago in December 2001. Again, his plan is to make measurements inside accelerators. But his larger mission—the purpose that drives his research—is to understand the fundamental forces raging through the universe. They are out there every second, whether we can see them or not, dancing over our heads in the infinite darkness.

> ... writing is the action of thinking, just as drawing is the action of seeing and composing music is the action of hearing. And all that is inward must be expressed in action, for that is the true life of the spirit and the only way we can be continually discarding our dead and mistaken (sinful) selves and progressing and knowing more.
>
> Brenda Ueland

Candace Savage, a writer based in Saskatoon, Saskatchewan, was born in northern Alberta. She is the author of twenty books, including *Aurora: The Mysterious Northern Lights*, *The Nature of Wolves,* and *Bird Brains.* She writes about wildlife, the environment, natural sciences, and women's history, and received an Honour Book Award, Children's Literature Roundtable, in 1991 for her book, *Trash Attack!*

I. *Response*

a. What knowledge did you have of the northern lights before reading this article? Have you ever seen them? If you have not, how important is it to you to see them? If you have, describe how you felt when you saw them.

b. If you had lived in times long past, how do you think you would have explained the northern lights? What must it have been like to see them then?

c. Create a diagram to illustrate the author's description of the plasma and/or the aurora.

2. *Writing* Technical Report

Explaining scientific or technical information for a general audience can be difficult to do well. How has this author made the science of the northern lights easy to understand? Write a brief report explaining another natural phenomenon. Do some research, if necessary, and use some of the techniques that Savage uses.

3. *Language Conventions* Parentheses and Apposition

In expository writing, writers often need to convey as much information as possible in a succinct way. If they are introducing new vocabulary, they sometimes need to offer brief definitions within their sentences. Skim the report to see how Savage has used parentheses to offer additional or qualifying information, and how she uses **apposition** to offer definitions of terms. Examine a piece of your own expository writing to see how you can use apposition and parentheses more effectively.

Apposition is the relation of two parts of a sentence when the one is added as an explanation to the other. For example, in *Mr. Brown, our teacher, is on vacation, Mr. Brown* and *teacher* are in apposition.

4. *Making Connections*

Use library or Internet resources to find two more literature selections—for example, a poem, story, folk tale, myth, or non-fiction item—that are about the northern lights. Discuss these works with a small group, comparing any descriptions of the northern lights and the role they play in the various selections.

An encounter with a weasel
leads to Annie Dillard's reflection
on how she would like to live her life—
by yielding only to necessity.

Living
Like
Weasels

Analogy by Annie Dillard

A weasel is wild. Who knows what he thinks? He sleeps in his underground den, his tail draped over his nose. Sometimes he lives in his den for two days without leaving. Outside, he stalks rabbits, mice, muskrats, and birds, killing more bodies than he can eat warm, and often dragging the carcasses home. Obedient to instinct, he bites his prey at the neck, either splitting the jugular vein at the throat or crunching the brain at the base of the skull, and he does not let go. One naturalist refused to kill a weasel who was socketed into his hand deeply as a rattlesnake. The man could in no way pry the tiny weasel off, and he had to walk half a mile to water, the weasel dangling from his palm, and soak him off like a stubborn label.

I have been thinking about weasels because I saw one last week. I startled a weasel who startled me, and we exchanged a long glance.

Near my house in Virginia is a pond—Hollins Pond. It covers two acres of bottomland near Tinker Creek with six inches of water and six thousand lily pads. There is a fifty-five mph highway at one end of the pond, and a nesting pair of wood ducks at the other. Under every bush is a muskrat hole or a beer can. The far end is an alternating series of fields and woods, fields and woods, threaded everywhere with motorcycle tracks—in whose bare clay wild turtles lay eggs.

One evening last week at sunset, I walked to the pond and sat on a downed log near the shore. I was watching the lily pads at my feet tremble and part over the thrusting path of a carp. A yellow warbler appeared to my right and flew behind me. It caught my eye; I swiveled around—and the next instant, inexplicably, I was looking down at a weasel, who was looking up at me.

Weasel! I had never seen one wild before. He was ten inches long, thin as a curve, a muscled ribbon, brown as fruitwood, soft-furred, alert. His face was fierce, small and pointed as a lizard's; he would have made a good arrowhead. There was just a dot of chin, maybe two brown hairs' worth, and then the pure white fur began that spread down his underside. He had two black eyes I did not see, any more than you see a window.

The weasel was stunned into stillness as he was emerging from beneath an enormous shaggy wild-rose bush four feet away. I was stunned into stillness, twisted backward on the tree trunk. Our eyes locked, and someone threw away the key.

Our look was as if two lovers, or deadly enemies, met unexpectedly on an overgrown path when each had been thinking of something else: a clearing blow to the gut. It was also a bright blow to the brain, or a sudden beating of brains, with all the charge and intimate grate of rubbed balloons. It emptied our lungs. It felled the forest, moved the fields, and drained the pond; the world dismantled and tumbled into that black hole of eyes. If you and I looked at each other that way, our skulls would split and drop to our shoulders. But we don't. We keep our skulls.

He disappeared. This was only last week, and already I don't remember what shattered the enchantment. I think I blinked, I think I retrieved my brain from the weasel's brain, and tried to memorize what I was seeing, and the weasel felt the yank of separation, the careening splashdown into real life and the urgent current of instinct. He vanished under the wild rose. I waited motionless, my mind suddenly full of data and my spirit with pleadings, but he didn't return.

Please do not tell me about "approach-avoidance conflicts."[1] I tell you I've been in that weasel's brain for sixty seconds, and he was in mine. Brains are private places, muttering through unique and secret tapes—but the weasel and I both plugged into another tape simultaneously, for a sweet and shocking time. Can I help it if it was a blank?

What goes on in his brain the rest of the time? What does a weasel think about? He won't say. His journal is tracks in clay, a spray of feathers, mouse blood and bone: uncollected, unconnected, loose-leaf, and blown.

I would like to learn, or remember, how to live. I come to Hollins Pond not so much to learn how to live as, frankly, to forget about it. That is, I don't think I can learn from a wild animal how to live in

---

[1] ***approach-avoidance conflicts:*** theory in psychology—a person has opposing urges to do something and hold back at the same time

particular—shall I suck warm blood, hold my tail high, walk with my footprints precisely over the prints of my hands?—but I might learn something of mindlessness, something of the purity of living in the physical senses and the dignity of living without bias or motive. The weasel lives in necessity and we live in choice, hating necessity and dying at the last ignobly in its talons. I would like to live as I should, as the weasel lives as he should. And I suspect that for me the way is like the weasel's: open to time and death painlessly, noticing everything, remembering nothing, choosing the given with a fierce and pointed will.

I missed my chance. I should have gone for the throat. I should have lunged for that streak of white under the weasel's chin and held on, held on through mud and into the wild rose, held on for a dearer life. We could live under the wild rose wild as weasels, mute and uncomprehending. I could very calmly go wild. I could live two days in the den, curled, leaning on mouse fur, sniffing bird bones, blinking, licking, breathing musk, my hair tangled in the roots of grasses. Down is a good place to go, where the mind is single. Down is out, out of your ever-loving mind and back to your careless senses. I remember mute- ness as a prolonged and giddy fast, where every moment is a feast of utterance received. Time and events are merely poured, unremarked, and ingested directly, like blood pulsed into my gut through a jugular vein. Could two live that way? Could two live under the wild rose, and explore by the pond, so that the smooth mind of each is as everywhere present to the other, and as received and as unchallenged, as falling snow?

We could, you know. We can live any way we want. People take vows of poverty, chastity, and obedience—even of silence—by choice. The thing is to stalk your calling in a certain skilled and supple way, to locate the most tender and live spot and plug into that pulse. This is yielding, not fighting. A weasel doesn't "attack" anything; a weasel lives as he's meant to, yielding at every moment to the perfect freedom of single necessity.

I think it would be well, and proper, and obedient, and pure, to grasp your one necessity and not let it go, to dangle from it limp wher- ever it takes you. Then even death, where you're going no matter how you live, cannot you part. Seize it and let it seize you up aloft even, till your eyes burn out and drop; let your musky flesh fall off in shreds, and let your very bones unhinge and scatter, loosened over fields, over fields and woods, lightly, thoughtless, from any height at all, from as high as eagles.

Annie Dillard was born in 1945 in the U.S. She studied English, theology, and creative writing at college, and graduated with a Masters in English in 1968. After a near fatal attack of pneumonia in 1971, she decided to live life more fully, and spent the next year in Tinker Creek. Life among the forests, creeks, and mountains led her, at the age of 29, to write her world-renowned book, *Pilgrim at Tinker Creek*. In 1975, Dillard won the Pulitzer Prize for general non-fiction. Some of her other works include an autobiography of her early years called *American Childhood*, and a book of poetry, *Ticket for a Prayer Wheel*. She works as an adjunct professor of English at Wesleyan University in Connecticut.

1. *Response*

a. Find an example of vivid description in this selection that allows you to see, almost like a picture or movie, what Dillard is describing. How has she made the picture real?

b. Identify the four parts of this selection, and note the shifts in focus and tone from part to part. How has the author achieved these shifts? How has she linked the last part with her introductory paragraph—what image is repeated?

c. In the third paragraph, the author uses the technique of contrast to make her point. Identify the series of contrasts and explain what she is contrasting, in a larger sense.

2. *Literature Studies* Analogy

This selection uses an *analogy*; it uses a subject (a weasel) as a representation of something else, or to show us a likeness between two things. What does the weasel represent? List two other examples of analogies in your own reading, in movies, or TV shows, or in the way you explain things to others, either verbally or in writing. Use an analogy to write a short essay about a subject of your choice.

3. **Language Focus** *Poetic Language* Dillard uses a number of stylistic devices to give her writing a rhythm and fluidity that is almost poetic. She uses vivid language and images, alliteration, and *consonance, and assonance* (similar vowel sounds repeated in the same sentence(s)). Many of her sentences are balanced: Two or more sentences in succession, or two parts of a sentence will have the same number of syllables, or close to it. See the opening two sentences, for example. Skim the selection to look for examples of these devices and of others that make Dillard's writing so evocative. Keep a record of the techniques so that you can refer to them when you do your own writing.

4. **Making Connections** In the second part of the selection (the eleventh paragraph), Dillard makes a subtle reference to Henry David Thoreau's famous work, *Walden*, in which he writes, "I went to the woods because I wished to live deliberately, to front only the essential facts of life, and see if I could not learn what it had to teach, and not when I came to die, discover that I had not lived." How does this compare with Dillard's thesis?

5. **Visual Communication** *Collage* "Living Like Weasels," "Hunter of Peace," and "Stone Faces" all have points of similarity. Choose sentences from these selections that express similar thoughts or themes, and input the sentences on the computer or write them out. From these sentences, or using just words and phrases from the sentences, create a collage of this text. Experiment with fonts, type styles and sizes, and colour.

Theme Connections

- *"The Large Ant," a story about following instincts to survive, page 150*
- *"The World Is Too Much With Us," a poem about rejecting civilization, page 219*
- *"Stone Faces," an essay about art transcending necessity, page 281*
- *"Hunter of Peace," a photo essay about leaving civilization behind, page 334*

Media

Societies have always been shaped more by the nature of the media by which men communicate than by the content of the communication.

Marshall McLuhan

As you read the following selection, consider the original audience and the purpose of this article. Who benefits from having this article appear in a local paper?

Follows Family Stages a Reunion

Newspaper Article by Harry Currie
from the *Kitchener-Waterloo Record*, June 2001

"We are a beastly family, and I hate us!"

So says a member of the Bliss family in Noël Coward's play *Hay Fever*, which is being rehearsed for a run at the Gravenhurst Opera House and at Guelph's River Run Centre.

But this is a unique production, for the Bliss family is being played by the Follows family, who are together both as a family and a group of thespians for the first time in years.

Ted Follows, father of the crew, now lives in Kitchener with his second wife Susan, and the others are spread out across North America. Ted's first wife, actress Dawn Greenhalgh, has joined the family for this production, and their children Laurence, Edwina, Megan, and Samantha are all present, along with Megan's partner Stuart Hughes and Samantha's husband Sean O'Bryan.

Ted and Megan took a few moments in a break from rehearsals to speak about the experience.

"We're not there yet," said Follows, "but we're getting to be a beastly family. We're plowing our way through. It's an awful lot of work, with many interruptions going on. Rehearsals are being held up, and I know it can't be helped when it's for public relations, but it definitely slows us down. But all in all it's coming along fine."

Follows feels that the difficulty in the play is that the real story is hidden below the actual dialogue.

"Because it's Coward, people tend to think that it's all superficial," he said. "But that superficial dialogue is masking the hidden tensions which are there constantly. A character may look as though he's falling asleep, but the energy which drives the characters is very, very powerful and completely unstated.

"With the Bliss family, filled with selfishness, each one wants to outweigh any thoughts for the others' needs or desires, yet this is never really stated. It's what's not said that's important."

Megan is probably the best-known of the Follows children, with her now-legendary role as Anne in the film version of *Anne of Green Gables*. She arrived here after finishing a movie that brought her from the glitz and glamour to Smalltown, Ontario.

"You know what?" she said. "It's wonderful. It really is a refreshing change."

The family hasn't acted together like this since filming three episodes of TV's *The Littlest Hobo* back in the early '80s when they were just kids.

"By the end of the day we're exhausted," she said, "but it's so unique, and so great being together. I'm so grateful to have this time with my brother and sisters, and particularly with my parents.

"I see different siblings at different times, but it's been a long time since we've all been together. It's wonderful to spend time with my mother and father together, because they've been separated since I was 11. I feel really grateful for that."

Megan finds working with the whole family in a play very interesting.

"We know each other extremely well," she said, "and we're having a lot of fun with one another. I think we all really appreciate each other's sense of humour. That's important, because that seems to be a stronger bond than anything— at least we're not getting on each other's nerves yet."

The film Megan has just finished was shot in Montréal.

"The working title was *The Stork Derby*," she said. "It's a great Canadian story about a man named Charles Miller who was a millionaire in the '20s. He left a million dollars in his will to the woman who gave birth to the most children 10 years to the date of his death. The newspapers called it the Stork Derby. It should be shown during the next season."

Patriarch Ted said this whole experience was like real-time déjà vu.

"I feel as though I've gone full circle," he said. "I was doing this back in the forties —performing together, living together—and here we are once again. It's hard to believe it's happened." ❿

> A camera is an instrument that teaches people how to see without a camera.
>
> Dorothea Lange

A native of Moncton, New Brunswick, **Harry Currie** is a graduate of four Canadian and British colleges and universities. He has been a Director of Music in the Canadian army, worked as an actor/singer/player/composer/arranger/conductor in Britain for ten years, taught high school music and English, published a thriller called *Debut for a Spy*. He is an entertainment writer for *The Record* in Kitchener/Waterloo.

1. Response
   a. Return to the introductory text at the top of this article and respond.
   b. What is a *thespian*? What connotations does this word have? What synonym could be used in the place of *thespian*?
   c. In your opinion, does this article provide a reader with enough information about the play *Hay Fever* and its production? Explain.
   d. Would you go and see a play you knew nothing about if an actor you really liked was playing the lead role? Why or why not?

2. *Media* Publicity The newspaper published this article because many of its readers would be interested in local theatre. The people producing the play would be eager to have this article in the newspaper, since it might increase the public's interest in seeing the play. This process of spreading news about a new play, movie, book, or product is known as *publicity* or *public relations* and is the responsibility of a marketing department. With a group, brainstorm ideas for spreading good publicity about a new play in your community. Which of your ideas do you think would be most effective? Why?

3. *Making Connections* Find a copy of Noël Coward's play, *Hay Fever*. Read at least two scenes and, with a partner, discuss why you would or would not like to see this play performed. Which actors would you cast in the main roles? Why? If you cannot find *Hay Fever*, research Noël Coward and his writing.

Richard Curtis, the screenwriter of *Four Weddings and a Funeral*, reveals all about writing movie scripts. This article appeared in *The Observer* (a British newspaper) the week before the movie was released in the summer of 1993.

Four Rules and a Suggestion

How-To Article by Richard Curtis

Everyone who ever wrote a film hates Sylvester Stallone most of all. Apparently, he locked himself in a room for three days and wrote *Rocky*, the first one, which is a marvellous script and an excellent movie. But mostly things don't happen that way. Writing a film script is a stupidly long process, and for everyone except Sylvester, a pretty agonising one.

Three years ago I started writing a film called *Four Weddings and a Funeral*, which comes out this Friday. I'm sure my experiences with it can't be generalised about—but just in case there are any prospective screenwriters amongst you, here is my simplistic stab at Four Rules and a Suggestion for screenwriting.

My first rule is that you let things stew. I've twice written films straight after I thought up the idea, and they were both disastrous. In 1989 I thought of an idea for a film about dreams, complete, at a petrol station on the A40. I drove home and started writing frantically. Six weeks later it was finished. Six weeks and one day later it was in the dustbin. I reread it, and I realised it was well-constructed twaddle, it meant absolutely nothing to me. On the other occasion, I wrote a film for America, to please Americans, which I made up on the way to a "pitch-meeting." Two whole years of writing later, I attended another meeting at MGM—they told me they absolutely loved the film, provided I could change the character of the leading man, the second lead, the cameos, the dialogue and the jokes. I said that only left the title. They said they wanted to change the title too. So that's the first thing—it helps to let things stew in your head a while to find out if you really care. The process of filmmaking is SO DETAILED and SO LONG, nothing fraudulent is going to escape discovery.

My second rule is—try not to pitch. If you can avoid it, try not to get commissioned. Now this is a tough one, because most of us need the money—but the problem with pitching things, and with treatments, is that two people can read the same bit of paper and sit in the same room having the same discussion, but they never hear the same thing. One of them leaves intending to write biting social satire—the other happily describes how he's commissioned a sexy pants-and-knickers farce. Then, as the writer writes, the film comes to life, and changes. It's no longer a social satire, it's a dead serious state-of-the-nation film, moved from the original Westminster location to the brooding Shetland Islands. So you deliver your film, and the person who commissioned it is INEVITABLY disappointed. The next year is spent reconciling a film now called *Earthworm* with the original treatment, called *Sir Peter's Trousers*. So if you can write the thing first, at least the people who buy it, if they buy it, are under no misapprehension about what they're paying for.

On to rule three. If you possibly can, get your work edited by someone you love. My first film, called *The Tall Guy*, was a four-hour muddle before my best friend, Helen, got her hands on it. Five different times she read it and cut it down. The film that was accepted was the fifth draft by me and her. *Four Weddings* is a co-operation between me and my girl, Emma. She read every draft of every scene from the beginning of the process to the end. For a year I lived in terror of the fatal initials "C.D.B." scattered through everything she read. "C.D.B." stands for "Could Do Better." Once again, you're lucky if you can get this—but the thing about a friend, girlfriend, boyfriend, wife, or husband is that they understand what you're getting at. They have no hidden agenda—they want the film to be good, and to be your film—not just profitable and a perfect vehicle for Steve Guttenberg.

> I stopped believing in Santa Claus when I was six. Mother took me to see him in a department store and he asked me for my autograph.
>
> Shirley Temple

Rule four is—don't count the rewrites or it will drive you mad. These were the rewrites on *Four Weddings*—five for Emma before it was ever handed in. One after talking to Duncan, my producer, and Debra at Working Title, the production company. Then two big ones for Mike Newell, the director, and Duncan, as we tried to give every character proper stories, rather than just jokes. Then there was one after the first round of casting: actors reading the lines tend to show just how clunky the script is! The next rewrite came after Channel 4 expressed worries about it all being a bit "smart." Then the film was delayed for six months, so there was one long rewrite to fill the time and to try to crack the really knotty problems with the end. At one point, Emma and I escaped to Europe, and spent a month on one 2-minute scene. Then there was another rewrite during the second round of casting. Then one when our budget went from £3.5 million to £3.2. Then another one when it went from £3.2 to £2.7, which consisted of cutting down the cast: "a vicar," became "the vicar you saw earlier." After the read-through (when no one laughed at 15 percent of the "jokes" and DID laugh at 25 percent of the serious bits), there was another hefty hack. During rehearsals another. That's seventeen, and I've got a nasty feeling I've forgotten one or two. And the horrible thing about this rule is part two of it—don't resent the rewrites—the awful painful truth is that the script probably did get a bit better each time.

And so on to the suggestion: **I suggest that**—after you have let an idea stew, written the film you wanted without the compromises of commission, let it be brutally edited by someone you love and then rewritten it fifteen times—**you cast Hugh Grant as the lead**. It doesn't matter what the character is—if she's a middle-aged cop on the verge of retiring, Hugh will be perfect. If he's an Eskimo schoolboy—Hugh is exactly what you are looking for. This weekend *Four Weddings and a Funeral* may pass the thirty-million-dollar mark in America, and relatives in New York tell me that's really down to Hugh. If only we'd been canny, and cast him in the Andie MacDowell, Simon Callow, and Rowan Atkinson roles as well, it could have been fifty million by now. And that's the hell of it. Whatever your script is like, no matter how much stewing and rewriting—if the punters don't want to sleep with the star, you may never be asked to write another one.

Publicity Shot from *Four Weddings and a Funeral.*

Richard Curtis is a well-known British scriptwriter. After graduation from university, he joined a team of writers to create *Not the Nine O'Clock News*. He also created the TV shows *Blackadder* and *The Vicar of Dibley*, and wrote the screenplays for the movies *Notting Hill* and *Bean*.

I. Response
   a. How helpful did you find Curtis's advice about writing a screenplay? What piece of advice was most helpful? Least helpful?
   b. In your opinion, does the humour within this selection make it more or less effective? Explain your answer to a partner.
   c. What does the image accompanying the article reveal about the movie?

2. **Film Study** Use Internet and library resources to find out more about Richard Curtis and *Four Weddings and a Funeral*. If possible, view the movie and then write a movie review for it. Examine the features and structure of movie reviews in your local newspaper and use them as a model.

3. **Writing** *How-To* In a humorous way, Curtis provides some very helpful tips for writing a screenplay. Think of some activity at which you excel. Write at least four rules and one suggestion about this activity that would help someone doing it for the first time.

4. **Media** *Movie Industry* With a small group, discuss the process of making a movie, starting with the information provided in this article. (You may also wish to check out what Emma Thompson reveals about moviemaking in the following article.) What various jobs or roles are there in the movie industry? Which job appeals to you most? Why? What motivates the various people involved in the movie industry? For example, consider what might have motivated Thompson or Curtis to write their screenplays.

There are two cinemas: the films we have actually seen and the memories we have of them.
—*Molly Haskell*

This selection is from Emma Thompson's (star and screenwriter of the movie *Sense and Sensibility*) diary that she kept during the pre-filming and filming of the movie.

The Making of
Sense and Sensibility

Production Notes

by Emma Thompson

Production meeting in Oxford Street on a raw wintry morning on Monday 15 January 1995. Lindsay Doran (producer), James Schamus (co-producer), Ang Lee (director) and I had met previously this month to discuss the latest draft of the script, which is what we're all here to work through. Tony Clarkson (locations manager) and Laurie Borg (co-producer) already know one another but this is the first time the core personnel of the shoot have met to prepare.

Lindsay goes round the table and introduces everyone—making it clear that I am present in the capacity of writer rather than actress, therefore no one has to be too nice to me. It's 9 a.m. and everyone looks a bit done in. Except Ang, who brings self-contained calm wherever he goes. Just looking at him makes me feel frazzled in comparison, as though all my hair's standing on end.

Our first point of discussion is the hunt (during which, in this version, we witness the accident that kills Mr Dashwood). Where do we get a hunt? It seems to require at least twenty-five male stunt riders—or we hire a real hunt, like the Beaufort which was used on *The Remains of the Day*. Ang wants villagers and labourers watching and to see the fox being chased. My idea is to start the film with an image of the vixen locked out of her lair which has been plugged up. Her terror as she's pursued across the country. This is a big deal. It means training a fox from birth or dressing up a dog to look like a fox.

Or hiring David Attenborough, who probably knows a few foxes well enough to ask a favour. Laurie finally says it's impossible.

What Ang wants next is even more expensive: he's desperate for a kitchen scene in Norland Park (home to the Dashwoods—to be filmed at Saltram House in Devon) which would show the entire staff of Norland preparing a huge meal. I want a bleeding Mr Dashwood to be brought in through the kitchen door and laid on the table surrounded by all the raw joints of meat. As Ang and I enthuse about symbolism, Laurie gently reminds us of expense. These are costly scenes and the film hasn't even started.

I look around the table and realise—perhaps for the first time—that it's actually going to happen. After five years' work on the script (albeit intermittent), the sense of released energy is palpable. There are budgets, an office and several real people here. I glaze over for a second, in shock. Pulled out of reverie by James asking, yet again, what physical activities can be found for Elinor and Marianne. Painting, sewing, embroidering, writing letters, pressing leaves, it's all depressingly girlie. Chin-ups, I suggest, but promise to think further.

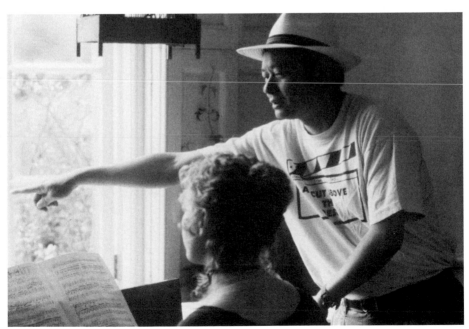

Photo from *Sense and Sensibility* by Clive Coote.

Examine this photo. How would you describe the relationship between the people in the photo?

We start to work through the entire script, adding, subtracting, bargaining, negotiating, trying to save money wherever we can. We get to the ballroom sequence and I suggest that we create several vignettes that occur in the background—a rich old rake forcing his attentions on a young girl whose greedy father affects not to notice, a fat matriarch surrounded by sycophantic cousins—a Cruikshankian taste of nineteenth-century greed and hypocrisy. More expensive than simply filling the room with extras but much more interesting. Laurie's eyes roll but he agrees that it's worth the effort and money.

I have a notion that it might be nice to see Colonel Brandon tickling trout—something to draw Marianne to him. Tickling trout is a mysterious old country method of catching trout; you tickle their tummies and when they're relaxed you whip them out of the water. I ask Laurie if it's possible to get trained fish. Lindsay says this is how we know I've never produced a movie. She tells us that two of her friends had read the script and thought I'd invented the pregnancy of Brandon's family ward for shock value. It's surprising to find such events in Austen, but after all, how many people know that there's a duel in *Sense and Sensibility*? When Lindsay asked me to adapt the novel I thought that *Emma* or *Persuasion* would have been better. In fact there's more action in *S & S* than I'd remembered and its elements translate to drama very effectively.

We get to the end of the script by 3.20 p.m. and Lindsay says, "Can we afford the movie we just described?" It's a long, complex script and the budget is pushing the limit. James is most worried about the number of shooting days. Doesn't seem enough. (In the event, our fifty-eight days stretched to sixty-five.)

Wander out into Oxford Street slightly dazed. "See you in April," I say to Laurie. Now everyone goes their separate ways to continue prep. Ang and James return to New York and work on budget and schedule from there. Lindsay returns to LA to produce and I go to West Hampstead and switch the computer on. Another draft ... I spend the rest of January in tears and a black dressing gown.

During February and March I revise the script constantly but the basic structure remains the same. Half a dozen new drafts hit the presses but by 2 April we settle on the final shooting draft. The hunt and kitchen scenes discussed at the January production meeting have both been cut due to budget and schedule constraints.

Never judge a book by its movie.

J.W. Eagan

In February, Ang, James and Lindsay return and the casting process begins. We start with Fanny. Everyone we see captures perfectly the balance of wifely concern and vicious self-interest. Ang says at the end of one day, "This is a nation of Fannys." It rings horribly true. Some characters are far more elusive, notably Lucy Steele and Willoughby, perhaps because of their hidden motives. Gemma Jones, Kate Winslet and Elizabeth Spriggs are so immediately Mrs Dashwood, Marianne and Mrs Jennings that we find it difficult to imagine anyone else in the roles. I'm excited about the fact that five of the actors I prevailed upon to perform a reading of an early draft last year are all hired by Ang: Hugh Grant (Edward), Robert Hardy (Sir John), Harriet Walter (Fanny), Imelda Staunton (Charlotte Palmer) and Hugh Laurie (Mr Palmer). Also that Hugh Grant, for whom I wrote Edward, has agreed to do it despite having become after *Four Weddings* the most famous man in the world. It's odd to be on the other side of the casting process. Even though Michelle Guish, the casting director, makes the circumstances as relaxed as possible, I am uncomfortably aware of how difficult it is for an actor to walk into a small room full of people staring at them. Lindsay is quite shy, James chats a bit, Ang seldom says anything at all and I make a lot of irrelevant noise whenever there's a long silence. Ang's principal criteria are unexpected. Physiognomy matters a great deal to him. Not whether a person is good-looking but the spaces between their lower lip and chin and between the bridge of the nose and forehead. Praxitelean proportions, virtually. After a first meeting with an actor there's a second during which we read scenes. I get the opportunity to play all the other roles and have a minor success with Sir John. Then a third when the scenes are put on video. Ang is not familiar with many British actors so we see people time and again until he's certain of what he wants.

"Can everyone in England act?" he says after a particularly engaging afternoon. Lindsay and I think about this one for quite some time before deciding that probably the answer is yes.

Ang presents a collection of intriguing contradictions. He does t'ai chi but his shoulders are constantly bowed, he meditates and smokes (not at the same time as far as I know), he hasn't an ounce of fat on him but eats everything going, especially buns. When I cooked roast beef for him he ate *all* the Yorkshire puddings—about eleven. He's forty years old and looks thirty.

As each role gets cast, the fact of the shoot becomes increasingly concrete. I rewrite scenes with the actors in my head. At the end of March I go away for two weeks, try to forget about the script and think about Elinor.

Emma Thompson was born in 1959 in London, England. She attended Newnham College at Cambridge University where she joined the Footlight Club, a group that performed comedies. Thompson, who is known first and foremost as an actress, won an Oscar for best screenplay for *Sense and Sensibility* in 1995.

1. Response

a. What is the most interesting or surprising detail about the production of movies that you discovered while reading this selection? Explain.

b. Discuss any references from this selection that you did not understand.

c. What impression of Ang Lee does Emma Thompson leave you with?

2. Film Study

With a small group, generate ideas for a movie that an audience of your peers would enjoy. Choose one idea and develop a proposal or pitch for it. Describe the genre (suspense, adventure, comedy, romance), theme, characters, and plot of your movie. Consider the tips provided in "Four Rules and a Suggestion" and "The Making of *Sense and Sensibility*."

3. Making Connections

Turn to the Drama unit in this book and find the scenes taken from *Sense and Sensibility*. Given these two examples, how would you describe Emma Thompson as a writer? Do you enjoy reading her work? Explain. How is her writing style different in both pieces? What are the reasons for these differences?

Theme Connections

- "*Four Rules and a Suggestion*," a how-to article about the movie script process, page 359
- "*The Movie I'd Like to See*," a satirical commentary about what would make a good movie, page 396
- "*The Dashwoods' Fate Is Decided*," an excerpt of the movie script written by Thompson, page 443

Many news programs aren't just concerned with hard-hitting stories or current events. Many news programs, like the following, feature the actions and accomplishments of personalities in our communities.

Interview With Artist George Littlechild

TV Interview
written and produced by Kamala Todd

(Logo, title, and music for First Story *come up on screen. Cut to shot of narrator, standing in front of Vancouver harbour)*

Tatiana: Hi. I'm Tatiana Housty. And you're watching *First Story*. The show that takes you to the heart of the Urban Rez.

(Pan skyline, ending with shot of George Littlechild running along waterfront boardwalk. Host voice-over:)

Today on *First Story*, George Littlechild, a renowned Cree artist, tells us about his unique creative process.

(Cut to shot of sculpture/painting, being worked on. With George voice-over:)

George: The Trickster, the transformer, transforms the idea that art is lesson and makes it become reality. That's what the Trickster is for me, that's my understanding of Trickster …

Tatiana: Stay with us; *First Story* will be right back.

(Fade to text: "First Story *will return" Music up. Cut to commercial. Commercials end, and logo of hands back, music up, title up. Cut to host walking along beach)*

Tatiana: Vancouver has an abundance of art and we're treated to its various forms and mediums. On a beautiful day like today you can really see how you can get outside and enjoy the lifestyle. And for this reason, artists come here. George Littlechild is a well-known name in the art scene. He's known for his vivid colours and his accessible art. And when you speak to him, you realize that George is greatly influenced by the Trickster. In fact, the Trickster kicks him out of bed each morning to come down here for a jog. Storyteller, Kamala Todd, caught up with George for a chat about how the Trickster influences him.

(Cut to George sitting talking, panning down from tree branches waving in breeze)

George: That whole idea of transforming oneself from animal to human, and in that relationship to the animals and their hierarchy and their importance and they're all symbolic. Those symbols are very pertinent or important in my art.

(Pan up to tree, to George running. Kamala voice-over:)

Kamala: The artist has a gift: to express the world around them in new and provocative ways ...

(Cut to George running along boardwalk)

... like George Littlechild, who is a renowned Vancouver artist of Cree heritage. He uses the power of the Trickster to influence how we look at the world.

(Cut to George sitting on beach, ocean in background)

George: The work is, in nature, it's intuitive. And I believe that as an artist, and as a vehicle for the information to come through.

(Cut to shot of can of brushes, bottle of paint with brush being dipped in. Pan up to sculpture being painted, golden head. Pan up to George as he speaks following lines. Medium shot of him, his paintings in background)

I'm very thankful for this talent. When I'm working on my art, it's a real place of serenity, calm. My studio, I think of it as a sacred place. A good place to go to and forget about what's going on out there.

(Cut to photo of George as a child)

I remember my artwork being shown in the display case in Grade 7, 8, or 9, I forget the year. And people would say, *"You* did that?"

All life's answers are on TV.

Homer Simpson

(Cut back to George, tighter head shot)

And to me that was the way that I won, in some regard. That people actually thought that, "Oh that person does have something good."

(Cut to George running along path, from behind. Music up. Cut to George from front, music down, George voice-over. During following speech cut to shot of feet running, move back to face)

George Littlechild at work in his studio.

This is a *still* (one frame captured from a movie or TV show) from the interview. Examine this image, and the directions included in this transcript. Discuss how the producers and directors tried to make this show appealing to its audience.

For me, running is sacred. To me it's like a real cleansing, and being in balance with the medicine world. And part of that is taking care of one's body, by exercising and you know nurturing it, and you love the end result. To me it's a real release. And here, *(speaking about ocean front park)* it's a place that just brings me back to the natural self of who I am, and how that environment … how it affects me.

(Pan skyline, shoreline, trees, ocean. Cut to George sitting in park as before, tree branches waving around him)

These rocks, these trees, this ocean, the mountains, the sky. Even when it's torpid grey, it still is so … beautiful. I think being brought up in the city you start to become so much of that environment that you don't really see nature around you. And one day I was looking at this … grove of trees and I started to see the spirit of the tree, and I had never seen that before. And when I did, it just suddenly made me realize that each and every one of these trees has a spirit. And it was the most phenomenally important thing that could have occurred. And what I started to do was I painted this series called the Tree Spirits, with faces in the trees. And just realizing that, the respect for the earth, and respect for mother earth especially, and that each of these trees are sacred and they're providing life for us, and they're our friends.

(Cut to shot of trees, cut to painting of horses. Kamala voice-over:)

Kamala: George derives much of his inspiration from the natural world. The horse is his special guide.

(George voice-over:)

George: It's a very important Cree symbol, a Plains First Nations symbol.

(Cut to George in park)

And, uh, it's the animal that transcends the vision to the artist in the Cree culture. For years painting the horse and never knowing why I was painting it. And just realizing that horse was my friend. It's the most powerful experience.

(Cut to painting of boxers. Kamala voice-over:)

Kamala: George's art is a powerful experience. He tells stories and asks questions that some people don't want to touch.

(Cut to George in studio, working on gold head sculpture, paintings in background)

It is the Trickster at work, pushing us to gain new awareness.

(Cut to George on beach, sitting on driftwood speaking the following. Superimpose image of him at work in studio)

George: I think as human beings, we judge. We judge very harshly each other—and just being aware of that, and keep working through that, and where does that come from. And finding out where that comes from in order to address and deal with it.

(Cut to painting of two women, close-up on part of image, move out to see whole image, women in boat, city in background. Kamala voice-over:)

Kamala: What I find so uplifting about George's work is the way he deals with difficult and painful issues. Through his colourful imagery he has shown me a new and refreshing approach to healing.

(Cut to other paintings one by one. Cut to George painting)

George: I mean you watch the news and just see ... how much catastrophe is going on, not only with mother earth but between nations, between people, and how we abuse each other, and I think the bottom line is to learn to respect and love each other, rather than continuously bringing each other down. I feel as an artist that ... my gift is to be able to share some of my perspectives, but also some of the teachings that I've been taught.

(Close-up on brush painting. Back to George painting)

Trickster is a transformer, that transforms the idea of the art as the lesson, and makes it become reality. I think that's what the Trickster is for me. That's my understanding of Trickster. And through that lesson we receive teachings and in those teachings it's up to us to grow. Yeah, I think a lot of that part of my history, of dealing with foster care and, um, that whole issue in my life. I mean I did an art piece in a way that was a catharsis to let go of that. And I called that the Sixties Scoop; and it was a huge installation with personal testimonies from different people that had been raised in the sixties scoop. It was their stories plus my own.

(Cut to painting of children in foster care. Cut to George painting)

And for me, that was the end—it was letting go. It was time to move on. And so I see the work in many ways, as a conduit, a way of informing people, and also it changes their awareness.

(Cut to many of his works, scanning some. Music up. George voice-over:)

You know within my art I like to play with that idea. Humour versus the serious quality of the work but also it works together.

(Cut to George speaking, waving paintbrush, back at work on gold head)

And I think that's where the colour comes. I mean people can see the issue, they can visually, if they're informed by what's going on, but the colour in many ways seduces them. I mean you can't always take it so seriously, otherwise it's over … it's too much; you have to bring people to a good place and not always leave them in a sad or place of desperation. This work is more spiritual or fun, and I like to work with both. Both fun, humour, sadness, it's part of our history.

(Cut to singers, drummers, in studio. Music up, Kamala voice-over. Pan paintings, people in gallery.)

Kamala: Recently, George unveiled his latest work to family and friends. A colourful transformation series. It is only one of many ways that he shares his gift.

(Cut to George speaking at gallery)

George: Thank you all for coming out this evening. Enjoy the art, enjoy the food. All the friends that have supported me over the years, the family. I have a brother here this evening. It's just wonderful to be so supported and so loved, and this work is my gift back to you.

(Cut from painting to painting. Music up. Cut to people looking at art. Cut to classroom, George at front, long shot)

Kamala: George's vision goes far beyond his studio. He is an active leader and a role model in his community.

(Cut to George close-up in front of class, cut to student close-up, cut to teenagers in his studio, looking at paintings. Cut to George, at beach)

George: As an artist I'm constantly educating. I never ever thought I'd be an educator. But I am.

> I think that one's art is a growth inside one. I do not think one can explain growth. It is silent and subtle. One does not keep digging up a plant to see how it grew.
>
> Emily Carr

(Cut to George flipping through pages of a book that shows his artwork. George voice-over. Cut to George midway through following speech:)

I become more increasingly aware that what I'm to do here is to transform ... the pain, or the history, the pain within the history. And it becomes more and more obvious in the work that I do in schools and lectures, is that ... you know and in the workshops that I do, that it's to transform that energy, that negative energy and to make it positive. And that, I really believe, is why I'm here ... what I was born to do, through this art, the gift that I was given.

And, um, one of the major themes that I like to go back to because I *enjoy* it—I really enjoy that transformation from human to animal spirit and in between and that essence, or that idea of what that would have been like years and years ago in traditional warfare trans-forming from self to animal spirit to attack your enemy, to go to places you couldn't go as a human. In relation to that, it's also those energies, and unblocking those energies that allow us to grow and ... and to change and to achieve and to become better persons.

(Cut to paintings, close-up on various images. Music up. Kamala voice-over:)

Kamala: George Littlechild offers us new ways of looking at the world, ways to empower ourselves and move beyond our pain.

(Cut to George)

George: When you discuss your pain, when you discuss this history you bring it out in to the public, in to the world and we all become part of it. Because my story is your story.

(Cut to trees. Kamala voice-over:)

Kamala: I'm Kamala Todd for *First Story*.

(Music up. Logo up. Cut to commercial)

Kamala Todd is of Cree descent. She lives in Vancouver and works as a freelance video producer. She is the producer of *First Story* for British Columbia's VTV.

1. Response
   a. With a partner, discuss this interview and what it reveals about George Littlechild.
   b. What else would you like to learn about Littlechild? List at least three questions you would like to ask him. Do some research on the Internet to find answers to your questions.
   c. Find examples of Littlechild's artwork and discuss the techniques he uses, as well as the content of the paintings.
   d. Does the interviewer exhibit any bias in the questions she asks? Explain. Would you have handled the interview any differently?

2. Media *TV Interview* Skim this article and list the ways in which a TV interview is like or unlike interviews in other media formats. View several other TV interviews and list any common elements. What makes this selection a particularly effective interview? Discuss what makes a TV interview interesting and engaging.

   With a partner or small group, develop a TV interview. You could interview someone of interest in your school, using a video camera to record the interview. You may wish to prepare questions beforehand.

3. Language Conventions *Interview Format* Examine the use of punctuation and other elements of design (such as the use of capitals, bold, or italic) within the transcript of this TV interview. List some rules for developing a TV script. Use those rules to script a short interview between yourself and a favourite actor or other personality.

4. Focus on Context This interview first appeared on the Aboriginal Peoples Television Network on a news program called *First Story.* Explain how the context in which this interview was developed may have affected its content. If CBC TV were to produce a documentary on Littlechild to be broadcast nationally, how do you think it might differ?

Theme Connections

- *"Art History," a speech about Aboriginal art in Canada, page 273*
- *"Stone Faces," an essay about the importance of art, page 281*
- *"Reviving Fridamania," an article about an artist, page 306*

Which newspapers do you read?
How often do you read a newspaper?
Which parts of the newspaper do you like most or least?

The Weekly

THE LAST COMMUNITY SIGNPOST

Newspaper Article by Catherine Dubé

Now that the mass media are busily scanning the four corners of the earth, the weekly newspaper is the only one still watching the neighbourhood. It is the one remaining link between the grass roots and the world.

A government minister serving food in a community kitchen is typical of the events covered by the local weekly newspaper. The news may seem trivial, except when the minister is Stéphane Dion and he receives a cream pie right in the face. Suddenly, the news takes on national scope.

Régent Gosselin, a photographer with *Les Nouvelles de l'Est*, owned by Transcontinental Group, was the only one to snap that memorable event on May 7, 1999, at Montréal's chic Resto-Pop restaurant. The next day, the photo from the Rosemont weekly made the front page of dailies across the country. Even media in Brussels, the world capital of pie-throwers, carried the item, along with the photo.

In close touch with events

Rarely does local news make its way abroad. The current generally flows the other way. "National and international issues filter down to the local news," says professor André A. Lafrance, head of the communications department at the Université de Montréal. "Local citizens know politics and the priorities of elected officials through the speeches of their members of parliament, ribbon-cutting ceremonies and community grants written up in their weekly paper."

Often a news item has to affect us personally before we pay attention, Lafrance says. Fifty years ago, conversations on the church steps filled that role. Events these days have international repercussions, however, and the weekly paper is the only medium able to reduce news to community proportions and thus link readers and current events. It is through its local athletes, for instance, that a community "participates" in the Olympic Games unfolding on the other side of the world.

Weeklies are not about to disappear. "Dailies have no interest in reporting small-town news," observes Florian Sauvageau, director of Université Laval's media research centre. "The local radio station could handle this role, but it has all but vanished, swallowed up by the big networks. The weekly is now the only medium that gives people news about their community."

The last village square

Small business openings and closings, the latest town council decisions, village festivals ... Leafing through the weekly paper keeps people abreast of what is happening right around them. "It's the last remaining village square!" says Lafrance.

Anyone who thinks the news reported in weeklies attracts no interest should think again! According to a 1997 study by PMB, 81% of Québecers and 74% of Canadians had read a local newspaper within the past month.

Weeklies do not fill the same role everywhere. "Although everyone appreciates neighbourhood papers, people living in towns with no daily paper naturally expect much more from their weekly," points out Serge Bragdon, former president of the distribution division of Transcontinental Group, the second leading publisher of weeklies in Québec. This can be seen without having to venture very far from the big cities. Laval, for example, is Québec's second-largest city, adjacent to Montréal, yet it still has no daily newspaper of its own.

The people in Laval get their information from their local paper and the Montréal dailies. "Our paper fills the role of a daily," notes Jocelyn Bourassa, news director of *Courrier Laval*, published twice a week. That paper, distributed throughout the local area, is in addition to six neighbourhood weeklies covering the community scene. The six weeklies are also owned by Transcontinental Group.

The weekly is free

Unlike the advertising in daily papers and on radio and television, the many ads appearing in weeklies are not seen as a necessary evil, but rather as a source of information by many people. According to a three-year survey which Descarie & Complices completed this past summer for the association of Les Hebdos du Québec, 42% of respondents said that they regularly consulted the ads in weekly papers—twice as many as read the ads in dailies. An additional 42% read those ads from time to time.

"As a rule, ads in the print media are more informative than what you find on television," Professor Sauvageau notes. Bragdon points out that "the weekly is the paper of choice for local merchants." People read the weeklies to find out about the businesses in their vicinity. "The advertising you find in the weeklies reflects local life just as much as the news items do," says Lafrance.

Like it or not, advertising is the reason weekly papers are free. "Since it is part of community life, people expect the weekly paper to be free, just as the little favours neighbours do for one another are free," adds Lafrance.

So, even when it comes to advertising, the weekly stands out as the one remaining community signpost, the only medium left at the grass roots.

1. *Response*

a. What conclusions about weekly newspapers does Catherine Dubé make? How does she support these conclusions? Do you agree or disagree? Explain.

b. What do you think the future of daily and weekly newspapers will be like?

c. Discuss the meaning and effectiveness of the title with a small group.

d. Examine the structure of this article, and comment on its effectiveness.

e. Skim the article and locate what Dubé compares weekly newspapers to. How effective are these comparisons?

2. *Vocabulary*
Define the following terms using the context in which they appear: *grass roots, signpost, national scope, village square, community scene,* and *necessary evil.* Compare your definitions to those of a partner.

3. *Media* Newspapers
Collect several examples of both weekly and daily newspapers. With a small group, discuss and analyse their features and content. What conclusions can you draw about the purpose, target audience, and effectiveness of these papers?

4. *Language Conventions* Using Quotations
Examine how Dubé incorporates quotations from others within her article. How are these quotations introduced? How are they punctuated? How effectively do you use quotations within your own writing?

*A media expert questions civic membership
in the age of globalization.*

The Accidental Citizen

Essay by Mark Kingwell

IT IS A COMMON EXPERIENCE in this, the age of casual multi-culturalism. There I was, on a crowded 767, heading to London from Toronto, when I realized that nobody around me was speaking English—nobody at all, except the Québécoise flight attendant, who looked as if she might have preferred not to. The two Germans next to me were reading Ken Follett novels in translation. The man across the aisle was talking to his little boy in a mixture of Spanish and French, for reasons that escaped me. The two women farther up were, as far as I could make out, arguing in Italian.

Tourists on their way to the next destination? Maybe. International shoppers off to Harrods and Jermyn Street? Possibly—a man in the departure lounge had let it be known that he was just zipping over to Amsterdam for the weekend to pick up a few things he needed. Or were they just a group of all-sorts Canadians on their way to England? In the arrival area later there was a flurry of passports, a shuffle of multiple identities. The passengers conjured their variable selves without hesitation. Some of them, armed with logo-embossed briefcases and branded golf shirts, were clearly servants of a higher, corporate power: citizens of the world as it now lies, carved up into markets and territories, catchment areas and satellite PCS coverage zones. These new global citizens, whatever their mother tongue and regardless of their sometimes halting command of English, the lingua franca of the New Internationalism, all speak fluently the language of the customs declaration and the luggage carousel. They know the grammar of taxis and hotel shuttles and courtesy cars. *Which passport? Whichever gets me through the barrier faster.*

It is time for us to rethink the idea of citizenship, to reconceive the structures of political commitment and membership against the background of our shape-shifting world. These sky-people, harbingers of the world we are fast creating, are the first clues as to why. They tell us that old ideas of civic membership no longer compel our attention or answer our needs. Their presence is a reminder that the political structures to which those old ideas were wedded are not yet dead, but they are suffering—and are as nothing compared to the real powers of our world, the real centres of loyalty for most people (however undeserved that loyalty may often be). And if we are the sky-people ourselves, the ones who have found a reasonably comfortable place amid all these changes, who have the frequent-flyer programs and the higher degrees and the international connections, then the challenge is that much more proximate.

We begin with what is not news. Corporations and firms have not simply taken over the mechanisms of production and consumption. They have equally usurped our private selves and our public spaces. They have created bonds of belonging far stronger than any fractured, tentative nation could now hope to offer, providing structures of identity, ways of making sense of one's place in a complex world. They are also far more powerful, and richer, than many nations: the annual budget of France was only three-quarters of the combined value of America OnLine and Time Warner when those two media giants merged in January 2000, and Kmart's 1998 U.S. sales were equal to the estimated budget of the entire Russian military. But corporations are not democratic, and they do not possess the political legitimacy that is necessary to justify that kind of power. We have global markets, however unjust and skewed; and we have a global culture, however banal and enervating. What we don't have, but desperately need, is a global politics to balance and give meaning to these troubling universal realities.

Mark Kingwell was born in Toronto in 1963. He has taught at Yale, York University, and the University of Toronto in Scarborough, and has been a contributing editor for the magazines *Shift, Descant,* and *Saturday Night.* His essays, reviews, columns, and articles have appeared in publications such as *UTNE Reader, Adbusters,* and *Harper's,* and he is the author of *Better Living: In Pursuit of Happiness from Plato to Prozac* (which won the Drummer General's Award for Non-Fiction in 1998); *Dreams of Millennium: Report From a Culture on the Brink,* and *A Civil Tongue: Justice, Dialogue, and the Politics of Pluralism* (which won the Spitz Prize in Political Theory in 1996).

1. Response

a. Mark Kingwell suggests that our loyalties are no longer connected to our nation or our citizenship. According to Kingwell, what are our "bonds of belonging" now connected to? Do you agree with this idea?

b. Do you think you have the power to resist these "bonds" that Kingwell says are so strong? Do you want to? Explain.

c. Kingwell uses the phrase "these troubling universal realities." Does what he has described in this piece trouble you? Explain.

d. What does Kingwell mean by *sky-people*?

2. Literature Studies *Structure* When you read the first paragraph, what did you think the piece was going to be about? Why might the author have started in this way? How does the opening paragraph connect to the subsequent paragraphs? Keeping in mind the purpose of opening paragraphs, do you think this one is effective? Explain.

3. Vocabulary The author refers to some places and people with which readers may be unfamiliar. Look up any references that you do not know, along with any vocabulary that you were unable to figure out from its context. Afterward, consider how important it was to your appreciation of the piece to understand these references and words.

4. Critical Thinking In a small group, discuss the meaning of *globalization*. Where do you hear and see the word mentioned? How aware are you of the term and the issues that are involved? To extend the discussion, look through newspapers, news and world issues magazines, periodical indexes, and the Internet to find articles about globalization. What do the issues seem to be, as reflected by your findings? How do the issues affect you?

It has been said that arguing against globalization
is like arguing against the laws of gravity.
—*Kofi Annan*

What TV shows *do* chimps like to watch?
Read this interview to find out the media habits
of some primates.

Media Diet:
Jane Goodall

Magazine Interview by Karen Olson

Long before reality TV brought us soap operas set in remote jungles, Jane Goodall was giving viewers a glimpse inside the steamy, cliquish, and otherwise very similar world of chimpanzees. During the 1960s, Goodall's work as a brilliant observer of chimps in eastern Africa first captured the popular imagination. Today, the project she began some 40 years ago at the Gombe Stream Research Centre in Tanzania has become the longest uninterrupted field study of any animal group in the wild. Goodall's insight that chimps feel emotions and possess distinct personalities, much as humans do, has revolutionized how we view animals in general.

Now one of the most respected and beloved scientists in the world, Goodall travels almost constantly, speaking out on behalf of chimps and other threatened animals. As the roving ambassador of the Jane Goodall Institute, she encourages her audiences to recognize the power of individual action in protecting the environment. One of her passions, the Institute's Roots & Shoots program, encourages children to take an active role in helping animals as familiar as the birds and squirrels in their back yards. Another cause is the ChimpanZoo project, whose purpose is to study and improve the lives of the world's captive chimps.

Goodall is the author of numerous books, including *Africa in My Blood: An Autobiography in Letters* (Houghton Mifflin, 2000). She talked with assistant editor Karen Olson during a recent visit to Minneapolis.

K.O.: What are you reading these days?

J.G.: It's hard to find time to read while I'm traveling, but lately I've been jumping between two books. One is *The Courage of Children* by Peter Dalglish, founder of Street Kids International—who I hope to work with to help children in Dar es Salaam, Tanzania. The other is *Into the Wild*, Jon Krakauer's account of a young man who disappears in Alaska. I'm fascinated by attempts to get back to nature, both those that succeed and those that fail. It wasn't an overly long book, which I also appreciated. Big fat books are really intimidating when you're traveling all the time.

K.O.: Where do you get your daily news when you travel?

J.G.: In places like China, Taiwan, and remote parts of Africa, I usually rely on CNN, or, if I can get it, the BBC World Service, which I think is better. The World Service's radio version is super.

K.O.: The public television nature show has become an established genre. Do these glimpses into animal life help or hinder your cause?

J.G.: They're helpful, by and large, but on the other hand, very few accurately portray what's really happening. They come in two kinds: One is all doom and gloom, which people don't want to watch, and the other portrays animals living their own sweet little natural lives. The best approach would combine both views and stress what people can do to help.

K.O.: Speaking of television, you were in a lighthearted commercial a few years back co-starring chimps watching TV.

J.G.: Yes. I was reluctant at first, but the chimps only had to be interfered with long enough to catch them on film. What's more, the commercial didn't feature the cute and cuddly baby chimps you usually see on TV, a practice that bolsters the pet trade, which is horrendous. You got Frodo, our biggest male ever, and no one would want him in their living room.

K.O.: How do chimps really react to TV?

J.G.: We'd never show wild chimps television, but captive chimps love it, of course. They love the films about the Gombe chimps. If the chimps on the screen are excited, the chimps watching get excited too.

K.O.: How do chimpanzees communicate?
J.G.: They have a large repertoire of sounds, each with a different meaning. These sounds are not words, but they do communicate emotions: An appeal for help. An indication of danger. Hello. Here I am. Where are you? Listening. Anger. Fear. They also rely on a rich repertoire of touch and posture and gesture—embracing, patting on the back, kissing, holding hands, swaggering, tickling, punching—very much as we do. And among both chimps and humans, it seems, these gestures are triggered by the same kinds of contact and mean more or less the same thing.

K.O.: Do chimps make music?
J.G.: In the wild, they drum on tree trunks, which can't be very satisfactory because it doesn't really sound like much except from a distance. Chimps also display a rhythmic movement that's almost like dancing—a swaying from foot to foot that can be very majestic and beautiful. When they're lying down for the night, they may start calling on one side of the valley and the sounds will be taken up by chimps on the other side. But that's the closest they come to music.

K.O.: You've done some chat room conferences on the Web.
J.G.: Yes. I've done one or two of those, but they're not direct enough for me. These disembodied questions come in, and I don't like it. I prefer lectures.

K.O.: How has fame affected your life?
J.G.: I hated it at first. It's very British, you know, not to like that kind of thing. But I gradually began to realize that it was important for the media to be on my side if I wanted to get a message across. I don't think I've ever had a bad relation with the media. I've faced what I might call intelligently penetrating questions, but I've never been addressed in a hostile way. I recall a time when AIDS activists were protesting my position against the use

> The greatest danger before you is this: You live in an age when people would package and standardize your life for you—steal it from you and sell it back to you at a price. That price is very high.
>
> Granny D. (a.k.a. Doris Haddock)

of chimps for medical testing. They argued that those trying to protect the animals were condemning people to die instead. But even in that highly charged instance I found that the protesters and the press were willing to discuss the issue with me.

K.O.: What do you do in your down time?
J.G.: I talk to journalists.

K.O.: As a private person with a very public life, what sustains you?
J.G.: First, I don't think I've chosen this life, I feel I've been pushed into it. And what nourishes and sustains me, primarily, is the sense of my life as a mission. I feel I'm meant to be doing what I do. Second, there are the amazing people I meet, including the children I've encountered through Roots & Shoots. Today, for instance, I talked to 700 kids, and all of them sat in silence, listening intently for 50 minutes. Afterward, one of them came up and whispered in my ear, "I loved your talk and I love you, and you inspire me." And I'm inspired by them.

K.O.: If you had to make one law, what would it be?
J.G.: Laws alone are useless. We already have animal-protection laws that mean nothing because they're not enforced—and they never will mean anything until we get to people's hearts. That's why I put so much energy into working with children. But if I could wish one thing into being, never mind the law, it would be that we'd stop overpopulating the planet. It's a terrible situation, compounded in some places by the vast numbers of people who can't afford to move and thus totally destroy the land they're trapped on. Meanwhile, the affluent societies are overconsuming in the most horrifying way. In either case, there are just too many people.

K.O.: What is the essence of the message you're trying to deliver today?
J.G.: That every individual can make a difference, and that if we continue to leave decision making to the so-called decision makers, things will never change.

Karen Olson is Associate Editor for the *UTNE Reader.*

1. *Response*
a. Use the information provided in this article to describe Jane Goodall to a partner.
b. What other questions would you have liked Goodall to answer?
c. With a partner, discuss the effectiveness of this interview and the features of an interview that make this selection different from other non-fiction.

2. *Oral Communication* *Interview* With a partner, choose three appropriate questions from the selection, and ask each other these questions. You can adjust the questions slightly to make them more relevant. Generate three more questions to ask each other. Practise your interview, then deliver it to an audience of your peers.

3. *Media* *Animal Portrayals* With three or four classmates, discuss the use of animals in commercials, TV shows, and movies. What are the **codes** and **conventions** that seem to govern the behaviour of animals in these media? Generate five rules that you think producers and directors are following when they use animals. For example, rule one could be that all cats in sitcoms must ignore their owners.

Codes and **conventions** refer to the different ways in which each media product typically conveys meaning to audiences. For example, we expect certain kinds of movies to open with certain conventions, such as an action movie opening with lots of action, special effects, and maybe a chase scene.

Theme Connections

Sontag wrote the following editorial for
The New York Times Magazine in 1996.
As you read the article, think about whether
you agree with her ideas, and if her predictions
about the future of cinema have come true.

A Century of Cinema

Editorial by Susan Sontag

Cinema's hundred years seem to have the shape of a life cycle: an inevitable birth, the steady accumulation of glories, and the onset in the last decade of an ignominious, irreversible decline. This doesn't mean that there won't be any more new films that one can admire. But such films will not simply be exceptions; that's true of great achievement in any art. They will have to be heroic violations of the norms and practices that now govern moviemaking everywhere in the capitalist and would-be capitalist world—which is to say, everywhere. And ordinary films, films made purely for entertainment (that is, commercial) purposes, will continue to be astonishingly witless; already the vast majority fail resoundingly to appeal to their cynically targeted audiences. While the point of a great film is now, more than ever, to be a one-of-a-kind achievement, the commercial cinema has settled for a policy of bloated, derivative filmmaking, a brazen combinatory or recombinatory art, in the hope of reproducing past successes. Every film that hopes to reach the largest possible audience is designed as some kind of remake. Cinema, once heralded as *the* art of the twentieth century, seems now, as the century closes numerically, to be a decadent art.

Perhaps it is not cinema that has ended, but only cinephilia, the name of the very specific kind of love that cinema inspired. Each art breeds its fanatics. The love that cinema inspired, however, was special. It was born of the sense that cinema was an art unlike any other: quintessentially modern, distinctively accessible, poetic and mysterious and erotic and moral—all at the same time. Cinema had apostles (it was like religion). Cinema was a crusade. Cinema was a world-view. Lovers of poetry or opera or dance don't think there is *only* poetry or opera or dance. But lovers of cinema could think there was only cinema. That the movies encapsulated everything—and they did. It was both the book of art and the book of life.

As many people have noted, the start of moviemaking a hundred years ago was, conveniently, a double start. In that first year, 1895, two kinds of films were made, proposing two modes of what cinema could be: cinema as the transcription of real, unstaged life (the Lumière brothers) and cinema as invention, artifice, illusion, fantasy (Méliès). But this was never a true opposition. For those first audiences watching the Lumière brothers' *The Arrival of a Train at La Ciotat Station*, the camera's transmission of a banal sight was a fantastic experience. Cinema began in wonder, the wonder that reality can be transcribed with such magical immediacy. All of cinema is an attempt to perpetuate and to reinvent that sense of wonder.

Everything begins with that moment, one hundred years ago, when the train pulled into the station. People took movies into themselves, just as the public cried out with excitement, actually ducked, as the train seemed to move toward *them*. Until the advent of television emptied the movie theaters, it was from a weekly visit to the cinema that you learned (or tried to learn) how to walk, to smoke, to kiss, to fight, to suffer. Movies gave you tips about how to be attractive, such as: it looks good to wear a raincoat even when it isn't raining. But whatever you took home from the movies was only a part of the larger experience of losing yourself in faces, in lives that were *not* yours—which is the more inclusive form of desire embodied in the movie experience. The strongest experience was simply to surrender to, to be transported by, what was on the screen. You wanted to be kidnapped by the movie.

The first prerequisite of being kidnapped was to be overwhelmed by the physical presence of the image. And the conditions of "going to the movies" were essential to that. To see a great film only on TV isn't to have really seen that film. (This is equally true of those made for TV, like Fassbinder's *Berlin Alexanderplatz* and the two *Heimat* films of Edgar Reitz.) It's not only the difference of dimensions: the superiority of the larger-than-you image in the theater to the little image on the box at home. The conditions of paying attention in a domestic space are radically disrespectful of film. Since film no longer has a standard size, home screens *can* be as big as living room or bedroom walls. But you are still in a living room or a bedroom, alone or with familiars. To be kidnapped, you have to be in a movie theater, seated in the dark among anonymous strangers.

No amount of mourning will revive the vanished rituals—erotic, ruminative—of the darkened theater. The reduction of cinema to assaultive images and the unprincipled manipulation of images (faster and faster cutting) to be more attention-grabbing have produced a disincarnated, lightweight cinema that doesn't demand anyone's full attention. Images now appear in any size and on a variety of surfaces: on a screen in a theater, on home screens as small as the palm of your hand or as big as a wall, on disco walls and megascreens hanging above sports arenas and the outsides of tall public buildings. The sheer ubiquity of moving images has steadily undermined the standards people once had both for cinema as art at its most serious and for cinema as popular entertainment.

In the first years there was essentially no difference between cinema as art and cinema as entertainment. And all films of the silent era—from the masterpieces of Feuillade, D. W. Griffith, Djiga Vertov, Pabst, Murnau, King Vidor to the most formula-ridden melodramas and comedies—are on a very high artistic level compared with most of what was to follow. With the coming of sound, the image-making lost much of its brilliance and poetry, and commercial standards tightened. This way of making movies—the Hollywood system—dominated filmmaking for about twenty-five years (roughly from 1930 to 1955). The most original directors, like Erich von Stroheim and Orson Welles, were defeated by the system and eventually went into artistic exile in Europe—where more or less the same quality-defeating system was now in place, with lower budgets; only in France were a large number of superb films produced throughout this period. Then, in the mid-1950s, vanguard ideas took hold again, rooted in the idea of cinema as a craft pioneered by the Italian films of the immediate postwar period. A dazzling number of ambitious, passionate, artisanally crafted films of the highest seriousness got made with new actors and tiny crews, went to film festivals (of which there were more and more), and from there, garlanded with festival prizes, into movie theaters around the world. This golden age actually lasted as long as twenty years.

It was at this specific moment in the hundred-year history of cinema that going to movies, thinking about movies, talking about movies, became a passion among university students and other young people. You fell in love not just with actors but with cinema itself. Cinephilia had first become visible in the 1950s in France: its forum was the legendary film magazine *Cahiers du Cinéma* (followed by similarly fervent magazines in Germany, Italy, Great Britain, Sweden, the United States, Canada). Its temples, as it spread throughout Europe and the Americas, were the many cinemathèques and film clubs specializing in films from the past and directors' retrospectives which sprang up. The 1960s and early 1970s were the feverish age of moviegoing, with the full-time cinephile always hoping to find a seat as close as possible to the big screen, ideally the third row center. "One can't live without Rossellini," declares a character in Bertolucci's *Before the Revolution* (1964)—and means it.

Cinephilia—a source of exultation in the films of Godard and Truffaut and the early Bertolucci and Syberberg; a morose lament in some recent films of Nanni Moretti—was mostly a Western European affair. The great directors of "the other Europe" (Zanussi in Poland, Angelopoulos in Greece, Tarkovsky and Sokurov in Russia, Jancso and Tarr in Hungary) and the great Japanese directors (Ozu, Mizoguchi, Kurosawa, Oshima, Imamura) have tended not to be cinephiles, perhaps because in Budapest or Moscow or Tokyo or Warsaw or Athens there wasn't a chance to get a cinemathèque education. The distinctive thing about cinephile taste was that it embraced both "art" films and popular films. Thus, European cinephilia had a romantic relation to the films of certain directors in Hollywood at the apogee of the studio system: Godard for Howard Hawks, Fassbinder for Douglas Sirk. Of course, this moment—when cinephilia emerged—was also the moment when the Hollywood studio system was breaking up. It seemed that moviemaking had rewon the right to experiment; cinephiles could *afford* to be passionate (or sentimental) about the old Hollywood genre films. A host of new people came into cinema, including a generation of young film critics from *Cahiers du Cinéma*; the towering figure of that generation, indeed of several decades of filmmaking anywhere, was Jean-Luc Godard. A few writers turned out to be wildly talented filmmakers: Alexander Kluge in Germany, Pier Paolo Pasolini in Italy. (The model for the writer who turns to filmmaking actually emerged earlier, in France, with Pagnol in the 1930s and Cocteau in the 1940s; but it was not until the 1960s that this seemed, at least in Europe, normal.) Cinema seemed reborn.

For some fifteen years there were new masterpieces every month, and one allowed oneself to imagine that this would go on forever. How far away that era seems now. To be sure, there was always a conflict between cinema as an industry and cinema as an art, cinema as routine and cinema as experiment. But the conflict was not such as to make impossible the making of wonderful films, sometimes within and sometimes outside of mainstream cinema. Now the balance has tipped decisively in favor of cinema as an industry. The great cinema of the 1960s and 1970s has been thoroughly repudiated. Already in the 1970s

Hollywood was plagiarizing and banalizing the innovations in narrative method and editing of successful new European and ever-marginal independent American films. Then came the catastrophic rise in production costs in the 1980s, which secured the worldwide reimposition of industry standards of making and distributing films on a far more coercive, this time truly global scale. The result can be seen in the melancholy fate of some of the greatest directors of the last decades. What place is there today for a maverick like Hans Jürgen Syberberg, who has stopped making films altogether, or for the great Godard, who now makes films about the history of film, on video? Consider some other cases. The internationalizing of financing and therefore of casts was a disaster for Andrei Tarkovsky in the last two films of his stupendous, tragically abbreviated career. And these conditions for making films have proved to be as much an artistic disaster for two of the most valuable directors still working: Krzysztof Zanussi (*The Structure of Crystals, Illumination, Spiral, Contract*) and Theo Angelopoulos (*Reconstruction, Days of '36, The Traveling Players*). And what will happen now to Bela Tarr (*Damnation, Satantango*)? And how will Aleksandr Sokurov (*Save and Protect, Days of Eclipse, The Second Circle, Stone, Whispering Pages*) find the money to go on making films, his sublime films, under the rude conditions of Russian capitalism?

Predictably, the love of cinema has waned. People still like going to the movies, and some people still care about and expect something special, necessary from a film. And wonderful films are still being made: Mike Leigh's *Naked*, Gianni Amelio's *Lamerica*, Fred Keleman's *Fate*, Abbas Kiarostami's *Through the Olive Trees*. But one hardly finds anymore, at least among the young, the distinctive cinephilic love of movies, which is not simply love of but a certain *taste* in films (grounded in a vast appetite for seeing and reseeing as much as possible of cinema's glorious past). Cinephilia itself has come under attack, as something quaint, outmoded, snobbish. For cinephilia implies that films are unique, unrepeatable, magic experiences. Cinephilia tells us that the Hollywood remake of Godard's *Breathless* cannot be as good as the original. Cinephilia has no role in the era of hyperindustrial films. For cinephilia cannot help, by the very range and eclecticism of its passions, but sponsor the idea of the film as, first of all, a poetic object, and cannot help but incite those outside the movie industry, like painters and writers, to want to make films, too. It is precisely this conception of movies that must be defeated. That has been defeated.

If cinephilia is dead, then movies are dead too—no matter how many movies, even very good ones, go on being made. If cinema can be resurrected, it will only be through the birth of a new kind of cine-love.

Crowds gather outside a theatre for the premiere of *The House of Seven Gables* on March 21, 1940. The film, based on Nathaniel Hawthorne's novel, is set in Salem.

Examine this image and discuss what going to the movies was like for people in this photo. What is going to the movies like for you?

Susan Sontag was born in New York City, U.S., in 1933. She was educated at universities in California, Chicago, and Paris, and at Harvard University. Her works include *Against Interpretation, Styles of Radical Will,* and *Under the Sign of Saturn* (essay collections); *Death Kit* and *The Volcano Lover* (novels); *On Photography* and *AIDS and Its Metaphors* (non-fiction books); and *I, etcetera* (a short story collection). Her novel *In America* won the National Book Award for fiction in 2000.

1. Response

a. With a partner, discuss Sontag's ideas and viewpoints in this editorial.

b. Which point from this editorial do you agree with most? Which point do you disagree with most? Explain why.

c. Define *cinephilia* to a partner. Discuss whether you consider yourselves cinephiles.

d. Discuss at least two reading strategies you used to read and understand this editorial.

2. Film Study
With a small group, list ten movies that you have all seen in the past year. Use Sontag's two categories (1. bloated, derivative, and witless; or 2. great and one-of-a-kind achievements) to create a chart organizing these movies. Does everyone in the group agree with the categorization of each movie? Explain.

Review the glossary terms following this selection and use them whenever you discuss films.

3. Making Connections
Find out more about one of the movies referred to in this article, using Internet and library resources. If possible, and if the movie is appropriate, view the movie. Write a short review of the movie, including your opinion of its quality.

4. Critical Thinking
With a small group, discuss the following quotation from the selection. Present your opinion about this idea to the group, using examples to support it.

> To be sure, there was always a conflict between cinema as an industry and cinema as an art, cinema as routine and cinema as experiment. But the conflict was not such as to make impossible the making of wonderful films, sometimes within and sometimes outside of mainstream cinema.

Film Study Glossary

A **Classical Narrative Structure** is the most common way of telling stories in Hollywood films. It is called classical not because it is the oldest way of telling stories or even the best, but the most common.

A **climax** is the point in a film where the story's main conflict develops into a dramatic confrontation. It is the point where key struggles are waged and an eventual victor is determined.

Closure follows a movie's climax, and is the point where all of the major conflicts, issues, or ideas in a story are resolved.

Codes and **conventions** refer to the different ways in which each media product typically conveys meaning to audiences. For example, we expect certain kinds of movies to open with certain conventions—an action movie opening with lots of action, special effects, and maybe a chase scene; or a horror movie opening with shots of mist and a haunted house, with creepy music in the background.

Continuity editing is a strategy for linking together all the individual shots that make up a movie.

Genre refers to a style or type of film or TV show; for example, westerns, comedies, action-adventures, or horror pictures.

High contrast lighting uses harsh lines of light and shadows combined with dramatic streaks of blackness. The effect of this lighting style is often haunting and eerie, creating a sense of anxiety and confusion.

High key lighting means most shots in the film are brightly lit, with few shadows. This is the most common lighting style in Hollywood and is often assumed to be the "natural" look of movies.

The **hook** is the opening sequences in a film using the Classical Narrative Structure. These scenes are called the hook because they are meant to "hook" the audience's attention, and draw them into the story.

Low key lighting uses shadows and directed pools of light to create atmosphere and suspense. This lighting style generally suggests a sense of mystery.

Mise en scène (French for "to put in scene") refers to how space is used in individual shots to create symbolic meaning or dramatic effect throughout a movie.

Montage editing is a strategy for linking together individual shots in a movie. Montage editing is different from continuity editing in that it does not put shots together with a seamless flow, but presents them in a way that requires audiences to make their own connections between the images.

Myths are stories that help to organize how we understand ourselves and our communities, and prioritize certain values that a society holds dear.

A **negotiated interpretation** of a media text questions the dominant or intended meaning of the text, but does not attempt to rework the text's meaning in any significant way.

An **oppositional interpretation** questions the dominant meaning or explanation of the text, and uses the text for purposes other than those intended by the creator(s).

A **preferred interpretation** of a media text replicates the meaning intended by the text's producer(s).

Representation means that all media are symbols, or symbolic systems that refer to the outside world.

Verisimilitude means creating a sense of reality between two realms of experience.

With a partner, discuss a recent movie you have both seen.
What was the most true-to-life scene in the movie?
What action or scene from the movie would never occur
in real life?

The Movie
I'd Like to See

Commentary by Geoff Pevere

In the movie I'd like to see, credits would include what people were paid to make the movie.

In the movie I'd like to see, we'd see people working out with personal trainers all the time, which would explain why people in movies look like they work out with personal trainers all the time.

In the movie I'd like to see, waiters would chase after people who leave bars and restaurants without finishing their drinks or meals. They'd demand payment, and ask them if they think they're in a damned movie or something.

In the movie I'd like to see, sometimes people wouldn't be home when other people knock on their doors to confront them. Or, if they're home, they'd ask the confronter why they didn't just phone like people outside of movies do. Then slam the door.

In the movie I'd like to see, someone would explain why people in movies always carry paper grocery bags instead of plastic ones, and why their bags are always full of unwrapped produce like lettuce and oranges. Especially oranges.

In the movie I'd like to see, Bill Murray would play the president of the United States.

In the movie I'd like to see, someone would explain why all the women over the age of 35 have disappeared from the face of the earth.

In the movie I'd like to see, Julia Roberts would be dumped for Janeane Garofalo.

In the movie I'd like to see, watching cartoons wouldn't be a symbol of witless trashiness, but watching CNN would.

In the movie I'd like to see, unspeakably rich movie stars would not be permitted to play feisty working-class single mothers.

In the movie I'd like to see, people who get drunk don't sober up as soon as they enter the next scene. And they'd have hangovers that last the rest of the movie.

In the movie I'd like to see, high school students would still be played by people in their 20s, but their teachers and parents would be played by teenagers.

In the movie I'd like to see, a cranky old misanthrope would not be redeemed by his relationship with a precocious young child. He'd want to kill the brat.

In the movie I'd like to see, telemarketers would be calling to interrupt people all the time, just like in real life.

In the movie I'd like to see, there wouldn't be subliminal product placements, people would simply hold products up to the camera and say: "Buy this. They paid us huge to tell you to."

In the movie I'd like to see, someone would explain why movie tears always come from the centre of people's eyes, while non-movie tears tend to run from the corners of people's eyes.

In the movie I'd like to see, people would forget what they're saying sometimes, or they'd ask other people to repeat themselves because they weren't listening.

In the movie I'd like to see, major movie stars would be recognized by other people in the movie as major movie stars. "Hi Mel … I mean, um, Dave …"

In the movie I'd like to see, moments and ideas stolen from other movies would be credited on screen while they occur. Since they do this for cleverly sampled music, this seems only reasonable for creatively bankrupt movies.

In the movie I'd like to see, unattractive people would fall in love and live happily together.

In the movie I'd like to see, two people you'd just love to see get together keep missing each other and never do get together. Maybe they never even meet.

In the movie I'd like to see, serial killers would be portrayed as the boring pathetic creeps they usually are.

What the mass media offer is not popular art, but entertainment which is intended to be consumed like food, forgotten and replaced by a new dish.

W.H. Auden

In the movie I'd like to see, people would react to each other's cosmetic surgery. "Man you look so weird."

In the movie I'd like to see, all attractive, well-heeled professionals in their 20s would be sent to Third World coffee plantations and multinational athletic equipment sweatshops at the first sign of an "emotional crisis."

In the movie I'd like to see, Cher would play the Frankenstein monster. If she insisted on singing, that would be even better.

In the movie I'd like to see, all evocations of the '60s would come with a choice of Jiffypop-nostalgia musical cues, so we wouldn't have to endure The Doors, Buffalo Springfield, The Temptations or Jimi Hendrix any more. Better yet, there would be no evocations of the '60s.

In the movie I'd like to see, letters would no longer talk when opened. They'd sing.

In the movie I'd like to see, the bystander who gets knocked down on the sidewalk by other people chasing each other with guns would chase the other people with guns and pistolwhip them for being rude.

In the movie I'd like to see, aliens would invade the earth only to flee when they realize how stupid the movie they're in—and the planet they're on—is.

In the movie I'd like to see, people would spend more time going to crappy unrealistic movies and then complaining about how crappy and unrealistic movies have become.

Is this asking too much?

Geoff Pevere is a movie critic with *The Toronto Star*.

1. *Response*
   a. Return to the discussion in the introductory text at the beginning of this article. How do you think Geoff Pevere would have responded to the movie you discussed?
   b. What item on Geoff Pevere's list did you agree with most? Why?
   c. Are there any items on the list that you thought were too extreme or radical? Explain.
   d. What do you think motivated Pevere to create this list?
   e. What is the overall tone of this selection? How is that tone achieved?

2. ***Film Study*** Review Pevere's list and discuss it in a small group. Together, brainstorm some ideas for additions to this list. List ten more items that you think should be added. Can you think of any movies that actually incorporate any of these items? If so, discuss the movie(s).

3. ***Media*** *Movie Trailer* Work with a small group to develop a proposal for a movie that incorporates at least five items from Pevere's list. Use that proposal to script and plan a movie trailer, remembering to feature Pevere's items. Discuss your production options, format, purpose, and audience. If possible, use a video camera to record your trailer, or present a live performance of the script. Ask your audience for some feedback on the production values of the trailer and the script.

4. ***Writing*** *Modelling the Selection* Use Pevere's commentary as a model to create a list of your own for another media form. For example, you could list what you would like to see in music videos, magazines, or sitcoms. Try to use a similar tone and structure to those used by Pevere. Discuss your list with others, assessing the effectiveness of your content, tone, and structure. Compare your list with a classmate who commented on another format. Are there similarities between your lists? If so, explain why this might be so.

5. ***Language Conventions*** *Parallel Structure* Examine the beginning of each paragraph and consider its effect on the reader. Why would Pevere choose to use a parallel structure for each paragraph? How effective is this use? Examine something you have written recently and consider how you could use parallel structure effectively.

Theme Connections

- *"My Old Newcastle," a memoir that refers to movie conventions, page 296*
- *"Four Rules and a Suggestion," a how-to article about writing a script, page 359*
- *"The Making of* Sense and Sensibility,*" a diary about the making of a movie, page 364*

*When it comes to portraying
individuals with disabilities,
Hollywood hasn't got a clue.*

Heroes
and Holy Innocents

Magazine Article
by Kathi Wolfe

Thanks to audio description and closed-captioning, blind and deaf moviegoers now are able to "see" and "hear" films. After a long struggle, people using wheelchairs are finding it easier to get into movie theaters. But once they're at the movies, people with disabilities rarely see true-to-life images of themselves.

Of course, Hollywood has presented unrealistic images of disabled people since its movie moguls first set up shop. Martin E. Norden, author of *The Cinema of Isolation: A History of Physical Disability in the Movies* (Rutgers University Press), writes, "the movie industry has perpetuated ... stereotypes ... so durable and pervasive that they have become mainstream society's perception of disabled people." Demeaning, patronizing stereotypes have marched across the silver screen for decades from that sweet innocent Tiny Tim in *A Christmas Carol* to Quasimodo, the villainous hunchback in *The Hunchback of Notre Dame* to the embittered blind veteran in *Scent of a Woman* (1992) and the idiot savant in *Rain Man* (1988). Disabled people aren't cheering as this parade of superheroes, venomous villains, and helpless victims goes by.

San Francisco State University history professor Paul Longmore says, "These stereotypes present disabled people as tragic, pathetic figures: Such films as *Whose Life Is It, Anyway?* (in which a man who has become quadriplegic begs to be allowed to kill himself) leave the audience thinking it's better to be dead than disabled." But disabled people today don't see themselves as symbols of evil, inspirational superheroes, or holy innocents (like that wise fool Forrest Gump). Though the disease-of-the-week flick still moves audiences to tears, most disabled filmgoers no longer view their lives as a two-hankie movie.

In the '90s movie *Living in Oblivion*, a comedy about the making of a small-budget picture, a dwarf named Mr. Tito complains about his role in a dream scene. He feels that he's only been cast because dwarfs symbolize weird emotions. Though Mr. Tito is a comic figure, his anger at being used as a symbol is shared by many with disabilities.

Leye J. Chrzanowski, editor-in-chief of the monthly newspaper *One Step Ahead—The Disability Resource*, asserts, "Hollywood has a hackneyed idea of disability. To add insult to injury, someone without a disability acting out this delusion is usually either an Oscar nominee or winner ... Every time we start breaking down stereotypes, we're slapped back into the 'helpless cripple' role by a *Love Affair* or a *Passion Fish*."

Are these views held only by the politically correct? Not at all, says George Covington, who was a special assistant to the quintessentially non-PC former vice president Dan Quayle. Covington, who is legally blind, says, "We're seen as 'inspirational,' and inspiration sells like hotcakes. My disability isn't a burden; having to be so damned inspirational is."

Mainstream Magazine editor William R. Stothers says, "If it was just entertainment, these images wouldn't worry me. But they help shape attitudes toward disability."

Do disabled people want to take the entertainment out of movies? To turn films with disabled characters into "eat your spinach" documentaries? No, says Mary Johnson, a former editor of *The Disability Rag Resource*, "but they want to see their reality reflected on screen."

Despite the stereotypes, some disabled people are hopeful about the movies. "As actors and writers, and from behind the cameras, we're pushing Hollywood hard to portray us in nonstereotypical ways," Stothers says.

Two recent independent films offer hope that this change can take place. *When Billy Broke His Head*, a dynamic documentary directed by Billy Golfus, has been shown on PBS and at film festivals. This film isn't (as Golfus himself says) an "inspirational cripple story." Instead the movie shows real-life disabled people: fighting for their civil rights, job hunting, and battling social service bureaucracies. *Twitch and Shout*, a touching but funny documentary directed by Laurel Chiten about people with Tourette Syndrome, has aired on the PBS program *P.O.V.* and at film festivals. The film shows not only what it's like to have this disorder but what it's like to encounter disability-based discrimination. The movie presents its subjects not as superheroes or objects of pity but as fully human human beings.

If the spirit of these films could somehow be transferred to Hollywood, the disabled wouldn't feel left out of the big picture on the silver screen.

Kathi Wolfe is a writer living in Falls Church, Virginia.

1. *Film Study* In your notebook, write a personal response to the points that Kathi Wolfe raises. Include your own experiences, ideas, and viewpoints about the portrayal of individuals with disabilities in movies you have watched.

   With a small group, discuss movies you have seen and how individuals with disabilities and other groups (teens, intellectuals, scientists, women) are portrayed, noting any stereotypes that you think exist. What stereotypes exist in the movies you like to watch most? What effect do these stereotypes have on you or other audience members? What do you think can or should be done about these stereotypes?

2. *Language Conventions* Loaded Language There are many groups and individuals who would object to the use of the word *disabled* as a collective noun, as Wolfe has chosen to use it. Many people would prefer terms such as *the physically or mentally challenged, individuals with disabilities,* or *people with special needs.* Discuss the issue of changing language trends, the language within this selection, and how **loaded language** can be used to stereotype or portray individuals negatively.

   Loaded language is language that is intentionally chosen to evoke a strong response in a reader—usually an emotional response. It is also language that is highly connotative, conjuring in the listener much more than its literal meaning.

3. *Making Connections* With two classmates, role-play a conversation between Pevere, Sontag, and Wolfe. Use the information in each of these authors' selections and make connections between the selections.

Artists from around the world react to the terrorist attacks on New York and Washington.

Artists Respond to September 11, 2001

An eerie silence...

An Eerie Silence ...
by Sally-Ann Maslen, Australia.
Manipulated photo. Sept 13, 2001.

Untitled 2,
by Bob Lake, United States.
Photo. Sept 30, 2001.

Eclipse 09.11.2001: Peace and Hate,
by Sergey Muravyev, Russia.
Painting. Oct 11, 2001.

Hope,
by Joy Yaffa, Canada.
Watercolour painting.
Sept 22, 2001.

Fire in New York,
by Blanka Lyszczarz,
Poland. Painting.
Sept 17, 2001.

No Words, 3,
by Gisela Vidalle, Argentina.
Pen-and-ink drawing.
Sept 23, 2001.

1. *Visual Communication* *Analysing Images* Discuss these images in small groups. What message does each image send to you? Does it send the same message to each member of the group? Why might the message be different for different people? How do these images make you feel? Which image is your favourite? Why? How do the captions for each image contribute to the meaning of the image?

2. *Research and Inquiry* Use Internet or library resources to find other works of art that were created in response to September 11, 2001. Choose one image and write an essay analysing its message, features, techniques, and content and how these elements work together. You should develop a clear thesis, an argument to support that thesis, and a conclusion.

Read the title and teaser below and consider whether you are being described here. Are you a skeptical youth? An information-age cynic? Discuss.

Peace a Hard Sell to Skeptical Youth

Opponents of the U.S. Star Wars scheme find out heartstrings and hippy-dippy nostalgia don't click with information-age cynics.

Newspaper Article by David Beers

from *The Vancouver Sun*, February 2001

The greying peace movement is looking for fresh blood to oppose America's latest "Star Wars" scheme. But how do you lure recruits who may have been playing with Cabbage Patch dolls and Transformer toys when the Cold War ended?

The answer stands 10 metres tall at the corner of Commercial and Broadway [in Vancouver], a day-glo image of a funky young guy kick-boxing a warhead beneath the words "Bombs Away." The billboard, similar transit ads and the Web site they promote are the direct result of a close study of how to sell nuclear fear, and activism, to 18 to 35-year-olds.

Irony works. Tugging at heartstrings doesn't. Make plenty of neutral-toned information available to your inherently skeptical audience. And avoid even a whiff of hippy-dippy. If there's one thing youth distrust more than the military industrial complex, it's their parents' nostalgia.

These are the findings of a Vancouver agency hired to research and craft a just-launched media campaign for the International Physicians for the Prevention of Nuclear War. The aim of the campaign is to mobilize youth against Canadian support for the U.S. national defence system, which sits at the top of President George Bush's agenda.

Proponents of NDM say the system will shield North America by intercepting nuclear-tipped missiles fired by "rogue" nations. Opponents claim the unproven technology is an expensive boondoggle in the making, may violate antiballistic missile treaties, and will trigger a new global nuclear-weapons buildup.

"If the U.S. goes ahead on this, China and Russia have said they will respond by heightening the arms race," notes 24-year-old Sarah Kelly, who was one of several Bombs Away campaign spokespeople on hand last Tuesday at the billboard unveiling. "Keep heightening the arms race," reasons the fourth-year medical student at the University of British Columbia, "and eventually a nuclear weapon will be used."

Articulate, imbued with energy not only to study medicine but wrestle with geopolitics, Kelly is just what the doctor ordered for a flagging movement.

Indeed, as the Star Wars debate rekindles, peace activists in North America and Europe see a golden opportunity to replenish their membership, which plummeted around the time the Berlin Wall came down. Fresh troops are essential, they say, to tackle their larger aim: abolishing nuclear weapons altogether.

Seizing public attention for that cause proved daunting in an era when "presidents Bush and Clinton told people that we no longer lived under the threat of nuclear war and that the world was a much safer place," says Lynn Martin, Communications Director for the U.S. branch of IPPNW.

"While it is true that the numbers of nuclear weapons decreased under these administrations," Martin says, "there are still 30,000 nuclear weapons in the world today and the nuclear war-fighting plans and strategies remain unchanged. The U.S. and Russia each have about 2,500 strategic nuclear weapons on hair-trigger alert status and these are targeted at hundreds of cities. If just one modern nuclear weapon exploded over a large city—either by accident or intent—millions of people would die and millions more would be injured. The threat of nuclear war remains the greatest immediate public health threat in the world today."

If so, not just politicians, but popular culture fails to reflect such urgency. In 1964, Stanley Kubrick's black comedy *Dr. Strangelove* made a splash by ridiculing the notion that America's nuclear arsenal was failsafe. In 1983, the television movie *The Day After* used realism to shock viewers into imagining the consequences of nuclear war. In cineplexes now we find *Thirteen Days*, a retelling of the Cuban missile crisis that gets good reviews, but implies nuclear doom was confronted 40 years ago and, through cool Kennedy thinking, defused.

Sarah Kelly was born 15 years after that near conflagration. She was but nine years old in 1986, when the International Physicians for the Prevention of Nuclear War received the Nobel Peace Prize. Forgive her, then, if the antinuclear movement of old is little more than a grainy *Life* magazine photo in her mind. She and her friends "have seen pictures of our parents' generation marching for peace." But for Kelly, the persistent risk of Armageddon comes as a fresh discovery, and she says she is hungry to know and do more about it.

Optimistic but ironic

The 18 to 35 age group that includes Sarah Kelly is the subject of much scrutiny by marketing types. A Toronto-based research firm called D-Code has named them the Nexus generation, caught as they are between the Industrial and Information Ages, and sandwiched between the Baby Boom and Echo generations.

This demographic is the focus, too, of Amanda Gibbs, whose job at the Vancouver-based Institute for Media, Policy and Civil Society is to help put together media campaigns for non-profit organizations. According to Gibbs, the Nexus generation is "realistic, confident, optimistic, activist" and "incredibly media literate. Yet members of the Nexus gang are also born skeptics, steeped in the irony of the age."

When the International Physicians for the Prevention of Nuclear War decided it needed to appeal to the Nexus generation, it hired Gibbs and IMPACS to figure out how.

Gibbs developed some campaign approaches, then hired D-Code to run the ideas by a Nexus-aged focus group. Among the group's six carefully selected members: A social activist who'd worked at addiction recovery and sexual-assault centres. An arts publicist who'd sailed the Pacific on a youth cultural exchange program. A restaurateur and wine grower who specializes in organic ingredients. A hip-hop artist studying commerce and information technology. A screenwriter/graphic designer. And the founder of her own ecological gardening company.

Gibbs herself casually throws around terms like "marketing to the Web" and "fashion forward" and would seem to be naturally in tune with these Nexusers. But at age 30, she felt a bit dated as the cultural biases of the focus group revealed themselves.

For example, Gibbs is in love with atomic kitsch like those 1950s instructional films telling school kids to "duck and cover" at the first sign of a nuclear flash, or that famous *Dr. Strangelove* scene of Slim Pickens riding a falling H-bomb like a bronco. But such retroiconography doesn't register with the Nexus group. "They thought it was mouldy," Gibbs says.

Nor, despite the success of "Joe Canada" beer commercials, did the group respond to a nationalistic, us versus big, bad America approach. This was unanimously rejected as self-righteous and cutting against their ideal of the "global citizen."

A concept called "We said No Nukes" was intended to connect younger people with the peace protests of the past. But it fared no better. "Several of the D-Coders [saw] the activism in the 1960s as largely ineffective and its adherents as sell-outs to big business (or worse, their parents)," read the final report.

Many in the group liked a concept that blamed corporate greed for driving the nuclear-arms industry. But they doubted the broader appeal of that message across their generation. "'Sticking it to the man' is not going to push your 'social hot-button' if you work in a bank," said the report. Some might "feel as though the campaign message is attacking them, their lifestyle, etc."

More popular was a straightforward approach declaring that we face, even today, immediate risk of a nuclear catastrophe. But again, a caveat specific to those of Nexus age: "The message was traumatic in the '80s when Nexus was growing up. It made them feel vulnerable to powers beyond their control and it could still elicit a disempowering response if not supported by actionable steps," D-Code reported. As the gardening company owner said: "No more missile horror messages for me ... I still feel traumatized by the nuclear war movies of the '80s. ... It was such a negative way to be brought up in this world, thinking that it might blow up any second because of power-freak grown-ups."

The group went so far as to brainstorm its own slogans, and came up with "Bombs away." Gibbs pored over the report and, working with graphic designer Darren Carcary, and Raised Eyebrow Web Design, produced a campaign she believes speaks to the essence of her Nexus targets. The total budget of $50,000 left only enough to buy one billboard here [Vancouver] and one in Toronto, but those plus bus and subway ads in both cities are designed to drive eyeballs to the real engine of the campaign, the Bombs Away Web site.

"Before you can activate younger people, you have to educate them," theorizes Gibbs. The younger half of the Nexus generation, those aged 18 to 25, "don't watch, much less trust, TV," Gibbs maintains. Instead, surveys show they get more of their information from the Web than anywhere else. The Web fits their skeptical, hype-averse nature by allowing them to read as deeply and broadly on a topic as they desire, and it can give them timely updates and action advisories. When a notice gets picked up and spread exponentially in cyberspace, Gibbs says, that is a sign that the "viral marketing" approach to "web activism" is working, and very inexpensively.

Such buzz phrases were foreign to Dr. Mary-Wynn Ashford, co-president of IPPNW, when she came to Gibbs and IMPACS for help. Ashford, who is 60 and lives in Victoria, intended to hire the group to make a 20-minute video, a standard tool for her group in the past. Now she fully buys into the Web-driven strategy for youth, whom she's come to see are "information savvy and steeped in irony."

It did startle Ashford to see this age bracket reject "our traditional approach: forthright and emotional, based on love for the planet, wanting to protect children. Young people said all this stuff sounds like the '70s and our parents' generation."

Likewise, Debbie Grisdale, the Ottawa-based executive director of Physicians for Global Survival, says she took to heart the focus group's demand "for straight information, and no sense of patronizing, speaking down." But the group's taste for "sarcasm" surprised her.

Sarcasm may be in the ear of the beholder. UBC education professor Peter Seixas likes what he thinks he hears from the Nexus focus group. The former high-school teacher, a baby boomer, believes students need to approach media messages critically, as a corrective to the emotional pull of today's dominant media, television and film. "Perhaps well-educated young people have taken the lesson: 'Don't hit us over the head with a one-minute ad, don't give us preachy talk about love or death—we exist in a much more critical mind than that.' If so, that is something to celebrate."

Exporting the message

Ashford expects lessons learned from Bombs Away to be applied in campaigns in the nine other countries. Top of that list is the United States, where public opinion is the only weapon against well-financed lobbyists for military contractors.

"We have to affect voting in the U.S. Congress," Ashford declares. "If we do, other countries will fall in line." If veteran nuclear dissenters are having to start from scratch with a new pool of potential activists, the U.S. military establishment suffers no such loss of institutional memory. Case in point: the point man on National Missile Defence is the new U.S. secretary of defence, Donald Rumsfeld—who held his same post in the mid-1970s under President Gerald Ford.

The new U.S. president vows to up military spending by a third, adding another $100 billion a year, and he has made NMD a cornerstone of his campaign. If the program goes forward, firms like Boeing and Lockheed stand to gain from at least $60 billion US in new contracts, according to a conservative estimate by the Congressional Budget Office.

Some of that money will be spent in this country, Bush has suggested. That is the carrot. The stick, should Canada not cooperate, is the subject of much concerned speculation in Ottawa. There are hints the U.S. might punish Canada by ending our NORAD air surveillance alliance, most of which is bankrolled by the U.S.

Canadian industry leaders also fear a backlash in trade dealings. Opposition to NMD will lead to "inevitable repercussions ... on such diverse issues as softwood lumber, or how long it takes for cars to get across the Canada-U.S. border," Yves Poisson of Human Resources Development Canada has predicted.

So far Minister for Defence John Manley is taking a wait-and-see attitude, watching European, Chinese and Russian reactions to the project. His predecessor, Lloyd Axworthy, is clearly against it. "Do you want to spend upwards of 100 billion dollars [Cdn] on a system that is not yet proven, for limited protection? And trade that for division among allies and a potential arms race in the nuclear field? That is not exactly a sound proposition," says Axworthy, now director and CEO of the Liu Centre for Global Issues at UBC.

Axworthy scoffs at the notion that the U.S. might boot Canada out of NORAD. "It's a fallacy. We've just signed a five-year extension." Nor is he cowed by the prospect of trade sanctions. "Prime Minister Pearson opposed the Vietnam War, and Canada is still in good standing with the U.S."

"It is important at this moment that we have a strong public debate," says Axworthy, who will host a gathering of international

Performance artist and activist Troy Jackson, 30, was involved in creating a billboard campaign that puts a new face on the peace movement and social activism to appeal to the post-Cold-War generation.

experts on the NMD issue at the Liu Centre next week, culminating in a public forum Friday evening.

Getting youth into that conversation, and mobilizing them to act throughout North America and Europe is, in Axworthy's view, "essential."

"Young people show a pretty strong understanding of global issues," he says. "A lot better than our generation did."

David Beers is a well-known Vancouver journalist who writes regularly for *The Vancouver Sun.*

1. *Response*
   a. Review what David Beers says about the Nexus Generation. Discuss the term *Nexus Generation.*
   b. What methods would you suggest for effectively selling peace to your generation? Discuss your ideas.
   c. What does *hard sell* mean? What connotations, if any, does the term have for you? Do you consider the use of this term appropriate or inappropriate? Explain.
   d. Discuss how you would have responded to some of the advertising campaigns that are described in the article.

2. *Making Connections* Consider what "Peace a Hard Sell to Skeptical Youth" says about your generation. Would you agree with the way in which the article describes today's youth? Why or why not? Write a short essay, letter, or poem in response to this selection.

3. *Research and Inquiry* Find out the current state of the U.S. Star Wars plan using Internet and library resources. Report your findings to the class in an innovative way—for example, using a poster, PowerPoint presentation, music video, radio news broadcast, collage, et cetera. Include a reference to recent world events and what impact you think these events have on Beers' argument.

4. *Media Selling to Youth* With several classmates, examine at least five ads that you think target teenagers. Discuss the strategies these ads use and develop ideas for selling some of these products, services, or ideas more effectively. Redesign at least one of these ads, using your ideas.

Nairobi's hip hop scene asserts its African identity in the face of the bland imports of the global music industry.

TRANSLATE THIS!

NEWSPAPER ARTICLE BY ADRIAN COOPER

Kenya's demand for music and television can't be met by under-funded local industries, so a flow of pop culture from the West, a culture of brands and products, fills the gap. It isn't a lack of talent that stops broadcasters from going home-grown: it's simply cheaper for broadcasters to buy the entrails of television from the West than it is to commission indigenous pro-gramme-makers or encourage a self-sustained music industry. Radio is judged for the speed it serves the latest Eminem, Will Smith or Britney Spears, not for introducing new, local artists. Record shops, magazine stalls and nightclubs are no different, their fodder shaped by the idea that current means playing catchup with the West.

Wayua Muli, a young Nairobi journalist says: "We're not quite sure where we belong, so our greatest influence right now is from the States and from Britain. That's what teaches who we should be."

At the core of this cultural crossfire, Nairobi's blossoming hip hop scene is the most visible example of how young urbanites are latching on to the styles, symbols and language of imported music, television and film. Its genesis, during weekend jam sessions and talent contests in Nairobi's clubs, was simple mimicry: rappers were hailed for their skill as a parrot, not their ability to invent new rhymes and sounds. You had to look and act the part too: baggy jeans, sports shoes, baseball cap and an imitation American accent.

In response, a group of journalists, musicians and television producers in Nairobi is searching for ways to counter the biased flow of pop culture into Kenya.

"What we're trying to do is encourage the young people to maintain the culture and morality that Africa has," says Jimmi Gathu, a television producer who has turned the spotlight on local talent through a string of music shows. This self-conscious attempt to create local icons for young Kenyans to identify with is paralleled by the recent launch of East Africa's first youth culture magazine *PHAT!* The title is an acronym of *Pamoja Hip Afrika Tunawakilisha*, Swahili for "Together we represent hip Africa." "There's never been a

Kenyan musician on the cover of any magazine in the world," says Blaze, assistant editor of *PHAT!* "Talent in Kenya doesn't get a chance to be seen." It hasn't proved easy for the likes of Jimmi Gathu and Blaze to convince financiers, venues and broadcasters to focus on new groups and music made in Kenya. "You'd literally have to pay DJs to play your records," recalls Gathu from his own musician days.

Not until 1995, when artist Poxi Presha released a single *Total Bala* (Total Chaos) in Luo, one of Kenya's 44 ethnic dialects, did people realize the potential of rapping and singing in local languages. *Total Bala* "just hit the country like bushfire," says Bruce Odhiambo, the record's producer. "It crossed all language barriers and people realized they could do it in their mother tongue." A realization that struck a chord with rappers from Nairobi's Eastlands slum estates, who formed the Mau Mau collective—named after Kenya's freedom fighters from the 1950s.

Mau Mau group Kalamashaka's song *Tafsiri Hii*—which means "translate this!"—evoked life in the Nairobi slums and became a major hit. Another Luo act, Gidi Gidi Maji Maji, released their debut album in 2001, *Ismarwa* (It's Ours).

Gidi Gidi Maji Maji researched the album by returning to their home province on the Kenyan shores of Lake Victoria, where they collected Luo myths and sayings, instruments and sounds that defined what Tedd Josiah, the producer of *Ismarwa*, says was a re-statement of identity: "If you're an African there are certain cultures, certain traditions that you've grown up with—our language, our musical styles—and we have to actually go back to those things."

The seeds that a new generation have scattered to define and encourage Kenyan culture are a direct response to the saturation of Western pop culture. *Umbia*, another track on a new compilation of Kenya's rising stars quotes the words of the late President Jomo Kenyatta: "Flare up as the flames of a fire. Consume the nation with your passion. Let the Kenyan culture sing loud and clear, echoing over the hills and ridges."

Adrian Cooper is a filmmaker and writer. In 1989, he worked on images for the documentary *The Forbidden Land*, which examined the growing divisions within the Catholic Church in Brazil. He is presently working on a music festival to help increase awareness of East African music and culture.

1. Response
   a. Study the first and final paragraphs. How are they connected, or how is the theme of the article expressed in each? Then skim the paragraphs in between and trace how the author has led the reader from the introduction to the conclusion.
   b. Why did some of the musicians in Kenya turn to their traditional cultural influences and move away from Western influences?
   c. According to the article, in Kenya's music and TV industry, Western imports dominate the local scene—that is, viewers and listeners experience more Western (American or British) media than local media. Explain why this is so. In your opinion, do Western media also dominate other media—such as radio, newspapers, or magazines?

2. Critical Thinking In small groups, discuss or debate one of the following topics:
   • Globalization threatens/enhances cultures.
   • The media teaches us who we should be.
   • Western influences are bad/good for other nations.

3. Oral Communication *Group Discussion* With a small group, discuss the article, using some of the following questions: What is meant by "the West," in global terms? What countries within these regions would you say hold positions of international power? Which countries' media texts dominate those of other countries? What effect do you think this has on other countries and cultures?

4. Media *Marketing Music* Imagine that, tomorrow, all music from the United States will be banned in Canada. In a group, plan an all-Canadian morning show for a radio station in your area that has a specific teen audience. Develop a sample *playlist*, (a list of the songs the station would play) arrange two interviews with guests, and write a brief mission statement (statement of intent) for your program.
   Alternatively, plan an issue of a new Canadian magazine along the lines of *PHAT!* (the magazine described in the article). Choose a title, design the cover, and list the articles you would include in that issue. Also write a brief mission statement for your magazine.

Drama

Drama assumes an order. If only so that it might have—
by disrupting that order—a way of surprising.

Václav Havel

Duel

Stephen Fry and Hugh Laurie are British comedians. The following script is taken from their comedy show, *Fry and Laurie.*

TV Comedy Sketch
by Stephen Fry and
Hugh Laurie

Hugh and Stephen in period dress (that is, dressed in the garb of seventeenth-century gentlemen) on a misty heath, about to duel. There is a referee, and possibly some seconds. Hugh plays "Sir David" and Stephen plays "Mr Van Hoyle."

REFEREE:	Gentlemen, I believe you both know the purpose of this meeting.
STEPHEN:	Thank you Mr Tollerby, but we have no need of explanation. The circumstances are well known to us.
HUGH:	Quite right. Let us be about the business.
REFEREE:	Very well, gentlemen. Sir David, I understand the choice is yours—sword or pistol?
HUGH:	Sword.
REFEREE:	As you wish.

Hugh takes the sword and swishes it expertly.

HUGH:	Ha. The only weapon for a gentleman.
REFEREE:	Quite so. That means, Mr Van Hoyle, that you have the pistol.
STEPHEN:	Thank you, Tollerby.
REFEREE:	When I give the command, I shall expect …
HUGH:	Wait a minute.
REFEREE:	Is there something wrong, Sir David?
HUGH:	Well …
STEPHEN:	Quick man, the hour grows late …
HUGH:	Well it's just that when you said sword or pistol, I sort of assumed that we would both have the same one, if you know what I mean.
REFEREE:	Ah.

STEPHEN: I'm not with you.

HUGH: Well I said sword, assuming that meant we would both have a sword …

STEPHEN: Oh I see.

REFEREE: Mmm. Thing is, I've only brought one of each, unfortunately.

STEPHEN: Oh damn and blast.

HUGH: Sorry to make a fuss, but it seems a bit unfair otherwise.

REFEREE: No, I take your point, Sir David.

STEPHEN: Well is there somewhere we could get a sword?

HUGH: I doubt there'd be anywhere open at this time … Excuse me!

Hugh dashes off and stops a pair of joggers in dayglo strip.

You wouldn't happen to have a sword on you, would you?

JOGGER: *(Not stopping)* Twenty past seven.

HUGH: Damn.

STEPHEN: Well … we're a bit stuck, really, aren't we?

REFEREE: Gentlemen, I realise that this is a bit of an improvisation, but needs must when the devil …

STEPHEN: Get on with it.

REFEREE: Right, how would it be if Mr Van Hoyle were to take the pistol but promise not to fire it?

HUGH: You mean, use the pistol as if it were a sword?

REFEREE: Exactly.

HUGH: Well, suits me.

STEPHEN: Wait a minute, wait a minute. That's hopeless. Wouldn't cut anything, look.

Stephen prods Referee with the pistol.

See?

HUGH: Perhaps you're right.

REFEREE: Well it was just an idea.

STEPHEN: You could try shooting with your … no, that won't work. Forget I spoke.

HUGH: Mm. How about fists?

REFEREE: You mean boxing?

STEPHEN: Oh Lord no. I'm no good at that at all. It hurts your knuckles.

HUGH: Well, I can't think of anything else … hang on I've got some matches here I think.

STEPHEN:	What, you mean set fire to each other?
HUGH:	Better than nothing. Oh no, actually, look, there's only one match left in fact.
STEPHEN:	We could nip across to that café and see if they have any forks …
REFEREE:	Gentlemen, if you'll bear with me—I have one last idea up my sleeve.
STEPHEN:	Well?

Referee reaches up his sleeve and pulls out a handkerchief.

HUGH:	A handkerchief?
REFEREE:	No, Sir David. *Two* handkerchiefs.
STEPHEN:	You're suggesting that we duel to the death with a pair of handkerchiefs?
REFEREE:	I realise it's not ideal, Mr Van Hoyle, but it would at least be fair …
STEPHEN:	It would take for ever. I've got to be in town by eight.
HUGH:	Well we haven't got anything else.

Stephen sighs.

STEPHEN:	Oh all right then. Better be clean, that's all.
REFEREE:	Perfectly clean, I assure you.

They each take a handkerchief.

Gentlemen, I believe you both know the purpose of this meeting?

Stephen and Hugh start hitting each other with handkerchiefs. ▶

… the theatre demanded of its members stamina, good digestion, the ability to adjust, and a strong sense of humor. There was no discomfort an actor didn't learn to endure. To survive, we had to be horses and we were.

Helen Hayes

Stephen Fry (left) and Hugh Laurie.

Hugh Laurie, born in Oxford, England in 1959, and **Stephen Fry**, born in London, England in 1957, met while attending Cambridge University. Emma Thompson (actor and screenwriter of *Sense and Sensibility*) introduced the two men. Since 1981, Laurie and Fry have been collaborating and performing together. They were both in the movie *Peter's Friends* and appear as Jeeves (Fry) and Wooster (Laurie) in the BBC production, *Jeeves and Wooster.*

1. Response

a. What serious point does this comedy sketch make? Do you think the authors intended to make this point? Explain.

b. How would you describe the humour in this selection? What comic techniques do the authors use?

c. Did you guess the general outcome of this sketch? If so, at what point, and what were the clues that suggested the ending?

d. Do you think you would enjoy the *Fry and Laurie* comedy show? Why or why not?

2. Drama *Voice*

Consider the emotion and emphasis you think the actors would have used in delivering this script. Choose four lines from one character in this selection and read them aloud as you think the actor would have done. Practise reading the lines, experimenting with different tones, expressions, and volumes. Deliver these four lines to an audience and ask for their opinion on the effectiveness of your delivery.

> PERFORMANCE TIP Before any performance, do a few exercises to relax your mind and muscles, and prepare yourself for your audience. Remember also that how you perform a scene not only depends on your interpretation of the author's words and intentions, but also on who your audience is (younger students, parents, peers) and where they are (classroom, auditorium, community centre).

3. Writing *Comedy Sketch*

In a small group, brainstorm ideas for a comedy sketch. Together, choose one idea and write a short script, using this selection as a model. What type of humour will you use? How will you make the script sound natural? Present your comedy sketch to the whole class.

4. Language Conventions *Interjections*

Examine the use of **interjections** in this script and analyse their effect on the reader. Remember to include interjections in the comedy sketch you are creating in activity 3. Note the use of interjections and their effect in other scripts within the unit. Form some conclusions about their use.

> **Interjections** are words—such as *oh, wow, ha, mmm*—that show emotion, often without any grammatical connection to other parts of the sentence.

Can reality programming go too far?

That's
Extraordinary!

One-Act Radio Play by Diana Raznovich

Translated by Rosalind Goldsmith

CHARACTERS

ALICIA	early forties
GASPAR	radio journalist, late twenties
MC	broadcaster, deep, rich voice

SCENE ONE

(SOUND: ALICIA walks, autumn leaves crackling under her feet. She pants as she climbs a hill. Wind in the tops of the trees. ALICIA stops.)

ALICIA: *(Inhales the fresh morning air)* It's nice here. Deserted. This is a good place to say goodbye to the world. Dawn. The rocks look black. The sky so dark and full of clouds. It seems somehow right for me to die under this stormy sky. *(Sings softly, sadly)* Goodbye beautiful clouds! We won't see each other again ... *(Pulls herself up)* Come on, let's not be gloomy at the last minute. *(Tries to be brave)* I'll die laughing! *(Laughs, tries to be cheerful, stops short. Admits to herself)* But ... I'm afraid. That's the truth. Those trees have turned their backs on me. They're hiding, and even the flowers shiver when they see my gun ...

(SOUND: She loads the gun.)

I'm trembling like you, my dear, beautiful red poppies!

(SOUND: She plays with the gun, loading it and unloading it.)

(Laughs anxiously) It's not easy to be the criminal and the victim at the same time! My own executioner ... Alicia's obedient assassin: Alicia. *(Breathes)* I must climb higher.

(SOUND: Stronger wind. ALICIA climbs. She stumbles into an enormous rock, sits on it)

(Out of breath) From up here my own life seems so far away, like someone else's story. *(Sighs)* Pitiful story. At least it could do with a dignified ending.

> *(SOUND: All nature seems to unleash itself. The trees creak and stir in the wind. Dry leaves blown everywhere; continues underneath)*

How much time I've lost in lost causes! I don't blame anybody ... no. They won't even notice when I've gone, since they never noticed me when I was there. *(With irony)* Someone will say: Miss Alicia didn't come today. Today she didn't cross the blue bridge clutching all her papers. Today she didn't eat alone at Joseph's restaurant. Today she didn't talk to her mirror. Today she didn't stay stuck to the telephone waiting for him to call. Today she has missed all her appointments. *(Overcome)* Today ...

> *(SOUND: Wind howls furiously, swish of leaves)*

(Speaks to the wind, her voice battling against the gale) Blow wind! Come on, blow! Take away all my fear! Take away my love—the love I gave to Peter that he never gave to me! Blow white wind and fill me with your rage, your power! Give me all the strength I need to pull this trigger! *(Decided)* I'll count to three and then I'll do it. Then it will all be over for me. One ... two ... two ... two and ... two and ... One, two and— *(Furious with herself)* I can't! I can't!

> *(SOUND: Wind drops. Calms. A gentle breeze, becoming more and more distant. A few birds chirp.)*

And now the wind has stopped! And the sun! The sun's coming out! *(Daunted, frightened)* How am I going to have the courage to say goodbye to the rest of my days in front of that beautiful sun? Oh God! Why do you make things even more difficult for me? Give me back my storm!

SCENE TWO

> *(MUSIC: Theme music of the radio program "That's Extraordinary!"—a catchy upbeat tune breaking the mood of the previous scene)*

MC: *(Professional, enthusiastic, false voice)* Good morning, ladies and gentlemen! And welcome to another morning with your friendly radio! Stay with us for "That's Extraordinary!" The hottest radio program on the international airwaves! *(With the same demagogic tone)* As always, at your service to bring direct into your home: *life itself!* And so ... *(Emphatic, inquisitive)* Isn't death just one side, one facet, we might say, of life?

(MUSIC: Suspenseful)

Because we believe that death is an intimate part of life, we are bringing to you today, direct, live and on location, an actual suicide.

(MUSIC: Well-known march)

Yes, ladies and gentlemen! The extraordinary and more and more extraordinary! Today we present "Suicide on a Hilltop."

(MUSIC: March)

What you have just heard was the fantastic but real testimony of a woman about to kill herself, captured by our secret microphones, especially arranged so that you can enjoy listening to a real suicide in the comfort of your own home.

(MUSIC: Suspenseful)

(In a salesman tone, with professional pride) Our program has stopped at nothing. We've been following Miss "A" for the last eight days, since the time we knew she had decided to take her own life. And now we can present to you, live and direct into your own home: her final words.

(MUSIC: Chords of triumphal march music between each of the following words)

Unique! Unrepeatable! Shocking!

(MUSIC: Suspenseful; builds underneath)

(Speaks invitingly, as if to each listener) She, of course, has no idea about our extraordinary report today. She doesn't know that her final words are being transmitted to thousands and thousands of eager radio listeners. Neither does she know that we have sent our own intrepid reporter, Gaspar Wolf, to the scene to interview her live and on location. Hello Gaspar? Are you there?

SCENE THREE

GASPAR: *(Enthusiastic, close on)* Good morning, William. I'm here, hidden behind some shrubs, and from my vantage point I can see today's interviewee quite clearly—in fact, she's only about a stone's throw away.

MC: We have heard directly her conversations with the wind, the poppies, the sun and God, and I must say it has been stupendous to follow her final emotions at such close range. But our curiosity has no end. Tell us—what does she look like?

GASPAR: *(Syrupy)* She … what does she look like? She's … tall, fair, blue eyes. She's very pale, really … not of this world, white as a sheet … She's been lifting the gun to her head and then … pulling it back. She's wearing a charming suit of autumn shades, she's a woman of about forty … Oh, she has an air about her … she's a classic beauty … But hang on—she's moving her lips, she's … *(Stops himself. ALICIA has done something unexpected.)* Oh!! No!! No!! You can't imagine what I'm seeing, my God! Just a minute! She's lifted the gun to her head with more conviction this time. *(Enthused)* She seems totally decided!! Here we go! She's going to do it!!!

(MUSIC: Suspenseful. Drum roll)

MC: *(Low, intense, like a golf commentator)* You are listening to "That's Extraordinary!"—the program with an impact! And for those of you who may have just joined us, "That's Extraordinary!" presents to you today a person just like yourself or myself, a person who, within a few precious moments, will actually cross over that barrier that separates life from death.

(MUSIC: Triumphal march; continues underneath)

Stay tuned! Don't lose a second! Every second could be the last!

SCENE FOUR

ALICIA: Now … yes. Now I feel ready … I can do it. *(Like a presentiment)* It's like a strange force is pushing me over the edge to the other world—a death-like energy inside me but from somewhere else … *(Forcefully)* One, two and—

GASPAR: *(Interrupts violently, as if sprung from the earth)* Just a minute! Don't do it! Not yet!

ALICIA: *(Terrified)* Who are you? Where did you come from? *(Furious)* Go away! Now! Go on, leave me alone! Don't you realize that this moment belongs to me?

GASPAR: *(Trying to placate her)* Miss, please believe me. It's not my intention to stop you or to dissuade you from your decision. On the contrary …

ALICIA: Get out of here! *(Discovers a mini tape-recorder on GASPAR. Panicked)* Why are you carrying a tape-recorder?

GASPAR: You're carrying a weapon and I haven't asked *you* why.

ALICIA: *(Furious)* A tape-recorder can also be a weapon.

GASPAR: Possibly … but not in my hands. *(Sincerely)* I am a good man. I earn an honest living.

ALICIA: *(Trying to calm herself down and to believe him at the same time)* If you're really a good man, please have consideration and respect for me.

GASPAR: Of course. Just tell me what you need.

ALICIA: *(With complete certainty)* I need to be alone.

SCENE FIVE

(MUSIC: Suspense music, with chords that finalize ALICIA'S last sentence)

MC: Well, dear listeners, we're at a crucial moment. *(Trying with each question to create emotional tension in the audience)* Will Gaspar succeed in his mission? Will he be able to offer us this direct and so-very-human testimony?

(MUSIC: "That's Extraordinary!" theme)

(In a hard-sell, advertising tone) You are listening to "That's Extraordinary!" The most successful radio program on the international airwaves.

(MUSIC: Catchy, upbeat "You have just won …" tune)

And why are we successful? Because we stop at nothing to bring to your ears, raw and untreated, reality itself! At whatever the cost!

(MUSIC: Smooth, romantic melody)

(Suggestively) Alicia needs to be alone. *(Ironically)* She doesn't know that thousands of people are following her every move.

(MUSIC: Suspense music returns)

SCENE SIX

ALICIA: *(Fed up)* Didn't you say you would leave me alone?

GASPAR: *(In a penetrating, sympathetic tone)* You are going to be alone forever. Really alone. What's your hurry? Let me offer you my company … as a friend.

ALICIA: There's no time left for that.

GASPAR: *(Wounded)* But I need you to help me.

ALICIA: *(Beside herself)* You want *me* to help *you*? Why don't you go and ask someone more …

GASPAR: *(Feelingly)* More … what?

ALICIA: More able to help you.

GASPAR: I need *your* help, Alicia.

ALICIA: *(Shocked)* How do you know my name? Who told you my name is Alicia?

GASPAR: *(Seductively)* When someone attracts me, really attracts me I mean, her name suddenly appears to me out of nowhere, as clear and bright as day. From the moment I saw you, I knew your name. I saw you … so distant, so beautiful, lost in the middle of this wood, at the very cliff edge of your own life, and I said to myself: Her name is Alicia.

ALICIA: *(Falling for the flattery for an instant)* Really? Nothing like this has ever happened to me before.

GASPAR: *(Leading her)* Nothing like … what?

ALICIA: *(Moved)* Nothing—magic. That someone could guess my name …

GASPAR: *(Taking advantage of the weak flank she has offered him)* It's not only your name that I can guess, Alicia …

ALICIA: *(Surprised)* What more can you guess?

GASPAR: *(In a carefully controlled, calculated voice)* Your deepest needs.

ALICIA: I don't need anything anymore.

GASPAR: I'm sorry to contradict you, but it seems so very clear to me that you do need something more, that you're asking for something, that you're even … crying out for something …

ALICIA: *(Shocked)* Me? Asking for something? For what?

GASPAR: *(Attempting to touch her in order to get the interview)* Love. Love, Alicia. Love. You are asking me for love.

> We are all actors now … Everyone in America now explains a moment in their lives by saying, "It was like a scene out of…"
>
> Peggy Noonan

SCENE SEVEN

(MUSIC: Romantic, something worn out and in bad taste;
continues underneath)

MC: *(Enthusiastic)* Yes! Oh yes! Now our own reporter Gaspar Wolf is really showing us how to reach the human soul. *(Demagogic)* I have tears in my eyes, and if my voice breaks … *(His voice breaks)* it's because *(With difficulty, as if about to cry)* I'm thinking of her, of Alicia. I can picture her enormous aquatic eyes mooring themselves in the penetrating gaze of Gaspar Wolf. His will be the last pair of eyes that she will see—the last pair of eyes that will look at her.

(MUSIC: Ends)

SCENE EIGHT

ALICIA: Why are you talking to me about love, now? I've looked for love all my life. Now I need to be alone, by myself.

GASPAR: *(Almost in secret)* Love cures all ills.

ALICIA: It's late … too late …

GASPAR: Give me a chance. *(Insistent)* Give yourself a chance.

ALICIA: A chance for what?

GASPAR: I want to do … an interview with you … before … before … you abandon us forever.

ALICIA: *(Bewildered)* An interview? With me? And who's going to be interested in this interview?

GASPAR: Lots of people, Alicia.

ALICIA: I don't understand …

GASPAR: You … could tell the world … what it feels like before you die. And since all of us are going to die sooner or later … who wouldn't be interested?

ALICIA: But what good is it to me to do an interview that won't come out until after I'm dead?

GASPAR: It will be for the good of humanity.

ALICIA: I have already said goodbye to humanity.

GASPAR: And above all it will be for the good of my family.

ALICIA: Your family?

GASPAR: *(Pathetic)* An interview like this could help us ... financially.

ALICIA: I don't understand.

GASPAR: Excuse my ... presumption, but you are in a position to do something really—an interview with someone who's about to take her own life—it's very original ... They would pay me very well for it, and that would help my family to get out of the financial mess that we're in. It would mean my children could eat ...

ALICIA: Your children are hungry?

GASPAR: *(Nervously)* Well, you see, I don't have any work right now. Well—actually—to be honest, it's been quite a while since I've had any work, since I've sold even a word.

SCENE NINE

(MUSIC: "That's Extraordinary!" theme)

MC: Extraordinary strategy of our reporter, Gaspar Wolf! He's demonstrating to us the techniques of the shrewd and clever journalist, the modern journalist without prejudice or fear ... Will he pull off this final interview with Alicia by pretending to be a poor, unemployed father?

(MUSIC: Suspenseful; building)

Stay tuned to "That's Extraordinary!" The program that investigates humanity in the service of humanity!

(MUSIC: Theme music)

SCENE TEN

GASPAR: Well, now I've confessed to you *my* tragedy. *(Snivelling)* Only you can help me, Alicia. But it's true you have no reason to help me. You have already broken free from the chains of reality. Why should you bother about me? You have every right to throw me out, to insult me ... *(Pitifully)* You could damn me to hell, Alicia, and I would understand perfectly.

ALICIA: Look, I—

GASPAR: *(False tears)* Yes?

ALICIA: I … never …

GASPAR: Do you want me to leave right now?

ALICIA: *(Confused, anxious)* Don't cry. Please don't cry, sir.

GASPAR: *(Cries)* It's nothing. It'll pass. Excuse my insolence. I'm going now.

ALICIA: I … look, don't go … I can do it … in a few minutes. I'll do the interview. At least my death will feed your children.

SCENE ELEVEN

(MUSIC: Happy, triumphant)

MC: *(As if GASPAR has scored a goal)* He scores! He scores! Our own Gaspar Wolf has broken through the defences of the unassailable Alicia, yes he has! Wonderful effectiveness in the approach, gentlemen, don't you think? This great offensive move on the part of our man means that we can now present to you a world première. Yes, for the first time anywhere in the world, ladies and gentlemen, an interview with a suicide a mere instant before her departure to the other world.

(MUSIC: Sports march)

Alicia leaves this world, valiant and resolute. And we will respect her unquestionable will. All we want is to be secret witnesses to her final confessions.

(MUSIC: Nostalgic, "We'll meet again"; continues underneath)

Alicia is not alone. Our white handkerchiefs are fluttering in the wind in gestures of: Farewell.

(SOUND/MUSIC: "Farewell" echoes and fades; harps, in bad taste)

We are like secret spies on her private journey of no return. Silent, hidden behind our radios large or small, you and I are the privileged witnesses to the unfolding of this final tragedy, while she, of course, is completely unaware of our presence.

(MUSIC: More intense, sentimental, nostalgic; continues underneath)

She is an unknown, an anonymous being from the anonymous city. But we have come to say goodbye. And although she doesn't know it, we have come to accompany her.

(MUSIC: Well-known children's tune; continues underneath)

Alicia too was once a little girl ... She too frolicked in the park with her little friends, surely unaware of what life had prepared for her.

(MUSIC: Children singing a well-known tune)

(Exploitingly) An innocent little girl who pranced about among the poppies, the same poppies that today bid her farewell.

(MUSIC: Sudden loud rock music; continues underneath)

And then Alicia became an adolescent. An adolescent who danced, happy and carefree, just like you ... or me, to the beat of rock and roll.

(MUSIC: Romantic Bolero music; continues underneath)

Until one day Alicia, also just like you or me, found love. The first love. The first kiss. *(Hums along with the music)* And perhaps it was then that she also came to know her first pain ...

(SOUND: Radio sound effect, intense rain; continues underneath)

Surely it was raining. And Alicia was walking in that rain, without her umbrella, thinking of him.

(MUSIC: "Singing in the Rain")

Then, one day, a day like any other day, it stopped raining. And Alicia, hardly realizing, began to laugh.

(SOUND: Radio sound effect, youthful, fun-loving laughter)

Whatever became of that youthful laughter? Who shattered it?

(SOUND: Radio sound effect, broken glass)

Who was it that suddenly slammed the door?

(SOUND: Radio sound effect, violent door slam)

Who was it that left her yet again in absolute and devastating solitude?

(SOUND: Radio sound effect, car starts, accelerates, screeches away)

Who? When? How was she brought to this final ending?

(MUSIC: "That's Extraordinary!" theme)

But enough of fantasies. Let's listen to the real Alicia.

(MUSIC: Soft music)

Let's hear what she herself has to say ...

SCENE TWELVE

(SOUND: Birds singing in the trees)

ALICIA: Well, what would you like to know, sir?

GASPAR: I was just listening to the birds singing and it seemed to me that their song was dedicated to you.

(SOUND: Singing and chattering of birds intensifies)

ALICIA: It's true. They're marvellous … with their feathers of all colours and their brilliant beaks … the way they fly. Look at that one perched on the top branch.

(SOUND: Happy cheeping of one bird)

If only I could perch on the highest branch and take to the air, flying towards the immense sky …

GASPAR: Have you ever tried?

ALICIA: Yes, I have tried.

(SOUND: Chattering of birds)

I have tried but I didn't get very far. And whenever I stopped to sing on the branches, usually I could only come out with a sort of "twip, twip," an insipid sound, not very joyful—or graceful for that matter. And most of the time the branch I was sitting on would break anyway, and I'd come crashing down to the ground.

(SOUND: Singing of birds intensifies)

They sing as if life were worth living … They sing innocently because they don't know anything about loneliness.

(SOUND: One bird sings alone, marvellously)

Can you hear that? That one sings better than the rest. He's a real virtuoso. *(Whistles to the bird, hoping for an answer)*

(SOUND: The bird answers, imitating Alicia exactly)

He heard me! He's answering me! *(Whistles again, this time a more complicated melody)*

(SOUND: The bird repeats the new tune)

GASPAR: He heard you! He is answering you!

ALICIA: Yes! I've made a friend! *(To the bird)* Let's see if you can do this tune. *(Whistles with more variations)*

(SOUND: The bird replies with exactly the same tune)

Oh! This is really incredible! What have I done all my life that I never paid any attention to the birds? Why did I have to come to this extreme before I could even notice how beautiful, how generous nature is?

(SOUND: Now the bird suggests a tune)

He's talking to me. Excuse me. I should reply. *(Whistles what the bird has just whistled)*

(SOUND: The bird speaks to her intently and at length)

Oh! I think I understand what the bird is saying to me.

GASPAR: *(Impatient)* You and I were going to have a little conversation.

ALICIA: I'm sorry, it's just that at the last minute I'm discovering things I never dreamed of. I've been deaf, dumb and blind all my life. I'm just beginning to realize how lazy I've been, how I've—

GASPAR: Do we do this interview?

ALICIA: Wouldn't it be better to listen to the birds?

(SOUND: A real uproar from all the birds, a riot of happy singing)

GASPAR: *(Fed up)* I didn't come here to listen to the birds sing, Miss.

ALICIA: I didn't either. But suddenly—

GASPAR: Let's just leave the little birdies aside …

ALICIA: Why?

GASPAR: What do you mean, why? You haven't come to this crucial point in your life just to amuse yourself with the singing of little birds. You came here to commit suicide. To commit suicide! Or have you forgotten?

ALICIA: I don't know …

GASPAR: What do you mean, you don't know?

ALICIA: Maybe I came here to discover the song of the birds.

GASPAR: That's not possible.

ALICIA: Everything's possible. *(Whistles to the birds)*

(SOUND: The birds answer her)

Do you hear them? They're talking to me. And do you know what they're saying?

GASPAR: They're saying that every person has an obligation to fulfil her destiny.

ALICIA: They're saying that life is worth the trouble …

(SOUND: Uproar of birds)

GASPAR: You're not seeing things clearly.

ALICIA: They're telling me to try again, not to be a coward, to wake up and live. Can you hear them? They're saying that life is always a risk … that to run away from this world is cowardice. That's what those birds are telling me.

(SOUND: Chattering of birds)

GASPAR: *(Losing control)* Enough of the stupid birds! Shut up! They're driving me crazy! I hate them!!

SCENE THIRTEEN

(MUSIC: "That's Extraordinary!" theme)

MC: *(Covering his anxiety)* It's all going according to plan, ladies and gentlemen. Our beloved Alicia has been deeply moved by the sweet singing of the birds, and this can only mean that in a little while she too will take to the air and fly, fly just like one of those little birds …

(MUSIC: Nostalgic)

One more bird among the thousands of birds that cross the night in glorious flight. She will fly … she will fly so high … and perhaps she will even reach the very source of light. Perhaps, from way up there, she will be able to see all of us, strolling through life … and perhaps she will even send us a sign so that we can recognize her.

(MUSIC: Vivaldi's "Gloria"; continues underneath)

She is ready to begin her flight. Her delicate wings have already begun to flutter. She is preparing herself for that eternal ascension …

SCENE FOURTEEN

ALICIA: You seem bothered, sir. What's the matter? It's not the birds, is it?

GASPAR: *(Trying to control his rage)* I was alone with you. Nobody was listening to us. It was like we were in our own glass bubble. And suddenly the place fills up with birds, talking birds, birds that talk to you. Look. You and I know that birds don't talk. You and I know that they chirp and that you are only hearing what you would like to hear.

ALICIA: Don't tell me you're jealous!

GASPAR: *(Romantic)* Very jealous.

ALICIA: *(Laughs)* Jealous of the birds?

GASPAR: Jealous of the birds.

ALICIA: They are asking me to live. And you?

GASPAR: I am not a bird.

ALICIA: Yes, I know that.

GASPAR: I am asking you to talk to me before you die.

ALICIA: To talk …

GASPAR: Yes, Alicia. I am asking you to talk to me in private before being silenced forever.

ALICIA: Of course. I understand. You want to appropriate my final words, isn't that right?

GASPAR: *(Implacable)* Good. I see you do understand. Speak to me, Alicia …

ALICIA: What do you want me to talk about? *(Lucid and ferocious)* You want me to entertain you with my romantic failures? Fine. The man I loved left me for my best friend. And now do you want to know about my personal frustrations? I wanted to be a dancer and I'm nothing. Do you know the taste, the smell of Nothing? Anything else? I have an alcoholic father who used to beat up my mother—who's paralysed. Is that the kind of news that sells?

GASPAR: Now we're on the right track, Alicia. It's the track of human beings, not birds, dear. So. Your father used to beat your mother?

ALICIA: And not only my mother, but my brothers and sisters too, and me. Are you taping? Is this what you want from me?

GASPAR: Yes, yes. I'm taping. Go on.

ALICIA: What else do you want to know?

GASPAR: Why did you come to this extreme, wanting to take your own life?

ALICIA: Because I didn't have birds around me …

(SOUND: Cheering of birds)

GASPAR: That's nonsense!

ALICIA: And because I was alone and confused … confused like I am now when I look at you.

GASPAR: I'm not confusing you.

ALICIA: You could tell me the same thing that the birds are telling me … Now … right now … if …

GASPAR: Alicia, we are human beings.

ALICIA: *(Desperate)* Say something … Please. Don't leave me alone!

GASPAR: Fine. I say goodbye and good luck.

ALICIA: *(Very anxious)* That's all?

GASPAR: Now it's your turn to say goodbye.

ALICIA: Will a shot in the head sell? Is that what you're longing for?

GASPAR: *(Panicked)* Look, there's no need to point that gun at me.

ALICIA: *(Decided)* Now you answer me. The reason you don't want to help me to live is because you don't want to lose this interview. It's business, isn't it?

GASPAR: Put the gun down. We are civilized people. I didn't come here to die. I came here to—

ALICIA: To see me die! You want me to put the gun to my head, am I right? *(Sudden)* Who sent you? Who do you work for? Answer me or I'll kill you!

GASPAR: It's not my fault! It wasn't my idea! I work for the radio program "That's Extraordinary!" It's the truth, I swear.

ALICIA: "That's Extraordinary!"? You mean thousands of people are listening to this!? You mean that all that stuff about the humble, unemployed journalist was a lie?

(SOUND: A shot)

GASPAR: My God! Help! She wants to kill me!

(SOUND: Two shots)

ALICIA: Run away! Run away, coward!

(SOUND: One shot)

Coward! You can't even stand up to me. You want to sell my death for a good price! Well, I'm not going to give you the pleasure! I'm going to follow the birds' advice.

(SOUND: Happy cheering from the birds)

I'm going to take a gamble on life …

(SOUND: Cheering of birds)

Alicia is going to dare to start over again! Attention, audience of "That's Extraordinary!", wherever you are … *(To herself)* I suppose there are microphones hidden around here somewhere …

(SOUND: Rustling of leaves, bushes)

No one's going to make a circus out of my death! Do you hear? I'm throwing away this gun! I'm going to live! I'm sorry to have to disappoint the morbid, bloodthirsty audience …

(SOUND: Rustling of bushes, very close on)

I know my life is no good for business, for this sinister program directed by—

GASPAR: *(Secretly, whispering)* Hello, sound? Cut. Sound, cut. Cut the—

ALICIA: Aha! There it is! Give me that microphone! Give it to me! Attention, all of you in the audience of—

GASPAR: Sound—cut cut cut!! Hey—

(SOUND: Grunts, rustling, etc. A scuffle, very close on, over the microphone; continues underneath)

GASPAR: Don't you—give me that mike right now. Give me that!!

ALICIA: No I won't!!

(SOUND: Scuffling)

SCENE FIFTEEN

(SOUND: Radio interference, static)

MC: There seems to be ... uh ... some interference on the line, ladies and gentlemen. Regrettably we are forced to interrupt our transmission.

(MUSIC/SOUND: Static. "That's Extraordinary!" theme, sped up. Chattering of birds as on location. Sound is picked up again. Static, then:)

GASPAR: *(Struggling)* Would you give that to me? It's not yours, it's mine.

ALICIA: I want to talk to the audience. I want to tell them—

GASPAR: Shut up! Just shut up! Cut the sound! Cut cut cut cut cut—

(MUSIC/SOUND: Theme music, a few bars, static)

ALICIA: I'm alive! You can't gag me! I'm alive!

(SOUND: They scuffle, close on over mike)

Give me that earphone! I want to hear what they're saying!

(MUSIC: Theme established)

MC: And so, ladies and gentlemen, we have saved a life today! And is this not perhaps the mission of a humanitarian program such as our own?

(SOUND: Static)

ALICIA: Criminals! Liars!

(SOUND: Static)

GASPAR: Cut cut cut!

(SOUND: Static)

MC: We're not actually hearing Alicia very well just now, but we know that she's grateful. We have a few technical problems, uh ... as I mentioned before there seems to be some kind of interference in our transmission. But doubtless if she could Alicia would want to say thank you to us all.

Drama of Trees by Robin Holtom. Oil.

Examine the painting above and consider its mood, style, techniques, and message. With a small group, discuss why it has been chosen to accompany this script.

There is no better indication of what the people of any period are like than the plays they go to see.

Edith Hamilton

(MUSIC: Triumphal march)

This has certainly been an unforeseen conclusion to our program today ... Marvellous! Alicia, grateful, deeply moved, is perhaps even now on her knees blessing "That's Extraordinary!" for saving her life ... And I must say it is wonderful to be able to do some good in this world, even from our own modest and humble program, "That's Extraordinary!"—the hottest radio program on the international airwaves! Until next week, friends!

(MUSIC: "That's Extraordinary!" theme)

Diana Raznovich was born in Buenos Aires, Argentina, in 1945. She published her first book of poetry by the age of 16. Because of the military regime, she left Argentina in 1976 and now lives in Spain. She is an internationally renowned playwright. This play aired on CBC Radio.

I. *Response*
a. Setting plays an important role in this selection. Discuss how the setting affects the action.
b. How is Gaspar's character different from that of Alicia? Which of these two characters earns the sympathy of the audience? Explain.
c. Do you think the ending is effective? Explain your answer.
d. Analyse the radio techniques and special effects the author has included, and assess their effect and effectiveness.

2. *Critical Thinking* This play deals with the sensitive subject of suicide in a humorous manner. Poll your classmates to see how many people think the subject matter and its treatment are or are not appropriate. Present these results in a bar graph. Along with the bar graph, write a paragraph in which you explain and analyse the results.

3. **Drama** *Satire* This play can be called a *satire*. What does it satirize? Is the satire effective? Share your findings with a partner. Discuss other examples of satires—plays, TV shows, novels, or poems. What do you like or dislike about satires in general? What might be difficult about performing a satire? With a small group, prepare a presentation of your favourite scene from this satire.

PERFORMANCE TIP Some comic scenes are funny to both the actors and the audience, while others could be described as *accidentally funny*—the audience might laugh at what happens to the characters, but the characters have to play the scene seriously. Consider how this advice applies to the scene you are presenting in this satire.

4. **Media** *Reality TV* This radio play is based on the idea of reality programming. Imagine that you work for a TV station that wants to come up with a new concept for a reality program. Write a memo to a studio executive in which you outline your idea. Include the advantages, as well as any possible drawbacks, to your idea. Assess the effectiveness and clarity of your proposal.

5. **Visual Communication** *Art Therapy* Reread this script, noting its use of symbols (birds, guns, trees, et cetera). Choose one of these symbols and create or find an image that depicts what the symbol represents in the script. Discuss your image with three or more classmates.

Theme Connections

The following script contains the opening scenes from the movie
Sense and Sensibility. Note that, in this selection, the structure is
different from stage plays and other selections you have already read.
As you read, refer to the abbreviations below
to help you understand the screenplay.

The Dashwoods' Fate Is Decided

an excerpt from the screenplay
for *Sense and Sensibility*
by Emma Thompson
(from the novel by Jane Austen)

ABBREVIATIONS

CAM	camera	EXT	exterior
cont.	continued	INT	interior
CU	close-up	POV	point of view
ECU	extreme close-up	V/O	voice over
EVE	evening		

0 EXT. OPEN ROADS. NIGHT. TITLE SEQUENCE.
*A series of travelling shots. A well-dressed, pompous-looking individual (JOHN
DASHWOOD, 35) is making an urgent journey on horseback. He looks anxious.*

1 EXT. NORLAND PARK. ENGLAND. MARCH 1800. NIGHT.
*Silence. Norland Park, a large country house built in the early part of the eight-
eenth century, lies in the moonlit parkland.*

2 INT. NORLAND PARK. MR DASHWOOD'S BEDROOM. NIGHT.
*In the dim light shed by candles we see a bed in which a MAN (MR DASH-
WOOD, 52) lies—his skin waxy, his breathing laboured. Around him two sil-
houettes move and murmur, their clothing susurrating in the deathly hush.
DOCTORS. A WOMAN (MRS DASHWOOD, 50) sits by his side, holding his
hand, her eyes never leaving his face.*

MR DASHWOOD: *(urgent)* Is John not yet arrived?

MRS DASHWOOD: We expect him at any moment, dearest.

(*MR DASHWOOD looks anguished.*)

MR DASHWOOD: The girls—I have left so little.

Mrs Dashwood: Shh, hush, Henry.

Mr Dashwood: Elinor will try to look after you all, but make sure she finds a good husband. The men are such noodles hereabouts, little wonder none has pleased her.

(They smile at each other. Mrs Dashwood is just managing to conceal her fear and grief.)

Mrs Dashwood: But Marianne is sure to find her storybook hero.

Mr Dashwood: A romantic poet with flashing eyes and empty pockets?

Mrs Dashwood: As long as she loves him, whoever he is.

Mr Dashwood: Margaret will go to sea and become a pirate so we need not concern ourselves with her.

(Mrs Dashwood tries to laugh but it emerges as a sob. An older MANSERVANT [Thomas] now enters, anxiety written on every feature.)

Thomas: Your son has arrived from London, sir.

(Mr Dashwood squeezes his wife's hand.)

Mr Dashwood: Let me speak to John alone.

(She nods quickly and he smiles at her with infinite tenderness.)

Mr Dashwood: Ah, my dear. How happy you have made me.

(Mrs Dashwood makes a superhuman effort and smiles back. She allows Thomas to help her out. She passes John Dashwood as he enters, presses his hand, but cannot speak. John takes her place by the bed.)

John: Father . . .

(Mr Dashwood summons his last ounces of energy and starts to whisper with desperate intensity.)

Mr Dashwood: John—you will find out soon enough from my will that the estate of Norland was left to me in such a way as prevents me from dividing it between my families.

(John blinks. He cannot quite take it in.)

John: Calm yourself, Father. This is not good for you—

(But Mr Dashwood continues with even greater determination.)

Mr Dashwood: Norland in its entirety is therefore yours by law and I am happy for you and Fanny.

(JOHN looks torn between genuine distress and unexpected delight.)

MR DASHWOOD: But your stepmother—my wife—and daughters are left with only five hundred pounds a year, barely enough to live on and nothing for the girls' dowries. You must help them.

(JOHN's face is a picture of conflicting emotions. Behind them is an ominous rustling of parchments.)

JOHN: Of course—

MR DASHWOOD: You must promise to do this.

(A brief moment of sincerity overcomes JOHN'S natural hypocrisy.)

JOHN: I promise, Father, I promise.

(MR DASHWOOD seems relieved. Suddenly his breathing changes. JOHN looks alarmed. He rises and we hear him going to find the DOCTOR.)

Still from *Sense and Sensibility* with (from left to right) Kate Winslet, Gemma Jones, Emilie Francois, and Emma Thompson.

Examine the costumes and set in the above still. Use Internet sources to access other stills from *Sense and Sensibility*, or view the movie. In small groups, discuss the costumes and set, and the challenges in producing a movie set in an earlier time period.

JOHN: Come! Come quickly!

(But it is we who share the dying man's last words.)

MR DASHWOOD: Help them …

3 EXT. JOHN AND FANNY'S TOWN HOUSE. LONDON. DAY.
Outside the house sits a very-well-to-do carriage. Behind it waits another open carriage upon which servants are laying trunks and boxes.

FANNY: *(V/O)* 'Help them?'

4 INT. JOHN AND FANNY'S TOWN HOUSE. DRESSING ROOM. DAY.
JOHN is standing in mourning clothes and a travelling cape. He is watching, and obviously waiting for, a pert WOMAN (FANNY DASHWOOD) who is standing by a mirror looking at him keenly.

FANNY: What do you mean, 'help them'?

JOHN: Dearest, I mean to give them three thousand pounds.

(FANNY goes very still. JOHN gets nervous.)

JOHN: The interest will provide them with a little extra income. Such a gift will certainly discharge my promise to my father.

(FANNY slowly turns back to the mirror.)

FANNY: Oh, without question! More than amply …

JOHN: One had rather, on such occasions, do too much than too little.
(A pause as FANNY turns and looks at him again.)

JOHN: Of course, he did not stipulate a particular sum …

5 INT. LAUNDRY. NORLAND PARK. DAY.
A red-eyed MAID (BETSY) plunges a beautiful muslin frock into a vat of black dye.

6 INT. NORLAND PARK. MRS DASHWOOD'S BEDROOM. DAY.
MRS DASHWOOD is rushing about, mourning ribbons flapping, putting her knick-knacks into a small valise. The room is in chaos. A young WOMAN (ELINOR DASHWOOD) looks on helplessly.

MRS DASHWOOD: To be reduced to the condition of visitor in my own home! It is not to be borne, Elinor!

ELINOR: Consider, Mamma! We have nowhere to go.

MRS DASHWOOD: John and Fanny will descend from London at any moment, followed no doubt by cartloads of relatives ready to turn us out of our rooms one by one—do you expect me to be here to welcome them? Vultures!

(She suddenly collapses into a chair and bursts into tears.)

ELINOR: I shall start making inquires for a new house at once. Until then we must try to bear their coming.

7 INT. JOHN AND FANNY'S CARRIAGE. DAY.
JOHN and FANNY are on their way out of London.

JOHN: Fifteen hundred then. What say you to fifteen hundred?

FANNY: What brother on earth would do half so much for his real sisters—let alone half-blood?

JOHN: They can hardly expect more.

FANNY: There's no knowing what they expect. The question is, what can you afford?

8 INT. NORLAND PARK. DRAWING ROOM. DAY.
A beautiful young WOMAN (MARIANNE DASHWOOD) is sitting at the piano playing a particularly sad piece. ELINOR enters.

ELINOR: Marianne, cannot you play something else? Mamma has been weeping since breakfast.

(MARIANNE stops, turns the pages of her music book and starts playing something equally lugubrious.)

ELINOR: I meant something less mournful, dearest.

9 EXT. ROADSIDE INN. DAY.
JOHN and FANNY are waiting as the OSTLERS make the final adjustments to their carriage. The LANDLORD hovers, waiting for a tip.

JOHN: A hundred pounds a year to their mother while she lives. Would that be more advisable? It is better than parting with the fifteen hundred all at once.

(He displays some coins in his hand. FANNY removes one and nods.)

FANNY: But if she should live longer than fifteen years we would be completely taken in. People always live forever when there is an annuity to be paid them.

(JOHN gives the coins to the LANDLORD.)

10 EXT. NORLAND PARK. MARGARET'S TREE-HOUSE. DAY.
ELINOR comes to the foot of a large tree from which a small staircase issues.

ELINOR: Margaret, are you there? Please come down. John and Fanny will be here soon.

(A pause. ELINOR is about to leave when a disembodied and truculent young voice stops her.)

MARGARET: *(V/O)* Why are they coming to live at Norland? They already have a house in London.

ELINOR: Because houses go from father to son, dearest—not from father to daughter. It is the law.

(Silence. ELINOR tries another tack.)

ELINOR: If you come inside, we could play with your atlas.

MARGARET: *(V/O)* It's not my atlas any more. It's their atlas.

(CLOSE on ELINOR as she ponders the truth of this statement.)

11 INT. JOHN AND FANNY'S CARRIAGE. DAY.
JOHN and FANNY joggle on.

JOHN: Twenty pounds now and then will amply discharge my promise, you are quite right.

FANNY: Indeed. Although to say the truth, I am convinced within myself that your father had no idea of your giving them money.

JOHN: They will have five hundred a year amongst them as it is—

FANNY: —and what on earth can four women want for more than that? Their housekeeping will be nothing at all—they will have no carriage, no horses, hardly any servants and will keep no company. Only conceive how comfortable they will be!

12 INT. NORLAND PARK. SERVANTS' HALL. DAY.
The large contingent of SERVANTS who staff Norland Park are gathered in gloomy silence as ELINOR addresses them.

> There are people, who the more you do for them, the less they will do for themselves.
>
> Jane Austen

ELINOR: As you know, we are looking for a new home. When we leave we shall be able to retain only Thomas and Betsy.

(CAM holds on THOMAS and BETSY, a capable woman.)

ELINOR: *(cont.)* We are very sorry to have to leave you all. But we are certain you will find the new Mrs Dashwood a fair and generous mistress.

13 EXT. NORLAND PARK. DRIVE. DAY.
JOHN and FANNY's carriage approaches Norland.

FANNY: *(V/O)* They will be much more able to give *you* something.

14 INT. JOHN AND FANNY'S CARRIAGE. DAY.
JOHN and FANNY are about to get out.

JOHN: So—we are agreed. No money—but the occasional gift of game and fish in season will be very welcome.

FANNY: Your father would be proud of you.

1. Response
a. Explain the relationships of each character to the others within the screenplay. Note the textual clues that reveal the types of relationships existing between the characters. Use a diagram or family tree to show how each character mentioned is related to the others. Discuss what the script reveals about each character.

b. In this opening segment of the screenplay, which characters do you think will be liked or disliked by the audience? In small groups, discuss your reactions to each character. Did each member of the group respond in the same way to the same characters?

c. What conflict is established in the opening scenes of this script? How do you think this conflict will be resolved?

d. The authors of this anthology chose the title "The Dashwoods' Fate Is Decided" for this excerpt. What do you think of this title? What else might this excerpt be called?

e. With a small group, discuss the tone of this selection and how that tone is established. Is the language the author uses appropriate for the setting? Explain.

f. List any words from the selection that you found unusual and develop definitions for them.

2. *Film Study* Watch the movie *Sense and Sensibility*. Does reading this screenplay add to your appreciation of the movie? Share your thoughts with your classmates.

3. *Drama* *Characterization and Conflict* Review your answers to 1.a, 1.b, and 1.c. With a small group, improvise a future scene between four of the main characters to perform for another group. Your scene should reflect the conflict and characters of the initial scenes in this movie. Make sure that your improvisation scene introduces or explains the conflict, and that the characters are then engaged in the conflict until some resolution is reached. Discuss the process of improvisation and the challenges of performing spontaneously.

> PERFORMANCE TIP Remember that conflict between characters is the basis for most action and the centre of the plot. Characters in conflict often want different things, so keep in mind what *you* want, as you perform. Actors in conflict act and react to one another, so consider how you will react to others as they voice what they want. Also remember that the personalities of the characters will be wrapped up in what they want, how they act, and how they react.

4. *Making Connections* Read the first three chapters of Jane Austen's *Sense and Sensibility*. In your opinion, did Emma Thompson successfully capture the tone of the novel and the essence of the characters? Explain.

5. *Language Conventions* *Abbreviations* Note the use of abbreviations throughout the screenplay. How do these help the reader? Is the use of abbreviations distracting at all? Explain. What reading strategies helped you read and understand this selection?

   Develop another scene for this screenplay using abbreviations, your understanding of the characters and their relationships, and your ideas from question 1.c.

Theme Connections

- *"Transients in Arcadia," a story in which characters worry about money, page 37*
- *"A Pair of Silk Stockings," a story in which a character worries about money, page 86*
- *"The Making of Sense and Sensibility," a diary that details part of the process of creating this script, page 364*

Discuss what you know about Stephen Leacock,
his writing style, and the time period
in which he lived.

The Raft

An Interlude

Burlesque Act by
Stephen Leacock

(The kind of interlude that is sandwiched in for fifteen minutes between the dances in a musical review.)

(The curtain rises and the light comes on the stage slowly, gradually revealing a raft in the middle of the sea. The dawn is breaking. The raft has the stub of a mast sticking up on it and there is a chair on it and a litter of boxes and things. On the raft is A MAN. He has on white flannel trousers, and a sky-blue flannel shirt, but no collar and tie. He stands up and looks all around the horizon, his hand shading his eyes. He speaks in a sepulchral voice.)

"Lost! Lost! Alone on the Caribbean Sea." *(In a more commonplace voice)* "At least I think it's the Caribbean. It looks Caribbean to me. Lost! And not a woman in sight ... I thought that in this kind of thing there is always a woman. Ha! Wait! There's one!"

(He is much excited and gets a long spy-glass and shoots it in and out at different lengths, searching the sea.)

"No!—it's only seaweed ... Ba!"

(He goes and sits down on a chair and yawns.)

"I call this kind of thing dull! There's really nothing to do."

(He gets a box of shoe polish and starts to polish his shoes with a rag. Presently—)

"I think I'll look around for a woman again. It really is the only thing to do, on a raft—or anywhere else."

It is to be noticed that this piece is all ready to put on the stage. Actors anxious for dramatic rights may apply by telegraph or on foot.

(He takes his spy-glass and looks again.)

"By Jove! Yes! Yes! There's one floating in the sea right there. Quick! Quick!"

(In great excitement he runs over to the mast, where a little looking-glass hangs, and starts putting on a collar and tie, and brushing his hair in terrible haste … He can't find his collar-stud, etc., etc., and keeps muttering—)

"I must keep calm—a woman's life depends on my getting this collar on."

(He looks over his shoulder.)

"She's floating nearer—"

(In the light of the rising sun THE GIRL *is now seen floating nearer and nearer.)*

"—and nearer—and she's a peach … I *must* save her! I must plunge in after her."

(He stands in the attitude of a person about to dive into the sea, swinging his arms and counting.)

"One—two—*three*—" *(nearly dives but checks himself and goes on)* "four—five—SIX … Ah, I forgot! I've no swimming costume … Wait a bit, though!"

(He picks up off the raft a long, long pole with a hook on the end.)

"Ha!"

(THE GIRL is quite near now. He hooks her on the pole and hauls her on to the raft … She sinks down flat on it, inanimate, her eyes closed, her face to the audience. Note: THE GIRL *of course is not wet: that would only mess the act up.)*

"What next? Ah, one moment."

(He runs over to a little bookshelf that is stuck up on the top of the mast, takes out a book, sits down in a chair, and reads aloud very deliberately.)

"'Rules for re—for, re-sus—for resuscitating the Damned—the Drowned: In resuscitating the drowned it must be remembered that not a moment must be lost.'"

(He settles himself more comfortably in his chair to get a better light to read by.)

"'Every minute is of vital—of vital'—humph, I must get my eye glass."

(He goes and hunts it up, polishes it and continues—)

"'Of vital importance. First, it is necessary to ascertain whether the heart is still beating.'—Ah!"

(He gets off his chair and on to the floor of the raft on his toes and hands, makes the motions of attempting to put his ear close down on THE GIRL'S *heart, but keeps withdrawing it with sudden shyness.)*

"Stop a bit."

(He goes and gets a cardboard box and takes out a stethoscope so long that, still standing up, he fixes it to his ears and it reaches THE GIRL'S *body. He listens and counts, his head on one side and with an air of great absorption.)*

"One."

(A long pause)

"One and a half."

(Another pause)

"One—eighty-five—right! She's alive!"

(He gets his book again and reads.)

"'The strength of the circulation being different in the male and the female sex, the first thing to do if the victim is a woman is to rub her— to rub her—'"

(He finds it difficult to read, and says conclusively—)

"The first thing to do is to rubber. Oh, yes I see: Now where shall I begin? I'll rub her hands."

(He takes one of her hands and strokes it very slowly in long loving strokes. After a moment he plucks at the lace cuff at her wrist.)

"Ah, a laundry mark! her name! I must read. Her life hangs on it. 'Edith Croydon!' What a beautiful name!"

(He goes on stroking her hand.)

"It doesn't seem to revive her. Oh, very well, there's nothing for it."

(He stands up with an air of great determination, and rolls back his cuffs.)

> Good drama must be drastic.
>
> Friedrich von Schlegel

"I must rub her legs."

(THE GIRL starts up.)

"Don't you dare! You're no gentleman!"

"Miss Croydon, you misunderstand my motives!"

(He walks away in a huff to the extreme end of the raft and stands with his back turned. THE GIRL meantime runs to the mirror and starts doing her hair, etc.)

"And for the matter of that, I *am* a gentleman. You'll find my card hanging there beside the mirror."

(THE GIRL picks down a large card that hangs beside the mirror and reads aloud.)

"'Harold Borus, Story Tale Adventurer, Rafts, Rescues and Other Specialities, Hairbreadth Escapes Shaved to Order.' Oh, Mr. Borus, I'm so sorry! Of course I know all about you—everybody does! I must apologize. Do come back to this part of the raft. Forgive me."

(BORUS, coming back, and taking her hand with emotion)

"Miss Croydon, there is nothing to forgive! If I have saved your life, forget it. Let us never speak of it. Think of me not as a hero, but only as a man!"

"I will!"

"And meantime, please make yourself comfortable. Do take this chair. The entire raft, I need hardly say, is at your disposition. You'll find the view from the east side most interesting."

"Thank you so much."

(They make themselves comfortable and intimate, she on the chair, he on the soap-box, with elaborate gestures of politeness.)

"And do tell me, Mr. Borus, how did you get here?"

"Very gladly. You won't mind if I begin at the beginning?"

"Must you?"

"It's usual ..."

"Oh, all right."

"Well then—" *(striking an attitude of recitation)* "Little did I think—"

"No, I suppose not."

"—when I left Havana in a packet—"

"Oh, Mr. Borus, who put you in a packet?"

"—in a packet-boat, that I should be wrecked on the dry Tortugas."

(THE GIRL, clasping her hands with agitation)

"The *Dry* Tortugas! Oh, Mr. Borus, have the Tortugas gone dry?"

"We had hardly left when a great storm arose … A monstrous wave carried away the bridge."

"Good heavens!"

"We struggled on. A second wave carried away the rudder, the propeller, the wireless apparatus and the stethoscope!"

"Great heavens!"

"We struggled on. A third wave carried away the bar. It was at once decided to abandon the ship and lower the boats."

(THE GIRL, perplexed)

"But why?"

"To look for the bar … In the confusion I was left behind. The storm subsided. I continued to make a raft out of a few loose iron beams fastened together by nuts."

"Fastened by nuts, Mr. Borus, but I thought you were the only one left in the ship?"

"—by nuts. This raft, Miss Croydon, cannot sink, it is all made of iron."

"How splendid! And now let me tell you my adventures."

"No, no, don't trouble, please. You're exhausted! Don't—you might faint!"

"Looking back" *(THE GIRL goes on very dramatically)* "it all seems a blank."

(BORUS, very hurriedly)

"All right, it's a blank. It's a blank. Let it go at that."

"Mr. Borus, I think you're terribly rude. You might let *me* tell *my* adventures!"

"Miss Croydon" *(very seriously)* "how many heroes are there in any story of adventure?"

"Only one."

"Well, I'm *it*. You must be something else."

(MISS CROYDON *pettishly*)

"I don't want to be. All I know is that I'm cold and I'm hungry, and I don't think that I'll stay!"

"Cold! Hungry!"

(He gets up and starts running round with animation, making preparations.)

"Cold! Ha! ha! I'll soon have a fire for you!"

"A fire, Mr. Borus, how can you possibly start a fire?"

(BORUS *laughs*.)

"A very simple matter, Miss Croydon, to a trained hero like myself."

(He has picked up an empty pan and set it on a box.)

"I do it simply with sticks rubbed together."

"By rubbing dry sticks together! How wonderful you are."

"I am."

(He picks up two or three very little dry twigs.)

"I take the dry sticks, *so*—"

"Yes! Yes!"

"And first rub them together, *so*—"

"Yes! Yes!"

"With a sort of twisting motion."

"Yes! Yes!"

"Then I put them in the pan with a bit of paper, *so*—" *(he takes out a matchbox as he speaks)* "and strike a match and light them."

(He lights the paper and the twigs and they blaze up in a little flame.
EDITH CROYDON and BORUS warm their hands at it; she speaks.)

"How really wonderful!"

"Yes. It's the Peruvian method! And now for food and drink."

(The little fire presently flickers out, and has nothing more to do with the act.)

"Have you food and drink on the raft, Mr. Borus? I think you are simply superb."

"I am. Now let me see." *(He starts taking things out of a box.)* "What have we here? Tinned pâté de foie gras."

"Lovely!"

"Canned asparagus. Do you like canned asparagus?"

"Oh, I worship it."

"Tin of boneless pheasant."

"Oh, Mr. Borus, I'm just mad over boneless pheasant!"

> *(BORUS, taking out the cans and reading the labels,*
> *with exclamations from THE GIRL—)*

"Boneless pheasant—finless fish—spineless sardines—tongueless tongue—now what shall it be first?"

> *(BORUS with great empressement has just laid a little white cloth*
> *on a soap-box, and quickly spread out glasses and dishes and knives*
> *and forks till it has the appearance of an appetizing preparation.*
> *They both accompany it with exclamations of interest and delight.*
> *MISS CROYDON says)*

"Let me see. I think I'd like first, pâté de foie gras and finless fish, and just a teeny bit of shell-less lobster—and—and—"

> *(When suddenly BORUS has sprung to his feet with a sort of howl)*

"Oh, Mr. Borus, what is it?"

> *(BORUS, casting his hands to heaven—)*

"I haven't got—I haven't got—"

"Yes—yes—"

"I forgot—"

"Yes—yes—you forgot—"

"The can opener! Great heavens, we have no can opener!"

(THE GIRL exclaims—) "No can opener!" *(and falls forward on the table.)*

(BORUS):

"Stop! Wake up! I can open them!"

(He makes a wild attack on the tins, beating them, and stamping on them, and biting them, etc., etc. Presently he subsides in despair and collapses on the soap-box.)

"It's no good, Miss Croydon. We must eat the tins. You eat first. You are a woman."

"No, Mr. Borus, not yet. We can at least" *(she speaks with tragedy)* "we can at least drink. Let us drink before we die."

"You are right. We can drink before we die. It is more than a lot of people can do."

(He recovers something of his animation and begins taking out bottles and setting them on the table.)

"There! Bottled ale. Bass's bottled ale!"

"Oh, Mr. Borus, how divine! I just worship Bass's bottled ale."

"Now then, get your glass ready."

"Right."

(Then he leaps up again with a howl.)

"What is it, Mr. Borus—Oh, what is it?"

"The thing—the thing you open it with! I haven't got one!"

(They both collapse, BORUS slightly recovering, but gloomily):

"There's a way of opening these bottles with a fifty-cent piece ..." *(feeling in his pocket)* "but I haven't got a fifty-cent piece."

(MISS CROYDON, brightly)

"Oh, never mind, I think I have a dollar bill in my purse."

(Business here of trying to open the bottle by holding a dollar bill over it. At last BORUS says):

"It's no good, Miss Croydon. We must resign ourselves to our fate. If we must die" *(he takes a noble attitude)* "you are a woman. Die first!"

(There is a sadness and then MISS CROYDON says):

"Mr. Borus, it's getting dark."

(BORUS looks up at the sky.)

"Yes, the sun will soon set."

"Already, Mr. Borus?"

"Yes, Miss Croydon. Night comes quickly in the tropics. Look, the sun is setting."

(The sun, seen as a round, red disk at the back of the stage, begins to set in jumps, about a yard at a time. When it has got near the bottom it takes a long whirl up again and then goes under. The stage is half dark.)

BORUS: "It is night!"

"Night! Here on the raft? Oh, I mustn't stay."

"Miss Croydon, I intend to treat you with the chivalry of a hero. One moment."

(BORUS takes an oar and sticks it up, and takes a big gray blanket and fastens it across the raft like a partition, so as to divide the raft in two.)

"Miss Croydon" *(says BORUS, looking over the top of the blanket)* "that end of the raft is absolutely *yours*."

"How chivalrous you are!"

"Not at all. I shall not intrude upon you in any way. Good-night."

"Good-night, Mr. Borus."

(They each begin making preparations for sleep, one each side of the curtain. BORUS stands up and puts his head over again.)

"You'll find a candle and matches near your bed."

"Oh, thank you, Mr. Borus, how noble you are."

"Not at all."

(After another little interlude BORUS puts his head over the top again.)

"I am now putting my head over this blanket for the last time. If there is anything you want, say so now. And remember if you want anything in the night do not hesitate to call me. I shall be here—at any moment. I promise it. Good-night."

"Good-night, Mr. Borus."

(They settle down in the growing darkness for a few minutes as if falling asleep. Then all of a sudden a bright light, a searchlight, comes shining over the sea, full on the raft. They both start up.)

"Oh, Mr. Borus, look, look, a light—a ship!!"

BORUS: "A light—a ship! They may have a corkscrew! We're saved. Look—it's a large yacht—a pleasure yacht."

(There are voices heard.)

"Raft, Ahoy!" *(and shouts)*

MISS CROYDON: "A pleasure yacht! Oh, then I recognize it!"

"You recognize it?"

"It's the yacht I fell out of this morning."

"Fell out of—"

"Yes. You wouldn't let me tell you …"

(There is a call across the water.)

"Raft ahoy! Stand by! We're lowering a boat."

BORUS: "Saved! Saved! But there is just one thing I want to say before we go aboard … Miss Croydon—Edith—since I've been on this raft I've learned to love you as I never could have anywhere else. Edith, will you be my wife?"

(MISS CROYDON, falling into his arms):

"Will I? Oh, Harold, that's what I fell out of the yacht for!"

(Curtain)

Dr. Stephen Butler Leacock was born in England in 1869 and immigrated to Canada with his parents in 1876. Although Leacock was a distinguished professor in the economics and political science department of McGill University, he is best known for his more than 60 books, particularly his humorous works. This great Canadian, who was considered the world's best-selling humorist during his lifetime, died in 1944.

1. Response

  a. Which of the two characters appeals to you more? Explain.

  b. What makes this play a **burlesque**? Is it successful as a burlesque? Share your responses in a class discussion.

A **burlesque** is a literary or dramatic composition in which a serious subject is treated ridiculously or with mock seriousness.

  c. Did you find the ending of this play predictable? If so, explain what clues allowed you to predict the ending accurately.

2. Drama *Performing Burlesque* With a small group, discuss how this burlesque might be presented and any challenges there might be in presenting it. How could these challenges be overcome? Work together to prepare a presentation of this script.

PERFORMANCE TIP Prepare for your performance by considering the gestures and movements you will make. Note that, in burlesque, the actions and emotions of the characters may be exaggerated. How will you use gestures, facial expressions, and movement to portray the emotions of the characters effectively? Practise displaying various emotions in front of a mirror.

3. Focus on Context *The Raft* was originally written in 1923. If this play were written today, how would it be different? What would account for these differences? Discuss these questions in small groups.

4. Language Conventions *Standard Structure* This play can be difficult to follow because Leacock has not used a conventional script structure. What has he done instead? Why might he have done so? Imagine you are planning to direct this show and you want to make the script easier for your actors to read. Do this by taking half a page of dialogue and writing it like a typical script. Use other scripts from this unit as models.

5. Making Connections With a partner, role-play a conversation between Borus from this selection and Aunt Bev from *Venus Sucked In*. Consider how the setting of each play and the time period in which it was written affect the characters' attitudes, actions, and beliefs. Which character do you find it easier to identify with? Why?

Just prior to the following excerpt, Cyrano arrived at a play and threatened a performer who offended him—Montfleury. Montfleury was halted just as he began to recite the opening lines of a play called *La Clorise* by Baro. This excerpt opens with the audience's reaction to Cyrano's actions and arrogance.

Introducing
Cyrano

AN EXCERPT FROM THE STAGE PLAY
CYRANO DE BERGERAC
FROM ACT 1, SCENE IV

by Edmond Rostand

CHARACTERS

YOUNG MAN
CYRANO
OLD BURGHER (business man)
LADY INTELLECTUALS
BELLEROSE (actor)
CROWD
JODELET (actor)
LE BRET (friend of Cyrano)
MEDDLER

YOUNG MAN: *(To Cyrano)* Tell me, sir, what reason do you have to hate Montfleury?

CYRANO: *(Graciously, still seated)* I have two reasons, my callow young friend, either of which would be sufficient. The first is that he's a deplorable actor who brays like an ass and wrestles ponderously with lines that ought to soar lightly from his lips. The second—is my secret.

OLD BURGHER: *(Behind him)* But you're high-handedly depriving us of *La Clorise*! I insist …

CYRANO: *(Respectfully, turning his chair toward the BURGHER)* Sir, your pigheadedness can't change the fact that old Baro's verse is worthless. I feel no remorse at having deprived you of trash.

LADY INTELLECTUALS: *(In the boxes)* Oh!—Our Baro!—My dear, it's ... How dare he!—Such insolence!

CYRANO: *(Gallantly, turning his chair toward the boxes)* Fair ladies, blossom and be radiant, fill our dreams with longing, soften death with a smile, inspire poetry—but don't judge it!

BELLEROSE: What about the money that will have to be refunded?

CYRANO: *(Turning his chair toward the stage)* Now there's the first sensible thing that's yet been said! Far be it from me to impose hardship on practitioners of the Thespian art. *(Stands up and throws a bag onto the stage.)* Here, take this purse and be quiet.

CROWD: *(Astonished)* Ah!—Oh!

JODELET: *(Quickly picking up the purse and weighing it in his hand)* At this price, sir, I'll be glad to have you come and stop our performance every day!

CROWD: Boo! Boo!

JODELET: Even if we must all be booed together!

BELLEROSE: Please clear the hall!

JODELET: Everyone out, please! *(The spectators begin leaving while CYRANO watches with satisfaction, but they soon stop when they hear the following scene. The ladies in the boxes, who have already stood up and put on their cloaks, stop to listen, and finally sit down again.)*

LE BRET: *(To CYRANO)* This is madness!

MEDDLER: *(Who has approached CYRANO)* What a scandal! Montfleury, the great actor! Don't you know he's protected by the Duke de Candale? Do you have a patron?

CYRANO: No!

MEDDLER: You don't have a ...

CYRANO: No!

MEDDLER: What? You have no great lord whose name protects ...

CYRANO: *(Annoyed)* For the third time, no! Must I say it a fourth? I don't rely on some remote patron for protection. *(Puts his hand to his sword.)* My protector is always near at hand.

MEDDLER: Are you going to leave the city?

CYRANO: That depends.

MEDDLER: But the Duke de Candale has a long arm!

CYRANO: Not as long as mine … *(Pointing to his sword)* … when I give it this extension!

MEDDLER: But surely you wouldn't dare …

CYRANO: I would.

MEDDLER: But …

CYRANO: Go now.

MEDDLER: But …

CYRANO: Go! Or tell me why you're looking at my nose.

MEDDLER: *(Petrified)* I …

CYRANO: *(Moving toward him)* Do you find it surprising?

MEDDLER: *(Stepping back)* You're mistaken, my lord …

CYRANO: Is it limp and dangling, like an elephant's trunk?

MEDDLER: *(Stepping back again)* I didn't …

CYRANO: Or hooked like an owl's beak?

MEDDLER: I …

CYRANO: Do you see a wart at the end of it?

MEDDLER: I …

CYRANO: Or a fly walking on it? What's unusual about it?

MEDDLER: Nothing, I …

CYRANO: Is it a startling sight?

MEDDLER: Sir, I've been careful not to look at it!

CYRANO: Would you please tell me why?

MEDDLER: I was …

CYRANO: Does it disgust you?

MEDDLER: Sir …

CYRANO: Does its color seem unhealthy to you?

MEDDLER: Sir!

A mold is used to make a mask of Cyrano de Bergerac's nose for
a performance of the Royal Ballet.

CYRANO: Is its shape obscene?

MEDDLER: Not at all!

CYRANO: Then why that disdainful expression? Do you find it, perhaps, a little too large?

MEDDLER: *(Stammering)* Oh, no, it's quite small ... very small ... diminutive ...

CYRANO: What! How dare you accuse me of anything so ridiculous? A small nose? *My* nose? You've gone too far!

MEDDLER: Please, sir, I ...

CYRANO: My nose is *enormous*, you snub-nosed, flat-faced wretch! I carry it with pride, because a big nose is a sign of affability, kindness, courtesy, wit, generosity, and courage. I have all those qualities, but you can never hope to have any of them, since the ignoble face that my hand is about to meet above your collar ... *(Slaps him. The MEDDLER cries out in pain.)* ... has no more glory, nobility, poetry, quaintness, vivacity, or grandeur—no more *nose*, in short—than the face that my boot ... *(Turns him around by the shoulders)* ... is about to meet below your waist! *(Kicks him)*

French dramatist **Edmond Rostand** was born in 1868 in Marseilles, France, and died during a widespread influenza epidemic in 1918. He is best known for his play *Cyrano de Bergerac*, written in 1897. Other plays include *The Romancers* and *Chantecler*.

1. *Response*
   a. In this segment of the play, Cyrano does not reveal his second reason for hating Montfleury. With a partner, speculate on Cyrano's second reason.
   b. How would you describe Cyrano's actions? How would you describe the reactions of those around him?
   c. Reread the description Cyrano gives of himself at the end of this selection. Would you agree with the qualities that Cyrano ascribes to himself? Explain.
   d. What do you think the author intended with this scene? Why would he have chosen to introduce Cyrano to his audience in this way?

2. **Drama** *Dialogue* This selection is an excellent example of dialogue. It might best be delivered in a *rapid-fire style* (delivered at high speed, with no pauses; very forceful on the part of Cyrano and timid on the part of the Meddler, with constant interruptions). With a partner, practise the exchange between the Meddler and Cyrano. Take turns assuming either role. In your opinion, which role is more challenging? Why? Reflect on other performances you have done during this unit. What did you learn about performing with others? Do you find it difficult? What strategies might help you work together to develop a unified performance?

> PERFORMANCE TIP When performing a scene, it is important to consider its context: When and where does it take place? What does the place look or feel like? What are the characters doing in this place? Where do the characters come from? What were the characters just doing? What will the characters do next? How much do the characters know? How much does the audience know? Reflect on these questions as you perform the scene between the Meddler and Cyrano.

3. **Focus on Context** With a small group, discuss the play and what you know of the whole story of *Cyrano de Bergerac*. Do you think this was a suitable excerpt to take from the play? Was the introductory text sufficient to help you understand the excerpt? Does the excerpt effectively introduce the character of Cyrano? Explain. To answer these questions, research this play on the Internet or by using print resources, if necessary.

4. **Language Conventions** *Imperative Voice* Examine how most of Cyrano's lines are phrased—short, emphatic commands in an imperative voice or mood. How does Rostand juxtapose the speech of others against Cyrano's lines? What effect does this have? How does the imperative voice help develop the reader's perceptions of Cyrano's character?

5. **Film Study** Several movies have been made based on this script. Investigate these movies using Internet or print resources. In a small group, discuss how you could use the story of Cyrano and give it a new slant for a twenty-first century audience. Develop a proposal for your movie, including notes about setting, costumes, actors, genre, and target audience.

Four women—all related—one small apartment

Venus Sucked In

A Post-Feminist Comedy

One-Act Radio Play by Anne Chislett

CHARACTERS

KATHY	sixteen
LIZ	Kathy's mother, forty-five
BETTY	Kathy's grandmother, sixty-seven
BEV	Kathy's aunt, thirty-seven

The play takes place in real time. We follow Kathy throughout. Everyone else is "on" or "off" in keeping with their spatial relationship to her. Fortunately, the apartment is small, with the entrance directly into the living room and the kitchen close by. The apartment is in a large, ordinary highrise in mid-town Toronto.

SCENE ONE
(Fantasy/speech)
(MUSIC: JOAN Baez, "Diamonds and Rust.")

(SOUND: Mike is raised. KATHY clears her throat. She adopts a public-speaking mode: quite natural and informal but with a touch of projection, opening up to an imaginary audience. She improvises the speech, sometimes with revisions and asides to herself.)

KATHY: *(Internal. Public address)* "Modern Women." Some modern women have deliberately decided to live in the world's crummiest apartment. Take my mother, for instance. If she had set out to find the place I would most absolutely hate to move in to, she couldn't have done better than this building. Her excuse is that it's in our old neighbourhood, and I'm still going to the same school. That's so I won't have *two* traumas to cope with. Well, if walking out of a perfectly good marriage and a perfectly great house were really going to make my mom into the greatest female artist since … *(Shrug)* I don't know who, uh … whom … ruining all our lives might be worthwhile. But as it is, the whole situation is just totally embarrassing. Like this afternoon, on the way back from the movie, Janet—she's my best friend—asked to come in so we could work on our speeches. I had to tell her that Sunday is now my mother's designated day for painting, and this apartment is so small her easel takes up our whole living room. I can't even have anybody in my room, because the walls are too thin. You see, on Sunday …

LIZ: *(Way off)* Kath?

KATHY: *(Internal. Public address)* … nothing, but nothing, is allowed to disturb Mom's concentration.

LIZ: *(Off)* Kath?

KATHY: *(To herself)* Wait a minute … how come the easel's covered up?

SCENE TWO
(Living room)

LIZ: *(Coming on)* Kathy, I asked you to get me a coat hanger.

KATHY: Sorry. I didn't hear you. *(SOUND: Closet door opens, coat hangers, plastic and wire; continues underneath)*

LIZ: What were you doing? Talking to yourself?

KATHY: Of course not.

LIZ: Your lips were moving.

KATHY: I was practising my public speaking. *(Passing hanger)* Here.

LIZ: Oh, not plastic. A wire one. I want to straighten it out. *(SOUND: Rummaging through more coat hangers)*

KATHY: Are coat hangers a new painting technique or something?

LIZ: Don't be sarcastic.

KATHY: I wasn't.

LIZ: Then don't be silly. *(Going off)* Come in the kitchen for a minute, will you?

SCENE THREE
(Small kitchen)

KATHY: Mom, I kinda need to work on my speech.

LIZ: *(Coming on as KATHY nears her)* Well, I kinda need you to hold the flashlight. *(Her voice becomes muffled as she sticks her head inside a dishwasher.)* Shine it in there where the hose connects.

KATHY: What are you looking for?
(SOUND: A coat hanger being poked into dishwasher's orifices. LIZ'S voice shows the strain of arm and neck stretching.)

LIZ: Whatever's clogging this thing.

KATHY: Yech.

LIZ: Yech is right. The dishes are dirtier than when I put them in.

KATHY: Is this going to take long? *(SOUND: Clinks and clanks; continues intermittently)*

LIZ: I hope not. *(Sounds of effort as she digs at clog)* So … are you going to win the contest again this year?

KATHY: Not with the topic I got stuck with.

LIZ: What is it?

KATHY: "Modern Women." I can't think of a single angle that hasn't been used a million times.

LIZ: You could talk about the sexism girls your age run into.

KATHY: I don't run into any.

LIZ: Sure you do. You must. *(SOUND: Clinks stop. Dishwasher door closes)*

KATHY: Not as far as I know.

LIZ: Give the dial a spin. *(SOUND: Dial turns. Mechanical sputter)*
Darn.
(SOUND: Dishwasher door opens. Clinks and clanks; continues underneath)
What about career choices? What if you want to be an engineer?

KATHY: I don't.

LIZ: But if you did … I can tell you I'd worry. *(Idea)* Hey, how about gun control? There's a feminist issue for you.

KATHY: The topic is "women," not "feminism." I want it to be upbeat.

LIZ: Well … we're sure to have more women prime ministers in future.

KATHY: I'd have a better chance with something that lets me smile a lot.

LIZ: Why? *(Outrage on the rise)* Are the boys expected to smile?

KATHY: *(Declining the challenge)* Look, thanks for trying to help, okay?

LIZ: No! It's not okay. Do boys look for topics that let them smile?

KATHY: How should I know! Mom, I have to be ready for the assembly tomorrow.

LIZ: Oh, Kathy. Why do you always leave assignments till the night before?

KATHY: I've been practising since Friday.

LIZ: Where? At the movies or at the skating rink?

KATHY: You were the one who suggested I call Janet.
(SOUND: Dishwasher door closes underneath)

LIZ: Because your father disappointed you. I'd have saved my sympathy if I'd known you had a speech to write.

KATHY: I don't "write" it, Mom. I prepare it, like … in my mind.

LIZ: In your mind?

KATHY: Yeah. It has to sound spontaneous, so I practise by making up stuff about whatever occurs to me.
(SOUND: Dial turns. Mechanical sputter)
So it doesn't really matter if I'm at a movie or at my desk.
(SOUND: Dishwasher door opens)

LIZ: Good. Then it won't matter if you're at the sink, washing dishes by hand.
(SOUND: Dishes taken from dishwasher to sink; continues underneath)

KATHY: What do we need dishes for? Aren't we sending out for pizza?

LIZ: There's been a change of plans.

KATHY: How come?

LIZ: Your Aunt Bev phoned while you were out. She invited herself to dinner.

KATHY: Oh, great!

LIZ: For you, maybe. I'd just mixed my paints.

KATHY: You could have said no.

LIZ: Well, she said she has some news …

KATHY: Why didn't she tell you on the phone?

LIZ: She wanted to see me in person. *(Beat)* All right, so I'm a sucker. I couldn't bring myself to say no.

KATHY: You still don't have to cook. Aunt Bev likes pizza.

LIZ: But it is Sunday. And I thought it wouldn't be much trouble to thaw a few chicken breasts.
(SOUND: Water taps turned on, water running; continues underneath)
That was before I discovered there wasn't a clean pot or pan in the kitchen.

KATHY: *(Hesitant)* Mom? …

LIZ: What?

KATHY: Maybe … if you called Dad, he'd come over and fix the dishwasher?

LIZ: *(Dismissive)* Come on, Kath, pick up a tea towel.

KATHY: He's probably finished at his office by now …

LIZ: Oh, don't be silly.

KATHY: I bet he could have that thing working in five minutes flat. *(SOUND: Taps turned off)*

LIZ: Kathy, you want to know about modern women? I'll tell you about modern women. They've ended up alone at forty-five in rotten cheap apartments, with rotten lazy superintendents. They've been brought up to believe they are utterly hopeless when confronted with a mechanical problem. But modern women are going to learn to make it on their own! They will wash every dish in the city of Toronto before they will ever again trade their personal integrity for some jerk who knows how to repair appliances.

KATHY: Cute, Mom. *(SOUND: Aggressive dishwashing; continues underneath)* Except I think the principal would dock me for false generalization.

LIZ: The principal is a man, naturally.

KATHY: No, she's a woman. It's just no big deal with her.

LIZ: What's no big deal?

KATHY: She doesn't think men are all jerks. And she's not paranoid about them trying to keep her in chains, either.

LIZ: I'm paranoid? Is that what you're saying?

KATHY: Well … I mean … maybe some men did try to keep your generation down.

LIZ: Maybe?

KATHY: Yeah, but the principal's younger, so her attitude is more "now."

LIZ: What do you mean "now"?

KATHY: You know, more like Aunt Bev's than like yours.

LIZ: *(Flaring)* Really! Then you should ask your Aunt Bev for help, shouldn't you? *(SOUND: Dishwashing fades out)*

SCENE FOUR
(Fantasy/speech)

KATHY: *(Internal)* Sisters. *(Public address)* "Modern Women and their Sisters." Have you ever seen that Bell Canada commercial? The one where this girl calls her sister because she needs a soft shoulder? Well, those two girls are definitely not my Mom and Aunt Bev. I figure it's because Mom is jealous. You see, Aunt Bev has her "personal integrity," which in my mother's mind means her chosen career, whereas Mom wasted fifteen years doing graphic art just to make money. She says that was Dad's fault because he insisted on a middle-class lifestyle. Except now, without him, she has to waste even *more* time on commercial stuff to pay the rent. The thing is—Aunt Bev makes twice as much money at her journalism, *and* she's got a great guy too. Sam not only does his share of the housework, he makes all their meals, on top of bringing her a long-stem rose every day. In other words, he's exactly the kind of guy Mom wanted my dad to be. But the weird thing is—Mom is always down on Aunt Bev for putting her own desires before anyone else's ... which is exactly why Mom walked out on Dad—so she could do the same herself. Not that she does. In fact, my mom can find more reasons not to do what she says she wants than anybody I ever heard of. *(To herself. Idea)* Hey ... maybe ... I could make a really fun speech about her totally screwed-up behaviour. Yeah ... like ... my mother says her art is going to be a priority in her life ... that is unless ... let's see ...

SCENE FIVE
(Kitchen)
(SOUND: Dishwashing fades back up; continues underneath)

KATHY: So, Mom, how much painting did you get done today?

LIZ: I told you. I hadn't touched the canvas when the phone rang ...

KATHY: *(Internal. Public address. Following her train of thought)* Unless the phone rings. *(SOUND: Apartment intercom buzzer; off)*

LIZ: What are you mouthing?

KATHY: That's the buzzer.

LIZ: Not already. Get it, will you? *(SOUND: Dishwashing noises recede)*

SCENE SIX
(Entrance way/living room)
(SOUND: Apartment intercom buzzer)

KATHY: *(Presses "Talk")* Who is it?

BETTY: *(Through intercom)* The Queen of England.

KATHY: Mom, what's Granny doing here? *(SOUND: Apartment intercom buzzer)*

LIZ: *(Coming on)* For heaven's sake, press the door button.

KATHY: *(To intercom)* You have to wait for the middle elevator. *(To LIZ)* Did she phone and invite herself too?

LIZ: I phoned her.

KATHY: I see.

LIZ: I thought if I was cooking for you and Bev ... I might as well cook for Mother.

KATHY: Mom, do you realize we've been here two months and you haven't finished one single picture?

LIZ: I would have today … if the dishwasher hadn't screwed up.

KATHY: I guess dishwashers want to keep women in chains too.

LIZ: That's a very snide remark.

KATHY: Well, you always blame Dad for not letting you paint. It seems to me *(Quoting)* "the problem is simply your own lack of commitment."

LIZ: Is that what your father told you?

KATHY: I mean, look at this afternoon …

LIZ: Yes, look at it! Who is supposed to take you out of my hair on Sunday?

KATHY: It's not Dad's fault he had to work.

LIZ: Kathy, I will not tolerate any quotations from that jerk about my lack of commitment, understand!

KATHY: What makes you think Dad said it?

LIZ: You didn't come up with an idea like that by yourself. If it wasn't your father, who was it?

KATHY: If you must know, it was Aunt Bev.
(SOUND: Knock on apartment door; off)

LIZ: *(Taken aback)* Bev told you I lacked commitment?

KATHY: I heard her tell Gran …

LIZ: Now come on. You're making that up.
(SOUND: Knock on apartment door)

KATHY: Here's Gran. Since you don't believe me—

LIZ: *(Overlapping)* Kathy!

KATHY: … you can ask her yourself.

LIZ: *(Overlapping)* Kathy!
(SOUND: Door opens)

KATHY: Hi, Gran. Mom wants to—

LIZ: *(Overlapping)* Don't you dare!

BETTY: *(Off)* Elizabeth, what's wrong?

LIZ: Nothing, Mother. Come in.
(SOUND: Door closes underneath)

BETTY: *(Moving on)* I could hear you two shouting since I left the elevator.

LIZ: We were having a discussion. The door is paper thin.

BETTY: Yes, I suppose. *(To KATHY)* Kathy, I'm surprised to see you home on a weekend.

KATHY: Dad had a computer crash.

BETTY: *(Judgemental)* I see.

KATHY: *(Defensive)* Well, he couldn't help it.

LIZ: Come and sit down, Mother. I'll move my easel …
(SOUND: Easel moved underneath)

BETTY: Oh, are you trying to paint again?

LIZ: What do you mean "trying"?

BETTY: *(Beat)* Trying to find time, of course. May I see it?

LIZ: *(Defensive)* No! *(Recovering)* Not yet. Not until it's finished. Open the closet door, Kath.

BETTY: Beverly and Sam aren't here yet?
(SOUND: Closet door opens. Rattle of coat hangers as easel is put in; continues underneath)

LIZ: Actually … Sam had to go see his father. He's back in hospital.

BETTY: I was wondering why Beverly was honouring us with her presence.

LIZ: *(Laughing)* You couldn't expect her to cook her own dinner. Speaking of which … I'd better get to it.

BETTY: May I give you a hand?

LIZ: No, no … you and Kathy have a chat.

KATHY: Mom, I need to work on my speech.

LIZ: Perhaps your grandmother can help you.

KATHY: It's about modern women, remember?

LIZ: Kathy!

BETTY: Never mind. *(Moving off)* I'm going to inspect your balcony for a bit.

LIZ: Mother, you haven't been here three seconds.

BETTY: *(Off)* Yes, but I couldn't smoke in the cab either.
(SOUND: Standard apartment balcony door opens. Hum of city noise, very low. Door closes)

LIZ: For Pete's sake, Kath, your speech has waited this long. Go out and try to be nice *(Moving off)* for a change.

KATHY: In a minute, okay?

SCENE SEVEN
(Fantasy/speech)

KATHY: *(Internal)* Anyway, where was I? Oh, yeah. *(Public address)* "Women's Confusing Behaviour." Teachers always tell us to talk about what we know, and the woman I know best is my mother. Well, I find the way she acts very confusing. She says her art is important, but not as important as answering the phone, fixing the dishwasher, or making dinner. Like today with Aunt Bev … Mom could have told her she was busy. I mean, I understood since I was a kid, if Dad has to work, he has to work, and there's no sense whining about it. I have to admit I didn't mind Mom being there. But it's like Dad says … if you want something you have to go get it. I guess the point is … well … if women want to—no.

If modern women want to get ahead in the world, I mean if they want to make it as artists or something, then they better not act like my mom. They should act like my dad instead. *(To herself)* Not bad ... but it's kinda ... it's a downer.

SCENE EIGHT
(Living room)

LIZ: *(Off)* Kathy!

KATHY: I'm on my way.
(SOUND: Balcony door opens. Hum of city noise; continues underneath)
SCENE NINE
(Balcony. Flick of cigarette lighter)

KATHY: Gran, are you on your *second* cigarette already?

BETTY: *(Puffs)* If it bothers you, feel free to go inside.

KATHY: *(Ironic)* Great view, eh? If you like parking lots.

BETTY: Perhaps your mother will find a nicer neighbourhood. *(Puffs)* When your house is finally sold.

KATHY: Dad says if Mom forces him to sell in today's market, we won't even cover the mortgage.

BETTY: Kathy *(Beat)* shouldn't you be working on your speech?

KATHY: Well ... *(Becoming intimate)* I'm sort of making one up about Mom, but ...
(SOUND: Balcony door closes. City noise continues underneath)

Gran, do you believe Mom has a chance of becoming famous?

BETTY: Well, she was "quite well known" once. She even had a one-woman show.

KATHY: Oh, that. *(Meaning ancient history)* That was before I was born.

BETTY: Really? What a coincidence.

KATHY: *(Takes point)* Okay, Gran. But women with commitment manage to have kids *and* a career. That is, if they have talent too.

BETTY: I think your mother has talent.

KATHY: *(Very intimate)* Go take a peek at that canvas in the closet ... just take a peek.

BETTY: I wouldn't dream of doing such a thing without permission!

KATHY: Gran, it's gross, really gross. The whole canvas is this nude woman ... being swallowed by an oyster!

BETTY: *Rising* from the oyster, surely. Like *Venus Rising?*

KATHY: No ... she's being swallowed ... the body is all stretched out and her mouth is open like she's screaming. Believe me, nobody, but nobody in their right mind is ever going to buy it.

BETTY: I'm not an expert in

modern art, and I doubt if you are either.

KATHY: Gran, please … listen, for Mom's own good, don't you think you should have a talk with her … you know … about the divorce?

BETTY: Kathy, I'm hardly in a position to give anyone advice.

KATHY: But you're her mother!

BETTY: I know I am. That's why she has to invite me over on Sunday afternoons. Now, if you've nothing more to say, I'm going back inside.
(SOUND: Balcony door opens. City noise continues for a moment, then fades)

SCENE TEN
(Fantasy/speech)

KATHY: *(Internal. Public address)* "Modern Grandmothers." Modern grandmothers aren't what they're supposed to be. They aren't grey-haired, they aren't

loving, and they're no help to their granddaughters at all. *(To herself)* Boy, is that ever a dead end.
(SOUND: Apartment buzzer; off. Hum of city noise comes up underneath)
Maybe Aunt Bev … if I can get her alone … *(Calling to LIZ)* It's okay, Mom. I'll answer it.
(SOUND: City noise fades)

SCENE ELEVEN
(Entrance way/living room)

KATHY: *(To intercom)* What's the password?

BEV: *(Intercom)* Chocolate Orange Ice Cream.
(SOUND: Door buzzer)

KATHY: *(To intercom)* All right! *(To LIZ)* Mom, I know you were joking when you suggested it, but would you be mad if I do a speech about Aunt Bev?

BETTY: I suppose you can't get more modern than your aunt.

Make them laugh, make them cry, and back to laughter. What do people go to the theatre for? An emotional exercise…. I am a servant of the people. I have never forgotten that.

Mary Pickford

LIZ: *(Comes to kitchen doorway)* The "me" generation belonged to the seventies, Mother.

KATHY: She's "now" enough to buy gourmet ice cream, and she does have a perfect relationship.

LIZ: *(Moves back into kitchen)* Oh sure … without any "commitment" on either side.

KATHY: *(Calling)* I knew you'd be mad.

LIZ: *(Off)* I'm not mad. I'm putting the potatoes on.
(SOUND: Angry rattle of pots; off)

BETTY: Kathy, you aren't thinking of telling your class about Beverly and Sam, are you?

KATHY: Why not? Oh, Gran … lots of people don't bother with marriage anymore. At least if she and Sam break up they don't have to go through a divorce.

BETTY: No, and your aunt will get even less out of the ordeal than your poor mother.

KATHY: Relationships are about love, Gran. Not money.

BETTY: Life is never so simple as when you're sweet sixteen.

KATHY: You don't have to patronize me.

BETTY: Then *you* stop patronizing *me*.

LIZ: *(Coming on)* What's going on? Kathy, are you being rude?

KATHY: She always talks to me as if I were a child.

BETTY: And she talks to me as if she knows the answers to everything. Well, you don't, little girl. You don't even know the right questions.

LIZ: Oh, come on, you two!

KATHY: Mom, what does she mean?
(SOUND: A knock)

LIZ: Nothing, Kathy. Nothing that concerns *you!*
(SOUND: Door opens)
(Tense) Hi, Bev. Come in.

BEV: *(Panting)* Liz, what's wrong?
(SOUND: Door closes)
(Panting) I could hear you three shouting from halfway down the hall.

LIZ: We were having a discussion.

BETTY: It seems the door is especially thin.

BEV: *(Starts to breathe more normally)* The door may be, but the tension in here is ten feet thick.

BETTY: Beverly, dear, you sound like you ran up the stairs.

BEV: Yes, I missed my workout this morning.
(SOUND: Closet opens, rattle of hangers; continues underneath)

LIZ: *(Slightly off)* Bev, I've put your stuff in the closet, okay?
(SOUND: Closet door closes)

BEV: Oh wait, there's a bottle in my bag ...
(SOUND: *Closet door opens*)
(*Slightly off*) Hey ... is that your painting stashed in there?
(SOUND: *Closet door slams*)

LIZ: Yes, it's stashed! Whose fault do you think that is?!

BEV: What?

LIZ: I had no "lack of commitment" till you phoned!

KATHY: Mom!

BETTY: Girls, are you arguing already?

LIZ: Mother, stay out of this!
(SOUND: *Clinking pot lid and hiss of water boiling over in kitchen; off; continues underneath*)

BEV: (*Confused*) Stay out of what?

LIZ: (*Moving off*) Damn. The potatoes!

BETTY: Let me—

LIZ: (*Off*) No, no, I'll take care of it.

BEV: Liz, I'm getting the feeling I'm not welcome here.
(SOUND: *Clanks, hiss; off*)

LIZ: (*Coming back on*) Bev, I've had a bad day ... I shouldn't have said anything.

BETTY: (*Changing subject*) Beverly, your gourmet ice cream must be starting to melt.

BEV: Oh, well, I'll put it in the freezer. (*Beat*) Here ... (*Hands LIZ bottle*) I brought us wine.

BETTY: Good. Your sister could use a drink.

KATHY: (*Sotto*) Mom, can I have a few minutes, just Aunt Bev and me?

LIZ: Okay, Kath, I'll stay out of the kitchen.

SCENE TWELVE
(*Kitchen*)

BEV: (*Coming on*) So kiddo, not out with Daddy today?
(SOUND: *Freezer door closes*)

KATHY: The system at his office went down.
(SOUND: *Cupboard door opens and closes*)

BEV: (*Knowing*) Uh huh.

KATHY: It's not fair of Mom, you know. She only gives him one chance a week.

BEV: (*Calling*) Liz, all I see in your cupboard is mugs.

LIZ: (*Off*) Oh lord, the wine glasses are still in the dishwasher.
(SOUND: *Dishwasher door opens*)
(*Coming on*) Hand me a few. I'll give them a rinse.

BEV: What's wrong with the dishwasher?

LIZ: It's broken.
(SOUND: *Taps, running water*)

KATHY: Aunt Bev, how would you define a modern woman?

BEV: Oh, I'm not into definitions. (*Referring to dishwasher*) Liz, want me to take a look inside? *(SOUND: BEV fiddles with the insides of the dishwasher, speaking with her head inside it)*

LIZ: *(Annoyed)* There's no point fooling with it.

BEV: I bet all this needs is a straightened-out coat hanger.

LIZ: I have one right here. *(SOUND: Clinks and clanks; continues underneath)*

BEV: Perfect.

LIZ: *(Over the last, insistent)* I tried that, Bev.

BEV: *(Head still in there)* Liz, trust me.

KATHY: *(Trying to get in)* So … Aunt Bev …

BEV: So, Kath … *(Yielding with a sigh)* What kind of woman do you have in mind?

KATHY: I guess … women like *you*.

LIZ: Middle-class white liberal yuppies.

KATHY: White liberal?

BEV: That's a sixties phrase, kiddo. *(SOUND: One big final clink) (Coming out of the dishwasher)* I think I've solved the problem.

LIZ: It means people who think they can solve problems they know nothing about. *(SOUND: Dishwasher door closes)*

BEV: Turn it on. *(SOUND: Dial is turned. Dishwasher behaves perfectly) (Triumphant)* There!

LIZ: *(Amazed)* What did you do? *(SOUND: Dishwasher turned off. Dishwasher door opens)*

BEV: I'll show you.

KATHY: *(Internal. Public address; over BEV and LIZ)* The true modern woman, not like my mother, but exactly like my Aunt Bev, is not hopeless when confronted with a mechanical problem.

BEV: *(Underneath Kathy's speech)* This hose was completely clogged.

LIZ: I figured that … but I couldn't get at it.

BEV: It takes a bit of flexibility.

KATHY: *(Internal. Public address)* She exercises regularly so she looks *twenty*-eight years younger … well, at least eighteen younger than Mom, instead of only eight. And …

BEV: Our kitchen had a machine like this before we remodelled.

LIZ: I sure envy you that kitchen.

BEV: Sam loves cooking in it.

KATHY: *(Internal. Public address)* Oh, yeah. Early in life she refused to learn to cook or to type, so she cannot be forced into any stereotypical roles such as Mother used to complain about.

BETTY: *(Coming on)* Why is everyone in the kitchen?

BEV: Liz and I are talking, Mother.
(SOUND: A pot clinks)

LIZ: Mother, what are you doing?

BETTY: Turning up the element.

LIZ: *(Irritated)* I just turned it down.

BETTY: But the potatoes have stopped boiling.

LIZ: *(Angry)* For God's sake, I know how to cook potatoes.

BEV: Mother, why don't you go and sit down? We'll bring your wine in a minute.

BETTY: *(Moving off)* As you wish.

KATHY: *(Internal. Public address)* The modern woman can take charge of any situation without sounding crabby like Mom.
(SOUND: Rattle of cutlery drawer)

BEV: Liz, where's your corkscrew?

LIZ: Oh, no ...

KATHY: *(Internal. Public address)* And also, unlike my mother, Aunt Bev would never forget to buy important things like corkscrews ...

LIZ: Kathy, the Seven Eleven will have one ...

KATHY: *(Cool)* I'm busy at the moment, Mom.

LIZ: *(Moving off)* Oh, for the love of heaven.

KATHY: *(Internal. Public address)* The modern woman is the perfect person to make the sixties woman see that it's too late for her to change her life now.

BETTY: *(Slightly off)* Liz, where are you going?

LIZ: Out!
(SOUND: Apartment door closes)

BETTY: *(Slightly off)* Wait for me.
(SOUND: Apartment door closes)
(In hall, off) Liz, you may think you're coping, but it looks to me as if ...

BEV: Lord, the door really is thin.

KATHY: Anyway, Aunt Bev, now that we have some peace ...

BEV: Kath, to tell you the truth, women's issues don't turn me on.

KATHY: Don't worry ... I've got that done ... I want you to give me your honest opinion of something entirely different.

BEV: What?

KATHY: In the living room.

SCENE THIRTEEN
(Living room)
(SOUND: Closet door opens, cloth is taken off painting)

KATHY: Here in the closet.

BEV: *(Coming on)* What are you doing?

KATHY: Look, Aunt Bev ... look what Mom has been working on for almost two months.

BEV: *(Astonished)* My lord ...

KATHY: So ... what do you think?

BEV: *(She hates it)* Well, I don't know much about painting.

KATHY: Do you like it?

BEV: *(Beat)* Is that the title on the bottom? *(Giggle)* The bottom edge, I mean?

KATHY: Where?

BEV: "Venus Sucked In" ... oh, I see. Now it makes sense.

KATHY: It does?

BEV: Yes, I think there's a famous painting on this subject.

KATHY: Gran mentioned it ... *Venus Rising*?

BEV: I only remember a Joan Baez song about Madonnas on the half shell ...

KATHY: That was before my time.

BEV: It was before my time too, but your mother was a great fan of Joan Baez. I guess this painting is some kind of parody.

KATHY: You mean it's a joke?

BEV: Your mother may be working out her hostility. The shell must represent old-fashioned male expectations of women.

KATHY: Yeah, but in terms of now ... do you think Mom can make it as an artist or not?

BEV: The subject matter is self-indulgent ... and ... perhaps a bit dated in its aggressive feminist metaphor.

KATHY: You mean it's crap.

BEV: Well ... it might work for today's market if her approach were less literal and a bit more ... playful.

KATHY: It's crap, Aunt Bev.

BEV: Oh. *(Beat)* Anyway, I think we should put it away before she gets back, don't you? *(SOUND: Painting is put back. Closet door closes)*

KATHY: What I think is that you should come straight out and tell Mom that she should throw out her oil paints and go home where she belongs.

BEV: It's a bit late for that, kiddo.

KATHY: No! The divorce isn't final. Legally they're still married.

BEV: But they don't want to be.

KATHY: Only because Mom's being selfish. I mean, Aunt Bev, maybe it's great for you being single, but you don't have a kid.

BEV: Actually, I might soon.

KATHY: Really? You want to have a baby?

BEV: I'm going to have one. *(SOUND: Door opens)*

KATHY: You mean *you're* pregnant?

LIZ: *(Coming on)* You're pregnant? *(SOUND: Door closes)*

BEV: *(Sotto)* Oh, lord, where's Mother?

LIZ: Gone, to the store by herself, she wanted more cigs anyway.

BEV: Thank god ... with her, I need to announce my wedding plans first.

KATHY: You're getting married?

LIZ: *(Mournfully)* I thought the last thing you ever wanted was to be tied down.

BEV: *(A light tone)* I'm not going to be tied down.

KATHY: *(Overlapping)* She doesn't have to be tied down.

BEV: I can afford a nanny, and Sam's promised to do his share of the parenting.

LIZ: Bev, you've no idea of what you're getting into.

BEV: Oh, Liz, I knew you'd be like this about it.

LIZ: Like what?

BEV: Negative, bitter. Look, it's Sam's idea, and he'll make a wonderful father. He's not like your Dave, you know.

KATHY: What's that supposed to mean?

BEV: Oh, nothing, kiddo.

LIZ: Kath, how about you go see what's keeping Gran?

KATHY: *(Overlapping LIZ)* Dad *is* a good father ... he's a good father.

LIZ: Of course he is. Now, Kathy, I want to talk to your aunt alone.

KATHY: I'm not leaving if you're going to say mean things about Dad.

LIZ: Please, Kathy, do as you're told.

KATHY: Okay.

SCENE FOURTEEN
(Hallway)
(SOUND: Door opens and closes)

BEV: *(From other side of door)* Funny how kids are devoted to people who don't care about them, isn't it?

LIZ: *(Under KATHY's speech)* Hush ... she might hear you.

KATHY: *(Internal)* Tell her she doesn't know what she's talking about. Dad loves me. You know he does.

LIZ: I find it heartbreaking, and there's nothing I can do about it except try to protect her.

BEV: She's going to see through those computer breakdowns sooner or later.

KATHY: *(Internal)* What's that supposed to mean?

She by Cat Jackson.

Cat Jackson created the above painting in response to *The Birth of Venus*, the painting by Sandro Botticelli (also referred to in this play as *Venus Rising*). Use library resources to find Botticelli's image and investigate what it represents. What do you think the image represents for Jackson? Find out how other artists have parodied or reproduced this image.

BEV: What if she runs into him out with one of his girlfriends sometime? I told you I ran into him last Sunday, didn't I?

KATHY: *(Internal)* No! No! It's not true.

LIZ: Yeah, you told me.

KATHY: *(Internal)* Maybe … it was somebody from work … maybe he was so lonely…

LIZ: *(Overlapping KATHY)* She'd probably find a way to excuse him. She'll probably say I drove him to it.

BEV: Why do you put up with it? If a kid of mine criticized me the way she criticizes you, I certainly wouldn't stand for it.

LIZ: She's been hurt enough already.

KATHY: *(Internal)* I'm not going to cry.

LIZ: Or maybe I'm a coward. Maybe I'm scared she'll say I deserved to be dumped …

KATHY: *(Aloud)* Dad walked out on her … *(Internal)* He dumped *her?*

LIZ: Maybe I'm scared she'll make up a speech about how her mother is such a fool … such a loser … such a statistic!

KATHY: *(Internal)* Oh, Mom …

BEV: *(Overlapping KATHY)* Liz, for pity's sake. You have to stop getting sucked into what other people want from you. You have to learn to make yourself your own priority.

LIZ: My daughter has always been my priority. I'm too old to change now. You can't have a child and still put yourself first, Bev.

BETTY: *(Coming on)* Kathy … what are you doing?

KATHY: Gran …

LIZ: *(Calling from other side of door)* Who's out there? Kathy?

KATHY: *(Sotto)* Gran, pretend we met by the elevator, okay?

BETTY: Why? What's the matter?

KATHY: *(Over her)* Please, Gran … trust me …
(SOUND: Door opens)

LIZ: Kathy, you weren't eavesdropping, were you?

KATHY: No! I was waiting by the elevator … Gran was on it when it came.

BETTY: *(Beat as she decides whether or not to go along)* Here you are. One corkscrew.
(SOUND: Door closes)

SCENE FIFTEEN
(Living room)

BEV: Give it to me, I'll pour.

LIZ: Kath, would you like half and half with soda?

KATHY: No, thanks, Mom.

LIZ: But we have to drink a toast to your Aunt Bev.
(SOUND: Cork extracted, glasses, wine pouring)

BEV: *(Upbeat)* Mother, you'll be thrilled to know I've finally said yes to Sam.

BETTY: That's wonderful!

LIZ: Kath, where are you going?

KATHY: To my room.

BETTY: Aren't you even going to congratulate your aunt?

KATHY: Congratulations.

LIZ: Sweetheart, you look upset.

KATHY: I'm fine, Mom. I just have to do that speech.

BEV: I thought you said you had it done?

KATHY: I changed my mind.

LIZ: *(Slightly off)* Okay, Kath. I'll call you when dinner's ready.

KATHY: Yeah, thanks.

BETTY: *(Fading off)* Beverly, tell us your plans. You're not being married in white, are you?

SCENE SIXTEEN
(Internal and from kitchen)

KATHY: *(Internal)* Who needs to write a speech about Aunt Bev anyway … Maybe Mom's idea was better … yeah … *(Public address)* In the new millennium we are sure to have a woman prime minister … What that will mean for women everywhere … or for our planet … or for girls growing up … I don't really know. You take my Aunt Bev. To be honest I don't think she'd be any better than the men.

BEV: *(Slightly off)* Liz, I'm starved. Did you ever put the chicken in the oven?

LIZ: *(Slightly off)* Oh, look, you guys wouldn't like pizza, would you?

BETTY: If it's less trouble.

BEV: *(Slightly off)* I could have stayed home and had pizza.

KATHY: *(Internal. Public address)* Because she only thinks about herself.

LIZ: Okay, okay …

KATHY: *(Internal. Public address)* Of course, someone like Mom might be different. So what if she can't get around to her painting, or even if she's any good at it … She really cares about other people … and that's what would be most important. I mean, what I'm saying is … that whether a woman prime minister is going to make a difference or not, well, it depends on the woman, that's all.

(MUSIC: Joan Baez up and out)

Anne Chislett was born and raised in St. John's, Newfoundland and Labrador. Her plays have been performed all over Canada and the United States. In 1983, she won the Governor General's Award for Drama for her play *Quiet in the Land.*

1. *Response*

a. Briefly summarize and discuss the plot of this play.

b. Describe the major and minor conflicts the play explores. How do these conflicts relate to ones with which you are familiar?

c. How did you feel about the characterization of the daughter? The other characters? Would you describe any of them as stereotypes? Explain your answer and the effect of these characters on an audience.

d. Discuss the meaning and effect of the title and subtitle with a partner. Now that you have read the play, how suitable do you think the title is?

2. *Drama* Present a Scene

Choose one scene from this play and prepare a presentation of it with two or three other classmates. You could plan your performance as an oral presentation only—since this was originally produced as a radio play—or you could plan a stage presentation, using visual elements such as costumes, props, movement, gestures, and facial expressions. Rehearse your scene several times, memorizing your lines, and experimenting with tone, expression, volume, and pace.

> PERFORMANCE TIP You need to know exactly what your character is like, and how to convey that information to your audience. What can the audience expect from this character? How does this character tend to think and act? What are his/her motivations or feelings?

3. *Oral Language* Speech

In this play, the main character, Kathy, is preparing a speech for school about modern women. Given the same topic, quickly jot down notes for a one-minute speech. Use those notes to deliver an impromptu, unrehearsed speech to a small group. With a partner, discuss the challenges of public speaking and the skills required to be a good public speaker.

4. **Writing** Comedy Reread the play and reflect on how Chislett has created humour within everyday family situations. Write at least one scene for a situation comedy about your own family or a fictional family; or write another comic scene for Kathy's family. Use the structure and comic techniques of this play as a model.

5. **Language Conventions** Ellipses and Dashes Examine the use of ellipses (…) and dashes (—) in one scene. Discuss how and why they are used, and their effect on the reader or listener. Examine other plays within this unit, noting how frequently dashes and ellipses are used. Consider how you can use this technique within your own scriptwriting to enhance clarity or emphasis, or to mimic normal speech.

Writing has been a way of explaining to myself
the things I do not understand.

—Rosario Castellanos

Theme Connections

What's your decorating tip for the day? Tom King answers that question tongue in cheek.

Tom King's Traditional Aboriginal Decorating Tips

Radio Comedy Sketch
by Tom King
from *The Dead Dog Café*

JASPER: It's time for King's Traditional Aboriginal Decorating tips with your Aboriginal Decorating expert, Tom King. So, Tom, what's your decorating tip for today?

GRACIE: Used bingo dabbers.

JASPER: What a great idea.

TOM: You want to decorate with used bingo dabbers?

GRACIE: In recent years, many non-Native homes have eschewed the more common uses of paint for interior walls and have gone to the avant garde techniques of sponging and ragging in order to create not only a complex of subtle and complementary colours but also to suggest a sense of depth and age.

JASPER: That sounds like a lot of work.

GRACIE: Indeed it is. Not only is it backbreaking, but you can never be sure that everything will come out even.

JASPER: So used bingo dabbers are the answer?

GRACIE: Exactly. When your bingo dabbers have served their purpose at the bingo hall, bring them home and use them to dab an accent line to complement the treaties.

TOM: Treaties? What treaties?

JASPER: Tom, remember when you showed our listeners how to wallpaper their walls with treaties?

TOM: Oh … yeah.

GRACIE: Treaties as a wall decoration is all well and good, but most treaties lack colour.

TOM: And used bingo dabbers have colour.

GRACIE: They do indeed. I especially like the new hot neon colours.

JASPER: This is great. Most people throw away their used bingo dabbers, so this decorating tip is environmentally sound as well.

GRACIE: Round up a variety of different coloured bingo dabbers and begin dabbing accent patterns on your walls at about the six-foot mark. Make sure to keep your colours co-ordinated, but don't worry about coverage. Being able to see parts of the treaties come through a hot pink dab can be quite effective.

JASPER: Should we just do straight lines or can we be more creative?

GRACIE: Straight lines of dab marks are simple and elegant, but patterns of any kind should be considered if the occasion and the room calls for it.

JASPER: Bingo dabbers ... who would have thought.

GRACIE: As an added bonus, once the dabber is completely used up, it can be set on bookcases or on a fireplace mantel or on an end table and passed off as an objet d'art.

JASPER: What a great tip, Tom. I'm going to start saving my used bingo dabbers right now.

TOM: Well, it was better than decorating with dogs.

Thomas King, born in 1943, has a father of Cherokee descent and a mother of Greek and German descent. King grew up in Northern California, but moved to Canada as an adult. He has written short stories and novels, most notably *Medicine River*. King teaches Native Literature and Creative Writing at the University of Guelph. Many Canadians are familiar with his performance on *The Dead Dog Café* radio show, which he writes for the CBC. The Dead Dog Café is a locale invented by King in an early novel.

1. *Response*

a. With a partner, assess the effectiveness of this radio comedy sketch.

b. What do you think King means by his last line? Develop two more lines of dialogue by other characters that might explain that line.

c. What do you think King is spoofing? In your opinion, how effective is this spoof?

d. What serious point does this selection make? With a partner, discuss how effectively humour can be used to deliver a serious message.

2. ***Making Connections*** Compare and contrast this selection with one other selection in this unit that uses humour. Consider content, subject, sources of humour, and techniques. Discuss your comparisons in small groups.

3. ***Media*** *Humour on Radio* In small groups, discuss radio shows you have enjoyed that were intended to be funny. What techniques did these shows use? What are the advantages or disadvantages of comedy in radio over comedy in other media?

4. ***Drama*** *Performing Comedy* Work with two other students to prepare a presentation of this sketch. Discuss how these lines should be delivered for comic effect. Rehearse your presentation, experimenting with the delivery of each line—your tone, volume, pace, emphasis, and expression. Record your final, polished performance on tape and play it for another group. Discuss the effectiveness of the presentation and the challenges of delivering a comic sketch.

> PERFORMANCE TIP When a performance involves only your voice, your voice becomes *really* important: certainly you must control your tone, emphasis, inflection, and expression to express emotion appropriately and effectively. However, your pronunciation and articulation are also important, since these allow others to understand your words or your character. Before a performance, you may want to practise some tongue twisters to challenge your pronunciation and articulation.

5. ***Focus on Context*** Research Tom King's background and writing career. Discuss what motivates him to create comedy sketches such as the one above. How does the content of the selection reflect his background? Visit the *Dead Dog Café's* official Web site and read other scripts for the show.

> A writer is a foreign country.
> —*Marguerite Duras*

In this innovative and amusing play,
Lindsay Price brings Galileo
to life.

Galileo
The Starry Messenger
A Play in One Act by Lindsay Price

SCENE ONE

*(A lone, blue back light comes up slowly. We can see the outline of
GALILEO but not his face. This is GALILEO in the final days before his
death. He is speaking to a former STUDENT.)*

GALILEO: Stop whispering. I can hear you. Voices ... murmur ....
murmur. I used to walk through the university and the whispers
used to speak to me in loving tones. Tell me about the wonders of
my mind, my experiments, my mistress ... Now they addle in my
ear and I am too weak to brush them aside.

Do you like my prison? Walls are walls, boy. It doesn't matter if
they are here in the villa or in a cell. They keep me in. The
pigeons have always wanted me helpless—always against me,
preventing my success.

Why did you open the window? I can feel the breeze, you fool.
What are you doing? Looking at the stars. The star. We used to be
such friends. That was long ago. Now they are just bitter. "Why
did you desert us Galileo? You left, recanted our existence. We
trusted you and we were betrayed." I can't shut them out. That
was long ago. Close the window! Close it. Don't let them in! I can
hear you ... I can hear you.

*(Lights slowly cross-fade into a wash on GALILEO'S studio. There is a
desk overflowing with papers and books and gadgets. There is a life-sized
pendulum hanging from a frame. There is also a telescope which is hidden
underneath a large cloth. We are now in the year 1609. GALILEO realizes
he is back in his studio in Padua. He moves around the studio, touching
the instruments and enjoying the space. He puts on his jacket and goes to*

his desk to resume writing a letter. He is sitting, writing furiously with his body turned away from the door. He speaks without looking up. This is the first visit of THE STUDENT.)

Wait … Wait … stop fidgeting. I can see you. *(He holds up a hand and gestures THE STUDENT into the room as he continues writing.)* … hold on … one more minute … *(He sneaks a look and watches THE STUDENT cross the room. THE STUDENT moves to touch the pendulum.)* Don't touch that. *(He chuckles and continues writing.)* … Almost there … Galileo … Gal-li-lei. *(Says his last name in syllables as he signs his name with a flourish)*

(He waves the paper in the air to dry the ink and gestures to the pendulum and comes across very sternly.)

If you touch that, it will move. *(Standing, he goes right up into the face of THE STUDENT.)* And the fitting is not so stable. It came crashing down last week on the foot of one of my students. Broke every bone in his foot. *(Turns away and looks up into the heavens)* He'll never walk right again. *(Demonstrating this as he speaks)* Always left, left, left … *(Turns to face STUDENT to see if he got the joke and chuckles)* What's under the cloth? *(Crosses stage and shoos STUDENT away from the pendulum)* I don't divulge every secret to every stranger that walks in. Besides, you haven't paid for your first lesson. Everybody comes here for lessons—why else would you come? *(Turning away from THE STUDENT and holding up the letter he has just finished)*

Here, be useful. Listen to this: *(Clears his throat and speaks in schmoozy tones)* To Belasario Vinta. *(Speaking slowly)* Vinta. Vinta. Belasario? He is the eyes and ears of the Grand Duke of Tuscany. You must know the Medici Family? *(Sizing up STUDENT as if not knowing who Vinta is, is a mark against him)* Hmm. *(Reading through the letter)* Blah, blah, blah … all right now … *(Goes back to speaking in schmoozy tones)*

My thought would truly be to get enough leisure and quiet so that I can complete, before my life ends, the great work … *(Grabs feather and changes the "the" into "three")* three great works that I have in hand, in order that they might be published, perhaps with some credit to me and to *him* who would favour me in these undertakings. Greater leisure than I have here at the University of Padua. So long as I am forced to derive the sustenance of my household from public and private teaching … the rotten little mindless no-neck buggers *(Looks at STUDENT and gives three short laughs)* … the freedom that I have here does not suffice since I am required, at anybody's request, to consume many hours of the day and, often, most of them. This Republic will never offer me such an ideal situation. These things I can only hope to have from a Prince.

(Grabs his carafe and swigs a mouthful. He cradles the carafe as he continues to read.) Of course, I don't want to appear to be asking unreasonable favours without giving something back in return. To obtain a salary from a Republic without rendering public service ... *(He pauses, puts the paper down again to rewrite.)* To obtain a salary from a Republic, however splendid and generous a salary, without rendering public service is not possible since, to draw benefits from the public, it is necessary to satisfy the public and not a particular individual. But I have so many and diverse inventions, only one of which could be enough to take care of me for the rest of my life ... I cannot hope for such benefits from anybody but an absolute ruler. *(Getting bored with reading)* Blah, Blah, Blah, Your humble servant, Galileo Galilei.

What do you think? *(Looks at THE STUDENT who just shrugs his shoulders)* Bah.

(Folds up letter and seals it) I am a brilliant suck-up. Cosimo de Medici used to be one of my students. Now he's the Grand Duke of Tuscany. Everyone talks this way when they want to suck something out of the Grand Duke of Tuscany. *(Looks through his papers)* And if I want to work for the Grand Duke of Tuscany, then I speak in dutiful suck-filled tones. *(Takes both letters and puts them together on the table and sits down on his stool to face THE STUDENT with his arms crossed)* All right, all right, stop fidgeting so. I know who you are. You want to study with me. Want me to teach you everything I know, do you? *(Puffs his chest out proudly)* You've heard stories about me perhaps? *(Deflates at the answer and is a little irritated)* Of course you have, no one comes to study with the great Galileo by chance. *(THE STUDENT says, "My father sent me.")* Yes, well, fathers are always sending their sons somewhere. I got sent to a monastery; you got sent to me. Which one of us is the luckier one, eh? Monasteries are wonderful places to study. It's quiet. No distractions.

(Stands up and walks around the table to stare down at THE STUDENT) But why did your father send you to me? There are many, many other teachers here at the university. Which story dazzled you the most, eh? The Leaning Tower of Pisa? Yes, that's a pretty good story, isn't it? *(To himself)* I almost wish I had come up with that one myself. *(Back to THE STUDENT, picking up two paper balls)* Do you want to climb to the top of the leaning tower of Pisa and be just like me? Throw some different weighted cannonballs off the top to see which gets to the

bottom first? Who is right—Aristotle or me? You're guessing. *(Drops both balls which land at exactly the same time)* All bodies accelerate at the same rate of motion. No playing favourites; you cannot sweet talk her with trips to the countryside or jewelry. Everything gets treated exactly the same. Cannonballs, feathers … it is the wind that bribes the feather away. Feathers bribe very easily. *(Turns to see THE STUDENT writing)* Don't write that down—I haven't accepted you yet.

I'm very expensive and you had better not be stupid. So, you better learn quick. *(Waving the letter)* I don't know how long I'll be here. *(THE STUDENT says he wants to stick it out.)* Determined, eh? Bah. Stupid, more like it. *(THE STUDENT'S face crumples.)* Oh, for heaven's sake. If you can't figure out when I'm serious and when I'm not, we'll never get anywhere. *(Kneels down to be at the level of THE STUDENT)* Look. *(Makes a serious face)* Serious Face. *(Makes a funny face)* Not serious face. Serious Face. Not serious. Which is this? *(Makes a face which is a combination of the two)* You're guessing.

(Counting off the rules on his fingers) Don't look at anything unless I tell you to. Don't touch anything unless I tell you to and don't try to steal anything, or I'll string you up by your thumbs. I can never be sure who is going to try and steal some of my genius away. You can try, of course—they always try—but the thing about genius is that it tends to disappear—poof—the instant it's away from its owner. *(Sarcastic and pompous)* So, are you trustworthy? Can I trust you? You're not going to sell my soul to the rag sheets, are you? Can I fill you with knowledge or will it pour out of you faster than I can pack it in? Will you study day and night? Will you take this journey with me? Once you do, you will never be able to turn back. You will never be able to study with anyone else. I will have corrupted you for life. Can you handle being corrupted for life? Can you touch your tongue to your nose? *(Breaking the mood)* Don't try, you look ridiculous. All right. *(Stands up, gets carafe and takes another swig)*

The first thing you can do is pay me. You've been listening to me for at least five minutes. That qualifies as a first lesson. You want to learn. *(THE STUDENT asks if he can see what's under the cloth.)* First the money, then the cloth. *(Fingers the cloth over the pendulum)* Place it on the table there.

(In response to whether GALILEO wants to count the money) Don't be rude; if it's wrong, you'll pay me double next time. And now … *(Uncovers the pendulum)* It is not a package on a piece of string. It's a pendulum. Don't you know anything? *(Starts the pendulum swinging)* We're going

to have to start at the very beginning, aren't we? (*Watching the swings and thinking of the past, his speech is as soothing as the words*) It's very soothing. It helps me think. Back and forth in equal swings of absolute perfection. Like myself. We've been together for a long time.

(*Breaks the mood and is pompous once again. He moves over to the table.*) Now, the next thing you can do is take that letter to the Duke's eyes and ears, and that one to my brother there. (*Sits down at the table and begins looking through books*) Go and find my landlady and give them to her. Her son is travelling south tomorrow. I can't get away right now.

(*Speaks as he begins to write*) Yes, yes, lots of family. It's very mundane; one brother, some sisters, one dead father who I wish was alive and one live mother who I wish was dead. Is your father well? Have you looked at his teeth lately? Oh dear. (*Looks up sharply*) You're not the first son in your family are you? (*The answer is no.*) Count your blessings. You don't have to support one live mother, one brother and some sisters.

(*Goes across the stage and takes a letter out of the bag near his cloak. Looks over it by the window. He is talking more to himself than to* THE STUDENT.)

(*He is reading a letter from his sister in which the threat is mentioned.*) I on the other hand … What is the most important ingredient in marriage? (*STUDENT says love*) Wrong. It's money. My sister's husband won't leave me alone. "When is the dowry coming, Galileo? Pay up, pay up, pay up!" (*He tears up the letter and goes back to the table.*) Why couldn't my brother be the first son? Why couldn't I have been in his shoes? Then I could go to him and pester him for money whenever I felt like it and refuse to help out the family. Off to Poland, off to Bavaria, off to wherever. Spend every last cent I have to marry an obnoxious braying cow. "Galileo, it's my wedding. I must have the best nuptial banquet." Blah, blah, blah, what a fool.

(*Stands up to go to the door and is surprised to see* STUDENT *still standing there*)

Are you still here? Go, go, you'll never learn if you sit around all day. (*Shoos* STUDENT *out the door*) How can I teach you anything if you won't go away?

(*The lights fade to spot.* GALILEO *is seen trying to pray but keeps getting distracted by the whispers and the rumours. He tries to shoo them away from his ears like gnats. He tries to block them out. But then he starts to listen. His face looks up into the light and the spot fades.)*

SCENE TWO

(GALILEO goes back to table and picks up two baskets. Inside the larger basket are lenses. The smaller basket is for the rejects.)

(Lights cross-fade back to the wash. GALILEO picks up two lenses. Holds one up to his eye and holds the other at arm's length. "No." He brings his outstretched arm in closer. "No." He puts the two lenses close together. He tosses the two lenses into the reject basket and picks up two more and starts the process again.)

(THE STUDENT wants to know about GALILEO'S life. GALILEO is sort of telling the story because he likes to talk about himself, but he is cheerfully talking on autopilot, while he is frantically trying to get the right combination. He has been up all night.)

Well, I was born, *(Arm's length)* no, *(Middle length)* no, *(Close-up)* no.

(Puts the two lenses in the reject basket. Picks up one lens and peers through it)

I was going to be a monk, then I wasn't. *(Brings out his handkerchief and starts to polish the lens)* I was going to be a doctor, then I wasn't. I was supposed to get a degree, but I didn't. *(Picks up another lens and holds it at arm's length)* Wait … wait … *(Peers through the lens)* No good.

(Puts the two lenses in the reject basket and sighs, using one hand to rub his neck while the other uses the handkerchief to rub his forehead. He then picks up two more lenses.)

I should have been an artist. Or a musician. But who needs a degree? I never did. "No, no, you need a degree." I need your father's money. *(Throws the two lenses into the reject basket in disgust)* Bah, these are not the right thickness; I can't get the right magnification. These are all wrong. *(Stands and paces. He moves to the pendulum and lets it swing.)* I'm going to have to get more made. It is so maddening! When you search for the truth, there is so much guesswork. No, if I wait until tomorrow, those wretched Dutchmen will get to Venice before I do and they will get all the credit.

(Removes his jacket, and sits once again at the table. Takes two lenses and holds one at his eye and one at arm's length. THE STUDENT is sitting on the floor, DSR.)

Are you finished that experiment I gave you? *(Arm's length)* You are not just rolling a ball down a plane, *(Middle length)* you are studying the acceleration of bodies *(Close-up)* and how they change their speed. *(Reject)* You are defying what other scientists have cast in stone. *(Picks up lens and wipes with handkerchief)* The problem is, you are lazy. You sit and listen to professors who give you all the answers and don't make you work. Well, here you have to figure out the answers all by yourself. I have to get rid of all your bad habits somehow …

(Drops hands and looks at THE STUDENT who has just said "I don't understand." GALILEO laughs.)

There are many things you don't understand. What exactly is it you don't understand today? Slow down, slow down! *(Stands up to talk to STUDENT. GALILEO truly believes that he is not in the wrong.)* It doesn't matter that I never invented this spyglass, far-seeing-whatever-the-Dutch-call-it thing. It matters that I can make it better. If I can make it better, who cares who invented it? Their spyglass has only three times the magnification. You can't even get a clear picture; there's a fringe all around the outside. The image appears upside down. It is a cheap tinker's toy. They should not be allowed to become rich with such an abomination.

Of course they will get rich. *(Stands up and returns to the desk)* They get richer every second they are in Italy and I get poorer. If only I had the time to take this to the Grand Duke of Tuscany. How he would regret not answering my letters. *(Arm's length)* They are going to make a presentation to the Doge in Venice. *(Middle length)* Well, they were, until I stopped them. I have friends in high places, my dear boy. *(Close-up)* It pays to have friends in high places so you can kick the teeth out of your enemies in low places. *(Rejects)*

(Looks up, exasperated at the nagging of THE STUDENT)

I am not cheating. You think in very absolute terms, my friend. Very narrow. I cannot even fit my head between the spokes of your thinking. I do not have a fat head. I know what this instrument can do;

> For the theatre one needs long arms; it is better to have them too long than too short. An artiste with short arms can never, never make a fine gesture.
>
> Sarah Bernhardt

I deserve to get the rewards. *(Arm's length)* You have to create your own opportunity. Well, perhaps *you* don't. *(Changes the lens at his eye)* All *you* have to worry about is that some irate peasants don't deem it fit that you should lose your head. *(Middle length)* Not as big as mine, but I think you would miss it all the same. I wonder how long you will keep your head. *(Rejects both lens and looks at* THE STUDENT*)* Have you ever had your horoscope done? I had one done for my daughter the day after she was born. Poor child.

Although, if I am right, you could make a fair amount just from being one of my students. You could sell your notes if anyone could read your handwriting.

(Holds up a lense. Notices the dust and starts to polish it) One instrument. That's all I need. Do you know how long I have been trying to find one instrument? Pendulum—no good. Thermoscope—no good. Lodestones—no good. I invented a machine for raising water and irrigating land; even got a patent for it: *(Imitating the language of a commercial)* "Very easy and convenient to use!" You only have to use one hose for spraying twenty buckets of water. I actually gave classes on how to use the blasted thing … but, no good; I only sold one.

(Sorts through the lenses) Military compass—no good. I thought that was going to do it for me. *(Discards a couple without holding them up)* I gave so many away … I had a man making compasses for me—worked him to the bone, but it was still no good. The thermoscope? It measures hot and cold. *(Holds up the lens)* There's a glass bottle about the size of an egg and a long glass neck … wait … almost. Almost.

(Keeps one lens and discards the other) You see, all I have to do is find the right buyers, and I am set for life. *(Picks up a lens. Holds at arm's length)* One instrument. *(Discards one)* This one is so simple. Two lenses in a tube make faraway objects appear as if they were right in front of your nose. *(Picks up another)* I'm sure I would have thought of it myself if I didn't have to spend all this time lecturing and teaching, and being bothered by students. *(Polishes the one he has just picked up)* You don't believe me. That's why I am a genius and you're not. The military alone will pay through the nose for something like this.

(Looks through at arm's length again) No, no, wait. Wait … *(Slowly stands up keeping the arm formation, and moves his arms in an arc)* That's it. The best Venetian glass. Ground. Polished. It matches. *(Looking through the lens)* Magnify. Magnify. Show me your wonders and pour gold through my fingers. This is the beginning.

(Lights fade to blue. GALILEO puts the two baskets on the floor. He then puts on his cape and hat, and exits through the doorway.)

SCENE THREE

(Lights cross-fade to wash)

(GALILEO is drunk. He is singing offstage. As he sings, he repeats one line over a couple of times, as if he is uncertain of the tune. He enters and stands in the doorway, swaying a little.)

"Tantalizing maiden, how shall I woo? ... All my heart is laden for love of you! Oh! I am all on fire with desire ... Tantalizing ... Tantalizing."

That's not right. That is not right. *(Sings the line again)* Where's my lute? *(Enters the space and searches behind the desk)* I know it's around here somewhere. *(Spins around)* Well, hello. You waited! *(Leans on the table)* Thank God you're here. We're celebrating! *(Totters away again, looking for something—he can't remember what)* I'm celebrating. I'm celebrating. You didn't do anything. *(Turns back)* I did it. I got the credit. I presented the spyglass, far-seeing-whatever-the-Dutch-call-it thing to the Doge of Venice. *(Imitates looking out of a telescope)* The top dog. *(Comes up close to the table still looking out of the "telescope")* I can see your nose hairs. Those wretched little Dutchmen didn't know what they were up against. They should know better than to fight a master. *(Arms out wide)*

It was a masterpiece! I am a masterpiece. The humble, middle-aged, dog-eared scientist presenting the lord and master with the sweat of his work. *(Does a sweeping bow)* The work of his life, or a week-and-a-half, depending on how you look at it. I had them in the palm of my hand. *(Shoos THE STUDENT back onto the stool and goes centre stage)* Sit down, sit down. All right? Here I am walking into the room.

(Walks pompously across the stage, stumbles a bit and rights himself. The Venetian court is SL.)

(Deep bow) "Good Morning. Good Morning. Good Morning." *(Looking back over his shoulder to THE STUDENT)* Everyone has their eyes locked on me. I am the centre of attention. *(Turning all the way around to face THE STUDENT)* There is nothing the matter with the way I dress! It's comfortable. Just because I don't trip over a toga every two steps; bah! I would rather go naked ... Now, where was I? Oh yes, the Doge. I am the centre of attention! *(Turns back to the court)*

(Speaking to the Doge, showing him how to use the telescope. They are both at a window looking out into the audience, being very serious.)

"Raise it to one eye and keep the other eye closed. What can you see? What can you see? The campanile and cupola with the façade of the church of Saint Giustina. Yes ... You can see people entering and leaving the church of Saint Giacomo, the gondolas at the Collona at the beginning of the canal of the glassworkers. *(High-voiced courtier)* "I see, I see. Quite remarkable." *(Low-voiced courtier)* "Quite remarkable." *(Looks at THE STUDENT and giggles a little. He clears his throat.)*

I have a letter for your honoured sirs. If it is no trouble.

*(Gives another deep bow, brings up a portion of his cape
to use as a letter. Schmoozingly)*

"Galileo Galilei, a humble servant of Your Serene Highness, now appears before you with a new contrivance of glasses drawn from the most recondite speculations of perspective, which render visible objects so close to the eye and represent them so distinctly, that those that are distant—for example, nine miles—appear as though they were only one mile distant.

This instrument is one of the fruits of the science which he has professed for the past seventeen years at the University of Padua, with the hope of carrying on his work in order to present you with greater ones, if it shall please the Good Lord and Your Serene Highness."

(Smiles and bows and falls over. A page has come over to GALILEO.)

Yes? The Doge has something to say to me? To me? *(Gives THE STUDENT a look, stands up and brushes himself off, and gives another bow)* Oh, my dear Sir, I am glad you appreciate my effort. Yes? *(This is a good thing.)* A raise in my salary? That is wonderful, I do appreciate ... A university position for life? *(Not such a good thing)* A university position for life. And ... *(He is waiting for more and gets nothing. He bows and backs away.)* You are most kind, most kind and generous. Most kind. Thank you for seeing me. You are most kind.

*(He gives a raspberry and flips the bird to the Doge.
He turns to THE STUDENT and laughs uproariously.)*

A raise in salary and a university position for life. There it is. *(Removing his cloak and hanging it up)* A raise in my salary and a university position for life. For life. *(With a little giggle)* It's an absolute disaster. How can I keep ahead if I am imprisoned within these walls? What if somebody creates a better instrument while I am chained to the lecturing table? Where does that leave me? All that sucking up for nothing! *(Starting to get riled up)* For life, for life, for life, for life!! … What a waste of time! *(Crescendo)* If I had known what the outcome was going to be, I would have left it for the wretched Dutchmen! *(THE STUDENT is reproachful, GALILEO turns away from him and crosses right. He gestures to the court.)* Don't look at me like that. Don't look at me like that. Venice is nothing. Venice is not even a stepping stone. *(Looks to the pendulum for support and a new idea)* A different approach. A stronger instrument. Yes, yes, that will work … Go to the glass blowers, boy; I need more lenses. Do not talk—go! Go now! I can do better.

(Lights fade. GALILEO stands DSC, holding his arms as if he is looking through a telescope. Slowly he raises his arms and looks at the sky. Shaken by what he sees, he runs offstage.)

SCENE FOUR

(Lights cross-fade to a wash as GALILEO re-enters, running.)

(Scattered, shaky, an octave higher than normal. At times he is fighting to maintain composure and failing. There should be nothing controlled in his actions or voice.)

Water, water, I need water. *(Lunging for the carafe)* … Beer. I need beer.

(GALILEO sits on the floor and drinks long and hard. He should be shaking. He turns the carafe over, trying to get the last drops out, and then hugs the carafe to his chest.)

Water? *(Looking around on the ground)* More beer; why isn't there more beer? *(Leaving the carafe and crawling over to the table)* Paper. Where is paper? No beer, no paper, this studio is a pigsty. Why doesn't anybody keep this place straight? *(Kneeling against the desk he gets a piece of paper and a feather)* Paper, quill, ink, write, write, write. I can't write; my hand won't stop shaking. *(To his hand)* Stop shaking. Beer, I need beer to calm my nerves. *(Looks towards the carafe)* There isn't any more. *(Looking under books)* Wine? Water? Nothing. Sit. Just sit. And don't move. *(He holds himself for a second and bursts out laughing.)* Paper! Hand! Stop shaking!! *(One hand holds the other wrist. GALILEO talks to the hand.)* I command you hand to commit yourself to steadiness. *(Hand speaks back)* "We're too excited, Galileo, we must wave! Bye-Bye." *(Slaps himself)* Get a hold of yourself. Write. The moon.

(Takes a deep breath and begins to write. He speaks and writes while trying to gulp in air. Everything is choppy.)

The moon. Cracks. Flaws. Mountains. Valleys. Crevices, Rough.

(Hears a noise behind him)

Who's there? Who are you? *(Trying to hide what he is writing and finding something to throw at the same time)* Get out! Get out! Get out! You have no business being here and I'll … *(Recognizes* THE STUDENT*)*. Oh. You. *(Takes a big breath and brings out his handkerchief to wipe his forehead)* What are you doing here? *(Stands and crosses right with the paper in his hands)* Your father, your father. No, don't tell me. I don't want to hear your simpering little problems. *(Shooing motion with his hand while still having his back to* THE STUDENT*)* I can't talk to you now. I can't possibly talk to you now. *(Stands still)* Why? Why? Why? Why? *(Crosses to stand in front of* THE STUDENT*)* I've done it. I've done it. Don't you understand? No. You don't. *(Waves the paper in front of* THE STUDENT, *taunting him)* I'm the only one who knows and I'm not going to tell you, *(Snatches the paper away and turns away to sit on stool)* not for all the ducats in the world. I'm going to show those old Aristotelian scholars who can't stop talking long enough to take their feet out of their mouths. *(Talking with one hand as if it were a puppet)* "I've found you out, you no-neck scholars. I have found you out! The moon is not as you say; it is not smooth, not uniform and precise. It is uneven, rough; there are mountains and valleys. In fact, it looks an awful lot like earth—what do you have to say to that?" *(Using the other hand)* "You were right, Galileo, all along. We were so very wrong." *(Laughing, turning to* STUDENT *and putting hands over mouth)* I've let it out. Very well, very well, come closer so the whole world won't hear me. *(Gestures to* STUDENT *to come to CS)*

I've looked up. Into the sky. With the telescope. *(Cuffs* THE STUDENT*)* No, not the one I gave to the Doge; that was too weak. Pay attention! Where have you been all of these months? What did you think I've been doing—teaching? *(Very conspiratorial)* I have magnified the lens nine times, ten times, twenty times, thirty times. I went up to the roof and I looked up into the sky. *(Getting excited again. Whispering, holding out his sheet)* The moon is not what we think it is. *(Breaking the mood as* THE STUDENT *spouts dogma)* Yes, yes, yes, the moon is a heavenly body. *(Speaking as a dutiful* STUDENT*)* The moon is perfect and incorruptible. You know that, because that is what you have been

> Drama is life with the dull bits cut out.
>
> Alfred Hitchcock

told. What you think you see. What you think you know. Who cares about what you know? Who cares about what you can spout? I am giving you something so new. *(Holding out sheet as a gift, which* THE STUDENT *rejects)*

Your head is stuck in your books and your shoes. *(Turns to the window)* The moon, it's so beautiful … it is spotted as the tail of a peacock, is sprinkled with azure eyes, and resembles those glass vases which, while still hot, have been plunged into cold water and have thus acquired a crackled and wavy surface. *(Breaking out of his reverie and goes to his desk to begin writing)* Say, that's rather good. I should write that down. I have to write all of this down. This is better than I expected.

(THE STUDENT starts to talk about Aristotle. GALILEO *is starting to get irritated.)*

Aristotle says, Aristotle says. The time for Aristotle is past. It is time for scientists to wipe the dust from their eyes and learn something. They haven't learned anything for years. They just keep spouting the ashes of a long-dead man. Aristotle was just a man. He saw with his eyes and he thought he knew what he saw. I have seen more in one night than Aristotle ever saw in his lifetime. He is the dust in our brains; he clouds everything we say and think and do …

(He turns and cuts off when he sees the face of THE STUDENT. *He takes a deep breath. Calmly and rationally, crossing toward* THE STUDENT)

The surface of the moon is not smooth. What they told you was wrong. The moon has never been smooth. Aristotle was wrong. All these months you've been experimenting and you didn't doubt me when I said Aristotle was wrong then, did you? How is this different? The principle is the same.

(Irritated) I know what I see, don't I? *(Under control)* I know what I have seen. *(Turning away, goes to table and writes again)* It's absolutely fantastic; I never dreamed … Stop questioning me! I am the master and you are the student. I am right and you are wrong. I know what I am talking about and you never did. *(Gets an idea)* Why don't you look at the moon yourself? Go up to the roof and look with your own two eyes so you can stop with this "Aristotle says." *(Encouraging)* Go ahead. *(Puzzled, stands, his eyes following* THE STUDENT *as he leaves the room)* Where are you going? Come back here! *(Goes to the doorway and shouts after* THE STUDENT) Don't you want to see with your own two eyes?

(Lights change)

Scene Five

(Galileo uncovers the telescope and looks through it when the lights change. The student enters. Galileo does not leave the telescope.)

You make so much noise when you are trying to lurk. Students, students! This place is like a boarding house sometimes. You have no grace. You should have taken dancing or fencing; something to give you more poise. Light on your feet. Maybe I'll ask Marina to give you some lessons. What would you think of that, eh? Even I would pay to see that. She could give grace to a slop pile. *(Sitting straight to think)* Although, she hasn't helped the girls any ... Virginia trips over her own shadow. They're still young I suppose ...

(Turns and looks at student. No joking) You have missed three lessons. I still expect to be paid. *(Cutting off the student, more calm than irritated, turning back to telescope)* I do not care what you tell your father, I still expect to be paid in full. *(Tired, waving hand)* Yes, Yes, I know I have changed my lecturing schedule. What of it? I have more important things to do.

Three days ago I saw three stars around Jupiter. Two to the east and one to the west. Two days ago, there were three stars to the west. Yesterday it was cloudy and today ... *(Waving hand at student while still looking through telescope)* Is there some paper over there? Write this down.

(Standing and stretching as he speaks) "On the 10th day of January in this present year, 1610, there were only two stars, both easterly." *(Heading to the pendulum and mumbling to himself)* Now what happened to the third star ... behind Jupiter? Perhaps, perhaps ... *(Looks over at the student)* What is the matter? ... You're not writing.

(Student is worried about the local gossip. Galileo is very calm.)

People always talk. Is that why you have come at such a late hour? What are they saying today?

(Cuts student off with a snort. Returns to the pendulum)

They may consider me an enemy, but I have no time for childish behaviour. Why should I care about enemies? Why should you? Are you being pelted with eggs in the courtyard because you study with me? The pigeons are restless; rumours flying at top speed around and around the university.

(Takes a big stretch and scratches his chest) What is happening with those stars? They have something specifically to do with Jupiter ... I know that ... *(Sees STUDENT looking at four moon drawings)* Do you like my drawings? *(Grabs one of the drawings)* The full moon was the hardest. With such a small field of view, I could only see a quarter of it at a time. That is something to work on. Something to change. *(Letting the picture drop, trying to add a bit of levity)* I should have been an artist. If only my father had been in your shoes, I could have painted nudes all day long and never finished one painting.

(Laughs and then looks at STUDENT) You take everything so seriously. Which face is this? *(Makes a face)*

All right. If you're not going to help me, perhaps I will help you. It's my generous nature; I give and I give and I give ...

(Wipes his forehead)

Have you ever heard of Copernicus? That is the lesson for today—Copernicus. If you are going to bother me at my studio at this hour, the least you can do is learn something. New lesson.

(Dips the cloth into the carafe. Squeezes some into his mouth and then goes on to wipe the telescope)

Nicholas Copernicus—ah, if only he had lived seventy more years ... what conversations we would have had. I've known about his theories for a long time; well, one theory in particular which is of great interest to me ... no boy, don't take any notes.

(GALILEO stares intently down the wrong end of the telescope, wiping and drying the lens. Not looking at THE STUDENT)

Nicholas Copernicus believed that the earth was not the centre of the universe. He believed that the sun was the centre and the earth revolved around the sun. That everything revolves around the sun ... Mars, Jupiter, Saturn, Venus ... *(GALILEO spits on the lens and wipes the lens clean)*

As you might imagine, this is not a popular philosophy. The church says that the earth is the centre of the universe, therefore the earth *is* the centre of the universe. The church says that the earth does not move, therefore the earth does *not* move. Who is right, eh?

(Galileo looks at THE STUDENT) Close your mouth boy; you'll let the flies in. That's better. *(Returns to the desk to a pile of notes)* So, I've been thinking about Copernicus and those stars I've been recording around

Jupiter. What if those stars are not stars at all? *(Throws notes down)* What if they are moons and they are rotating around Jupiter? What if it were possible for planets to revolve around something that is not the earth? I have seen those stars move with my own eyes. What if the earth is not the centre of the universe? *(Brings hand down to look at fingers)* What if everything we have ever known has been slipping through our fingers? What if we look at our fingers and find out they are not just flesh and bone, but made of something that we have been brought up to reject?

(Moving away from THE STUDENT, *still examining his hand)*

I have lectured that the earth is the centre of the universe. I have lectured that the earth does not move. I have known men who have been burned at the stake for saying otherwise. That will make things difficult, but not impossible.

(Sitting down at desk with the notes)

What did I say before? On the 10th day of January ... *(THE STUDENT interrupts.)* I'm making notes. It will be awfully hard to publish a book with incomplete notes. Do you think I'm doing this for my own amusement? What good is discovering something if I don't tell anyone about it? I have a duty as a scientist ... I am not a stupid man. I am not going to make mistakes. I am just going to publish my findings in a ... you don't understand. I cannot be satisfied with just the moon, because the universe does not consist of the earth and the moon.

(Returns to taking notes)

I must do what I must do. If you do not like it, you are free to leave. *(Slams feather down)* Fine, fine. I should never have invested so much time in the small-minded intellect you possess. *(Turns back on* STUDENT *and waves him away with the back of his hand)* Tell your father that I refuse to teach you anything else. Damn! *(Running to the doorway)* Wait. Wait! Come back! Come back. You still owe me for three classes!

SCENE SIX

(Lights change. GALILEO *picks up some of the balls of paper that are scattered around his desk. He sits on* THE STUDENT'S *stool shooting the paper balls across the stage.)*

"All things are hard: man cannot explain them by word. The eye is not filled with seeing, neither is the ear filled with hearing." *(Shooting the paper ball)* Parabola. *(Picking up another ball)* "What is it that hath been? The same thing that shall be. What is it that hath been done? The same that shall be done." *(Shooting ball)* Parabola. *(Picks up two balls, peeks to see what is written on the paper and re-crumples them)* "Nothing under the sun is new, neither is any man able to say: Behold this is new. For it hath already gone before in the ages that were before us ..." *(Shooting a ball)* Parabola. "The perverse are hard to be corrected: and the number of fools is infinite."

(Looks up at THE STUDENT*)* Well, well, well. *(Bends down to pick up another ball)* You came back. Ah yes, you heard about the book. *(Aiming for* THE STUDENT*)* Parabola. It's sitting on the table there. I would show it to you if I felt like it, but I don't. *(Shoots it high in the air)* Parabola. That sounds very poetic, doesn't it? Parabola. *(Picks up another and shoots it high in the air)* Science and poetry often go hand in hand. The equal sign in an equation is a metaphor. One thing being equal to another.

(Takes a ball in one hand and pops it to the other) Parabola. *(Showing the piece of paper to* THE STUDENT*)* I invented the parabola. *(Shifting from hand to hand)* I have invented and discovered. *(From hand to hand)* Invented and discovered. I am surrounded by my inventions. Knee-deep in the mire of discovery, clinging to my days and stinking up my breath. *(Lets the ball go)*

(Picks up a ball and stands) Aristotle says—there's that phrase again—that objects only travel in one direction and when they stop feeling like going in that direction, they drop to the ground. *(Drops the ball)* Boof. If that were true, I could take my brand new book here from the table *(Picks up the book and pretends to throw it across the stage)* and project it across the room and it might go and go and go. *(Watching it go)* The science in this book would take me to the greatest heights. But it's not true. Ah, the truth. You never questioned me on projectiles did you? Objects go in two directions—they go forward and they go down at the same time. My book goes forward into science and is pulled down, down, down, by religion. *(Picking up three paper balls)* No matter how hard I try to throw, it always curves back to earth.

(Shoots a ball) Parabola. Can't get away from science. *(Shoots a ball)* Parabola. I can't leave the church. *(Shoots a ball)* Parabola. Which is more important—science or the church?

(Goes to the pendulum) The pendulum! When I was in school, I invented the pendulum. *(Lets the pendulum go)* If only a pendulum had made me famous. Aristotle never said anything about the pendulum. No one was

ever burned at the stake because of a pendulum. Well, perhaps they were; that would make a good story too. *(Stops movement)* But if I were to take my book and tie it to the end of a rope and let the book go … *(Lets it go)* … It swings from side to side: science, religion, science, religion. But no matter how short the swings get, the rhythm never gives weight to one side or the other. You see? The period of the swings is the same. Science, religion. Science, religion. Each part of the problem receives equal weight. How can I make a proper decision, when everything is weighed so equally? *(Gets two balls and then goes and stands on his chair)* What about the leaning tower of Pisa? I throw science and religion off the top of the tower and *(Drops the paper balls)* they both reach the ground at exactly the same time. *(Gets two more balls and balances them in his palm)* I throw different sizes of ice science and ice religion into water and they both float. They always float! Science, religion. Science, religion. Catholic, scientist. Catholic, scientist. *(Throws them down)* Do I flip a coin? Which am I supposed to choose? Why can't I be both?

(Looks at THE STUDENT and laughs gently at himself. Looks at the studio and the mess he has made. He gives a sigh. As he talks, he picks up the paper balls and puts them into a pile.)

God gave to me the capacity to look up into the sky. The church upholds human reason. I must use my reason to find the truth. What else should I use it for? *(Turns to THE STUDENT)* Why must I let my reason rot just because it goes against the world? Just because I am intelligent, I should waste away? *(THE STUDENT does not answer.)*

Hmmm. *(Looks toward the book)* This will amuse you.

(Going to book and opening to first page, reading in a commanding voice)

"The Starry Messenger. Revealing great unusual and remarkable spectacles, opening these to the consideration of everyman and especially of philosophers and astronomers; as observed by Galileo Galilei, Gentleman of Florence, Professor of Mathematics in the University of Padua, with the aid of a spyglass lately invented by him. In the surface of the moon, in innumerable fixed stars, in nebulae and, above all, in four planets swiftly revolving about Jupiter at differing distances and periods and known to no one before the author recently perceived them and decided they should be named The Medician Stars."

(Looks up) What do you think? I have dedicated the satellites of Jupiter to the Medici family in Florence. The Medicea Sidera. If that

doesn't get me a position in Florence, I don't know what will. *(Closes book and brushes off the cover)* I plan to present the Grand Duke with a personally crafted telescope with the instructions that I will be at his beck and call to teach him how to use it. The damn fool needs me to be there; why can't he see that?

I did not lie. I practically came up with the idea for the instrument. Besides, nobody remembers the wretched little Dutchmen anymore. I have to make the title page impressive. As far as the world is concerned, I did invent it.

(Leans down to stare at THE STUDENT)

Did you know there are seven kinds of torture used by the inquisition, all in the name of truth? The first is the pit—an underground cave twenty feet deep and entirely without light. The second is a cell, so small that a person cannot enter it standing up. The third is the rack, which draws the limbs of the sufferer in opposite directions. The fourth, an iron ring which brings the head, feet, and hands together to form a circle. The fifth is an iron glove which encloses the hand with great pain. The sixth consists of manacles attached to the arms. The seventh, of fetters attached to the feet. This is all, of course, before they march you through the street on an ass, then burn you alive. Or put you in prison for the rest of your life and take away everything you have. *(Walks away to look at telescope)*

This book will change the world. I will be responsible for changing the world. Why would I want to give up an opportunity like that? Besides, I'm running out of time. Sooner or later, someone else will realize and look up into the sky, instead of out at the sea. I will look like a fool if I don't do this now. Galileo knew about this and he let it lie? Galileo knew years ago and he sat on it like a bump on a log, like a frightened old man. I am telling them the truth. Why should they reject the truth? All they have to do is look through the telescope and know that I am right. And the church?

(Hides his shaking hand)

I must tell what I know. This is it. I am tired of being a speck on the wall of this university. A poorly paid, overworked speck of nothing— of dust and dirt—and now I have the power to change the world.

(Regains control and looks at THE STUDENT)

I will publish only a small number of copies. Five hundred or so. In Latin. It's only a book. One book. Why should the church have a problem with one book? I know what I know. I know what I see. I know that I am the one who is right.

SCENE SEVEN

(Lights change. GALILEO is packing for Florence.
He is covering the telescope with the cloth.)

Marina, we used to lie on the roof and watch the sky at night. Pointing out the light slashing across the sky. Marvelling at the beauty of the moon. We drank wine, balancing the cup on your swollen belly. Listening to the girls try and sing themselves to sleep, and everything seemed just right. Why do I only miss you sometimes, Marina? Why can't I miss you every hour of my life? I would love to show you these stars, Marina, up close. Through my window, up and far beyond. I know you never liked my works, but still you would love the stars.

(Noticing STUDENT and continues to look through books,
and tearing and piling papers)

I didn't hear you come in. You're getting better. My daughters are outside? *(Puts on jacket)* Excellent. Excellent. Yes, I am taking them with me. The boy can stay with Marina for a few more years, but I must see about that convent for the girls. No more dowries; my sisters have cured that in me ... I am not teaching today. I am not teaching again ever. I am done with this university. Bye-bye. My debts are paid; I am a free man, and you are on your own.

(Picks up the carafe)

A toast. We must have a toast to the Chief Mathematician and Philosopher, to the Grand Duke of Tuscany. I am going to Florence! *(Drinks and points to books at the end of the table)* Pass me those books, will you? What? You're shocked? You knew nothing about it? No one knew. I don't open my big mouth all the time. I know, I know; it's not even been a year since the top dog rewarded me with such wonderful prizes. Venice is nothing, not even a stepping stone. Don't look at me like that. Are you going to pass me the books or not? Not. *(Gets them himself)* Fine.

I know people are talking. But people always talk. If it wasn't about me then they would find someone else to talk about. I love being the topic of conversation. *(Speaking loudly)* Besides, the ones with the loudest voices always have the smallest minds. As soon as I'm packed, I will vacate this miserable memory.

(He puts his cape on and looks around.)

I have spent eighteen years here. You gather so many things. I can't take it all with me. I have something for you. I want to leave you something. I know you won't look through the telescope, so see that Marina gets it, will you? She won't look up, but she likes to spy on her neighbours. I want you to have the pendulum. I want you to have it. Use it when you study. It's very soothing.

(Lets the pendulum go)

Can't you even be a little happy for me? I won. No matter what the grumblers might have said, the church did not string me up. The church did not ban my book. Ah, I have only opened the door a crack. There is so much more to say. And now who can stop me with the Duke by my side? *(Goes to the table and picks up a pile of books and the carafe)*

I have enlarged the scope of science a hundred and a thousand times; why should I stop there? I have taken a man's beliefs and made them real. Don't you believe in anything? Wait. You still owe me for a lesson. On the table there. Who will you study with? Hmmm. It will never be the same. You see! I have corrupted you. There is no turning back. This is the beginning.

(The lights fade slowly to back light. GALILEO is returning to his "prison" from the beginning of the play. He removes his cloak and jacket. He fondly caresses the pendulum and stands in the same spot as at the beginning of the play.)

(Lights fade to black)

Lindsay Price is a Canadian playwright and member of the Playwrights Union of Canada. She is involved in Theatrefolk, a stage company in Toronto that specializes in theatre in education. She is currently teaching a playwriting course on the Internet to high school students.

1. Response
  a. Examine Galileo's first five lines. What do they reveal about his personality? Are these lines effective in capturing the audience's interest? Explain.
  b. Imagine that you are Galileo's student. What do you think Galileo would be like as a teacher? Explain.
  c. At one point in the play, Galileo says, "Aristotle says, Aristotle says. The time for Aristotle is past ..." Who is Aristotle? Why would Galileo have negative thoughts about Aristotle? If necessary, conduct research to answer these questions fully.

2. *Drama* *Adding Lines* A number of times in the script, the student says something to Galileo but his lines are not presented in the usual script form. Why do you think Price chose to do this? Choose three such incidents and write some lines for the student that would match how Galileo responds. Consider how both characters might move around or gesture during this scene. Present this revised script to a small group and discuss the effectiveness of the added lines.

> **PERFORMANCE TIP** When performing before an audience, it is important to remain comfortable and balanced while moving and to gesture in a natural way. Your posture is also revealing—are you proudly standing straight, or are you slumped in defeat? Mime several everyday activities to check your movement, posture, and balance. Relaxation exercises will also help you prepare your body for the presentation of a scene.

3. *Research and Inquiry* From this play, what do you learn about Galileo and his accomplishments? Research Galileo further. Does the author, Lindsay Price, exhibit any bias in what she reveals or conceals? Explain. How is this portrayal of Galileo affected by its having been created by a woman living in the twenty-first century?

Theme Connections

- *"When I Heard the Learn'd Astronomer," a poem about the study of astronomy not being as meaningful as gazing at the stars, page 231*
- *"Thoughts on Education," an essay about the importance of seeking and distributing knowledge, page 312*
- *"Living Like Weasels," an essay about living a simple, unexamined life, page 350*
- *"Media Diet: Jane Goodall," an interview that explores the life and work of a scientist, page 383*

A monologue gives an actor the chance to deliver thought-provoking or moving lines while enjoying the audience's complete attention. Think of some examples of outstanding monologues you have heard in plays or movies. What made them effective? How did these monologues move or affect you?

What Will Your Verse Be?

Monologue by Tom Schulman
from Touchstone Pictures' Feature *Dead Poets Society*

MR. KEATING: Now, my class, you will learn to think for yourselves again. You will learn to savor words and language. No matter what anybody tells you, words and ideas <u>can</u> change the world. Now, I see that look in Mr. Pitts' eye like… like nineteenth-century literature has nothing to do with going to business school or medical school. Right? Maybe. Mr. Hopkins, you may agree with him, thinking, "Yes. We should simply study our Mr. Pritchard[1] and learn our rhyme and meter and go quietly about the business of achieving other ambitions." I have a secret for you. Huddle up. HUDDLE UP! We don't read and write poetry because it's cute. We read and write poetry because we are members of the human race. And the human race is filled with passion. Now medicine, law, business, engineering, these are noble pursuits, and necessary to sustain life. But poetry, beauty, romance, love…these are what we stay alive for. To quote from Whitman, "O me, O life of the questions of these recurring. Of the endless trains of the faithless of cities filled with the foolish. What good amid these, O me, O life?" Answer: "That you are here. That life exists and identity. That the powerful play goes on and you may contribute a verse. That the powerful play goes on and you may contribute a verse." What will your verse be?

---

[1] **Mr. Pritchard:** The author of the book they are studying.

Tom Schulman is a Hollywood screenwriter who won the Best Original Screenplay Oscar for *Dead Poets Society*. He based the character of Mr. Keating on one of his favourite English professors.

1. Response
a. Based on this speech, how would you describe Mr. Keating as a teacher? Do you think he would be a good teacher? Explain.
b. Mr. Keating quotes Walt Whitman. Who is Whitman and why do you think Keating quotes him?
c. Answer Keating's final question: "What will your verse be?"

2. Drama *Presenting Monologues*
Prepare a presentation of this monologue or another of your choice. As you plan your performance, remember that monologues consist of one actor communicating strong feelings or ideas to an audience. Ask your audience to record their thoughts on your performance. With your audience, discuss how you might improve your performance.

> PERFORMANCE TIP Pronunciation, articulation, and the projection of your voice are all especially important in presenting a monologue. You may find it helpful to think of your voice as something tangible, like a ball, that you are throwing to an audience, using the power of your lungs, diaphragm, and voice. Remember that volume is an important part of projection, but it is just as important to be able to project a whisper as a shout. Practise projecting a whisper across a crowded room.

3. Focus on Context
You have just read a monologue that is part of a much larger movie. Discuss how your response to the monologue, in reading it out of context, might vary from your response to it if you watched the whole movie. What advantages and disadvantages are there in reading part of a movie?

4. Film Study
Dead Poets Society remains a popular movie many years after its release. Watch Robin Williams delivering this monologue, or watch the whole movie and comment on its popularity. Who is the movie's target audience? How might the target audience respond to this monologue? To the whole movie?

Glossary

In the **active voice**, the subject of a sentence does the action. For example, the dog ran into the street. Use the active voice when possible. It uses fewer words and is more precise than the passive voice. See **passive voice**.

An **allegory** is a simple story, such as a fable or parable, whose major purpose is to teach a moral lesson. An allegory can always be read on two levels—one literal, the other symbolic. The underlying meaning can be parallel to, but different from, the surface meaning.

Alliteration is a repetition of the same first sound in a group of words or line of poetry. For example, The sun sank slowly.

An **allusion**, in a literary work, is a reference to another literary work, or a person, place, event, or object from history, literature, or mythology. For example, If you take the last piece of pie, you can expect WW II all over again.

An **analogy** is the illustration of one idea or concept by using a similar idea or concept. An analogy can be phrased as a simile.

The **antagonist** of a narrative or dramatic work is the primary person in opposition to the hero or **protagonist**.

Apposition is the relation of two parts of a sentence when the one is added as an explanation to the other. For example, in *Mr. Brown, our teacher, is on vacation, Mr. Brown* and *teacher* are in apposition.

An **archetype** is a theme, symbol, character, or setting that can be found throughout literature, folklore, and media so often that it comes to reflect some universal human character or experience. For example, Robin Hood is an archetypal hero.

Assonance (also known as *vowel rhyme*) is the repetition of similar or identical vowel sounds within the words of a poem or other writing. For example, mellow wedding bells.

Bias is the author's inclination or preference toward one stance that makes it difficult or impossible to judge something fairly. For example, a Sylvester Stallone fan may be unable to write an objective or balanced review of Stallone's work.

A **burlesque** is a literary or dramatic composition in which a serious subject is treated ridiculously or with mock seriousness.

A **cacophony** is a harsh or clashing combination of words, often caused deliberately for effect. For example, finger of a *birth-strangled* babe.

A **caesura** is a pause in a line of verse, generally agreeing with a pause required by the sense. For example, England — how I long for thee!

Climax See **plot.**

Closure occurs when a story ends without ambiguity. The main crises and/or conflicts are neatly wrapped up, and the reader has a sense that the story is truly finished. In an *open-ended story,* the reader is uncertain about what might happen next; several outcomes are possible.

Codes and **conventions** refer to the different ways in which each media product typically conveys meaning to audiences. For example, we expect certain kinds of movies to open with certain conventions, such as an action movie opening with lots of action, special effects, and maybe a chase scene.

Consonance is the repetition of similar or identical consonants in words whose vowels differ. For example, *gripe, grape, grope.*

Diction refers to the way an author expresses ideas in words. Good diction includes grammatical correctness, skill in the choice of effective words, and a wide vocabulary.

A **dynamic character** is one who undergoes a significant and permanent change in personality or beliefs.

Enjambment occurs when there is no strong punctuation at the end of a line of poetry, allowing a phrase or sentence to carry through that line and into the next without a pause. For example,

> Let me not to the marriage of true minds
> Admit impediments. Love is not love
> —Shakespeare

A **eulogy** is a tribute to someone who has just died and is often delivered as a speech at a funeral.

A **fact sheet** presents key information about a particular topic, issue, or organization. It provides concise answers to basic questions. Some fact sheets are written in point form, others in full sentences.

Figurative language uses words to paint a picture, draw an interesting comparison, or create a poetic effect. **Literal language** says what it means directly. Language can be figurative or literal.

See the **Film Study Glossary** on page 395 for glossary items related to movies.

Free-verse poetry is written without using regular rhyme or rhythm. Images, spacing, punctuation, and the rhythms of ordinary language are used to create a free-verse poem.

Foreshadowing is a plot technique in which a writer plants clues or subtle indications about events that will happen later in the narrative.

Imagery is the pictures or impressions that writers create in the minds of their readers. To create these pictures, they use descriptive techniques such as figures of speech (simile, metaphor, personification, oxymoron), onomatopoeia, alliteration, and allusions.

Irony occurs when a statement or situation means something different from (or even the opposite of) what is expected. Another type of irony is called **dramatic irony**. It occurs in plays when the audience knows something that the characters do not.

Interjections are words—such as *oh, wow, ha, mmm*—that show emotion, often without any grammatical connection to other parts of the sentence.

Juxtaposition is the intentional placement of dissimilar words or ideas side by side for a particular purpose—to emphasize contrasting ideas, for example.

A **literary essay** presents an interpretation or explores some aspect of one or more works of literature.

Loaded language is language that is intentionally chosen to evoke a strong response in a reader—usually an emotional response. It is also language that is highly connotative, conjuring in the listener much more than its literal meaning.

A **loaded word** is a word intentionally chosen to evoke a strong response in a reader—usually an emotional response.

A **logo** is an identifying symbol used as a trademark in advertising.

Mass media is any method by which a message is communicated to a large audience at the same time—movies, radio, TV, books, magazines, the Internet.

A **media text** is any media product—movie, radio show, CD, TV program, et cetera—that is selected for critical examination.

A **metaphor** is a comparison of two things that are not alike. The comparison suggests that they do share a common quality: *His words were a knife to my heart.*

An **oxymoron** is a figure of speech that is a combination of contradictory words. One of the most common examples of an oxymoron is "jumbo shrimp."

Parallelism is the intentional use of identical or similar grammatical structure within one sentence or in two or more sentences. For example, She likes dancing, singing, and jogging.

Parallel structure is the repeated use of the same phrase or sentence, or the repeated use of a similar sentence structure. Parallel structure can be used to create balance or place emphasis on certain lines.

In the **passive voice**, the subject of the verb receives the action: *The fire was extinguished.* See **Active Voice**.

The **persona** is the voice or character that represents the narrator in a literary work. A persona is often described as a mask an author deliberately puts on in order to narrate a particular story or poem.

Personification occurs when objects, ideas, or animals are given human qualities: *The sun smiled down on me.*

Plot refers to the events in a story. Plot usually has five elements: exposition, rising action, climax, falling action, and resolution.
- The **exposition** or introduction sets up the story by introducing the main characters, the setting, and the problem to be solved.
- The **rising action** is the main part of the story where the full problem develops. A number of events is involved that will lead to the climax.
- The **climax** is the highest point in the story where something decisive occurs.
- The **falling action** follows the climax. It contains the events that bring the story to its conclusion.
- The **resolution** or denouement is the end of the story and traces the final outcome of the central conflict.

A **point of view** is the vantage point from which the author tells a story. The four most common points of view are *first person* (I, me), *omniscient* (all seeing), *limited omniscient* (all seeing from the viewpoint of a group of characters), and *objective* (he, she, they, it).

A **précis** is a concise summary of a text. It is written in full sentences, but contains only the most important information.

A **process analysis** shows how something is done. It gives information about a process, usually in the same order as the process itself.

A **proverb** is a short saying that expresses a basic truth or useful principle. For example, Look before you leap.

Racist language is any language that refers to a particular cultural group or ethnic group in insulting terms, but racism also exists in more subtle forms. To avoid even subtle racism, remember the following:

- Mention a person's race only if it is relevant to the context. If a person's race or ethnic origin is relevant, be specific:
  Irrelevant/Vague: *Dago is African.*
  Relevant/Less Vague: *Dago is proud of her Nigerian heritage.*
- Avoid making generalizations about any racial or cultural group:
  Stereotype: *The Welsh are great singers.*
  Better: *The Welsh have a long tradition of singing.*

Register refers to the level of formality of language. Language can be characterized according to the social context for which it is appropriate. For example, language with a colloquial register might contain slang expressions and unconventional grammar.

Resolution See **plot.**

A **rhetorical question** is one that is asked for effect, and that does not invite a reply. The purpose of a rhetorical question is to introduce a topic or to focus the reader on a concern. For example, How do I love thee? Let me count the ways.

Rhythm is the arrangement of beats in a line of poetry. The beat is created by the accented and unaccented syllables in the words used in each line.

A **satire** is a work that criticizes something—for example, a person, a characteristic, an institution, or a government—by depicting it in a humorous, sarcastic, or scornful way.

Sexist language is language that degrades or unnecessarily excludes either women or men. It is best to avoid generalizing about males and females unless the claims are based on scientific facts. To avoid sexist language, remember the following:
- Whenever possible, replace words such as *fireman, policeman,* and *man-made* with non-sexist alternatives such as *firefighter, police officer,* and *fabricated.*
- Avoid using the masculine pronouns *he, him,* or *his* to refer to both men and women.
  Sexist: A doctor must always be polite to his patients.
  Non-sexist: Doctors must always be polite to their patients. **Or**
                 A Doctor must always be polite to his/her patients.

A **stereotype** is an oversimplified picture, usually of a group of people, giving them all a set of characteristics, without consideration for individual differences. For example, the nerd scientist, the rebellious teenager, and the bratty younger brother are all stereotypes.

Style is the overall texture of a piece of writing; the particular way in which the ideas are expressed. Style is made up of many elements including diction, figurative language, sentences, and tone.

Suspense is a feeling of tension, anxiety, or excitement resulting from uncertainty. An author creates suspense to keep readers interested.

A **symbol** is something that represents something else—for example, the lion can be a symbol of courage.

The **symbolic meaning** of a work is developed through the symbols that the author includes.

A **synopsis** provides an overview or summary of a longer work.

A **theme** is a central thesis or idea that is expressed directly or indirectly in a literary work.

The **thesis** of an essay is the main idea or argument that the author is attempting to prove.

Tone is the implied attitude of the writer toward the subject or the audience. Tone differs from mood, which describes the emotional feeling of the work more generally. The tone of a piece of work can be described, for example, as *angry, satiric, joyful,* or *serious.*

Transition words—such as however, in conclusion, and on the other hand—indicate relationships between ideas. Writers use them to suggest links between sentences or paragraphs.

A **unifying device** connects different parts of a narrative. It can be a metaphor, a symbol, an image, a character, or even an important word or phrase.

Verbals look like verbs but function as other parts of speech. There are three kinds of verbals: infinitives, participles, and gerunds. An infinitive can function as a noun, adjective, or adverb, and takes the form of a verb preceded by "to": "I'll continue to hope for good weather." A participle functions as an adjective and takes the form of a verb + "ing" (present participle) or "ed" (past participle): "I am hoping for good weather." "I hoped for good weather." A gerund functions as a noun and takes the form of a verb + "ing": "Hoping is something I do all the time."

Index of Titles and Authors

Acknowledgments

Every reasonable effort has been made to trace ownership of copyrighted material. Information that would enable the publisher to correct any reference or credit in future editions would be appreciated.

12 "Groom Service" from *Working Men* by Michael Dorris, © 1993 by Michael Dorris. Reprinted by permission of Henry Holt and Company, LLC. **26** "The Shining Houses" from *Dance of the Happy Shades* by Alice Munro. Copyright © 1968 by Alice Munro. Reprinted by permission of William Morris Agency, Inc., on behalf of the author. **44** "The Return" by Ngugi Wa Thiong'o from *Secrets Lives and Other Stories* by Ngugi Wa Thiong'o. Reprinted by permission of Heinemann Educational Publishers. **51** "Two Words" by Isabel Allende. Reprinted with the permission of Scribner, a Division of Simon & Schuster, Inc., from *The Stories of Eva Luna* by Isabel Allende, translated by Margaret Sayers Peden. © 1989 by Isabel Allende. English translation, © 1991 by Macmillan Publishing Company. **60** "A Marker on the Side of the Boat" by Boa Ninh. Originally published in *Tap Chi Van Nghe Quan Doi*, 1994. Reprinted by permission of the author. Translation © 1990 by Linh Dinh. **70** "On a Rainy River" from *The Things They Carried* by Tim O'Brien. © 1990 by Tim O'Brien. Reprinted by permission of Houghton Mifflin Company. All rights reserved. **86** "A Pair of Silk Stockings", from *The Awakening and Selected Stories* by Kate Chopin, Introduction by Barbara H. Soloman, © 1976 by The New American Library, Inc., Introduction. Used by permission of Dutton Signet, a division of Penguin Putnam Inc. **92** "Dressing Up for the Carnival" by Carol Shields. Extracted from *Dressing Up for the Carnival* by Carol Shields. © 2000 by Carol Shields. Reprinted by permission of Random House Canada, a division of Random House of Canada Limited. **100** "The Spaces Between Stars" by Geeta Kothari. Reprinted by permission of the author. **112** "The Chrysanthemums" by John Steinbeck, 1937, renewed © 1965 by John Steinbeck. from *The Long Valley* by John Steinbeck. Used by permission of Viking Penguin, a division of Penguin Putnam Inc. **124** "Touching Bottom" by Kari Stutt. Reprinted by permission of the author. **134** "The Forest of Arden" by Hannah Grant. Reprinted by permission of the author. **143** Reprinted with the permission of Simon & Schuster from *Life After God* by Douglas Coupland. © 1994 by Douglas Campbell Coupland. **150** "The Large Ant" by Howard Fast. Reprinted by permission of Sterling Lord Literistic, Inc. © by Howard Fast. **160** "A Drowning" from

Hearts Larry Broke by Mark Ferguson (published by Creative Book Publishing). Reprinted by permission of the author. **164** "Red Bean Ice" by Nancy Lee. Reprinted by permission of the author. **174** "If a Poem Could Walk" from *Angels of Flesh, Angels of Silence* by Lorna Crozier. Used by permission of the Canadian Publishers, McClelland & Stewart, Toronto. **177** "After the Wedding" by Marisa Anlin Alps. Reprinted with permission of the author. **178** "Brian at Eighteen" from *The Blue Machines of Night* by Rick Hillis (Coteau Books, 1988). Reprinted by permission from the author. **182** "Pride" by Marilyn Cay from *Farm* (Thistledown Press, 1993). **183** "Silent, but..." by Tsuboi Shigeji from *The Penguin Book of Japanese Verse*, translated by Geoffrey Bownas and Anthony Thwaite. Reproduced by permission of Penguin Books Ltd. London: Penguin Books, 1964. **184** "On the Value of Fantasies" by Elizabeth Brewster is reprinted from *Sometimes I Think of Moving* by permission of Oberon Press. **186** "The Swimmer's Moment" from *Winter Sun/The Dumbfounding Poems 1940-1966* by Margaret Avison. Used by permission of McClelland & Stewart Ltd. The Canadian Publishers. **186** "Symposium" from *Hay* by Paul Muldoon. © 1998 by Paul Muldoon. Reprinted by permission of Farrar, Straus, and Giroux, LLC. **188** "The Layers" by Stanley Kunitz. Reprinted by permission of the author. **189** "Young Soul" by Amiri Baraka. Reprinted by permission of the author. **191** "Since Feeling Is First" © 1926, 1954, 1991 from *Complete Poems:1904-1962* by E.E. Cummings. Used by permission of Liveright Publishing Corporation. **192** "Love Is Not All" by Edna St. Vincent Millay. From *Collected Poems*, HarperCollins. © 1931, 1958 by Edna St. Vincent Millay and Norma Millay Ellis. All rights reserved. Used by permission of Elizabeth Barnett, literary executor. **194** "I Wish to Paint My Eyes" 6 lines, by Anonymous, Trans. By Willis Barnstone, from *A Book of Women Poets from Antiquity to Now* by Willis Barnstone and Aliki Barnstone, © 1980 by Schocken Books. Used by permission of Schocken Books, a division of Random House, Inc. **200** "Variations on the Word *Love*" from *Selected Poems 1966-1984* by Margaret Atwood. © Margaret Atwood 1990. reprinted by permission of Oxford University Press Canada. **202** "First Person Demonstrative by Phyllis Gotlieb. Reprinted by permission of the author. **207** "Because I Could Not Stop for Death" by Emily Dickinson. Reprinted by permission of the publishers and the Trustees of Amherst College from *The Poems of Emily Dickinson*, Thomas H. Johnson, ed,. Cambridge, Mass.: The Belknap Press of Harvard University Press,

© 1951, 1955, 1979 by the President and Fellows of Harvard College. **208** "Miss Dickinson Goes to the Office." Reprinted with permission of the author. **209** "Do Not Go Gentle Into That Good Night" from *The Poems* by Dylan Thomas (J M Dent). Reprinted by permission of David Higham Associates. **210** From "He Went Gentle" by Geraldine Rubia (excerpt from poem "He Went Gentle), published in *Skating Among the Graves*, Killick Press, St. John's, NF. Reprinted by permission of the author. **211** "The World" from *Collected Poems* by Kathleen Raine. Reprinted by permission of the author. **212** "Acquainted With the Night" from *The Poetry of Robert Frost* edited by Edward Connery Lathem © 1928, © 1969 by Henry Holt and Co., 1956 by Robert Frost. Reprinted by permission of Henry Holt and Co., LLC. **213** "ABC" from *Jersey Rain* by Robert Pinsky. © 2000 by Robert Pinsky. Reprinted by permission of Farrar, Straus and Giroux, LLC. **220** "Modern Edifices" by Maria Holod, from *Yarmarok: Ukrainian Writing in Canada Since the Second World War*. Reprinted by permission of the author. **222** "Kindly Unhitch That Star, Buddy" © 1935 by Ogden Nash, renewed. Reprinted by permission of Curtis Brown, Ltd. **223** "To Be of Use" by Marge Piercy, from *Circles on the Water* by Marge Piercy, © 1982 by Marge Piercy. Used by permission of Alfred A. Knopf, a division of Random House, Inc. **225** "I Am a Rock" by Paul Simon. © 1965 Paul Simon. Used by permission of the publisher: Paul Simon Music. **226** "The World Is Not a Pleasant Place to Be" from *The Selected Poems of Nikki Giovanni* © 1996 by Nikki Giovanni. Reprinted by permission of HarperCollins Publishers Inc., William Morrow. **228** "I'm Sorry Says the Machine" by Eve Merriam from *Chortles: New and Selected Wordplay Poems* by Eve Merriam. © 1962, materials requested and acknowledgment: 1964, 1973, 1976, 1989 by Eve Merriam. All rights renewed and reserved. Used by permission of Marian Reiner. **231** "Advice to the Young" from *Collected Poems* by Miriam Waddington. © Miriam Waddington 1986. Reprinted by permission of Oxford University Press Canada. **234** "Original Thought" by The Four Dancers. reprinted by permission of Theytus Books Ltd. **235** "Anything Worth Knowing © Kevin Major **236** "Did I Miss Anything?" by Tom Wayman from *Did I Miss Anything? Selected Poems 1973-1993*, Madeira Park, BC: Harbour Publishing, 1993. Originally published in *Poetry Northwest*. **240** "The Love Song of J. Alfred Prufrock" from *Collected Poems 1909-1962* by T.S. Eliot. London: Faber and Faber Limited. **244** "Loneliness" by Emma LaRocque from *Writing the Circle* , edited by Jeanne Perreault and Sylvia Vance. Reprinted by permission of the author. **246** "Auto Wreck" by Karl Shapiro from *Poems 1940-1953* © Karl Shapiro by permission of Wieser & Wieser, Inc.

247 "Provisions" from *The Animals in That Country* by Margaret Atwood. © Oxford University Press Canada 1968. Reprinted by permission of Oxford University Press Canada. **249** "Circular Saws" by Fred Cogswell. Reprinted by permission of the author. **250** "Night" by Yvonne Trainer from *Everything Happens at Once* © 1986 by Yvonne Trainer by permission of Goose Lane Editions. **256** "What I've Learned from Writing" © Shauna Singh Baldwin. Reprinted by permission of the author. **273** "Art History" by Doreen Jensen from *Give Back: First Nations Perspectives on Cultural Practice: Essays*, Gallerie: Women Artists' Monographs, Issue 11 (Vancouver BC: Gallerie Publications, 1992). Reprinted with permission of the author. **281** "Stone Faces" from *Coyote's Morning Cry: Meditations and Dreams from a Life in Nature* by Sharon Butala. Published by HarperCollinsPublishersLtd. Copyright © 1995 by Sharon Butala. All rights reserved. **284** "Making Poetry Pay" from *I Wonder as I Wander* by Langston Hughes. © 1956 by Langston Hughes. Copyright renewed © 1984 by George Houston Bass. Reprinted by permission of Hill and Wang, a division of Farrar, Straus and Giroux, LLC. **289** "A New Perspective" by Janice Fein. Reprinted by permission of *Fresh Ink*, The University of Akron, Ohio. **292** "Only Daughter" by Sandra Cisneros © 1990 by Sandra Cisneros. First published in Glamour, November 1990. Reprinted by permission of Susan Bergholz Literary Services, New York. All rights reserved. **296** "My Old Newcastle" by David Adams Richards. Reprinted by permission of the author. **306** "Reviving Fridamania" by Chris Kraul (April 24,2001). © 2001, Los Angeles Times. Reprinted by permission. **309** "The Akward Sublime" by Margaret Atwood. © Margaret Atwood. Used by permission of the author. **320** "Rink Rage" by James Deacon from Maclean's Magazine, March 26, 2001. Reprinted with permission from Maclean's Magazine. **327** "Coffee" by Alan Durning. Reprinted from Adbusters Quarterly, Winter 1995, Vol. 3, No. 3, pp. 72-74. **330** "Blue Gold" from *If the Gods Had Meant for Us to Vote They Would Have Given Us Candidates* by Jim Hightower © 2000 by Jim Hightower. Reprinted by permission of HarperCollins Publishers Inc. **345** "Night Spirits" by Candace Savage. First published in *Canadian Geographic* in March/April 2001. Reprinted by permission of the author. **350** "Living Like Weasels" from *Teaching a Stone to Talk: Expeditions and Encounters* by Annie Dillard © 1982 by Annie Dillard. Reprinted by permission of HarperCollins Publishers Inc. **356** "Follows Family Stages a Reunion" by Harry Currie from *The K-W Record*, June 2001. Reprinted with permissionof The Record, Waterloo, Ontario. **364** "The Making of Sense and Sensibility" Diaries © 1985 by Emma Thompson. All rights reserved. Material reprinted